SYSTEMS
Analysis, Administration, and Architecture

SYSTEMS
Analysis, Administration, and Architecture

John W. Sutherland

Van Nostrand Reinhold Company
New York/Cincinnati/Toronto/London/Melbourne

Van Nostrand Reinhold Company Regional Offices:
New York Cincinnati Chicago Milbrae Dallas

Van Nostrand Reinhold Company International Offices:
London Toronto Melbourne

Library of Congress Catalog Card Number: 75-12792
ISBN: 0-442-28074-2

Manufactured in the United States of America

Published by Van Nostrand Reinhold Company
450 West 33rd Street, New York, N.Y. 10001

Published simultaneously in Canada by Van Nostrand Reinhold Ltd.

15 14 13 12 11 10 9 8 7 6 5 4 3 2

Library of Congress Cataloging in Publication Data

Sutherland, John W.
    Systems: analysis, administration, and architecture.

    Includes bibliographical references and index.
    1. System analysis.   I. Title.
QA402.S9   003   75-12792
ISBN 0-442-28074-2

Although the words here
are for so many,
Susan and our October child
will know that they are perhaps
more for them than anyone.

life is short
the art long
timing is exact
experience treacherous
judgment difficult.

—Hippocrates—

. . . the occasion urgent.

Preface

This book is designed to give the widest possible overview of the system sciences to the widest possible audience. As such, the subjects elected for discussion are those aspects of the system sciences that are context-independent . . . those that will be of interest and hopefully of benefit to individuals of virtually all disciplines, backgrounds, or ambitions. The book is thus an inventory of system concepts. At the conceptual level at which we shall be operating, the system sciences emerge as much more than a simple amalgamation of tools and techniques. They become a new methodology—coherent, complete, and differentiated—a methodology particularly well suited to the treatment of the complex problems characterizing our times, yet easily and efficiently at home with simpler problems as well.

This book is thus for those who must make decisions, set policy, or solve problems . . . or for those who are studying to do so. It is for the sociologist, the economist, the psychologist, the political scientist, the administrative theorist, and the computer scientist, or for any one—practitioner or student—whose ambition is to solve real-world problems or contribute to their solution.

The unique aspects of the system sciences' methodological platform will thus be of primary concern to us here. The first aspect of its uniqueness is found in the fact that the system scientist will walk an interdisciplinary path, for he recognizes that the problems that nature and man pose seldom fall within the neat but artificial demarcations of academic faculties. In fact, many of the real-world problems that are currently pressing us would fall rather neatly *between* defined academic areas, to be neglected in the interstices. Thus, many of the models and discussions here will be concerned with both the system scientist's ability to construct interdisciplinary models, and the provisions the system approach offers for the development of perspectives that are syntheses of parochial disciplinary views. The result, hopefully, will be a heightened awareness of the role that the generalist can play in problem-solving . . . the role he *must* play.

A second aspect of the system methodology is the imperative that the system scientist cultivate an eclectic analytical capability. He must thus be prepared to draw on instruments from both the quantitative and qualitative domains, using each in isolation or in combination as appropriate. To this extent, the system scientist is not content to be a mathematician, at the expense of insight and comprehensiveness; nor will he allow himself to be a rhetorician at the expense of discipline. Thus, in these pages, we shall be blending the mathematical, statistical, and engineering bases of the system sciences with the qualitative, deductive, metaphysical, and idiographic capabilities we normally associate with the social or behavioral scientist. As a result, many sections of this book will allow the quantitative analyst an opportunity to become aware of the sensitivity and creativity of the qualitative scientist, and at the same time will offer the "soft" scientist an opportunity to appreciate the very real discipline and precision that elements of the quantitative methods can bring to problem-solving exercises.

This emphasis on a syncretic approach to problem-solving, on a cojoining of quantitative and qualitative appreciations, simply reflects a third major aspect of the system science methodology, the dictate that the properties of the problem at hand should determine the analytical approach we take, not any *a priori* methodological biases nor any convenient preferences we happen to hold independent of emerging problem realities. In effect then, we shall here be pointing out the ways in which we can bring all the structure and order possible to the problems we face, without bringing so much that real complexities are sacrificed to analytical expedience . . . a sacrifice that usually results in sub-optimal decisions, dysfunctional policies, or ill-considered theories.

A fourth aspect of the system sciences' methodological platform is the demand that scientists, decision-makers, analysts, policy-makers, and problem-solvers in general adopt an *holistic* appreciation of the subjects with which they are forced—or have elected—to deal. In essence, this means that the basic unit of analysis for the system scientist is extremely broad, treating phenomena as unreduced *wholes*. In dealing with wholes, the analytical problems are immense. There are the connections among broadly diverse components to consider; there are the questions about hierarchical orderings that find no real-world system entirely independent of influence from other systems, and no real-world action we take that can be regarded as lacking impact for other systems; there are issues of the "organic" quality of most social, economic, and political systems, a quality that translates into an inability to isolate components from other factors without losing significance. In short, holism means complexity, and complexity is the game that the system approach is designed to play.

Thus, the system scientist is not simply a technocrat trying to computerize or mathematize every aspect of the world he encounters. Rather, he looks at this increasingly complex and protean world of ours—at the deep-seated problems accelerating and concatenating on every dimension—and tries to answer the challenge laid down by Julius Stulman in Evolving Mankind's Future:

We have to develop and apply widely a new methodology for thinking that leads us from the singular viewpoint to a system of thinking, from system to an organization of systems to synthesis, and from synthesis ultimately into metamorphosis—in other words, a methodology of integrated thought and action in which there is a continuing feedback and flow forward to deal with constant changes at all levels.*

This demand for a new methodology is echoing more and more widely these days, as man and his world are gradually seen to be vastly more complicated than was once thought. In modern psychology, simple stimulus-response theories no longer suffice to explain the range of behaviors of which men are evidently capable. On the social, economic, and political dimensions, we are now asked—and now see—a world where physical distances are being shortened by new transportation technology and where innovations in communication are causing heretofore isolated aspects to collide and interact in often unpredictable ways. In short, we are asked to see the world in terms of a *global village*, the product of some natural integrative process assisted by jet airplanes and satellite television. This concept of the global village is then used to demand greater sophistication in decision- and policy-making activities, greater attention to the incredibly complicated cause and effect sequences that arise in a world where all parts are potentially connected to all others, and where an action in one part of the organism is sure to set off a complementary, sympathetic, or compensatory reaction elsewhere. The system sciences, in the broadest possible sense, are the scientific community's answer to this kind of complexity.

In the perspective taken in this book then, the system approach, system theory, and the repertoire of system science concepts will all be directed toward the solution of problems, asking that we seek always to comprehend complexity before we contemplate action . . . and in some cases asking we exhibit the sensitivity and wisdom *not* to interfere with certain natural processes or asking the courage to intervene where self-interest might dictate withdrawl. The contributions that can be legitimately expected of the system sciences to policy-making, or problem-solving in general are inferentially available to us by a review of the demands that the system approach makes on its practitioners . . . irrespective of the particular organization they serve or the level at which they operate:

- It demands that they have the ability to develop eclectic appreciations for complex phenomena, not being restricted solely to a particular academic discipline or to any irrational *a priori* stance about the nature of the subject at hand.
- It demands that they appreciate the contributions that can be made by both quantitative and qualitative instruments in the solution of complex problems, not merely being content to use one to the exclusion of the other as a matter of expedience or bias.

*Published by J. B. Lippincott, 1967.

- It demands that they be prepared to exert every effort to solve problems completely, not just a piece at a time, suboptimally, or for some short-run.

In essence, then, the system sciences simply ask that their representatives—in government, industry, research, science, or society—practice that most fundamental but elusive virtue of the educated man in a world depending on him: *integrity*.

This book, then, will attempt to make the system sciences approach to problem-solving a viable alternative for three populations: (a) practicing scientists who contribute, either directly or indirectly, to decision or policy issues; (b) the people who have the line responsibility for making policy or decisions ... the manager, the administrator, or the executive in either private or public enterprise; and (c) those young men and women who are studying to become contributing members of one or the other of the first two groups. This broadly defined audience means that the discussions here can be neither too erudite and specialized, nor too trivial. And, they must meet the criteria of the system sciences approach itself: they must reflect an interdisciplinary appreciation; they must seek to wed concepts from both quantitative and qualitative analysis; and they must be those that promise to be of immediate use.

The structure of the book reflects, as largely as possible, these somewhat ambitious and elusive criteria. In the first chapter a brief attempt is made to set forth some of the more basic and important aspects of the system approach itself. Particularly stressed are the imperatives for the interdisciplinary attack on complex problems, and the necessity for not being bound to any particular methodological alternative.

We next approach the substance of system sciences as a discipline in its own right. Here will be introduced the key concept of the isomorphism, i.e., a property that is shared between two or more superficially different systems that tends to allow us to approach them as a defined "class" of phenomena. To the extent that meaningful isomorphisms can be found, single theories or models can be advanced that pertain to numbers of different systems, and hence the cause of efficiency in problem-solving is served. We first, in Chapter 2, approach the identification and exploitation of isomorphisms by exploring the several different structural modalities that the majority of real-world systems tend to exhibit; and then move on, in Chapter 3, to the several different behavioral or dynamic isomorphisms that predominate among real-world phenomena.

Thus, for example, hierarchical organization becomes an instance of structural isomorphism, as the properties of hierarchical structure are shared by many diverse systems. On the behavioral dimension, cybernetic engination is an appropriate isomorphism, as it indicates a certain behavioral characteristic shared by many systems that may otherwise be very diverse. It is the concern and facility with handling isomorphisms that makes the system scientist the "generalist" in the scientific community. As the two eminent system theorists Zadeh and Polak explain:

... system theory is a discipline in its own right—a discipline which aims at providing a common abstract basis and unified conceptual framework for studying the behavior of various types and forms of systems.*

In this statement, the key words are "common abstract basis," for the elements in such a basis will turn out to be points of isomorphism among widely diverse systems. Thus, for Zadeh and Polak, the system theorist does not care what particular superficial properties a system exhibits, but

what matters is whether it is linear or non-linear, discrete-time or continuous time, lumped or distributed, deterministic or stochastic, continuous-state or discrete-state, passive or active, etc. In short, it is the mathematical structure of a system and not its physical form or area of application, that is of interest to a system theorist.†

The important point here is that the terms used above are all in effect sources of isomorphisms, as they seek to describe *generic* system structure or behavior. Thus, the terms linear or nonlinear, discrete time or continuous time, etc., provide abstract references against which the properties of individual systems may be compared. When a fit is found between the real-world properties of a system and the properties postulated for the abstract isomorphism, we may use the body of theory or information pertaining to the abstract ideal-type to treat that system. In effect then isomorphisms serves the cause of *efficiency* in science by allowing us to discover rules of structure or behavior pertinent to large numbers of systems, rather than having to treat each phenomenon as unique or unprecedented.

The *efficiency orientation* of isomorphisms, however, takes on more meaning when we realize that instances of isomorphism may allow us to employ one of the most powerful tools in the scientific arsenal: the *analogy*. For isomorphisms are the building blocks of analogies that, when appropriately conceived, can hope to move science gradually toward that very much-desired end where the largest number of phenomena are explained by the fewest number of unique formalizations. Analogic models serve the cause of *simplicity* in the theoretical realm as well as *efficiency* in the operational realm. It is this point that leads Anatol Rapoport to defend the potential utility of mathematical general systems theory:

If it happens that several phenomena of widely different content can be described by some mathematical model, both simplicity and generalization have been affected. Therein lies the power of mathematical general systems theory, based on the principles of mathematical isomorphisms, the completely rigorous version of analogy.‡

*Zadeh and Polak, eds., *System Theory* (New York: McGraw-Hill, 1969), p. vii.
†Ibid.
‡The Search for Simplicity," *Main Currents in Modern Thought*, 28 no. 3 (January-February 1972), pp. 79–84.

With isomorphisms and analogies as part of our methodological arsenal, Chapter 4 takes us into the realm of integrated systems . . . those phenomena in which structural and behavioral properties are treated simultaneously. We approach the difficult and critical task of treating complex systems as "wholes" through the use of one of the major modalities of modern science: the hypothetico-deductive method. The ambition here is to develop an array of system ideal-types that is broad enough to exhaust the majority of real-world systems we might encounter, but small enough to be manageable. In response to the system sciences' emphasis on interdisciplinary constructs, this array of ideal-types must carry social, economic, political, and administrative implications; and it must also have significance for us in terms of a problem-solving methodology. In short, the ideal-types are asked to carry an awesome burden, and so considerable time is spent in their development.

With the array of generic ideal-types defined and elaborated—serving pretty well to summarize the conceptual base of the pragmatic system sciences—we are ready to turn to a consideration of the methods and instruments available to the system scientist to accomplish the work he has been assigned or that he has elected to perform . . . and to a detailed discussion of the procedural and operational aspects of system sciences. And because the system approach is basically a thoroughly eclectic one, the entire instrumental arsenal of the modern sciences is available to the system scientist. The only dictate that he follows is that which suggests that it is the properties of the problem at hand that should determine the selection of instruments employed. This brings us clearly to the concept of *analytical congruence*.

Analytical congruence is the subject of Chapter 5. The chapter is concerned with the efficiency and effectiveness of the instruments we employ in the production of information pertinent to the solution of a decision or policy problem. We begin with the concept of the scientist as one whose ambitions are to build models that are either predictive, or descriptive, or both. A predictive model, to be a good one, must minimize the variance between events that it predicts and events that actually occur; a good descriptive model, on the other hand, will have a high morphological correlation between the structure of its own components in abstract, and the structural components of the real-world system it is attempting to allegorize. In either case, the scientist employs the analytical instruments at his disposal to develop these models and it is here that the concept of congruence comes into play. For we are concerned with the selection of those instruments that, at each point in the model-building process, promise to produce the greatest amount of information for the least cost.

Here it will be shown that the attempt to use instruments that are not powerful enough in the face of the properties of a particular problem leads to a condition of ineffectiveness (where the instruments simply cannot get the information required for an adequate comprehension of the problem). On the other hand, the use of instruments that are too powerful results in inefficiency or "overkill," which is tantamount to a misallocation of analytical resources.

Chapter 5 will also introduce the concept of the learning curve, whereby we may empirically audit the rate and efficiency of our learning about a problem. When learning curves are properly employed, they give us an opportunity to bring within the confines of scientific experimentation a range of methodological issues that, in the absence of the learning-curve concept, remain condemned to the realm of rhetoric. This fifth chapter also gives us an opportunity to give the nonmathematical reader an *intuitive* appreciation of the inventory of analytical instruments available to the modern scientist, in the hopes of stimulating him on to further reading and study in areas such as game theory, optimization, simulation, linear programming, adaptive programming, scenario-building, heuristic problem-solving procedures, etc.

Chapter 6 will introduce what is called the *system architecture* platform. This, basically, is a procedural paradigm for problem-solving, with special emphasis on a systematic approach to the solution of extremely complex problems. The system architecture approach will take us step-by-step from the initially heuristic attack on an ill-structured problem or system, to the point where we have exhausted a great deal of its complexity through research and may thus employ the simpler and more expedient optimization techniques. Here, however, the concentration will be on the front-end of complex problem-solving exercises, those aspects that are generally ill-treated or ignored in the traditional literature ... the problems of constructing unprecedented interdisciplinary models and dealing with indeterminacy in a disciplined way.*

Chapter 7 will then offer a system-based methodology for policy-setting and decision-making. The significant differences between these two activities are pointed out, and suggestions are also offered as to how these activities may be joined within a single procedural framework. The intention here is not to displace any of the excellent existing works on the theory of policy and decision, but simply to offer a concrete procedural paradigm that reflects the unique perspective of system sciences.

Especially critical, simply because they are not well precedented, are the sections that point out pragmatic means by which problems involving values or opinions may be subjected to scientific treatment; such problems have traditionally been approached largely through rhetoric only. Essentially, then, it is here that we attempt to make the system approach a fully operational one, and lend specific substance to many of the conceptual constructs that occupied earlier pages.

Equipped with paradigms for problem-solving, policy-setting, and decision-making, we are now prepared to deal with the last areas of interest in this book: system administration and control. Chapter 8 will stress the immediate potential of system sciences for extending the bounds of managerial rationality ... in both the commercial and noncommercial sectors. In short, what we shall emerge with is a general theory of system administration and control, one whose

---

*E.G., Delphi processes, scenario-building, defactualization, heuristic procedures, or other essentially deductive techniques.

basic postulates are as pertinent to business management as to the management of hospitals, government agencies, educational institutions, creative enterprises, service bureaus, etc. It is here then that we speak directly to the manager, the bureaucrat, the industrial psychologist, the organization theorist; to the information system designer, political scientist, and policy-maker . . . whereas some of our previous work could as easily have been applicable to the biologist, engineer, or mathematician.

The first section of Chapter 8 will attack a central interest of the system sciences: *system control*. As things stand today, there are at least two almost diametrically opposed ways to approach the control problem. First is what we might call the engineering-economics perspective, built largely around the concepts of system reduction quantification, and marginality. We shall explore the utility of this approach under the general heading of *cybernetic* processes, largely through the elaboration of the limits of the utility of what is generally known as the servo process. In so doing, we shall be closely examining the closed-loop—feedback-based systems that are so much a part of modern systems control—but we shall find them limited in application.

The second perspective on the problem of system control deals with the social, behavioral, and ideological instruments available to us, those that may serve to complement the cybernetic processes or, in many cases, displace them. In either case, any book on systems would be incomplete without noting the differences between engineering and social contributions, and without saying something about the conceptual and operation interfaces that may be formed between them.

The second and final section of Chapter 8 will consider aspects of system administration. The basic logic will find us trying to isolate relevant properties of various types of systems we might legitimately expect to encounter in the real-world, and setting out some conditions that should lead to *administrative congruence* (where the approach taken is responsive to the emerging properties of the system to be managed, and not to any *a priori* biases).

The net result of this concluding chapter will, hopefully, be the appreciation of enterprises and organizations as proper systems, and a rather complete if somewhat generalized set of concepts pertinent to their systemic management. At any rate, the discussions, arguments, and propositions set out here should serve pretty well as a set of practical precepts that the system scientist may take with him when he goes to work in the field. For they are the perspectives that should distinguish, positively, the solutions that he evolves and the contributions that he makes to a world so desperately needing competence, conviction, and disciplined creativity.

John W. Sutherland
Highland Park, N.J.

Acknowledgments

Many of the key constructs and models presented in these pages were tested on my professional colleagues in the pages of the academic literature. Particularly, the concepts of analytical congruence and the array of system sciences instruments were first presented in the 1973 issue of the General Systems Yearbook. The editor of this publication, Anatol Rapoport, has been of great assistance in maturing my work for the past several years, and his own writing has been a source of great inspiration. The managing editor of this publication, Claire Adler, deserves a very special vote of thanks, for her kind of courtesy and support is extremely rare in the field.

The section of Chapter 8 dealing with the socioeconomic control modalities derived from a paper earlier published in Human Relations, the journal of the Tavistock Institute, London. The American editor is Eric Trist, now director of the Management and Behavioral Science Center at the Wharton School of Finance, University of Pennsylvania (Philadelphia). Over the past six years, my obligations to him have continued to grow and grow. Initially, he was a member, some years ago, of my doctoral committee at the University of California at Los Angeles. Throughout the interval, his work and integrity have served as a constant reference for my own efforts. I think he is my friend as well as my mentor, and for this I count myself lucky.

Several years ago I had the pleasure of meeting my first general system theorist, George Klir, a professor of systems and engineering at the School of Advanced Technology of the State University of New York (Binghamton). Chapter 4 is, in large measure, an attempt to do for the social sciences what his own work did for the engineering sciences ... to generate a system structure that simultaneously carries both theoretical and practical significance. He was kind enough to publish this first effort in the fine journal he edits, the *International Journal of General Systems* (1, 2). In the interval between the publication of that paper and the completion of this book, the original models were expanded and made a bit more elaborate, and at least some portion of this elaboration is due to the fact that George and I were able to spend some time together as visiting professors at the System Science Ph.D. program of Portland State University.

The director of this program, Harold Linstone, is also the editor of the very significant journal of *Technological Forecasting and Social Change*. During my stay at PSU, and as a product of much interchange between myself and Dr. Linstone, I was able to develop the concept of normative system architecture which appears in Chapter 7, and accomplish something I had long sought . . . the wedding between the Delphi process and subjective probabilities. This was particularly important, for to my mind this merging is the best bet we currently have for injecting some initial discipline into our attack on very complex systems. The first effort at this was published in the Spring 1974 issue of Harold's journal **(6)**. While at PSU, I benefitted greatly from the association with the fine array of Ph.D. system students. One among them Mr. King Yi, is particularly responsible for part of the section on the concept of the modality shift presented in Chapter 7. I am eagerly awaiting the completion of his dissertation on this subject, as he should be able to take its substance far beyond the little which I have been able to do.

The concept of the heuristic managerial modality presented in the body of Chapter 8 was derived essentially from a paper I had the opportunity to prepare for one of the most promising and exciting journals in the entire academic arena . . . *Fields Within Fields . . . Within Fields*. This publication is sponsored by the World Institute Council in New York, whose president is the very remarkable Julius Stulman. I have long enjoyed access to Stulman's immensely stimulating ideas, and to his almost epically poetic grasp of the role that the system sciences must play in the future of this troubled world of ours. Stulman has been, directly or indirectly, the catalyst for so many of the propositions that the reader will find in the pages to come, and for this I am truly grateful (and honored that he should have given me benefit of his own appreciations of complexity, organic systems aspects, and scientific integrity).

I must also reexpress my gratitude to Ervin Laszlo, certainly the most prolific and one of the most interesting authors in the system field. Ervin edits the International Library of Systems Theory and Philosophy for George Braziller, Inc. (New York), and is a professor of philosophy at the Geneseo campus of SUNY. Largely under Professor Laszlo's guidance, I was able to publish a volume in his series in 1973: *A General System Philosophy for the Social and Behavioral Sciences*. This work gave me the opportunity to search among the literature of system sciences and science in general in an effort to attempt a formal systems epistemology. In large measure, the very structure of this book and many of the arguments dealing with methodology are attributable to this work done on a systems' philosophy. The debt I owe Ervin Laszlo is, therefore, a continuing and substantial one.

Finally, I must thank some institutions. First, Rutgers University lent the financial support to produce a first draft of this volume, and Portland State

University, through its system science Ph.D. program, really put the thing to-gether. Karen Showers, our secretary and general assistant there, not only typed a large portion of the manuscript but made a valiant effort to correct my spelling and grammar, and to clear up the incomplete sentences, dangling participles, and indefinite antecedents which I produce with such regularity and apparent skill.

And thanks must go to five years of students; we teachers owe them so very much. They offer us the opportunity to become precise, desciplined, and hope-fully relevant in our presentations. The index of our own growth is measured only by the index of their comprehension and, ultimately, by the distance they leave us behind. I have been so fortunate. There is not a page or a phrase of this work that does not somehow bear the stamp of their insight and their interest. And there is not a single word here that is not for them, and for those to come.

Contents

SYSTEMS
Analysis, Administration, and Architecture

PART I

CONCEPTUAL ASPECTS

The four chapters that follow attempt to lend the reader a broad appreciation of the system approach as the analytical modality most appropriate to the demands made on modern scientific enterprise. Chapter 1 explores some of its key logic properties, concentrating especially on the interdisciplinary and syncretic attributes associated with it. Particularly important is the proposition that the inductive and deductive methods represent complementary rather than competitive branches of scientific inquiry, and they respond to differences we note in real-world phenomena. This will be followed by two chapters that have a more or less definitional intention. Chapter 2 introduces the array of system "types" that operate on the structural dimension, while Chapter 3 discusses the various different behavioral modalities that real-world systems tend to approximate. In short, if the first chapter provides the philosophical foundations that will carry us throughout this book, the second and third chapters give us a vocabulary to work with. Chapter 4 concludes Part I, and concentrates on the provision of a *general* system theory, introducing a set of abstract ideal-types against which virtually all entities we might encounter may be compared. These abstract ideal-types then serve as the foci for most of the substantive work in Part II.

1

Some Key Properties of the System Approach: An Introduction

1.0 INTRODUCTION

The system scientist is basically one who adopts and exploits a unique method-ological vehicle known generally as the *system approach*. This methodology is available to anyone who wishes to adopt it. There is nothing mysterious about its properties, and there is nothing arcane about its objective. As for the latter, put in the simplest possible way, the system approach attempts to increase the efficiency of our problem-solving exercises. The possibility of its achieving this goal depends on the extent to which we are willing to abide by three simple dictates that pretty well sum up the substance of the system approach:

(a) The proper focus for the system scientist is holistic . . . where he is con-cerned not solely with the system itself, but with the stream of determi-nants impinging on it, and with the concatenation of impacts the system has on the environment in which it is resident or on other systems with which it may interact. In practice, this focus means the full exploitation of interdisciplinary contributions and, as a consequence, a direct attack on academic parochialism.

(b) The system scientist should be eclectic on the analytical dimension, draw-ing freely from both the quantitative and qualitative methods, and pursu-ing both theory and practice within the same general frame of reference. In short, the emergent properties of the phenomenon at hand, and not *a priori* epistemological or axiological biases, should determine the methods he employs. The models he builds will generally be Janus-faced, one face concerned with articulating a theoretical (hypothetico-deductive) contri-bution, the other with opportunities to validate deductive components through empirical (inductive) experimentation and field experience. These models, when developed, serve to populate the neglected middle-range between theory and practice, and between qualitative and quantita-tive approaches, resulting in a direct attack on polarization within aca-demic disciplines.

(c) The system scientist should explicitly search for (and subsequently exploit) isomorphisms among the "universe" of phenomena, this in the hopes of increasing the efficiency of science through the generation of broadly significant analogies. As the general system theorist George Klir explains,

> certain concepts, principles and methods have been shown not to depend on the specific nature of the phenomena involved. These can be applied, without any modification, in quite diverse areas of science, engineering, humanities, and the arts, thus introducing links between classical disciplines and allowing the concepts, ideas, principles, models, and methods developed in different disciplines to be shared.*

Thus, when we speak of the system scientist, we do so with respect to a methodology that is both portable and relatively precise. Its portability stems from the fact that it is not restricted to any particular phenomenon or class of phenomena; it is as at home in the physical sciences as it is among the human sciences, and is as relevant at the level of atomic structure as it is at the level of the multinational corporation or suprastate. The precision of the system approach stems from the fact that there are certain properties that serve to distinguish it from other methodological or procedural modalities the modern scientist might employ.

It is the definition, elaboration, and defense of the properties constituting the system approach that will occupy most of the pages of this book. We will, in this initial chapter, briefly introduce just a few of the more important of these properties.

1.1 THE INTERDISCIPLINARY AND SYNCRETIC IMPERATIVES

One distinguishing property of the system approach is the system scientist's preference for an *interdisciplinary* appreciation of phenomena. He will generally refuse to be bounded by disciplinary lines, except in those rare cases where the phenomenon at hand is one that can be totally explained by the constructs of a single discipline. In short, he is always searching for opportunities to make links between heretofore isolated disciplines. He does this in the recognition that science, through the past several centuries, has been primarily interested in the partitioning of real-world phenomena into successively smaller and more narrowly bounded units; this in response to the widely held belief that "wholes" could be gradually built up from an analysis of the individual parts. While this is true for essentially simple systems, it has been found to be often untrue for systems with any degree of complexity. Therefore, while normal science continues to serve the cause of *analysis*, per se, which often results in a knowledge

*George Klir, *Trends in General Systems Theory* (New York: John Wiley & Sons, 1972), p. 16.

about isolated parts at the expense of a comprehension of entities as operating wholes, the system approach seeks to give some attention to that other major aspect of science, *synthesis*.

Another distinguishing property of the system approach is that it is *a priori* uncommitted to either quantitative or qualitative analysis as the basic vehicle of scientific enterprise. Rather, the system scientist operates under an epistemological dictate laid down by Aristotle over 2400 years ago. In his *Nichomachaen Ethics*, he suggested that

> it is the mark of an educated man to look for precision in each class of thing just so far as the nature of the subject admits. It is evidently equally as foolish to accept probabilistic reasoning from a mathematician as to expect from a rhetorician rigorous proofs.

It may seem somewhat surprising that a thoroughly modern scientific movement is harking back to a philosophy that is centuries old. But it is equally surprising that the common sense displayed here has been ignored for so many centuries. What the system scientist has come again to realize, in the most explicit way, is that for anything except essentially trivial phenomena, quantitative analysis cannot provide us with a complete and accurate comprehension of system structure or behavior. By the same token, he realizes that opportunities for precision and discipline which quantification represents, should not be foregone, and that there are opportunities even within the most complex systems to inject such discipline at certain points. Thus, the models that the system scientist builds will be *syncretic*, as fully as possible exploiting opportunities for quantification. But where the properties of the problem do not admit to such techniques, he will be complementing the mathematical and statistical appreciations with qualitative constructs. He is thus not wed to any particular epistemological bias (an *a priori* concept of what constitutes a proper scientific method), but is free to let his analytical methods respond fully to the emerging properties of the problem at hand.[1]

In a word, what the system approach demands of its practitioners on the methodological dimension is *congruence*. Congruence refers to the problem solver's ability to use the right tool at the right time . . . to identify that specific instrument that should be most effective and efficient in dealing with the point-in-time properties of some problem or system he must treat.

On a broader dimension, in addition to being able to freely move between both quantitative and qualitative techniques, the system scientist should also be equally at home in those two usually isolated arenas of scientific enterprise . . . the *inductive* and *deductive* processes. The ability to work in the area between these two diverse analytical modalities is of critical importance, for the history of science has shown us that very little can be accomplished by using one, to the exclusion of the other.

In order to better understand this assertion, it is necessary to engage in a typical (if minor) system science exercise. Thus, in the next section we shall first say a few words about the difference between system complexity and system simplicity, and then advance the proposition that simple systems are most amenable to treatment using the empirical-inductive method, whereas its polar modality, the hypothetico-deductive, is most appropriate for essentially complex systems.

1.2 SYSTEM SIMPLICITY AND COMPLEXITY

The following discussion is meant to convey something of the "spirit" of a system science exercise, rather than its substance. For many of the terms used, and the basic logic, will not be familiar to a majority of readers this early in the game. Nevertheless, the way in which we distinguish simple from complex phenomena is immediately important, for it sets the stage for some methodological propositions we must make even in this introduction to our subject.

In general, the complexity or simplicity of a system with which we are forced to deal will be determined by certain properties that it exhibits on three dimensions. First are the conditions of its relationships (interfaces) with the outside world. We are concerned here with the system's ability to maintain itself within well-defined, tangible boundaries, and to protect itself against incursions of unpredictable or uncontrollable forces arising from the field or environment in which the system is resident. A simple system will thus be one whose perimeter is well defined and relatively impervious to environmental (or exogenous) intrusions. A complex system, on the other hand, will be one whose perimeter is more or less "open" to environmental or exogenous influences, especially when these are themselves complex.

The second dimension of interest refers to the structural properties of the system, (e.g., the nature of its components, the method of their distribution, and the prevailing relationships among them). Without yet going into great detail, it is clear that when the parts or constituents comprising a system are homogeneous in nature and morphology, and are arrayed in some neatly allegorizable distribution (e.g., arrayed hierarchically), we have at hand a system that is likely to be structurally simple. When, on the other hand, the system constituents are heterogeneous and distributed asymmetrically (and exhibit multidirectional, recursive, or reflexive relationships, for example), we have a system that will be unamenable to simple structural mapping.

The final dimension of interest is the dynamic aspect of a system. Here we are concerned with the changes that take place on the structural dimension through time, and in the probability of being able to accurately allegorize the causal trajectories driving those changes. So, when the behavioral repertoire available to the system constituents is highly limited, or when their functions are highly proscribed, the system in aggregate is considered simple on the dynamic dimension. On the other hand, a system would be considered dynamically complex when the interfaces and functional alternatives available to the parts is very wide such that their behavior, in the face of any given stimuli-set (any set of starting-state conditions), would be difficult to predict or control.

The inherently most simple system which we might expect to encounter, then, would be one that is *closed* to exogenous forces, structurally *homogeneous* and *symmetrical*, and functionally limited to only a single behavioral state. This system sounds very much like the artificial automata or "mechanisms" designed by engineers, systems whose prime criterion is *predictability*.

In the worst of all possible worlds, we might be forced to encounter a system whose perimeter is open to influences arising from a highly complex and protean environment, whose structure is highly differentiated, and whose parts are relatively autonomous. Many natural systems appear to be complex according to these criteria, and the legitimate tendency is to consider most social or human

ATTRIBUTES	MECHANICAL IDEAL-TYPE	ORGANIC IDEAL-TYPE
1. Interface Conditions	Usually exists within well-defined, tangible boundaries which may be adjusted endogenously for greater or lesser selectivity with respect to entering or exiting forces.	Highly open with respect to environment and exogenous forces. External determinants that affect the system may, therefore, be too far removed (spatially or temporally) to be analytically observable at any point in time.
2. Structural Characteristics	Generally has its components arrayed in a neat, observable hierarchy, with relationships among the various levels being essentially deterministic.	Parts are not arrayed in a neat, stable hierarchy but stochastically, with the magnitude and direction of interrelationships among parts altering constantly and opportunistically with respect to local changes.
3. Dynamic Properties	Parts are usually highly constrained, having only a limited repertoire of responses permitted them; causal trajectories and paths of interaction are generally fixed, controllable, and exclusive; driving forces are generally tangible and measurable.	Parts have potential for inaugurating opportunistic or strategic behavior in response to local parameter changes; causal trajectories may be altered locally and interactions may be equifinal; dynamic (driving) forces may be transparent rather than tangible and manipulable.
4. Normative Analytical Properties	—Observability —Measurability —Manipulability	—Empirical inaccessibility —Imperfect controllability —Immeasurability
5. Amenability to Analysis via Empirical-Inductive Modality	Given a set of starting-state conditions or a set of historical properties, future states may be induced with a high probability of accuracy.	Future-state conditions cannot be accurately or completely inferred from starting-state conditions, or from historical states.

Figure 1.1 The antonymical system ideal-types.

systems as being *potentially* the most complex entities with which we might have to deal.

These arguments are summarized in Figure 1.1. The dimensions of interest are arrayed as the rows of the figure, while the columns represent two abstract and polarized ideal-type systems, the *mechanical* and the *organic*. In this figure, it can be seen that the mechanical ideal-type acts as an abstract agent for system simplicity, whereas the properties associated with the organic ideal-type illustrate conditions of system complexity. These two ideal-types might be thought to represent the best and worst of all possible analytical worlds, such that the majority of the real-world systems we might expect to encounter would fall somewhere within the range defined by these two extremes . . . on a continuum of system complexity.

Some of the terms employed in the figure will certainly be unfamiliar or vague for most readers at this point, yet the organic and mechanical ideal-types should nevertheless convey fundamentally different implications. Particularly, they should set the stage for consideration of the basic proposition with which we begin: systems inhering different properties will be best approached by analytical modalities that themselves are significantly different in terms of their resolution power and the prerequisites for their employment.

Specifically, we now want to try to show, in a very crude way, that real-world systems approximating the mechanical ideal-type are properly approached via the empirical-inductive analytical modality, while organic systems demand, at least initially, that we employ the other major scientific method at our disposal, the hypothetico-deductive modality.

1.3 THE EMPIRICAL-INDUCTIVE MODALITY

Basically, as was illustrated in Figure 1.1, a "simple" system from the standpoint of a system scientist will be:

1. A system whose properties, both structural and behavioral, are fully empirically accessible to us, such that there is no aspect that is unobservable.
2. A system whose properties are amenable to quantification or precise qualification, such that we may develop numerical or qualitative surrogates of great precision to codify its characteristics.
3. A system that is amenable to experimental manipulation within what amounts to a controlled laboratory context.

When a system or phenomenon with which we are concerned meets these three criteria, it may be described as one which is analytically tractable. That simply means it presents little challenge to the imagination or instruments of the modern system scientist; it is, in fact, highly predicable. Its being entirely accessible to empirical observation—the first criterion—means that, operationally, the system analyst can develop a well articulated and highly elaborate "map" (or snapshot portrait) of its structural properties. Given this, we will be able to analyze in great detail and with great accuracy the dynamic properties of the system as reflected in changes in the structural map through time.

The *efficiency* with which we can deal with an empirically accessible system will depend in part, of course, on our ability to reduce and codify its properties to numerical values (or to other forms of symbolization that will permit us to use the instruments of modern mathematics and statistics)—the second criterion. The ability to reduce a system to quantitative terms enables us to operate on the system in abstract and achieve essentially the same results as if we were manipulating the system itself, a process which the modern electronic computer makes both feasible and economical.

The third criterion, however, is perhaps the most important, for it reflects our ability to make accurate predictions about the behavior of the system under a wide range of different circumstances. For when we can replace it in a laboratory environment—and can shelter our experiments from confounding factors or from outside influences whose effect cannot be controlled and hence accounted for—we are able to emerge with a highly accurate allegory of the system as an operating entity. Thus, in summary, the more completely a system meets the three criteria set out above, the more "simple" it is from the standpoint of the system scientist.

These criteria are pertinent because they help ensure the scientist access to an adequately accurate and relevant *data base* (i.e., an ordered collection of empirical observations taken on the phenomenon of interest), upon which inductive inferences must be based. For the inductive inference process aims ultimately at the production of laws or principles that have their roots in the observations of specific phenomena. Thus, in the world of normal (empirical-inductive) science, the researcher is presumed to have focused somehow on a class of phenomena that interests him and to have inaugurated a set of empirical observations on those subjects.

Similarities in structures or behaviors that emerge from these empirical observations then serve as the basis for the generation of an hypothesis. This hypothesis is then used to structure and discipline an experiment or set of experiments aimed at the empirical validation of the observed similarities—their breadth and depth—in the hope of arriving at a law or principle pertinent to an entire class of phenomena. Should subsequent empirical research validate the substance of the hypothesis, its implications and assertions become candidates for entry into the arsenal of scientific theory; theory being an ordered set of assertions about a generic behavior or structure assumed to hold throughout a significantly broad range of specific instances. In short, then, empirical-inductive science tends to think of itself as that enterprise that elicits theory from facts and facts from observations, such that (at least in principle) the derogatory influences of prejudice, opinion, or bias are effectively minimized.

As most readers probably already know, empirical-inductive procedures have monopolized science since Francis Bacon and Galileo ushered in the "Age of Reason." For, as Gardner Murphy reports:

> Modern science took shape by observing and describing the world outside us . . . it became 'exact science' when it was grasped that things observed can become things measured. . . . With these observational skills go mathematical skills, such as those used by Einstein in the establishment of relativity theory. Today, experimental and theoretical physics, shot through and through with mathematical sophistication, have convinced us that the 'real' world is that *physical* world which observation, measurement and calculation have established.[2]

In short, the only reality which *normal* modern science hopes to obtain is that which is available to us through the manipulation, codification, and extension of empirical observations. And thus, under the empiricist banner, the scientific method has become virtually identical to the exploitation of the inductive inference process.

1.4 THE HYPOTHETICO-DEDUCTIVE MODALITY

The alert system scientist will suggest that there is a relatively significant class of phenomena (i.e., essentially "organic" systems) that simply do not meet the above criteria, and hence are not proper targets for empirical-inductive analysis. In treating such systems as these, the scientist is forced to adopt an analytical modality that does not depend for its significance on the availability of a high-quality data base . . . the *hypothetico-deductive modality*.

The hypothetico-deductive modality is characterized by the generation of hypotheses whose origins are not derived exclusively from observation. Rather, the hypothesis owes at least some portion of its substance to cognitive devices such as imagination, fabrication, intuition, subjectivity, speculation, metaphysics, or other essentially idiosyncratic or idiographic intellectual methods. In short, if the inductive-empirical methods asks us to manipulate percepts (e.g., sense data; sets of observations), the hypothetico-deductive method allows us to manipulate concepts and still be scientific. For the *hypothetico* component suggests that our concepts are not to take the form of dogma or categorical imperatives, but true hypotheses . . . structures that may serve as the guides and bases for investigation and whose ultimate validity or rectitude depends on the extent to which they are subsequently empirically validated. Thus, the hypothetico-deductive modality frees the scientist from the strictures of empiricism but, at the same time, demands that he maintain integrity by subjecting his speculations or deductive constructs to the same type of empirical testing to which we subject inductively-predicated hypotheses. This is all that can be asked of a scientific, as opposed to a casuistic, effort.

But the system scientist really need not engage in such arguments, for his case that the hypothetico-deductive modality should be exploited to the fullest can be made in a very concrete and immediate way. For whenever we come upon systems that significantly exhibit properties that we associated earlier with "organic" entities, he has little choice but to employ (at least initially) the hypothetico-deductive modality. Among such properties would be the following:

1. When the phenomenon under investigation is one whose future behavior is unlikely to be any calculable function of its historical behavior.
2. When a phenomenon is empirically inaccessible (e.g., cosmological or teleological issues; extraterrestial systems; prehistoric cultures).
3. When, under the auspices of structural or cross-section analysis, the properties of the observed (or empirically accessible) portion of a phenomenon are unlikely to be reproduced in the unobserved or unobservable portions . . . e.g., where the observed properties are heterogeneous, distributed asymmetrically and/or undergoing rapid morphological change.
4. Where certain properties of phenomena, or even phenomena themselves, are empirically transparent in the absence of a structuralizing *a priorism* (e.g., the empirical evidence which lent subsequent support to the Darwinian hypothesis was available to many researchers; it was Darwin's unique conceptual "mask" that enabled him to see relationships and implications which were transparent to others).
5. Where the phenomenon at hand is too large or complex to be treated empirically as a single unit of analysis, but where its reduction to artificially isolated parts is impermissible. (As with, for example, many organismic as opposed to mechanistic systems).

Thus, so long as scientists and problem-solvers continue to bind themselves to a methodology that demands that their subjects be empirically accessible, measurable, and controllable (manipulable in an experimental setting), they automatically constrain themselves from dealing effectively with most of the significant social, political, and economic problems which plague our age . . . for these, almost without exception, must be classed as organic rather than mechanical in nature. And it might be added here that, fortunately, many of the truly great scientists did not heed this *a priori* methodological constraint.

In summary, then, there is absolutely nothing to be gained by *a priori* restricting ourselves to either the inductive or deductive modalities, nor by restricting our competence to either quantitative or qualitative analysis alone.

Rather, the properties of the phenomenon at hand should determine our approach. Thus, those scientists who neglect the deductive potential and demand that all truth be sought solely through observation and inductive inferences drawn from those observations, work against ultimate success as surely as do those rhetoricians who deny observation any role (e.g., those who distrust all sense data as being delusionary). Such restrictions contravene logic as well, for there is always some positive (if not often significant) probability that reason, speculation, intuition, or imagination might arrive serendipitously at a truth with greater efficiency than empirical trial and error operated on by induction.

In fact, where the problem at hand is an extremely complex one, characterized perhaps by nonhierarchical structure, nonalgorithmic behavior, or equifinal potential, the probability of arriving most expeditiously at an adequate explanatory/predictive allegory may very well shift in favor of nonempirical methods. Thus, the inductive and deductive methods are not so much competitors as complementary modalities. For, in essence, the deductive approach is employed only when we lack the predicates for the inductive, and is employed in the thought that hopefully our operations on the deductive dimension will ultimately allow us to employ the more precise and generally more accurate inductive methods. In short, in the face of extremely complex phenomena, the hypothetico-deductive modality is not a substitute for the inductive, but a prerequisite.

1.5 POLARIZATION AND PAROCHIALIZATION

The fact that a system scientist holds no *a priori* methodological bias in favor of either of these modalities gives him the platform that he needs to be able to successfully attack one of the most debilitating problems in modern scientific enterprise (particularly among the social, behavioral, and administrative sciences)— *polarization*. Secondly, if we can solve the polarization problem, even partially, this might constitute a direct attack on the other major symptom of debilitation in modern science—*parochialization*.

Polarization owes its origin to the tendency for individual scientists—and in general, disciplines—to adopt one analytical modality to the effective exclusion of the other. Polarization works primarily *within* disciplines, splitting resident scientists into two camps. In the social and behavioral sciences, for example, those scientists who adhere strictly to the empirical-inductive modality generally tend to approach their subjects quantitatively.* Whereas those scientists who work deductively generally tend to adopt a rhetorical approach (which is simply the hypothetico-deductive method minus the hypothetico component). When polarization is strong, the area between these two methodological poles is largely unpopulated, such that no bases for communication exist between the inductivists and deductivists. For those at the empirical-inductive pole will tend to employ the vocabulary of concepts and operations inherent in experimental research (e.g., hypothesis-testing), whereas those at the deductive pole will tend to employ idiographic, fuzzy, or broad qualitative concepts and constructs that the empiricist-inductivist usually sees as having no scientific merit.

---

*Another way of saying this is to suggest that their interest lies in structuring experiments that may be engined by operations of statistical inference, or in defining their units of analysis so as to permit treatment using the instruments of the physical sciences, etc.

On the other hand, the qualitative scientist will look dubiously at the quantitative scientist, perhaps suggesting that the limited hypotheses of the latter hold very little interest for science and very little promise for explanation of complex system behavior. Nowhere is polarization more evident than in the social sciences, as this statement by sociologist Robert Merton so well points out;

> On the one hand, we observe those sociologists who seek above all to generalize, to find their way as rapidly as possible to the formulation of sociological laws. Tending to assess the significance of sociological work in terms of scope rather than the demonstrability of generalizations, they eschew the "triviality" of detailed, small-scale observation and seek the grandeur of global summaries. At the other extreme stands a hardy band who do not hunt too closely the implications of their research but who remain confident and assured that what they report is so. To be sure, their reports of facts are verifiable and often verified, but they are somewhat at a loss to relate these facts to one another or even to explain why these, rather than other, observations have been made. For the first group the identifying motto would at times seem to be: "We do not know whether what we say is true, but it is at least significant." And for the radical empiricist the motto may read: "This is demonstrably so, but we cannot indicate its significance."[3]

Now, both the deductive grand-theory builder and the inductive hypothesis-tester may simply be responding to essentially *a prioristic* assertions about the natures of the subjects they have elected to treat. It may be, then, that there are no middle-range constructs[4] to connect these two extremes simply because, before the advent of the system approach as an epistemological platform, there was no eclectic, moderating scientific philosophy . . . just the two polar extremes.

Thus, again with reference to the field of sociology, so eminent a scholar as Pitirim Sorokin can out of hand deny the contribution of the mathematical-statistical instruments for, to him

> . . . there is the fundamental difference between sociocultural and physio-chemical—or even purely biological—phenomena. It consists in a profound difference between the componential structure of sociocultural phenomena on the one hand, and that of physiochemical and purely biological phenomena on the other. Any empirical sociocultural phenomena consists of three components: (1) immaterial, spaceless and timeless meanings; (2) material (physio-chemical and biological) vehicles that "materialize, externalize, or objectify" the meanings; (3) human agents that bear, use, and operate the meanings with the help of material vehicles.[5]

In short, sociocultural phenomena, from Sorokin's standpoint, are numinous and empirically transparent, and therefore generally unamenable to treatment by instruments of the type that the physicist or chemist might employ. He has therefore cautioned explicitly against importing the methodological principles or analytical instruments from the physical sciences into the social sciences. Thus Sorokin may be thought to act as an agent for the deductive (rhetorical) pole of the social sciences. That this position has a long and honored tradition is indicated by the fact that one of the earliest and certainly most eminent of sociologists, Max Weber, operated under the belief: "an objective analysis of cultural events, which proceeds according to the thesis that the ideal science is the reduction of the empirical reality to law" is meaningless.[6]

There are, of course, *a prioristic* defenses made for the use of the inductive-empirical modality in the social sciences, thus establishing the other pole. The logic behind this position—and hence the demand that social science subjects be approached as if they were reducible to the same form as the subjects of classical physics, etc.—is presented by the sociologist George Lundberg:

> All phenomena are different in some respects. All of them are similar in one highly vital respect, namely, in that they are all known, if at all, through sense experience conceptualized and organized into the patterns determined by the nature of the human organism as conditioned by all its environments .... Are the means by which we know societal phenomena fundamentally different than the means by which we know physical phenomena? If they are not, then it is as irrelevant . . . to enumerate "differences" between "physical" and societal phenomena as it would be to claim that the differences between ants, spiders, and grasshoppers preclude a science of biology.[7]

Thus, within just one discipline, we have one group for whom their subjects remain empirically elusive and who therefore argue for an essentially subjective approach, while another group argues just as strongly that sociocultural phenomenon are just as amenable to objective (e.g., reductive, statistically disciplined) analysis as any other aspect of the world in which we live. When scientists are thus so divided on basic epistemological issues, it is small surprise that there is the disturbing absence of the type of middle-range construct that Merton and others have advocated. Thus we find, in the sociobehavioral sciences, not one sociology but two, not one psychology but several, not one economics or anthropology but two, etc. And, to a lesser extent, much the same thing may be said of some of the disciplines in the "hard" natural and physical sciences.

It is into the ignored middle-range, then, that the system scientist brings his concept of the syncretic analytical modality, which simply asks that the properties of the problem at hand determine our analytical approach and not any epistemological biases we happen to hold. Under the syncretic modality then, whenever we set about modeling a system—in the attempt to understand or predict its behavior or simply in an effort to describe its structure—we are asked to treat mathematically or statistically those aspects of the system that will lend themselves to such precision, and to employ our deductive techniques in the approach to those aspects of the system that are too complex or "fuzzy" to be reduced to quantitative terms. In actual practice, this means that we initially approach a complex system using a hypothetico-deductive modality, in order to gain some comprehension of the whole *before* we proceed to attempt to comprehend the parts. Thus, the broad structure and causality of the system is captured analytically (and abstractly) in terms of a hypothetico-deductive model which will be used to guide and structure our subsequent empirical researches. These empirical researches must be aimed at gradually translating the hypothetical or subjective portions of the model to objective, empirical validated ones.

Clearly, the extent to which a system can be reduced ultimately to quantitative terms depends largely on the inherent properties of the system itself. But generally speaking we expect that our ability to precisely and accurately capture the properties of any system will depend largely on the amount of analytical resources, time, and effort we are willing to spend in its resolution. Therefore, at virtually all points in the problem solving or system analysis process undertaken by the system theorist, the "reality" of the system is approximated by a model that simultaneously involves both qualitative and quantitative components. The construction of such models obviously means that the historically unpopulated middle-range between empiricists and rhetoricians now must be occupied. For the type of construct approved of by the system theorist will be a Janus-faced one, with one face pointing toward the opportunities for integration and articulation with higher-order theories, while the other face scans the empirical domain for the opportunities to validate or invalidate the hypothetical or deductive components. In short, the system theorist holds a feedback-based concept of science, where experiment and empirical research lend an element of experience that may then bend back and alter, modify, or displace the essentially deductive components through which the first tentative analytical feel for a complex phenomenon was gained.

The system theorist must also be Janus-faced, appreciating the expedience and precision associated with reductionism, surrogation, quantification, and controlled experimentation, and appreciating the contribution from the disciplined development and manipulation of concepts whose origin is "defactual," i.e., conceptual rather than perceptual. Thus, with respect to the phenomenon of polarization, the first evidence of a system approach being adopted within a discipline emerges with those scientists who have thrown off the shackles of the particular epistemological platform on which they were initially raised and who manage to synthesize—within themselves—the sensitivity and conceptual elasticity of the deductivist with the precision and discipline of the empiricist. As more and more scientists move towards such a syncretic position, the symptoms of polarization may be expected to gradually disappear, such that we will no longer have two psychologies, two biologies or two economics, etc., but disciplines unified around the complimentary relationship between quantitative and qualitative analysis and between the inductive and deductive modalities in general. It is in such a cause that the system scientist may most directly and immediately benefit the community of knowledge.

Polarization, however, is not the only problem that adversely affects modern scientific enterprise. There is also the problem of *parochialization* (which may, in many cases, be a derivation of polarization). Parochialization refers to the partitioning of complex real-world systems into parts that are then distributed among existing academic disciplines, disciplines that seldom interchange or communicate with one another. When we review the structure of modern science, we tend to see the individual academic areas as residences for large collections of essentially *intradisciplinary* models, where the variables of other academic disciplines usually are entered as unspecified exogenous effects. Thus, explanations of system behavior tend often to be relevant to system partitions that in the real-world, simply do not exist. For example, it hardly makes sense to talk about an economic system bereft of behavioral or social influences, just as it makes little sense to talk about a purposive social system without bringing in concepts developed by economists. Yet economics and sociology seldom cojoin, so the concept of a socioeconomic system is yet to be treated except in the most desultory way, though they are the most frequently encountered and most important organizational phenomena in the modern world.

In terms of countering parochialization, the biological and physical sciences are somewhat advanced of the social and behavioral, for there are many new disciplines springing up that act as interfaces between existing academic partitions, among them biophysics, biochemistry, bioengineering, psychophysics, physiochemistry, etc. Such hybrid disciplines help compensate for the long generations of *analytic* reduction through which real-world systems were gradually reduced to parts at the expense of the comprehension of systems as wholes. In short, the hybrid disciplines directly serve the cause of *synthesis*, as their units of analysis are, generally speaking, more encompassing and complex than those of the individual disciplines of which they are comprised. To continue and extend such work must be one of the prime areas of focus for the system scientist.

Just how critical the need for such integration is can be reflected in a debacle whose effects are still being felt by all of us. Several years ago it was recognized that inflation was becoming a serious problem in the United States. The president turned to economists for an answer, and they returned with a solution right out of the textbook . . . the imposition of a surtax. According to traditional economic theory, a surtax would reduce disposable personal income that, in the process, would result in a lower effective demand for goods and services (largely because the individual consumer would have less dollars to bid). This lowering of demand, again according to economic theory, would result in a decrease in inflation, resulting directly from the reduction in prices associated with a lowering demand schedule.

The issue to be resolved in terms of policy was not whether the surtax itself would prove a functional strategy—economic theory had no doubts about that— but rather what level surtax should be imposed to get the proper degree of reduction in inflation without incurring deflation. Econometric models were developed to simulate the effects of various levels and, finally, a specific surtax was agreed on and implemented. The results were inexplicable from the standpoint of the economists: despite the surtax, inflation kept rising. But what had happened was perfectly clear from the standpoint of the sociologist or behavioral scientist. They recognize that every element of economic theory, when applied in the real-world, must be mediated by a factor that is transparent to, and hence usually disregarded by, the economist: *expectations*. In this particular case, the need for a surtax was interpreted by consumers as just another sign of emerging economic chaos and instability. In short, *the fact that a surtax was proposed at all led to increasingly adverse expectations* for large numbers of consumers. Under adverse expectations about the future, the consumers (despite reduction in disposable income) wished to make purchases now and pay later with what they thought were sure to be cheaper dollars. Thus many compensated for their reduced incomes by two ancillary moves that had not been foreseen by the economists. First, they acquired current buying power by drawing on their savings accounts; secondly, they went deeper into debt, radically increasing consumer credit. Both these factors, and especially the latter, put direct pressure on prices and kept inflation rising.

The point in this anecdote is as simple as it is compelling: the degree of parochialization one finds among disciplines results in advice (e.g., policy or decision premises) from science to the real-world that occasionally proves dysfunctional. In this particular case, formal links between the economic and sociobehavioral disciplines would have avoided this error . . . it is inconceivable that even the most mediocre sociologist or psychologist could have failed to demand that the policy-makers receive a prediction about the possible effects of the expectation operator. Thus, when the system scientist stresses the need for interdisciplinary attack on real-world problems—when he condemns academic parochialism as either precarious or dysfunctional—he may do so with reference to a long list of policy failures in the real-world.

It was mentioned earlier that parochialization may be viewed as a derivative of polarization. The rationale behind this assertion is simple. Partitioning and reduction of systems to lower-order units of analysis ultimately serves the causes of observation, measurement, and manipulation, which in turn serve the cause of empirical-inductive science. Empirical-inductive science, then, when carried to its logical conclusion would naturally result in a fractionation of science . . . a secularly increasing degree of specialization. Specialization is reinforced by the fact that analytic instruments have become so powerful in modern science, while instruments of synthesis have lagged well behind in terms of sophistication and operationality, such that system reduction is usually a far simpler process than system synthesis. So, following the historical condemnation of deductive instruments as unscientific, and lacking other means for gaining synoptic appreciations of complex phenomena, "science" became reduction, and the disciplines became proudly parochial. In short, the end of parochialization can only be seen as the end to that downward spiral that finds the vast majority of scientists emphasizing analysis at the expense of synthesis.

But because synthesis will demand the development of a methodology for treating complex phenomena as wholes—as instances of organized complexity— it apparently must wait on the sophistication and gradual maturation of the system sciences themselves, the vehicles for dealing with complex, nonreduced entities that are nonmechanical in nature. It appears, then, that the answer to polarization may also be the answer to parochialization . . . the development of *syncretic* methodologies that simultaneously accommodate both qualitative and quantitative contributions to the extent that both are valuable. In this sense, then, the system theorist emerges primarily as an epistemologist whose utility will be at least partially reflected in the extent to which he is able to cause a reduction in the degree of polarization and parochialization associated with modern scientific enterprise.

1.6 BEYOND TECHNOCRACY

The empiricist dominance of modern science has militated against the development of an appreciation of complex phenomena as wholes and, as discussed, has been responsible for the instances of parochialization and polarization we note among disciplines . . . especially those of the social, behavioral, and administrative sciences. The result is a separation between science and community, between academics and applications. As things now stand, the policy- or decision-maker looking for specific direction from the social or administrative sciences, direction that considers problems as "wholes" in the same frame of reference as does the man responsible for solving them, is likely to be very ill-served indeed . . . as were those government officials who relied on inputs from theoretical economics to treat inflation. He will find competitive paradigms, each purporting to be *the* explanation for a particular problem, and this multiplicity of proffered solutions extends across the board, whether he is concerned about treating behavioral pathologies, economic underdevelopment, social casualties, or political conflicts. For there is not a single economics, a single psychology, or a single sociology; but multiple, warring, and often uncommunicating "schools" within each of these disciplines. Thus, the causes cited for a problem—and the ostensible solutions offered—depend not so much on what particular discipline one turns to as on what school within the discipline one consults.

Parochialization in our disciplines may operate then on two planes: first, there is the glaring lack of articulation among the disciplines themselves; secondly, the lack of articulation and coordination among the polarized schools within the disciplines. And this not only contributes to the elements of redundancy and inefficiency we associate with the sociobehavioral and administrative sciences, but to the generally dismal reputation they enjoy among practical men with real problems, and also among members of the exact or hard sciences. For, from their perspective, these disciplines do not appear to be the evolving, concatenative enterprises of the physical sciences, but rather *theatrical* enterprises where the "truths" of matters dealt with go in and out of style with their ideological-emotional currency.

These are harsh words, but compelling. For the hallmark of our times is the coexistence of great triumphs in the technological and physical domains, and dismal failure in the fields of morals, politics, values, socioeconomic development, etc. Those who have no firm understanding of the inherent complexity of such subjects may properly ask, should we not turn social and economic development over to the computer scientists and engineers? Cannot the same techniques that put men on the moon and mice in orbit around Mars clear up slums, dismount alienation and anomie from the great horse of state, and automate welfare, health, and education? The answer is, of course, a resounding *no*—not unless we want more Apollo III's or Edsels than we already have.

One of the principal reasons for our doubt about the ability to engineer solutions to social, economic, behavioral, and political problems is a sutle but critical one—the engineering sciences generally deal with phenomena that lend themselves quite well to deterministic treatments, that are mechanical in nature. That is, the subjects they have traditionally dealt with *successfully* represent an entirely different genre than those that are the concern of the social and behavioral sciences. For the subjects of the engineers are usually fabrications of man himself, constructed from some blueprint and comprised of components that have little choice except to do what the engineers designed them to do. In most situations then, arguments about "ends" are gratuitous; it is the search for effectively optimal "means" to achieve already given ends that occupies most engineers, whether they are working on pollution control devices for automobiles, longer-life color television tubes, or rockets with greater payload capacities. And for our immediate purposes here, the critical characteristic of such problems is that they permit the employment of what we have called the *analytic modality* . . . the gradual emergence of an optimal system structure or problem solution by varying only one factor at a time, holding all others constant.

This modality fails, however, at the point where the essentially *mechanical* subjects of the engineering sciences turn into the essentially *organic* subjects of the social, behavioral, or administrative sciences. Thus, as opposed to the analytic-deterministic approach of the engineers, the sociobehavioral systems analyst, for example, is going to have to operate under a radically different analytical modality, one characterized by the following dictates:

- Until empirical investigation indicates otherwise, treat all social, behavioral, economic, or political phenomena as effectively unreducible, and hence as unamenable to any analytic approaches that deny the simultaneous and inseparable quality of *all* determinants. Hence, social, behavioral, economic, or political phenomena become proper targets for an *holistic* approach . . . one that treats the entity as a whole, whose substance is jointly determined by the interaction of variables from many different disciplines.

- Develop constructs or system models that meet the criteria of the middle-range. Such constructs will both scan the empirical domain for opportunities to validate or invalidate the theoretical or deductive premises, and search the conceptual or theoretical hierarchy of the several disciplines for points of conceptual interchange or analogy (this latter to counter redundancy and inject greater theoretical efficiency into the several disciplines).
- Finally, develop models that employ a methodological *mix* that reflects the distribution of the subject system's properties into those that will permit precise quantitative treatment and those that must be approached via qualitative instruments (e.g., verbal analysis, comparative statics, metaphorical model-building).

To add what is probably a gratuitous caveat: the methodological treatment we give our subjects should reflect the emerging properties of the entity itself, not the epistemological prejudices of some "school" or metaphysical platform.

Thus, the system scientist is not simply a glorified engineer or operations researcher, trying to impose mathematical and statistical models on every phenomena he encounters. Nor are all system scientists committed to the computer as the saving grace of civilization, or to quantification as the *sine qua non* of science. He recognizes that different problems require different solution modalities, and is hence problem-oriented rather than tool-oriented. And while he might disagree with Sorokin that all sociocultural phenomena are *a priori* unamenable to any kind of quantitative treatment, the true system scientist would applaud Sorokin's view that

> mere mechanical borrowing and importation of principles from the natural sciences cannot serve the purpose of the scientific study of sociocultural phenomena; for when literally transposed from one field to the other, they prove to be inadequate. The invariant result is the distortion of these principles as they are given in the natural sciences; the creation of an amateurish and superfluous pseudophysics, pseudomechanics, pseudomathematics, and pseudobiology, running parallel with the real natural sciences; and, finally, a virtual failure to grasp the essence of sociocultural phenomena in their static and dynamic aspects.[8]

With this very brief introduction to some of the more important epistemological predicates of system science, we may now move toward the first of the key substantive concepts . . . the identification and exploitation of isomorphisms and analogic models.

1.7 NOTES AND REFERENCES

1. For more on this point, see my *A General Systems Philosophy for the Social and Behavioral Sciences* (New York: George Braziller, 1973), especially Chapter 2.
2. Gardner Murphy, "The Inside and Outside of Creativity," *Fields Within Fields . . . Within Fields*, 2 no. 1, pp. 7-9.
3. Robert Merton, *Social Theory and Social Structure* (New York: Free Press, 1968), p. 139.
4. *Ibid.*, p. 139ff.
5. Pitirim Sorokin, *Sociocultural Causality, Space and Time* (New York: Russell & Russell, 1964), p. v.
6. Henderson and Parson's translation of Max Weber's *The Theory of Social and Economic Organization* (New York: Oxford University Press, 1947), p. 88.
7. George Lundberg, *Foundations in Sociology* (New York: Macmillan Publishing Co., 1939), p. 40.
8. Sorokin, *op.cit.*, p. 236.

2

Modalities of System Structure

2.0 INTRODUCTION

Recall from the Preface, that one of the keystones of the system approach is the search for, and exploitation of, isomorphisms among systems. It is worthwhile to repeat here Zadeh and Polak's statement that

> . . . a system theorist is a scientific generalist whose interests and expertise cut across many established fields of science. It does not matter to him whether a system is electrical, mechanical, economic, biological, or whatnot in nature. What matters is whether it is linear or nonlinear, discrete-time or continuous time, lumped or distributed, deterministic or stochastic, continuous-state or discrete-state, passive or active, etc. In short, it is the mathematical structure of a system, and not its physical form or area of application, that is of interest to a system theorist.[1]

While we shall later relax the implication that the system scientist looks solely for mathematical structures, it is clear that when we consider real-world systems with reference to abstractions such as linearity or nonlinearity, etc., we are on the track of *generality* and *simplicity*. For the concept of a linear system, for example, is not restricted to any particular field of activity . . . real-world systems of approximately linear behavior extend from the lowest-order units of analysis in physics to some relatively highly evolved sociocultural systems.

In short, when two superficially very different systems can both be shown to behave linearly, then there is isomorphy between those systems. So far as that particular aspect of behavior is concerned, then, we can develop a single causal model whose properties are pertinent to both systems, presuming we know something about linearity as a *generic* phenomenon. If a significant number of widely diverse systems may be shown to be special cases of this generic linearity model, then the cause of scientific efficiency has been served through generalization. In this sense, the system theorist is at work trying to displace myriad localized, specific models with a fewer number of generalized models. In doing this, he directly attacks disciplinary parochialism, for linearity, as a property, is not exclusive to the subjects of any particular discipline or area of application.

The same arguments apply to a wide range of other generic system abstractions, among them the other cases cited in the Zadeh and Polak statement, and this chapter is concerned with their definition and elaboration. In the process of introducing these referents against which structural properties of real-world systems may be compared, the utility of abstractions in their own right is also stressed. In the world of the layman, the process of abstraction takes on pejorative overtones. It seems to reflect the undue complication of a subject, or its removal from the realm of relevance. In the scientific domain, just the opposite situation prevails . . . abstractions, properly employed, become engines of simplicity.

The objective that scientific abstractions seek is economy of allegorization relative to accuracy of description. Specifically, we want to isolate from among all properties of a system those that will permit us to give a reasonably accurate portrayal of the system's structure or behavior using the fewest possible variables (and postulating the fewest possible relationships among those variables). An allegory (e.g., model) is always a simplification until it becomes an oversimplification . . . where we remove so many complexities from the real-world entity in constructing our model that the model no longer adequately reflects reality. Nevertheless, an *appropriate* degree of abstraction allows us to operate on a simplified model of the system while making the assumption that these abstract manipulations are to a certain extent, roughly equivalent to having manipulated the real-world system itself. In this sense, virtually all the models of science become abstractions, and hence simplifications of reality; and virtually all the instruments available to us (mathematical programming, statistical analysis, simulation, etc.) are designed to manipulate abstractions. Thus, when we look at real-world systems as instances of linear behavior, stochastic-state structure, etc., we are abstracting in the name of both simplicity and generality.

The problem however is in determining—for any given phenomenon or class of phenomena—just what the *appropriate* level of abstraction might be. The tendency is always to try to inject simplicity into analytical operations by imposing the simplest and most tractable abstraction on a system. Thus, for example, we might try to treat some problems that are clearly nonlinear as linear, so that we may employ the neat and expedient instrument known as linear programming; or we might feel that we are warranted in assuming a system that is actually stochastic-state to be a finite-state system so that we can treat it using the well-developed instruments of finite-state system analysis. In either case, analytical expedience is traded off against the ultimate accuracy of the descriptions or predictions. It was the recognition that abstractions offer both benefits of simplicity and generality, while carrying the potential of misinformation, that Anatol Rapoport laid down this dictum for the system scientist, ". . . seek simplicity and distrust it."[2]

In a later chapter much more will be said about the problem of determining "appropriate" levels of abstraction, and also about methods of calculating objective trade-offs between descriptive (or predictive) accuracy and analytical expedience. Here we simply introduce a set of abstractions most commonly employed by system scientists . . . those that have historically proven most fruitful in leading toward structural isomorphisms among widely diverse systems, and hence toward opportunities for generalization and simplification. The abstractions introduced here, referred to as generic system structural referents, have thus become key elements in the system sciences' conceptual vocabulary, and will serve as points of departure for many discussions in subsequent chapters.

2.1 THE STRUCTURAL DIMENSION

The most frequently employed model in the system sciences is given in Figure 2.1. Very simply, a system is seen as a causal sequence which finds a stream of

Figure 2.1 The "Black Box" model.

inputs being transformed into a stream of outputs by some process (the proverbial "black box"). Structural analysis asks that we take a "snap-shot" of the system at some specific point in time (or space). When we switch to a consideration of the behavioral or dynamic aspects of systems (as in Chapter 3) we then are concerned with the nature of the relationships between inputs and outputs or, more broadly, with the time-dependent *changes* in system structure. And, in Chapter 4, we see that proper systems analysis consists in simultaneously considering both structural and behavioral properties. Nevertheless, the admittedly simplistic consideration of a system as an ordered combination of inputs, outputs, and process is useful in these formative stages of our inquiry into the system sciences.

When we are concerned with the *structural* dimension of a system, we are interested in making a *map* of the contents of the process box. This *map* should show what components comprise the system, and indicate the nature of the prevailing relationships among them.

In developing a system map, there are basically three tasks we must perform. First we must isolate the system boundaries and, in the process, identify the major components of the system (e.g., the parts comprising a machine; the individuals of which a social group is constituted; the subsystems that, when integrated, yield a macrosystem of some sort). Secondly, given the system boundaries and the array of system components, we must then develop a (spatial) distribution that illustrates where each component resides relative to every other. Thirdly, we must represent the prevailing relationships among the system components, or at least those that tend to be relatively stable through time. Thus, we might be interested in which components of the system can potentially interact with which others, and describe any constraints on these interactions (e.g., component *a* can interact with component *b* in a positive fashion only, such that an increase in the value of *a* leads to an increase in the value of *b*). In the third aspect of the structural analysis process, then, we are interested in the *interface conditions* that exist among system components, especially as concerns the permissibility of interactions and their nature.

To use a simple analogy, the structural analysis of a system is roughly equivalent to a geographical map, where the various sovereign nations might represent system components and where the spatial projection employed gives an idea of the relative placement of each. If we were then to impose something such as the relatively permanent patterns of trade among these nations or the various treaty alliances, etc., we would have the geographer's counterpart to the "prevailing relationships" sought by the system scientist.

With these basics at hand, we may now proceed to explore some of the more important structural modalities used by system scientists, beginning initially with two very abstract but very important classifications: (a) discrete vs. continuous-state systems, and (b) linear vs. nonlinear systems.

2.1.1 Discrete and Continuous-State Systems

We cannot yet provide a formal definition of system state. It is a very complex concept which will not become fully operational until Chapter 5. Nevertheless, one of the most important structural aspects of systems refers to the concept of state, so we approach it tentatively and quite crudely here.

Consider, initially, that every system has properties that serve to distinguish it as a unique entity. In the most basic sense, the collection of these properties—at a specific point in time—constitutes the *state* of that system at that time. When properties change through time, this constitutes a state-change that results, in effect, in a redefinition of the system. These changes may be either quite significant or negligible; nevertheless, when properties alter, the system scientist must be prepared to alter his conception (or model) of that system.

What concerns us here is the fact that system scientists tend to distinguish between two types of states which systems may generate: *discrete* and *continuous*. The general system theorist, George Klir, has defined discrete systems as those whose quantities," . . . acquire a finite number of discrete values and are known only at discrete instants of time." Continuous-state systems are, on the other hand, those with, ". . . quantities that are regarded as continuously variable in continuous time over the whole range of activity."[3] These definitions become very important to the system scientist, for continuous- and discrete-state systems are approached using very different operational tools and they demand basically different modeling technologies. While this point may be immediately clear to those with a mathematics, statistics, or engineering background, it may escape those without such a background. So it is worthwhile to provide a simple elaboration of these concepts.

First of all, the idea of discrete and continuous systems evolves from the statistician's concept of discrete and continuous variables. A discrete (random) variable is one that assumes *point* values at specific *points* in time. In general, these values will be real numbers. In effect, then, a discrete-state system is one whose states may be defined as a point in time and assigned real values. Such systems are frequently encountered in the real-world. A roulette wheel or a poker hand, for example, constitutes a system that resolves into discrete states; so does a business enterprise when we consider its state to be represented by a balance sheet or income statement. In roulette, the slot the ball falls into, at a specific point in time, gives a specific number. A poker hand, at a specific point in time, is defined by the cards held. A business, when evaluated at the end of a fiscal year, becomes intelligible in terms of the distribution of assets and liabilities which resolve to real numbers.

When we speak of a discrete-state system, then, we are speaking of one that may be made intelligible in terms of a set of random variables that, at specific points in time, have positive probabilities of assuming specific, real values. Where these values may only be integers (i.e., whole numbers), we speak of a system as being an *integer-state system*, as with the roulette wheel. This concept derives directly from the way in which the statistician defines a random variable. Hoel, Port, and Stone define it,

let X be a discrete real-valued random variable. Thus, for any number x, $\{w: X(w) = x\}$ is an event. Indeed, if $x_1, x_2, \ldots$, are the values that X can assume, then $\{w: X(w) = x_i\}$ is an event by the definition of a discrete real-valued random variable.[4]

They then extend this definition to incorporate the positive probabilities associated with values that discrete random variables may assume:

The real-valued function f defined on R by $f(x) = P(X = x)$ is called the discrete density function of X. A number x is called a possible value of X if $f(x) > 0$.

In summary, this means that we arrive at the state definition of a discrete-state system by elaborating a function such as the following:

$$S_t = f(X_1, X_2, X_3, \ldots, X_n)_t$$

where:

$P(X = x_i)_t > 0$
$X \in R$
R is the domain of real numbers.

Note, then, that an integer-state system would impose the added condition that $x = 0, 1, 2, \ldots, n$.

Klir suggests that, for discrete-state systems

> ... it is possible to express relations between the principle quantities by equations of some particular logic algebra. ... Problems of composition and decomposition of the relations are then solved within the respective algebra.[5]

While this proposition may not be clear to some readers at this point, it will be treated at some length in subsequent chapters. What is important here is to note the distinction in treatment Klir makes with respect to the *continuous* state system, where, "... the relation between the quantities are generally expressed by differential equations."[6]

Good examples of continuous-state systems are thermostats or hour-glasses. In the case of a thermostat, temperatures are constantly fluctuating around some point value, or may be thought to have a *limiting* value approaching some specific (discrete) temperature. In an hourglass, the sand flows constantly, such that there is no specific point in time at which a meaningful measurement can be taken ... the system is continuously in a state of change, just as is the thermostat. Other measurement (as opposed to counting) variables that must be treated as continuous are: spatial coordinates, velocity, time, voltage, pressure, etc. For variables such as these, we must employ calculus; whereas discrete variables are approachable algebraically.

This becomes clear when we consider the fundamental differences between discrete and continuous systems so far as probabilities of events occurring (e.g., values assumed by random variables) are concerned. Remember that for a discrete-state system, states could be evaluated in terms of point values at specific points in time. However, when we refer to continuous systems—comprised of continuous variables—point values at specific points in time have absolutely no probability of occurrence, such that:

$$P(\{X = x_i\}) = 0, \quad \text{for:} \quad -\infty < X < +\infty.$$

However, while point values have no relevance with respect to continuous-state systems, the following formulation does have importance for us:

$$P(\{X \gtreqless x_i\}) > 0, \quad \text{for:} \quad -\infty < X < +\infty.$$

This suggests that we *can* arrive at a positive probability that a random variable in a continuous system will take on a value less than or greater than some value. In short, in moving from discrete to continuous systems, the equalities associated with the former are replaced by inequalities in the latter.

The normal procedure in dealing with continuous random variables is to consider the probability of a value falling within some *interval*, say $P(a < x < b)$. This probability is evaluated by subtracting the value of the boundary probability density function, or,

$$P(a < X \leqslant b) = F(b) - F(a); \quad a \leqslant b.$$

What is essentially different between discrete and continuous random variables is the way in which the probability density functions are calculated, with the function for the continuous variable being an integration function such that:

$$\int_{-\infty}^{+\infty} f(x)\,dx = 1.$$

Given this, the formulation for the calculation of the probability that X (as a continuous random variable) will take on some value in the interval between a and b is given as,

$$P(a < X \leqslant b) = \int_{a}^{b} f(x)\,dx; \quad a \leqslant b.$$

Discrete and continuous-state systems differ mainly in the procedure by which we assign values to the variables of which they are comprised. For the continuous-state system, point values are replaced by interval values, and the concept of a specific point in time with which that value is associated is replaced by the concept of an interval of time. Thus, the *states* of a continuous-state system become intelligible in terms of *events* arrayed along a continuous probability distribution; whereas events associated with a discrete-state system may be distributed according to the frequency distribution (see Figure 2.2).

It should be clear from the figure that there are opportunities for transforming discrete-state systems into equivalent continuous-state systems, and vice-versa. When we begin to define discrete events ever more precisely, such that the difference between them gradually diminishes, we approximate a continuous-state system. By the same token, when we concern ourselves with categorical intervals (e.g., age between 40 and 50 or weight between 100 and 125 pounds) rather than limiting estimates, then we treat an inherently continuous-state system as if it were discrete.

As we shall later show, there are occasions when such transformations become

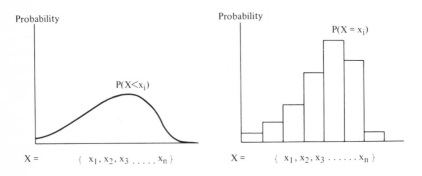

Figure 2.2 Continuous vs. discrete distributions.

analytically expedient. Most often, the transformation is from continuous-state to discrete-state systems, as when we speak of age in years, temperature in specific degrees or weight in pounds. Age, temperature, and weight are inherently continuous random variables, though for convenience sake we convert them to discrete variables for many applications. As a general rule, we may make this transformation when the importance of nondiscrete values declines below some level of significance. By the same token, there are times when discrete-state systems are conveniently transformed into continuous ones, especially where the number of discrete states is very large or where the differences between successive states falls below some level we assign. For example, we might use a formulation like this to determine a change in state:

$$\sum \frac{|x_i - x_{i+1}|}{n} < \theta$$

This says that when the mean absolute value of the sum of the first differences between successive pairs of states (events) falls below some value theta, a shift from discrete to continuous representation occurs.

We have now completed the first of our structural definition tasks in distinguishing between discrete and continuous-state systems. We shall have occasion to return to these distinctions, and amplify them. For the moment, however, what has already been said about discrete- and continuous-state systems is enough. So we now turn to a discussion of the next structural dichotomy: linear vs. nonlinear systems.

2.1.2 Linear And Nonlinear Systems

Linearity and nonlinearity may pertain either to system structure or behavior. In the present case, being concerned only with the structural dimension of systems, the definitional tasks are fairly simple. Structurally a linear system is simply one where the components comprising a system are related *additively*; whereas a nonlinear system involves a more complex relationship among its parts.

This interpretation of linearity may seem a bit alien to those with a traditional engineering background, for linearity there is generally defined solely in terms of the relationships between inputs and outputs. Here, however, we are concerned with the nature of the process which mediates between inputs and outputs. Particularly, we are here working on the third aspect of structural analysis, on the nature of the relationships prevailing among system components.

Earlier it was suggested that a system state could be described as,

$$S_t = f(X_1, X_2, X_3, \ldots, X_n),$$

where for discrete-state systems the Xs took on integer or real values, and for continuous-state systems took on interval values (or were approached in terms of inequalities). In either case we were concerned in the previous section with being able to assign values to the random variables, $X_1 \ldots . X_n$.

Now we are concerned with the nature of the relationships among them, or with the morphology of the function f. For a system to be linear, the function f must be additive (or subtractive), such that all the variables are related by either (+) or (−) operators. In short, the perfectly linear system, on the structural dimension, would be one like this:

$$S_t = X_{1_t} \pm \ldots, X_{n_t}, \qquad \text{for the discrete-state system.}$$

When we are concerned with continuous-state systems, essentially the same logic holds, but there is the added condition that the relationships among system components be reducible to a set of linear differential equations,

$$S_t = \frac{dx_1}{d_t} + \frac{dx_2}{d_t} + \cdots \frac{dx_n}{d_t} \equiv \sum_i^n \frac{dx_i}{d_t}.$$

Structurally linear systems will be among the simplest entities we are likely to encounter. In effect, they will be systems where "the whole is roughly equal to the sum of the parts"; little is gained by associating the various elements of the system into a working collectivity, at least from the productivity perspective.

When we begin to consider the administrative and control aspects of systems, however, we find that certain socioeconomic systems that exhibit structured linearity have been historically important and continue to be so. Particularly, when we discuss the concept of the segmented system in Section 2.2.1, the administrative utility of linear structures will become immediately apparent. In short, linearly structured systems may generally be thought of as those where the system components, in simultaneous association, provide little that could not be provided where they simply isolated components activated sequentially. Symbolically this can be written,

$$S_t = f(X_1, X_2, \ldots, X_n) \equiv X_1 + X_2 + \cdots + X_n.$$

As was suggested, linearity will assume more importance when we treat it as a behavioral modality, so little more will be said about it in this section. Instead, we may now introduce the more interesting complement to the linearly structured system, the nonlinear modality.

In a rhetorical sense, if linearly structured systems impose an additive relationship among their components, nonlinearly structured systems involve the concept of *synergy*. When a system is synergistic, it may be thought of as generating a whole that is *more* than the sum of its parts, such that the components in simultaneous association (e.g., the integrated system) are not equivalent to the isolated components activated sequentially . . . they are greater.* Symbolically it can be

---

*Sometimes, of course, there may be a competitive relationship among parts, such that the whole is dimensionally less than the sum of the parts.

written,

$$S_t = f(X_1, X_2, \ldots, X_n) > X_1 + X_2 + \cdots + X_n.$$

More specifically, when the system is a discrete-state one, the relationship among the parts cannot be reduced to linear form; were it a continuous-state system, the relationships would have to be expressed in terms of nonlinear differential equations.

The implication to be drawn here is this: nonlinear systems represent a higher level of complexity of organization than linear, yet this increase in complexity is usually the only way to achieve the property of synergy. Nonlinear structure is a necessary (but not sufficient) condition for synergism among system components.

Another way of phrasing this is to suggest that the additive relationship among components of linear systems becomes *ampliative* in nonlinearly structured systems. Specifically, the (+) and (−) operators joining components of linear systems are replaced by the other operators: division, multiplication, and exponentiation.*

In summary of the discussions of structural linearity and nonlinearity, consider the following formulation:

(a) The state of a system, at time t, is given by $S_t = f(X_1, X_2, \ldots, X_n)$, where the X_i's are major components of the system, or *state-variables*.

(b) Let F, be the set of all operators available for establishing relationships between the set of state-variables comprising a system, such that: $F = \{+, -, \times, \div, \exp.\}$. Now we may define two subsets of F:

$$f_L = \{+, -\}$$

$$f_N = \{\times, \div, \exp\}.$$

(c) Consider that the functional relationship among the components of a system, f, will itself be a set of functions relating all state-variables that are capable of interacting; such that: $f = (f_1, f_2, \ldots, f_n)$, for all interacting X_i's.

(d) We may now define a structurally linear system as one where all f_i's are elements of the set f_L:

$$\forall f_i \in f_L \text{ (linearity)}.$$

A structurally nonlinear system will then be one where any (or all) of the f_i's are drawn from the set f_N, such that at least one of the interacting pairs of state-variables is functionally related by something other than an addition or subtraction operator, as such: any $f_i \in f_N$ (nonlinearity).

The distinctions between discrete-state and continuous-state systems, and between linear and nonlinear systems, give rise to extremely important *classes* of systems.

---

*Note that this is an operational as opposed to a formal definition of linearity; only the exponent operator defines a non-linear system in mathematical terms.

Whether a system is linear or nonlinear, or discrete-state or continuous-state, will have great importance when we finally move into the instrumental and operational aspect of the system sciences in subsequent chapters.

For those who are still having trouble with the distinction between structural linearity and nonlinearity, the sections that immediately follow should be of great help. For when we begin to discuss the two evolutionary modalities associated with systems, we shall find that segmented systems are generally cases of linear structure, while most differentiated systems will exhibit nonlinear relationships among their components.

2.2 EVOLUTIONARY MODALITIES

The concept of an evolutionary modality associated with systems is very important, especially when we consider that virtually all systems appear to evolve through one of two processes: *segmentation* or *differentiation*. These two processes lead to systems with radically different structural characteristics, such that even the most cursory analysis of a system's existing structural properties should enable us to say something about the process of its development through time (e.g., whether it has tended to emphasize segmentation or differentiation). Once this has been determined, the system analyst will be able to make some important assertions about that system, independent of the specific type of system or the specific context in which he finds it. In short, the concepts of segmentation and differentiation provide us with immensely important sources of isomorphisms among widely diverse entities. They also give the opportunity to introduce another concept critical to the system sciences, the difference between operational and coordinative dimensions of systems.

Let us first consider that every system, whether it is social, physical, electrical, or whatnot, has some of its components devoted to maintaining the coherence or integrity of the system as a whole, and some components that actually do work or perform functions. In broader terms, of the total energy or resources available to a system, a portion will be used to perform work, accomplish survival functions, etc., while the residual will be dedicated to coordinative, administrative, control, or integrative tasks. We may consider system resources or energy devoted to the latter tasks as constituting *system overhead*, while that energy or those resources available to operating or functioning units may be thought of as directly *productive*.

As a rule, segmented systems will tend to economize on system overhead, leaving a larger proportion of their total resources available for productive investment. Differentiated systems, on the other hand, will tend to compensate for the greater proportion of energy or resources associated with system overhead by using the productive residual more efficiently. Thus, segmented and differentiated systems become primarily meaningful when we realize that they represent basically different strategies for system organization and operation, as well as distinct developmental modalities.

We may dispose of segmented and differentiated systems without recourse to mathematics, for they arose not from the engineering sciences, but from anthropology, through the work of L. A. White.[7] White was concerned about the way in which cultural systems evolved, noting that, historically, they tended to follow one of two paths. The first he called segmentation, systems enlarging themselves (or evolving) by a replication of already existing components, such that all the operational parts constituting a system tended to be similar in both structure and function. Segmented systems evolve through replication. The second, differentiated systems, tended to evolve parts that were structurally and functionally unique, such that fundamentally new components were added to the system through time. This latter modality is clearly more inherently complex than the former.

So we may extend White's work to suggest that segmented systems tend to be associated with more primitive cultures and earlier times than do differentiated systems. Indeed, the latter form the basic units of operation in the industrial world, while segmented systems tend to be found today only in subsistence agricultural areas or other regions insulated from the technological mainstream.

Yet the case is by no means this clear-cut, for there are examples of segmented systems in the modern world, just as there are some examples of differentiated systems in the underdeveloped regions. For the most part, however, we expect that an empirical analysis of real-world systems would result in a scatter-diagram heavily weighted toward the association between modernity and differentiated systems, etc. As was suggested, segmented and differentiated systems carry significantly different implications for the system analyst, and are concepts that are by no means restricted solely to the treatment of human, social, or cultural systems. Indeed, physical, chemical, biological, engineered systems, etc., will also tend to approximate the segmented or differentiated referents to be developed here, though we shall be concentrating on human systems.

2.2.1 Segmented Systems

First consider the *fully-segmented* system. This will be one where all components not only look alike structurally, but perform alike functionally. Each individual component may be distinguished only in that each occupies a unique point in space, or a unique "geographical" position. An example of a fully-segmented system might be an amoeba colony evolved by strict replication of a prototype. In the social world, we have only scattered examples of fully-segmented systems on which to draw, and these are only approximate. Among the most notable would be grass roots political organizations. Here we find a replication of a prototypical "cell," with each cell distinguished from every other largely on the basis of its particular geographic location. Each cell is structured exactly like every other, and each performs essentially the same set of tasks as every other. Other examples which might come to mind are national fraternal organizations, certain charitible systems, or ad hoc movements, such as those organized to fight pollution or sponsor the causes of minority groups.

What is empirically distinct about most fully-segmented systems that survive in the modern world is their ideological or axiological basis.[8] In most cases, members *volunteer* their time, as membership in these organizations offers social rather than economic benefits. What is also distinct about fully-segmented systems is the fact that they perform immense amounts of work with essentially minimal administrative or control overhead.[9] Here, the administrative infrastructure which supports most modern socio-economic systems is largely gratuitous, for when all units are structured alike and asked to perform essentially the same function, the same array of command and control instruments (e.g., directives, policies, proscriptions) may be used to discipline all components or subsystems. In the political arena, then, a relatively small cadre of professional campaign managers can administer an immense number of localized political cells, widely scattered geographically; a lesson that has not been lost on political organizers either in the United States or abroad. In the same way, a few paid professionals in systems such as the Red Cross or the United Fund serve to minimally manage a vast collection of local "branches," such that a larger porportion of donated resources goes directly into productive employment than would be the case were a non fully-segmented modality employed.

So, fully-segmented systems take on a somewhat unique organizational structure, much like Figure 2.3. There are basically just two levels with which we are concerned: (1) a relatively small collection of directors or managers at the top, (X_0) and (2) a potentially vast number of noninterfacing branches, cells, or subsystems at the operating level of the system, $(X_{1,N})$. Thus we can add (e.g., replicate) system components—and therefore enlarge the system as a whole—without incurring any significant increases in administrative costs and without necessitating radical changes in the nature of the control instruments employed, etc. In this way, then, the fully-segmented system may be thought to reach a theoretical minimum so far as costs of system "administration" relative to system size is concerned, yet the conditions of its employment in the real-world are very restricted (as we shall see in Chapter 4).

It should also clear that the fully-segmented system stands an excellent chance

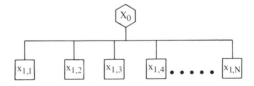

Figure 2.3 Segmented system morphology.

of being *linear*, such that the system as a whole is roughly equal to the sum (or aggregate) of its parts. This is especially true for the social, economic, and political systems falling under the fully-segmented category; for the various subsystems comprising them are usually operating independently of one another. Thus, what happens to the political cell in Omaha may have no effect on the cells in New York, Portland, Minneapolis, etc. By the same token, nothing is taken away from the basic structural character of the system should one system component be erased or another added, etc. The function which combines the subsystems into a working system is still just *additive*, with only the number of elements rather than the "quality" of the system being altered.

To a great extent, the same thing can be said to be true of certain ecological or biological instances of full segmentation (e.g., as with amoeba colonies, coral formations, or certain amalgamations of lower-level organisms). To this extent, then, the concepts of segmentation and linearity serve as sources of isomorphisms, combining to make a large number of superficially diverse systems intelligible in essentially the same terms, and allowing us to cross disciplinary lines and displace myriad localized, context-specific models with generic, abstract ones.

There is a much larger number of systems that are structurally segmented but functionally differentiated, such that all the system components look alike but not all of them perform the same tasks. In fact, a majority of the real-world systems we encounter in our political, social, or economic sectors are of this type; among them military systems, religious systems, and formal bureaucracies. Military systems, though perhaps less now than in the past, tend to be replications of platoons. While each of these platoons is structured in the same way as every other, they may do different things. One platoon, for example, may be a rifle platoon responsible for engaging enemies on the battle line, while another might be a military band, or perhaps a collection of road builders. In the same way, bureaucracies tend to be exercises in *departmentalization*, such that different tasks are performed by entities all organized into structurally replicative departments, with roughly corresponding positional hierarchies, promotion rules, communication and command algorithms, etc.

Structurally-segmented systems differ from fully-segmented systems in primarily two ways. First, rather than just a two-layer vertical dimension, yielding the effectively *flat* distribution of fully-segmented systems, structurally-segmented systems will have a *strongly hierarchical structure*, with multiple levels mediating between the executive and operational system components. Secondly, the administrative and control economies associated with fully-segmented systems will be somewhat diluted when we consider systems that are segmented only on the structural dimension. True, most military, religious, and bureaucratic systems will possess a *book* which prescribes broad behavior to be maintained by organizational members and subsystems (e.g., the Military Code), and sets the strategic envelope for all system parts. But while such an instrument might suffice in entirety for a fully-segmented system, it has to be supplemented by specific dictates outlining procedures or prescribed behavior unique to each functionally differentiated unit. Such special orders and designations proliferate in bureaucratic, religious, and military systems, as the reader is surely (and perhaps cynically) aware.

Nevertheless, because of the morphological correlation among units comprising a structurally-segmented system, *generic* coordinative or control instruments may be employed to economize somewhat on administrative and control efforts. Thus, while the structurally-segmented system is not as absolutely economical on the administrative dimension as the fully-segmented one, it is somewhat less expensive to manage and control than the fully-differentiated system, largely because addition of new units (system enlargement) simply involves a replication of existing coordinative units in some ratio to new operating units.

2.2.2 Differentiated Systems

The fully-differentiated system is evolved from the differentiation rule, which demands that each functionally unique task be performed by a subsystem that is structurally unique. Thus, whenever a component is assigned a task that differs from that performed by other system units, it is assumed that a structural innovation will be inaugurated for the newly evolved part. Such differentiated systems are uniquely modern and predominate in industrialized cultures. The very concept of system differentiation owes its articulation to an adjunct of the industrial revolution: the proposition that the productivity associated with systems may be increased through *specialization*, or division of labor among subsystems.

A fine example of fully-differentiated systems is the modern professional football team. There we find three structurally unique systems operating to perform three basically different tasks: (a) the offensive team concerned with making points; (b) the defensive team concerned with keeping the opponent from scoring points; and (c) certain specialty teams concerned with managing tasks such as kickoff returns, or punting. Each of these subsystems operates under a different set of rules, is organized differently, and involves different players (whose basic physical or mental characteristics may also differ in certain important respects). This, as most readers will no doubt realize, is a very different situation than that which prevailed a few decades ago, where the same men played both offense and defense and where the "specialty" team was unheard of.

Differentiation, then, as a modality by which systems evolve, is indicated by increasing specialization of structure and function among system components, or by a more thorough application of the dictum that "structure should follow function." Segmented systems, on the other hand, evolve in a way that becomes intelligible as the process of replication, where nothing essentially *new* is added but where originative properties are simply reproduced or extended. On the coordinative dimension of human systems, this difference becomes especially important. Consider, for example, that when the system under treatment is a structurally-segmented one, we can accommodate new components simply by replicating new control or administrative units . . . for both the control and operating units will simply be reproductions of already existing system components, and there will be some already established ratio between number of operating units at a certain level and number of coordinative or control units required at the next level, etc. But when each component of the system is essentially unique—or where the system evolves or enlarges itself at least partially through the introduction of unprecedented elements—then we must assume that coordinative and control subsystems associated with unique operating subsystems will themselves be unique. Thus, we gradually lose the ability to manage a system through replication of instruments.

An additional problem of system coordination is reached when we consider that relationships between components of differentiated systems will usually involve more than simple additivity or sequential connection, and that the task of adequately managing nonlinear relationships consumes significantly large amounts of resources. Thus, just to maintain the integrity or coherence of a complex differentiated system means a considerable investment in administrative overhead, such that the ratio of productive to unproductive resource expenditures in differentiated systems becomes quickly less favorable than that associated with structurally- or fully-segmented systems.

It is important to realize, however, that the additional expenses associated with the coordination of a differentiated system may be more than offset by the increase in system productivity that occurs when we inject specialization of function and structure, and when we allow system components to interact simultaneously and nonlinearly rather than sequentially and additively. It may be suggested then, and will later be shown to be something of a system postulate, that segmented systems tend to economize on the costs of coordination, whereas differentiated systems tend to emphasize efficiency of production or function. This increase in operating efficiency is generally gained, however, at the expense of the system analyst, for differentiated systems require a great deal more energy, effort, time, and imagination to accurately *map* than segmented systems. Thus, for example, physicists have run up against the three-body problem, simply because the simultaneous interaction of three heterogeneous subsystems requires more mathematical sophistication than is currently available to us. By the same token, an accurate *map* of the human body is not yet built, assuming it ever can be, simply because the number of interactions among components, and the nature of the interfaces between differentiated components, exceed both our mathematical and logical comprehension. Thus, the neat hierarchies of the structurally-segmented system, much less the effectively *flat* structure of the fully-segmented system, gradually give way to highly complex and often unallegorizable structures when we enter the differentiated domain.

Consider, for example, that a structural map of a complex differentiated system would have to take heterogenous system components, distribute them according to some possibly very complex spatial algorithm, and then portray simultaneous, usually nonlinear relationships among large numbers of these components. This is a vastly more complex task than that associated with the mapping of fully-segmented systems, though some structurally-segmented systems may present limited difficulties when their size is great. So, as a general rule, and one that will be qualified later, it may be suggested that structural segmentation considerably eases the task of constructing descriptive "snapshot" models of systems, and may in some cases simplify the prediction problem as well.

In summary, then, the differentiated system must be thought of as being something more than the mere sum of the properties of its parts; whereas the fully-segmented system is intelligible as an aggregate. The differentiated system must be treated as potentially nonlinear; whereas the fully-segmented system is effectively just additive. The components comprising a differentiated system may often interact with each other in very complicated ways, whereas those components associated with fully-segmented systems generally do not interact simultaneously, but are exercised sequentially. For socioeconomic systems, particularly, the energy or resources devoted to system coordination, coherence, or control, as a proportion of the total available energy or resources, is usually lowest for fully-segmented systems, highest for differentiated systems, and intermediate for structurally-segmented systems. And, finally, the model required to capture the structural properties of the fully-segmented system will be simpler than that for the structurally-segmented system which will, in its turn, be simpler than that required to treat differentiated systems. We shall be reintroducing the segmented and differentiated system in Chapter 4 (and again in Chapter 8 where we discuss system coordination), so it is enough now to simply keep in mind the broad differences between these two structural referents as we turn to a discussion of the boundary modalities available to systems.

2.3 BOUNDARY MODALITIES

Here we will be concerned with the nature of the boundaries that systems establish, and more broadly with the nature of system relationships with the world outside themselves. There are, as with our previous structural referents, a pair of distinct alternatives to consider here: *open* systems vs. *closed* systems. As the reader might expect, an open system is one that depends, to a lesser or greater extent, on interchanges with its environment, and with other systems that might be present there. Closed systems, on the other hand, tend to be self-contained or only minimally responsive to outside influences. What this means, in practical terms, is that determinants of an open system's *states* might be far removed in time or space from the immediate locale of the system itself, whereas determinants of closed systems are generally local or proximate to the boundary of that system. In general, then, the mapping operation associated with open systems will be more difficult than that associated with closed systems. But there are more subtle implications we will have to explore before open and closed systems are adequately defined.

Initially, openness and closure have been approached in two ways by system scientists. From what might be called the general system perspective, Ludwig von Bertalanffy is primarily concerned with open systems as the appropriate referent for biological and, by extension, social systems, thereby relegating the closed system to what might loosely be called the laboratory sciences (including, from his view, experimental physics). The insights he draws are important for us.

Conventional physics deals only with closed systems, i.e., systems which are considered to be isolated from their environment. Thus, physical chemistry tells us about the reactions, their rates, and the chemical equilibria eventually established in a closed vessel where a number of reactants is brought together. Thermodynamics expressly declares that its laws apply only to closed systems . . . However, we find systems which by their very nature and definition are not closed systems. Every living organism is essentially an open system. It maintains itself in a continuous inflow and outflow . . . . This is the very essence of that fundamental phenomenon of life which is called metabolism, the chemical process within living cells. . . . Obviously, the conventional formulations of physics are, in principle, inapplicable to the living organism *qua* open system . . . [11]

The implication of this statement is clear . . . animate systems must be approached as open and. in the process, the traditional theoretical and instrumental emphases of classical physics must be replaced.

But there is, as we suggested, another approach to system openness and closure. This comes from the engineering sciences by way of Jay Forrester; for Forrester, the closed system is equivalent to a "feedback" system, whereas the open system becomes, in effect, a nonfeedback system. He explains:

an open system is one characterized by outputs that respond to inputs but where the outputs are isolated from and have no influence on the inputs. An open system is not aware of its own performance. In an open system, past action does not control future action. . . . An automobile is an open system which by itself is not governed by where it has gone in the past nor does it have a goal of where to go in the future. A watch, taken by itself, does not observe its own inaccuracy and adjust itself—it is an open system. . . . A feedback system, which is sometimes called a "closed" system, is influenced by its own past behavior. A feedback system has a closed loop structure that brings results from past action of the system back to control future action. One class

of feedback system—negative feedback—seeks a goal and responds as a consequence of failing to achieve the goal. A second class of feedback systems—
positive feedback—generates growth processes wherein action builds a result
that generates still greater action.[12]

He then goes on to give some elucidating examples

The heating system of a house is controlled by a thermostat which responds
to the heat previously produced by the furnace. Because the heat already produced by the system controls the forthcoming generation of heat, the heating
system represents a negative feedback system that seeks the goal of proper
temperature. A watch and its owner form a negative feedback system when
the watch is compared with the correct time as a goal and is adjusted to eliminate errors. An engine with a governor senses its own speed and adjusts the
throttle to achieve the preset speed goal—it is a negative feedback system.
Bacteria multiply to produce more bacteria which increase the rate at which
new bacteria are generated. In this positive feedback system the generation
rate of new bacteria depends on the bacteria accumulated from past growth of
bacteria.

Now the difficulty here is all too apparent. An open system from von Bertalanffy's standpoint may be either an open or closed system from Forrester's
perspective.

For what von Bertalanffy is primarily concerned with is the relationship of the
system to the world outside itself (the system's ecological aspects, as it were). If
such relationships exist, the system is an open one. If they do not, the system is
closed. Forrester, on the other hand, is primarily concerned with the connections between past and future behavior. If such a connection exists, the system becomes closed (through feedback). If no such connection exists, it is an
open system. But an open system by this definition could be a closed for von
Bertalanffy. For example, a random-number generator is effectively isolated
from environmental influences (except for the trivial requirement that it be provided with some electricity), and thus becomes closed in von Bertalanffy's terms.
Yet each successive number generated (e.g., each action taken) is entirely independent of previous generations (e.g., the states of the system are sequential
and independent), such that it is open from Forrester's standpoint.

To avoid ambiguity, we can elect to use von Bertalanffy's definition of open
and closed systems as being determined by the ecological properties of the system (e.g., the nature of external dependencies). But Forrester's definitions also
have importance for us. So we will rephrase his open system to read *open-loop
system*, and his concept of a closed system to read *closed-loop* (indicating a feedback condition). Under such an arrangement, open or closed systems may be
either open-loop or closed-loop. It is best to begin our more detailed discussions
with a consideration of the higher-order pair: open vs. closed systems, per se.

2.3.1 Open vs. Closed Systems

It is useful to recognize that openness and closure represent relativistic or limiting concepts. Clearly, no system exists in the real-world that is totally closed to outside influences for any significant interval of time. By the same token, no completely open system can exist, for to be completely open would be tantamount to being dissolute . . . effectively incoherent. So when we speak of a closed system, we really mean one that is minimally dependent upon outside influences, or one whose internal properties are well-buffered against external (exogenous) intrusions. So an open system will be defined as one that is highly dependent upon external events or operators, or one whose growth or survival depends on a constant interchange with environmental factors.

Another way of looking at this is to consider what might be called the *selectivity* of the system's interfaces with the outside world. Every system, to be a proper system, must somehow be distinguishable from the milieu in which it resides. It must be bounded in some way, having a perimeter which serves to define the domain of the system. Exogenous or external forces must pass through this perimeter to influence the system's structure or behavior; by the same token, outputs from the system must pass through this perimeter to reach the outside world. The points where exogenous determinants pass into the system, or where endogenously generated forces pass into the environment (milieu), are known as *interfaces*. They are, as it were, the doors and windows of the system. So when we speak about the selectivity of the interfaces associated with some system, we are referring to the ability of the interfaces to distinguish acceptable from unacceptable inputs and outputs, and to let pass, in either direction, only those that have been deemed desirable. In a sense, then, interface selectivity refers to the system's regulation of its interchanges with external entities.

Most machines designed by men, become effectively closed systems under such a definition. They are designed to accept only certain inputs, or to respond to only a limited set of externally-generated stimuli (e.g., the pushing of a button). They are also designed to produce a highly limited set of outputs. By the same token, some social systems are able to regulate their perimeters with great authority and success; examples would be exclusive country clubs, secret government agencies, certain criminal or extralegal systems (e.g., bookmakers' parlors), certain professions or unions, fraternities, etc. Such systems may be viewed as effectively (rather than absolutely) closed. This does not mean that they do not rely to some extent on outside inputs or that they are completely insulated from external perturbations or events. It simply means that they are highly "protected."

Open systems, on the other hand, would be those that are unable (or unwilling) to regulate their interfaces with great authority and precision . . . systems whose interchanges with the outside world are somewhat unspecific. This means that when we set about trying to make a map of an open system, we have to assign a relatively wide range of exogenous factors some positive probability of affecting the system's structure or behavior; whereas maps of effectively closed systems need usually consider only a single set of determinants (e.g., inputs or environmental stimuli) as significantly probable.[13]

For open systems, determinants may become very complex, and input or stimulus "events" may often take the form of simultaneously interacting sets. This may mean that system's outputs or impact on the milieu may be complex, such that maps of open systems tend to be highly *probabilistic*. Clearly, the more open the system, the greater the number of potential input and output events we must consider, and therefore the lower the probability associated with any one alternative. So, whereas inputs and outputs associated with closed systems tend to be linear and exclusive due to their highly selective interfaces, those associated with open systems will be more fan-shaped, as shown in Figure 2.4.

This, generally speaking, is the significance of the difference between open and closed systems for the system scientist, reflecting the differential amenability of the two system types to structural analysis. In general terms, then, closed systems become easier to model or allegorize than open systems. And open systems will be *more* difficult to model the less specific the interfaces and the more inherently complex the environment in which the system is resident. In Chapter 4, a great deal more will be said about the *ecological dimension* of general systems.

There is another aspect of open systems which may be discussed here, one touched on in the previous chapter. If open systems' states rely heavily on exogenous influences—or if they maintain strong and constant and potentially protean interchanges with the external world—an *holistic* analytical perspective becomes imperative. Whereas we may properly assume that most closed systems may be readily isolated from the environment in which they reside, and studied in effective isolation from external influences (e.g., with external factors assumedly held constant or introduced in the forms of exogenous constraints), this is an extremely perilous practice when the phenomenon being treated is an open

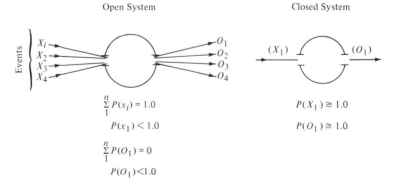

Figure 2.4 Open vs. closed systems.

system. Here it becomes important to extend the boundaries of the unit of analysis (e.g., the system, per se) to incorporate as many external variables as possible. In doing this we as completely as possible *endogenize* factors that would normally be left exogenous in a closed system analysis. Thus, von Bertalanffy saw in the concept of the open system a strong argument against reductionism.[14]

The natural and biological sciences have also been affected by the emergence of the open system concept. Thus, for example, the traditional biologist may be content to view living systems as closed, ignoring what happens outside that system and neglecting to explicate the network of interactions in which each living system is engaged. Yet, as all readers must surely be aware, it was precisely this failure to come to grips with openness in systems that spurred the development of ecology as a discipline attempting to provide explanations for natural phenomena *qua* open systems. For the ecologist, as for the system scientist concerned with open systems, the relevant unit of analysis extends far beyond the physical boundaries of the system itself. It involves often complicated and always concatenative sequences of inputs and stimuli arising from the field in which the system is resident, (some of which may be far removed in time or space); it also incorporates the range of effects (e.g., resonations) that systems may have on the field itself or on other systems (which also may be far removed in time and space).

The open system demands that the scientist *open*, as it were, his perspective, including factors that nonsystem scientists might be expected to ignore. Thus the study of open systems becomes the study of interactions, resonations, concatenations, and complex causal sequences, all terms to which we shall return in later pages.

There is a final aspect of the difference between open and closed systems which concerns us here. This difference revolves around the concept of *entropy*. Entropy derives from the second law of thermodynamics which postulates, that for a closed system, the quantity "entropy" must secularly increase to a maximum until an equilibrium is reached. We may add that the nature of this equilibrium will be a state of maximum disorder that, for closed systems, constitutes the most probable distribution of system properties. What this means, in effect, is that closed systems will eventually reach a state where there is no organization, just randomness or some other variant of chaos. To understand this we must return to the distinction between productive and coordinative energy (or resources) available to systems. Where the energy with which a system begins is fixed and invariant (as it would be for the perfectly closed system), free energy available to either productive or coordinative functions will gradually be used up. When this occurs, the energy used to configure system components into a coherent (nonrandom) state will no longer be available, and the individual components will no longer be held in check or otherwise disciplined by the system, per se. In this case, the system dissolves, such that only the components are left. Thus, for a closed system, we invoke the teleological (or limiting) principle that the system will gradually move from states of greater organization (negentropic* states) to states of lesser organization (entropic states).

Now much stir has been raised by scholars who have suggested that open systems (such as living organisms or social systems) contradict the second law of thermodynamics. They suggest that in the biological and social world, the inverse holds, such that systems pass from successively less organized states (entropic) to more organized (negentropic) ones. They generally support such arguments by suggesting that the history of civilization (if not the history of biological evolution) lends evidence that social systems are becoming more highly centralized and more "ordered," as if there were some secular negentropic engine at work. Examples of the concentration of industry into fewer, larger firms, and the gradual development of fewer, more encompassing nation-states support this contention. The fact is, however, that only a basic misunderstanding of the second law could have led them to the conclusion that such examples serve to abrogate it.

The first point of misunderstanding is the obvious one . . . the laws of thermodynamics are applicable only to closed systems, whereas economic, political, and social systems are clearly open. The second point of misunderstanding is more subtle but equally important. Entropy is a teleological or limiting concept, one that holds only as an ultimate condition. Thus, any system, even an effectively closed one, may contravene the second law of thermodynamics in the short-run or in any finite interval, without casting aspersions on the validity of the second law itself. In the same way, no matter how much centralization we note among existing systems, no matter how clear the historical tendency toward greater degrees of organization among the world's social systems (or any other elements), such systems cannot be used as sufficient evidence against the second law . . . for it applies only to an ultimately empirically inaccessible (teleological) future.

So, for our purposes here, an entropic system is one that is secularly "running down," one tending to disintegrate or weaken. A negentropic system may then be thought of as one where the degree of organization or coherence, is increasing, possibly along with an increase in size as well. But there are many factors that can intervene to transpose a negentropic system into one eventually exhibiting that postulated equilibrium state of maximum entropy and disorder. Even the most casual glance at the history of civilization indicates that highly organized systems have come and gone; some great empires have reached tremendously strong states of cohesion, only to gradually dissipate. Others have attained high degrees of organization and then shattered, suddenly, like a crystal. Similarly even moderately closed systems can potentially escape the entropic equilibrium state by falling into a *steady state*. In a steady state, the amount of energy that is consumed in system coordination or in the process of system

*Implies negative entropy.

functioning (or work), is exactly replaced by new energy or resources drawn from the environment.[15] Thus, the system neither grows nor diminishes; it is, while in the steady state, neither entropic nor negentropic.

2.3.2 Closed-Loop and Open-Loop Systems

We may dispose of the open-loop system first. In the most fundamental sense, open-loop systems do not learn. They act, but they do not assimilate the effects of previous actions in order to discipline or direct future actions. To this extent, we would consider open-loop systems to be *nonintelligent.* Such systems, to use the old phrase, "wake up in a new world every morning," for they lack the capability to draw inferences from experience. In a statistical sense, each action taken by the system is *independent.*

For our purposes here, open-loop systems are of scant interest, for those we are likely to encounter will generally be mechanisms designed to meet specific and invariant performance criteria. In a later chapter, however, we shall reinvoke the concept of the open-loop system to allegorize the behavior of certain types or organizations that recognize and respond to only a limited set of stimuli and that operate on these in a more or less automatic way. We shall also find that where environmental or contextual conditions are expected to remain constant, and where the components of the system may be expected to behave only as commanded or designed, "learning" becomes gratuitous. Thus, action may be properly unaccompanied by provisions to evaluate its effects, and system behavior thus becomes invariant.

In moving from open-loop to closed-loop systems we move into another order of complexity and sophistication (which is the implicational inverse of moving from open to closed systems as von Bertalanffy defined them). System structure now becomes more complex because we actually add new components to the system, components that enable it to learn.[16] Particularly, in moving from an open-loop to a closed-loop system, we must equip the system with some sort of monitoring and decision capability, and an assimilative capability as well. Thus, structurally, closed-loop systems are distinguished by the presence of these three components, whereas open-loop systems generally just have an action element.

In this respect, consider Figure 2.5. We can enter the figure at *action.* This represents some action which the system has taken, whose effects or impacts will be sensed by the *monitor.* The *assimilator* then is responsible for incorporating the information from the monitor, and structuring it as a premise for determining future action . . . the determination of which is accomplished in the *decision* subsystem. In short, a link has been established between past and future, and the system becomes *intelligent* in that its actions become objects of judgment rather than automation.

Now the difference between negative and positive feedback systems becomes explicit when we consider the normative morphology of the learning curves that

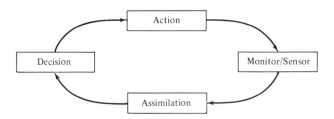

Figure 2.5 The closed-loop system.

result from a feedback-based process. Recall that in Forrester's terms, the negative feedback system was one that attempted to converge on a specific goal. We may extend this to suggest that a negative feedback system might also be one that attempts to maintain some specific property in the face of external perturbations (e.g., as a thermostat attempts to keep room temperature at a certain level despite factors constantly acting to either raise or lower it). Thus, as a negative feedback system proceeds through time, we may characterize it as trying to minimize deviations from some established "levels," as in Figure 2.6. This system is self-correcting, where the utility of the feedback provision (the productivity associated with the monitor, assimilation, and decision subsystems) is found in its ability to reduce variance from the desired variable value to a lower level than would be the case were the system an open-loop one.

As for the learning curves we associate with the positive feedback system, they generally tend to be *ampliative*, similar to the curve in Figure 2.7. This curve reflects a situation where we know where we want to be (e.g., the desired variable value) and, after each action, so long as we perceive that we are moving in the right direction, we *accelerate* our movement along that trajectory. In short, the positive feedback system is one which amplifies successful actions. At the point where the desired level is attained, the negative feedback process could then be kicked in to keep us cylcing around that value as nearly as possible, as in Figure 2.7.

In summary, then, the open-loop and closed-loop systems differ structurally in that the former incorporates more components than does the latter, with the

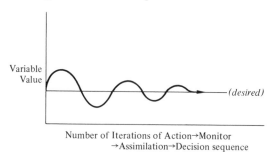

Number of Iterations of Action→Monitor
→Assimilation→Decision sequence

Figure 2.6 Deviation-minimization model.

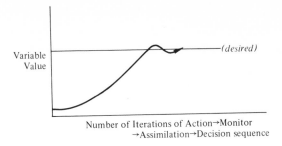

Figure 2.7 Positive-feedback learning.

resultant difference in the *maps* that systems of each type produce. The reader may recognize that when we talk about closed-loop or feedback-based systems, we are entering the domain of cybernetics, one of the cornerstones of control theory. However, we shall be treating the cybernetic system as a behavioral modality rather than a structural one, reserving a discussion of its properties until a later section. So we now proceed to treat the last pair of our major system structural referents: hierarchical and nonhierarchical organizational modalities.

2.4 ORGANIZATIONAL MODALITIES

If, as many suggest, systems are instances of *organized complexity*,[17] then here we are interested in the dominant patterns of organization that they establish for themselves, or that are imposed on them. This involves the determination of the lines of communication and control that extend throughout a system, and the patterns of potential influences among system components.

Among all the organizational modalities that have emerged, one stands out as preeminent . . . *hierarchical* structure. For as Herbert Simon has pointed out,

> . . . nature loves hierarchies. Most of the complex systems that occur in nature find their place in one or more of four intertwined hierarchic sequences. One . . . starts with observable chemical substances. Analyses of these discloses sets of component molecules. Within the molecules are found atoms, nuclei and electrons, and finally—or is it momentarily?—within nuclei are found elementary particles. . . .
>
> A second important hierarchy runs from living organisms to tissues and organisms to tissues and organs, to cells, to macromolecules, to organic compounds, to a junction with the molecules of the first hierarchy. A third, intertwined hierarchy leads from the statistics of inheritance to genes and chromosomes, to DNA, and all that.
>
> A fourth hierarchy, not yet firmly connected with the others, leads from human societies to organizations, to small groups, to individual human beings, to cognitive programs in the central nervous system, to elementary information

processes—where the junctions with the tissues and organs of neurobiology remain largely to be discovered.[18]

Hierarchical structure stands as one of the most powerful generic system referents available to the system scientist, and as a major source of isomorphisms among the widest possible range of real-world systems.

2.4.1 Hierarchical Systems

The first question might be just why hierarchical organizations are so frequently encountered in both natural and artificial systems. As for the natural systems, apparently products of biological or physical *evolution*, Herbert Simon cites evidence that suggests that " . . . hierarchies will evolve much more rapidly from elementary constituents than will nonhierarchic systems containing the same number of elements." He arrived at this by simple mathematical analysis.

> . . . on the simplest assumptions, the mathematical model shows that if a system of k elementary components is built up in a many-level hierarchy, and s components, on the average, combine at any level into a component at the next higher level, then the expected time of evolution for the whole system will be proportional to the logarithm to base s of k. In such a hierarchy, the time required for systems containing, say, 10^{25} atoms to evolve from systems containing 10^{23} atoms would be the same as the time required for systems containing 10^3 atoms to evolve from systems containing 10 atoms.[19]

There are distinct reasons for the popularity of hierarchically organized manmade systems. Particularly, the task of managing a complex enterprise is generally considerably simplified when that enterprise can be broken down into subsystems, just as a complex problem is generally solved by breaking it into subproblems that are, individually, more analytically tractable. There are reasons of efficiency as well. For example, computer scientists know that the computation of an optimum solution to a large scale (many variable) problem is more efficiently accomplished when the solution steps are modularized . . . where they try to obtain a solution by successively coupling N sets of M variables each rather than simultaneously attacking the whole $N \times M$ variables. In industrial or governmental organizations, the hierarchy principle is predicated on the realization that individuals in positions of authority or control have only a limited "span of management"; in recognition of this we tend to break organizations down into sets of functional or structural subsystems, which themselves may be hierarchies. Thus a manager may indirectly control many individuals by exercising only a few associations with the highest-level members of each of those subsystems. The result is a more manageable organization than were no intervening levels present between the highest-order and lowest-order system components.

Basically then, a hierarchy is an assembly of components that may be looked at in terms of *levels*. These levels serve as subsets into which system components of a particular class are organized. A level may have only one or many component elements.

There are four major types of hierarchical structure. The first suggests that a property of proper hierarchical systems is the *dominance* of higher-order components over lower-order. In this view, the highest level of the system denotes the focus of ultimate authority, with the lowest levels exhibiting the least autonomy, etc. Such a hierarchy may be called a dominance hierarchy, predicated on the complete control of higher-order components over lower-order, throughout the system. Dominance hierarchies have properties that are very appealing to the system analyst, as is here noted by the economist, Albert Ando.

> The possibility of identifying 'causal' relations is intimately related to the possibility of classifying variables into a hierarchy of sets, levels I, II, III, and so on. Variables belonging to higher-numbered sets are influenced by those in the lower-numbered sets, but the former do not influence the latter . . . when such a stratification exists, then we may say that the variables in the lower-numbered sets are the 'causes' of the variables in the higher-numbered sets. This type of hierarchical structure also provides the justification for ignoring the variables in higher-numbered groups when the object of an investigation is restricted to the behavior of variables in lower-numbered sets.[20]

In such a system, every level except the highest level becomes effectively *deterministic*, if we know the constraints that the higher level imposes on the structure and behavior of the next lower level. This logic may be distributed throughout the system, with each successively lower level being, in effect, the "slave" of the higher level. The neat thing about such an arrangement is that we do not need to worry about any reflexivity among the various levels; causality is in one direction only, such that lower-order components cannot exert any meaningful influence on higher levels. Such a system would resolve into what is known as a partially-ordered set, which can be interpreted as a "tree." There exist mathematical tools, grouped under the instruments of topology, to resolve and allegorize such systems.[21]

Unfortunately, examples of a dominance hierarchy, in the strict sense, are difficult to find in the real-world. Some instances, however, come to mind. The clearest would be systems that are engineered and fabricated to convey the property of unilateral causality. These would be machines, where lower-order components exercised in some sort of sequence, have no option but to behave as dictated by the preceeding or exercising component. In the social world we are tempted to think of strict bureaucracies as instances of dominance hierarchy, especially those that are militaristic in tenor (as was the Prussian military from which Weber evolved the concept of the bureaucratic ideal-type). In such systems, there is a one-way (downward) chain of command and a single channel of communication, which means that such systems place an extremely low emphasis on *feedback*, stressing instead a "do or die" attitude among their members. In short, dominance hierarchies are open-loop systems.

As all readers are surely aware, the strict bureaucracy has come under intense fire, both from behavioral scientists and from economists concerned with the efficiency of such organizational structures.[22] There is some considerable merit in their arguments, for as we shall see in Chapter 4, the dominance hierarchy is useful primarily only in the face of a set of iterative, well-precedented processing demands, to which an entirely predictable response on the part of system members is desired. Extending this somewhat, the strict bureaucracy is warranted most fully, if at all, to the extent that the mission accepted or imposed on the organization is an especially critical one (e.g., national defense; law enforcement; firefighting). Thus, in terms of their basic effectiveness and efficiency, open-loop, dominance-oriented hierarchical systems have a very limited repertoire of tasks for which they are suited, and are seldom found in pure form.

What we tend to find, rather, is another type of hierarchical system, a system with components that cannot be assumed to be completely constrained by higher-level units, or hierarchies in which the various levels are not connected by a unilateral chain of command or communication. Such systems abound in the social world, and Arthur Koestler has termed them *holarchies*.[23] In the holarchy, each level of the system has a Janus-faced quality. To those system components at higher levels, they appear to be tools to be exploited, but also sources of information and recommendation; to system components on the lower-level, they appear to house the authority of command or control. This situation replicates itself throughout the system, at all levels, except the very lowest and the very highest.

The important thing about the holarchy is that it gives us the opportunity to bring our appreciation of hierarchical systems a bit closer to the situation that appears to predominate in the real-world. For we now have a condition of *bilateral* influence . . . with the lower-order components having some potential to affect the behavior of higher-order components. Such a situation seems very approximate of the political, social, and industrial systems we empirically investigate. Thus, for example (following arguments as old as Plato, Rousseau, and Marx), a government or political authority of any kind may be seen to hold power only so long as the humor of the constituents permit. In such a case, the attitude of the lower-order components of the systems, and the limits of their tolerance, will determine not only what instruments of government may be employed by higher-level components, but may also determine the very existence of the higher-order elements. In much the same way, we note the "acceptance theory of authority" lent us by Barnard with respect to industrial organizations.[24] Under this scheme, higher-order components are allowed by the lower-order components to exercise authority only so long as it is perceived to be legitimate or acceptable. In such cases, then, lower-order components most definitely are perceived to carry the potential for influencing higher-order, such that the dominance hierarchy (with its unilateral lines of determinancy) becomes a perilous oversimplification of reality as social, political, and behavioral scientists are coming to know it.

In the biological world, we tend to encounter another type of hierarchical structure, one that finds higher-order components evolved from lower-order components. Such hierarchies are called *neogenetic*, and are apparently reflective of the kind of structuring through which organic systems pass.* Each new generation of life, for virtually all species or classes of organic phenomena, begins with a "seed" of some sort which apparently carries the ability to determine the ultimate development and form of existence. The seed may be a very complex system in its own right, replete with DNA, RNA, various protein strings, and a set of relationships among these components. Yet, by no means, is the seed as structurally complex as the mature organism which it ultimately generates. Here, then, we encounter the mystery of ontogenesis . . . the means by which a less differentiated system gives rise to a more differentiated system within a single generation, and the problem of the links between generations. In regard to this problem of ontogenesis, the eminent biologist Clifford Grobstein finds the concept of the neogenetic hierarchy central to any explanation we might eventually develop.

. . . organisms deal with the problem of replication of higher levels of order by replicating information at relatively low levels of order and then successively translating and transforming this information to generate higher levels of order . . . new properties constantly appear, frequently under circumstances which suggest some mysterious emergence. . . . Formal analysis shows that emergence relates to what may be called set-superset transitions. In these, determinate association of components provides new collective sets with relationally transformed information not resident in individual components. The new information frequently can be read only in a context or frame provided by another, often also newly formed, level of order. As an example, enzyme activity of proteins is an emergent property dependent upon amino acid sequence but manifested only after establishment of a specific configuration and in the presence of a suitible substrate. Hierarchical organization in biological systems thus is characterized by an exquisite array of delicately and intricately interlocked order, steadily increasing in level and complexity and thereby giving rise neogenetically to emergent properties.[25]

The important point here is that in neogenetic hierarchies, the origin and substance of higher-order components is to be found in the evolutionary impulses associated with lower-order elements. Thus, in nature, a set of initially simple

*Modern theoretical physics is now attempting to structure neogenetic explanations and models for the physical world, perhaps taking a clue from biologists and biosystemic models.

agents can band together, share information, and in contexts of specific situations, generate a new level that serves as the first step toward the development of an ultimately hierarchically organized system. In this way, for example, the human body gradually emerges as a complex, multi-level, highly differentiated hierarchical system, having begun initially from what, at one level of description, could only be described as a set of largely undifferentiated cells (or seeds) constituting only a single level.

There are immediate parallels in the social world, as when a group of initially undifferentiated peers elects one of its members to become a chief or leader, thus generating, *ab intra* and *ab initio*, a new level. It was much in this spirit that the Bible tells of the generation of the ten tribes of Israel. At any rate, as the system increases in size, new levels are generated from the old, and serve to further separate the lowest-order components from the highest-order, and so on.

Clearly, in neogenetic hierarchies not only do the lower-order components initially give rise to the higher-order components, but the health of the various levels is interdependent. Consider, for example, that if an organ (e.g., higher-order component) of the human body does not function properly, it can lead not only to the demise of the parts it regulates or supplies, but eventually to its own death as well. In dominance hierarchies, on the other hand, it is possible to conceive of each higher-order component as at least partially insulated from the behavior or state of the lower-order components it controls. Thus, in dominance hierarchies we can readily ignore reflexivity, whereas reflexivity becomes an essential property of any map pretending to adequately reflect the structure of either neogenetic or holarchic systems.

There is another class of hierarchy, the *identity* hierarchy, which we deal with only reluctantly, as it entails a problem that is by no means satisfactorily solved as yet. Howard Pattee, a hierarchy theorist, considers that the central problem in hierarchy theory is ". . . the relation between the structural and descriptive levels" of hierarchical systems.[26] What this means, in essence, is that there are some hierarchical systems where the levels of description we use to lend it structure may not be functionally or substantively relevant to the real-world phenomenon itself. In short, some things that we perceive as being levels may not really be so. In this case, the concept of level and in turn the concept of hierarchy become analytical expedients rather than reflections of reality. This seems to be particularly a problem in what we refer to as identity hierarchies.

As opposed to the dominance, holarchic, and neogenetic modalities we have previously defined, the identity hierarchy is one with a very special property: successive higher-levels of a hierarchy simply become aggregates or sums of the lower-order components which they encompass. Here we have a variant of a case with which we are already familiar . . . the linear system. In a linear structure, the existence of any levels intervening between the highest- and lowest-order components is gratuitous, for the system, per se, involves nothing more than the summation of the lowest-order components. In short, the intervening levels add nothing, and therefore simply become conveniences of scientific expression. Without going into great detail, it may be that some of our hierarchical appreciations are of this type. For example, we tend to order planets and stars into galaxies, but a galaxy, per se, may involve no properties that are distinct from the aggregation of the properties of the individual components of which it is comprised. In the same way, biological levels such as phylum, species, and family, for example, represent conveniences of ordering that have no structural or functional significance in the real-world. In some physical systems, if all molecules can be made comprehensible simply in terms of the properties of the atoms which comprise them, and the atoms in turn made comprehensible simply in terms of the properties of their elementary particles, then nothing substantively new is added at the atomic or molecular levels, such that the concept of a molecular system *qua* hierarchy has only expository rather than explanatory significance. As a general rule, then, we will distinguish between a true hierarchy and an identity (or analytic) hierarchy by a simple rule: each level of a true hierarchy must involve structural or functional properties that are differentiated from those of the lower-order components it is seen as encompassing or controlling. Whenever a hierarchy or a level of a hierarchy may be reduced to the sum or simple aggregation of the properties of its parts, it is simply an identity hierarchy.

This leads us directly into a proposition that is perhaps the key element in modern hierarchy theory . . . the properties of higher-level components cannot be completely inferred (i.e., induced) from an appreciation of the properties of the lower-level components it encompasses, serves, controls, or was generated by. The inverse also holds. Thus Mesarovic and Macko can set out a highly specific dictate for the analysis of hierarchical systems:

> . . . the principles or laws used to characterize the system on any stratum cannot in general be derived from the principles used on other strata. For example, the principles of computation or programming are not derivable from the physical laws that govern the behavior of the computer on the lower strata and vise versa. Similarly, the grammar and syntax are not derivable from the physical laws of sound generation nor are the rules for a literary composition derivable (solely) from the grammar and syntax.[27]

In a similar way, it is rather ludicrous to expect to be able to describe an entire social system in the same terms that we use to describe the cellular behavior of the lowest-order components of which the individuals comprising the social system are themselves comprised. In normal circumstances, sociological terms, underivable from the biochemical terms used to describe cellular structure and behavior, become appropriate at the level of the social system, per se, but entirely inappropriate at the level of the cell or molecule.

In the absence of the realization that new levels spawned by old levels inhere new properties (not simply extensions or extrapolations of those already existing at the lower levels), we find the impulse toward scientific reductionism we have so often deplored. The hierarchical theorist Robert Rosen explains,

> . . . to what extent does a knowledge of the *lowest* relevant level of system activity determine its properties at higher levels? This is the essential problem of *reductionism* in biology, seen most clearly in the claims of molecular biology. Their assertion is that the lowest relevant system description is at the biochemical (or even quantum-theoretic) level, that such a description is effectively attainable and effectively determines all higher-level descriptions.[28]

He then goes on to suggest that while he has discussed the infeasibility of arriving at adequate biochemical descriptions in the first place, others (e.g., Elsasser and Polanyi) have been concerned with the mechanics of drawing meaningful inferences from them as if such descriptions were feasible. In summary then, we can say at this point, that one of the characteristics of proper hierarchical systems is the fact that *different levels demand different descriptions*.

This brings us to another point. In general, higher-order levels of the system will be comprehended mainly in terms of the significance of the system as a whole, relative to the field in which it is resident or the relationships it entails with other systems. As we move upward through the hierarchy, we sacrifice detail in description. On the other hand, as we investigate successively lower-levels of the system, we may expect to be able to employ more precise terms and analytical instruments, and gain a more thorough explanation of their operational rather than their relational significance. Thus Mesarovic and Macko can suggest that

> by moving up the hierarchy, the description becomes broader and refers to larger subsystems and longer periods of time. The analysis of a literary composition, starting from the alphabet, becomes richer as one comprehends and uses the principles of higher strata: grammar, syntax, rules of style . . . and composition.[29]

We shall later have much more to say about the issue of wedding information taken at different levels of description—using different media of explanation—into integrated system models.

At this point, we may introduce a formal property of proper hierarchical systems through the use of Figure 2.8 . . . asymmetry. The condition reflected in the figure is that structurally different components of a hierarchical system will appear with different frequencies, with higher-order components (those exercising higher levels of authority or status, etc.) appearing with successively lower frequencies. In this formulation, the question of direction of influence no longer becomes a necessary definitional component; at any interval of time, low-order components may be exercising an influence on higher-order, or the reverse. The precise direction of influence between any two levels (any X_i's) depends on *contextual conditions* that must be specified for a sufficient determination.

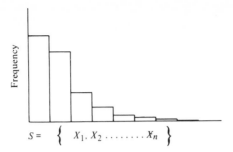

Figure 2.8 Simple hierarchical morphology.

In any case, with the X_i's of Figure 2.8 constituting system levels, proper hierarchical systems will always map out as a pyramidal organization (see Figure 2.9), with the sharpness of the angles of the resultant pyramid being determined by the successive differences between frequencies of appearance of the components at different levels. The first requirement for a hierarchical system, would now be that the successive pairs of X_i's (e.g., contiguous levels) have an existing or potential interface which they can exercise. In this sense, the lowest and highest levels of the system are interconnected, *but not directly.* Indeed, when the mediating levels between highest and lowest disappear, such that every system component is capable of interacting with every other directly, we move away from hierarchical structure and into what we shall call, in the next section, the reticulated system (a nonhierarchical organizational modality).

The second requirement is the necessity to accommodate the noninferability principle we just introduced, the proposition that demands that there be some differentiation between the laws or principles governing the structure and/or behavior of the several levels. In this sense, we may suggest that the functions

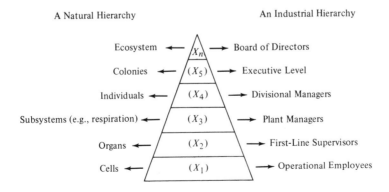

Figure 2.9 The pyramidal system.

governing the relations between the various $x_{i,j}$'s constituting a level must be different, *or* the components of the various levels must be morphologically different (e.g., qualitatively distinct). The limits on the ability to induce structural and/or behavioral properties across system levels will then be related to the degree of difference we note on either of these dimensions.

A third aspect of hierarchical systems is the frequency of occurrence of components within each of the system levels (e.g., the number of components constituting a set, X_i) and the provision of an interface between successive pairs of levels. This says nothing about the nature of the relationship between the $x_{i,j}$'s which comprise a level (each $x_{i,j}$ being the j'th component of the i'th level, or the j'th element in X_i). Components may have no contact whatsoever with one another, and may even be unaware of each other's existence. In short, the precise nature of the relationship among the system components, organized into levels, is *a priori* unconstrained in this general formulation.

From this perspective then, the conditions under which two hierarchical systems become *structurally* isomorphic are simple to evolve. First, the number of unique levels must be the same, such that both have the same number of X_i's. Secondly, each of the corresponding X_i's must contain the same number of components ($x_{i,j}$'s). In this way, the relationship between system components and system levels is the same for both systems. We may characterize a hierarchical system, on the structural dimension, by the function that relates appearance of components to appearance (or generation) of levels. Thus, two divisions within a military system may be considered to be isomorphic systems (or subsystems, depending on our perspective) when each contains squads with the same number of men giving way to platoons with the same number of men, etc. We may even wish to look for isomorphic hierarchical structures between systems drawn from very different sectors, as for example between social systems and biological entities.

Functional isomorphy may occur with or without structural isomorphy. When it is accompanied by the latter, two systems would be *equivalent* . . . isomorphic in all respects. What we would be concerned with in functional isomorphy would be the nature of the interface conditions relating the various pairs of contiguous levels. When these relationships are identical for two systems, we have functional isomorphy. In this perspective, each of the levels of a hierarchical system becomes a "system" in its own right, with the interfaces available to each entered as boundary conditions. This generally enables us to reduce a complex hierarchical system to subsystems which are more manageable (or more analytically tractable) than the system as a whole. This kind of reduction is permissible to the extent that we are able to accurately allegorize the interface conditions among subsystems, so that the system, once broken-down, may be resynthesized without loss of real complexities. In short, it is at the interfaces among levels of hierarchical systems that we find conditions of synergy, and there that we must identify the nonlinear, nonadditive functions that really make a proper hierarchical system something much more than the simple aggregation of its parts. In a proper hierarchical system, then, the highest-order component is not identical with the system, per se, but is only one of its structurally and/or functionally differentiable levels.

In summary, then, any proper hierarchical system will be structurally mapped in the following way: first, we must identify the levels *qua* subsystems by isolating structural and/or behavioral uniqueness; secondly, we must assign system components to each of the levels on the basis of the generic properties associated with the levels, recognizing that the basic instruments of explanation for the various levels will probably themselves have to be unique, perhaps even coming from basically different disciplines; thirdly, we must establish the nature of the interface conditions *among* the various levels, thus developing the vehicle by which we may analytically synthesize previously reduced complex systems (usually involving interdisciplinary analysis); and finally, the nature of the components and relationships *within* levels must be allegorized as the lowest-level mapping task associated with hierarchical system analysis (a task that, again, will probably involve the use of basically different disciplinary perspectives and instruments within the different subsystems or levels). A strongly hierarchical system will then be one where the structural-functional properties assigned to each level are highly differentiated, and where the interface conditions among the various contiguous pairs of levels (subsystems) are also highly differentiated. A weakly hierarchical system will be one where the variances between levels are not terribly significant.

With this relatively brief introduction to hierarchical systems, we now go on to an even briefer examination of the instances of nonhierarchical organization that occur in the real world.

2.4.2 Nonhierarchical Systems

There are basically three types of nonhierarchical systems with which we need to be concerned. The first we have already discussed . . . the *fully-segmented* system of Section 2.2. There, it will be recalled, segmentation enabled us to develop very large but structurally and functionally simple systems, systems with basically just two levels: (a) a proportionately very small executive authority, and (b) a potentially immense number of replicative operating units. Examples of systems more or less fitting this pattern in both the political and social sectors were given. Also, in the biological domain the example of the amoeba colony as a fully-segmented, obviously nonhierarchical system was given. In the inorganic world similar systems exist, as in the coagulation of essentially undifferentiated particles as represented by a clay mass or a sand compact.

In general then, fully-segmented systems are always effectively nonhierarchical, simply because they have only one or two meaningfully differentiated levels, with an enormous difference in frequency of appearance between the higher and lower components. Hence we get a somewhat "flat" distribution, such as that shown earlier in Figure 2.3. The organizational description of such systems would not produce the strongly pyramidal organizational pattern associated with adequately hierarchical systems (and in cases of fully-segmented systems, such as the amoeba colony, there would be no pyramidal influence at all).

A second class of nonhierarchical systems exists. In this class are the systems which are expected to gradually displace the hierarchic bureaucracies in the post-industrial era . . . the *adhocracies* postulated by Toffler, and advocated by social scientists such as Warren Bennis[22]. Such organizations will be structured, or will emerge, as a situation demands, and be just as quickly dissolved as soon as the need passes. The nonhierarchical characteristics of such systems will be reflected in their exploitation of differentiated expertise among system members organized as *peers*, containing "professionals" for whom a constraining superstructure promises to be dysfunctional. This type of nonhierarchical system, as we will see in a later chapter, is generally associated with tasks that demand creativity, or with situations where the emphasis is on the generation of original solutions to effectively unprecedented problems. If we read the situation of post-industrialism correctly, more and more emphasis will be placed on such problems, and less and less need will be found to maintain bureaucracies that have proven congruent only with effectively precedented problems for which solutions may be pre-programmed (e.g., secondary industry). As the distribution of employment and investment gradually shifts in favor of creative, research or service (tertiary) enterprise—or as post-industrial government becomes more an exercise in socioeconomic *development* than in maintenance or control—more and more nonhierarchical organizations may be expected to emerge.

In a sense, these adhocratic organizations will reflect an organizational phenomenon that, in a relatively quiet way, has been with us for some years. This is the project-oriented or *matrix* organization. Unlike the traditional pyramidal organizational structure, that may be viewed as a single hierarchy, the matrix organization represents the *union* of vertically-structured functional hierarchies and an array of distinct projects cutting across them, as shown in Figure 2.10. In this figure we have arbitrarily set up an organization that has three unique

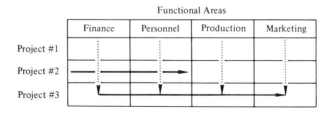

Figure 2.10 The matrix organization.

projects underway, and four functional areas. Each of the various projects, represented as rows, may be thought of as a lateral hierarchy, with a project director occupying the highest level, and a group of line workers at the lowest level, with various mid-management and staff positions in mediating roles. In a similar way, each of the functional areas may be thought of as vertical hierarchies, with a vice president of marketing, etc., and staff and mid-management people interposed between him and the lowest-level line functionaries. Each of the elements in the matrix may thus be thought to represent the interface between a project and a specific functional area, with the project exercising demand on the resources of the functional areas, while the higher-order elements of the functional hierarchies are responsible for managing the supply to meet demands. Thus, in a sense, control over enterprise resources is shared jointly among projects and functional areas, with the functional areas now all basically acting as *service* agents for the projects.

As the reader may expect, such structures have been historically important in the aerospace industry and other fields where the enterprises survive on the basis of effectively unprecedented projects. Aerospace firms—or other purveyors of extremely advanced technology directed at meeting unprecedented needs—may be viewed as rather exotic and terribly complex *job shops*, very different, as such, from the firm that exists by continuously producing the same product or set of products according to time-tested, market-tested parameters, and within the technological state of the art. The operational demands made on these two types of organizations are different enough to impose the matrix organization on the former and the pyramidal, traditionally hierarchical structure on the latter. To this extent, then, the matrix organization is best explained and represented as a relatively significant departure from hierarchical organization, a departure which has been explored in more detail elsewhere.[30]

The last of our nonhierarchical systems is the most complex of all structural referents that we must be prepared to face. It is called the *reticulated* system, distinct mainly in that every component of the system is "equipotential" with respect to every other. In simpler terms, this means that only contextual factors dictate which components will interface in which ways with which others at what times . . . there are no *a priori* structural constraints. A fully-reticulated system would then be intelligible in terms of a *network* where potentially every part could connect more or less directly with every other. The individual components would have a relatively wide repertoire of alternative behavioral states available to them, perhaps being able to alter their behavior in the face of every different interface situation that emerges. The number of alternative structural states that may emerge, and for which the system scientist would have to account, thus becomes some permutation of the number of system components and the number of alternative behaviors each could evoke; a situation that may easily defy our mathematical capabilities as they exist today.

Reticulated systems are not really representable as neat pyramids, for they do not meet the basic conditions we earlier laid down for a proper hierarchy. Rather, they can be conceived of as an array of components *qua* nodes, with effectively circular interconnections, and with potentially direct lines of communication and co-determination between all elements . . . and with "subsystems" that are determined differently at different points in time, according to conditions and algorithms that are possibly entirely unpredictable.

The only analogy that we can give at this point would be that of an immense cocktail party, with guests who are highly differentiated, whose associations are unconstrained, and who may exhibit a potentially unique behavior to each different guest with whom they happen to have an interchange. A weak analogy is reflected in the realization that some ostensibly bureaucratic (e.g., hierarchical) systems have an *informal system* structure that operates sub rosa, through which the majority of the work really gets done. Just how important these partially reticulated informal organizations are is given substance when bureaucracies *work to rules* . . . when they, in effect, abandon the informal, *ad hoc* connections among mèmbers and begin to observe the chains of command and communications laid down by the "book." Productivity plummets! The important point here is that these informal organizations act to obviate the formal hierarchy, horizontally connecting subsystems at critical levels so as to prevent having to go upward in the chain of command each time a coordination or interchange is needed. Good examples of the informal network appear in the military, where *arrangements* exist between corresponding members of essentially different functional units, or in manufacturing concerns where the various departments engage in a type of casual interchange of information and priviledge which is not envisioned or accounted for by the formal organizational chart.

At any rate, this concept of the reticulated system should remain in the reader's mind as we close this second chapter, for we shall return to it in another guise when we lay out the properties for the worst of all possible analytical worlds in which the system scientist might find himself. And now having introduced the most complicated and perhaps most elusive of our structural referents, we may consider our problem of defining the structural aspects of system at an end. We now turn to a somewhat easier task, easier largely because of the work we have already done . . . that of exploring the dynamic dimension of systems, and providing the reader with a set of behavioral referents.

2.5 NOTES AND REFERENCES

1. Zadeh and Polak, eds., *System Theory* (New York: McGraw-Hill, 1969), p. vii.
2. Anatol Rapoport, "The Search for Simplicity," *The Relevance of General Systems Theory*, ed. Ervin Laszlo (New York: George Braziller, 1972), p. 30.
3. George Klir, *An Approach to General Systems Theory* (New York: Van Nostrand Reinhold Company, 1969), p. 71.

4. Hoel, Port, and Stone, *Introduction to Probability Theory* (Boston: Houghton Mifflin Company, 1971), p. 50.

5. Klir, *op. cit.*, p. 71.

6. *Ibid.*

7. Leslie A. White, ed., *The Evolution of Culture* (New York: McGraw-Hill, 1959).

8. This point is amplified in Chapter 4, suggesting that primitive system structures tend to be associated with control through ideology, and with axiological (e.g., affective, value-driven) bonds between member and system, per se. For a more complete discussion of this point, see my "Toward an Array of Organizational Control Modalities," *Human Relations,* **27** no. 2 (1974).

9. White, *op. cit.*

10. In this regard, see Shirley Terreberry's "The Evolution of Organizational Environments," *Administrative Sciences Quarterly,* **12** (March 1968).

11. Ludwig von Bertalanffy, *General System Theory* (New York: George Braziller, 1968), p. 39.

12. Jay W. Forrester, *Principles of Systems* (Cambridge, Mass.: Wright-Allen Press, second preliminary edition, 1968), pp. 1-5.

13. Such considerations may, through logical extension, lead to a basis for classifying systems in general. For more on this, see my "Beyond Systems Engineering: The General System Theory Potential for the Social and Behavioral Sciences," *General Systems Yearbook,* **XVIII** (1973). Also see Section 4.1 of this book.

14. von Bertalanffy, *op. cit.*, pp. 86-87; see also the brilliant volume edited by Koestler and Smithies, containing a collection of the most important arguments against scientific reduction: *Beyond Reductionism: New Perspectives in the Life Sciences* (New York: Macmillan Publishing Company, 1969).

15. von Bertalanffy, "General Systems Theory: A Critical Review," *Modern Systems Research for the Behavioral Scientist*, ed. Buckley (Chicago: Adline Publishing Company, 1968), pp. 11-30.

16. For a somewhat mathematical but highly intriguing examination of learning system theory (predicated on Bayesian transformations, a subject we shall discuss in Chapters 7 and 8), see K.S. Fu, "Learning System Theory," Zadeh and Polak *op. cit.*, pp. 425-463.

17. In this regard, see Walter Buckley's *Sociology and Modern System Theory* (Englewood Cliffs: Prentice-Hall, 1967) especially Chapters 1 and 2.

18. Herbert Simon, "The Organization of Complex Systems," *Hierarchy Theory*, ed. Howard H. Pattee (New York: George Braziller, 1973), pp. 3-27.

19. *Ibid.*

20. Quoted by Lancelot Law Whyte, ed., in *Hierarchical Structures* (New York: American Elsevier Publishing Co., 1969), p. 7.

21. See Hocking and Young's *Topology*, (Reading: Addison-Wesley Publishing Co., 1961), Chapter 1; or any other reference to topological spaces.

22. In this regard, see Chapter 7 of Alvin Toffler's *Future Shock* (New York: Random House, 1970); or either of the following by Warren Bennis: "Beyond Bureaucracy," *Transaction* (July-August 1965) or *Changing Organizations* (New York: McGraw-Hill, 1966).

23. Koestler and Smithies, *op. cit.*

24. See Chester Barnard's *The Functions of the Executive* (Cambridge, Mass.: Harvard University Press, 1938). See also the so-called Barnard-Simon

model of organization motivation in *Organizations*, ed. March et al., (New York: John Wiley & Sons, 1958).

25. Clifford Grobstein, "Hierarchical Order and Neogenesis," Pattee, *op. cit.*, pp. 31-47.
26. Pattee, *op. cit.*, p. 136.
27. Mesarovic and Macko, "Foundations for a Scientific Theory of Hierarchical Systems," Pattee, *op. cit.*, pp. 29-50. See also Mesarovic, et al., Theory of Hierarchical, Multilevel Systems (New York: Academic Press, 1970).
28. Robert Rosen, "Hierarchical Organization in Automata Theoretic Models of Biological Systems," Pattee, *op. cit.*, pp. 179-199.
29. Mesarovic and Macko, *op. cit.*, p. 35.
30. For a good discussion of project management principles, see Cleland and King's *System Analysis and Project Management* (New York: McGraw-Hill, 1968).

3

Modalities of System Behavior

INTRODUCTION

In dealing in the previous chapter with the structural aspects of systems, we found a set of abstractions (generic system referents) that real-world systems were said to more or less approximate. In essence, this meant that we could look forward to the possibility of constructing maps for large numbers of specific systems using an appropriate collection of generic referents. Such a process becomes more feasible the closer the approximation of real-world systems come to the generic referents or, more specifically, the greater the exhaustion, by the referents, of the range of structural configurations we might expect to locate in the real-world.

Naturally, when we work strictly with dichotomies, such that a system is deemed to be either segmented or differentiated, or either linear or nonlinear, etc., we are indulging in oversimplification. But such is the way of science. While we recognize the possibility of uniqueness for each and every phenomenon we might encounter, we also recognize the imperative for evolving, from this world of differences, certain aspects which *classes* of phenomena may share. What is hoped, then, is that the structural referents we introduced will serve to majorally exhaust the array of real-world systems we might encounter, while also recognizing that there will be some systems that are simply unable to be accommodated in crude dichotomies.

What we shall later find is that complex systems need not really be looked at solely with respect to such dichotomies. Rather, systems may be usually broken down into subsystems, or even further broken down, and these lower-order units of analysis stand a much better chance of reflecting the properties of the abstractions we set out. Thus, a complex system may emerge as an amalgamation of parts, some of which may approximate one member of the dichotomies we set out, some of which may approximate the antonyms. Thus, for example, a socioeconomic system may have some subsystems which are structured linearly, other nonlinearly; some component subsystems may reflect conditions of segmentation, others may be structured in terms of differentiation, etc.

This situation does not really affect the utility of the abstract referents we set out for the structural dimension of systems, nor will it inhibit the contribution we can expect from the behavioral modalities we shall be developing here. Rather, wherever they emerge, at whatever level, and within whatever specific context, they help serve the cause of generalization, and hence make available to us the powerful potential of analogy-building.

The major difference between structural and behavioral referents is that the former pertain to the problem of mapping the configurational or static properties of systems, while behavioral referents attack systems in their dynamic aspects. Here, then, we are interested in the time-dependent behavior of systems, whereas in Chapter 2 we were really concentrating on *space-dependent* properties (the focus of structural analysis).

Let's amplify this. Recall that in the previous chapter we were using the analogy of taking a "snapshot" of a system, yielding a point-in-time inventory of system components, the configuration of their distribution within the confines of the system's boundaries, and also a portrayal of the lines of communication and influence among the components. Now, intuitively, we realize that a map is really representative of the function that finds system properties varying through some space which the system occupies. In this sense, an amoeba colony would be represented by an extremely simple space-dependent function, for the properties in any one segment or area are replicated in all other segments. When however we spoke about complex hierarchical systems, much less the nonhierarchical systems, the space-dependent functions generating the structural attributes of the system are themselves very complex . . . for heterogenous components are distributed asymmetrically, etc. Thus, our structural maps are generated by functions that allocate system properties through points in space, whereas the functions pertinent to the behavioral dimension of systems are those that distribute properties according to their variation through points in time.

Such a perspective loosely corresponds to what is often called functional analysis. In undertaking a functional analysis of systems, we are not concerned with what they look like, but with what they do. Hence, on the behavioral dimension we speak in terms of purpose, work, change, achievement, process . . . in short, dynamic concepts. But there are two distinct subdimensions of functional analysis, both equally important to the system scientist. The first of these subdimensions we shall refer to as the *macro-analytic* level. Here we are interested only in the nature of the relationship between system inputs and system outputs, or more broadly between a set of starting-state conditions at some time t and ultimate or concluding-state conditions at some time $(t + n)$. In either case, what we look at here is not the *process* that mediates between inputs and outputs, or between successive time-dependent states, but merely the quantitative or qualitative relationship between these pairs of entities. In other words, we assume that the structural map of the system remains the same through the interval, an assumption that is warranted for the majority of systems we will expect to encounter. In such a case, the structural aspects of the system may be ignored, and we move into the "black-box" analytical modality, where the components and mechanics of the transformation process remain transparent to us.

On the second subdimension, naturally enough referred to as the *micro-dimension*, we are interested in the structure of the system, and specifically interested in any changes that take place in that structure through time. Thus, a micro-behavioral analysis would involve developing a model to explain any changes that took place in an interval in any of the following:

(a) The nature of the components of the system.
(b) The distribution of the components.
(c) The nature of the prevailing relationships among these components.

In short, when we may assume the map of a system to remain constant, we work at the macro level. When, on the other hand, there is some probability that the very structure of the system will alter, we must move down to the more detailed and time consuming micro level.

As a general rule, we tend to treat artificial systems (e.g., machines or highly regulated bureaucracies) on the macro level, for the structural characteristics of such systems are not highly susceptible to change through time. Other phenomenon must be treated as black-boxes, on the macro level, simply because we do not have access to the processual structure that mediates between inputs and outputs, or between starting and concluding states. The example that immediately comes to mind is the genetic trait-transfer process. The macro relationships are predictable with some degree of statistical precision. Thus, for example, we know what the concluding state (or output) will be if we put parents with certain genetic traits together . . . i.e., parents with brown eyes, for example, have a 75% probability of giving birth to a baby with brown eyes; if one of the parents has blue eyes, the probability is 50% that the baby will have brown eyes. The same statistical regularity can be observed with respect to other genetically transmitted properties, yet we still do not know the nature of the transformation functions—the processes—by which these well-behaved input-output relationships are obtained. In other words, the genetic code remains a "black box" for modern science, while the genetic process itself may be treated as *macro-deterministic*.[1]

On the other hand, there are classes of systems that will usually have to be approached on the micro level. These include many natural systems and the majority of social, political, and economic systems . . . all of which are highly susceptible to structural changes through time, which may or may not effect changes on the macro level. (As will later be shown, some systems may produce the same outputs from a given set of inputs despite physical changes in the mediating process). As a general rule, however, we must expect that changes that occur in the structure of a system (on any of the mapping levels) will have an effect on the nature of the input-output relations, or on the relationships be-tween any starting-state conditions and the concluding state that will emerge. Thus, the reorganization of the sequence of processing a product, or perhaps the reorganization of the management subsystem of a corporation, is undertaken in the hopes of positively affecting the efficiency of the enterprise which means, in effect, improving the input-output ratio (which may be extended into meaning an increase in the rate of return on investment, etc.). By the same token, when the constituents or members of an athletic teams change, we expect, with some confidence, that the performance of that team will be altered in some way; just as a change in the power-weight ratio of a car (a structural effect) would presum-ably alter variables such as mileage and acceleration (input-output parameters).

One more point should perhaps be dealt with a bit more fully in this introduc-tion. Remember we said that behavioral analysis deals with the changes that have taken place between successive snapshots of a system. But then we also suggested that one level of behavioral analysis, the macro, is not really concerned with the properties of the system structure as exhibited by the snapshot. The logic still holds, for when we are dealing on the macro level, the initial or refer-ence snapshot is that which shows the configuration of the input properties, while the concluding-state snapshot shows the configuration of the outputs. On the micro level, the snapshots would be those directed not only at the configura-tion of inputs and outputs, but at the configuration of the mediating process as well. In this sense, the two levels of analysis differ mainly in the depth or scope of their focus. They both still attempt to capture the relevant dynamic proper-ties of the system, recognizing that where the macro level is appropriate, struc-tural properties become effectively irrelevant. Thus, the output from a macro-level analysis will simply be a function relating inputs to outputs, and will usually take the form of a linear or nonlinear equation, per se. When we define our unit of analysis more broadly, incorporating structural states of the system that pertain at the beginning and ending points of an interval, we move into a somewhat different level of sophistication. For there we will be concerned about the set of transformation functions that allegorize basic state changes through time, or about those that will explain the process by which funda-mentally different systems maps were arrived at.

A general formulation of the problem for behavioral analysis could then be arrived at this way. First, let us consider that the starting-state conditions perti-nent to a system at some time t comprise not only the structural properties of that system (as per the map), but also the inputs available to the system at that point-in-time. In this sense, the concluding-state conditions at some time $(t + 1)$ would be not only the configuration of the output(s), but also the structural properties of that system as constituting the system map at time $(t + 1)$. Now, where there is no difference between the successive maps, or where the qualita-tive differences are negligible, an adequate conclusion of the behavioral analysis process will simply be the equation relating inputs to outputs. Where, on the other hand, the successive maps show significant qualitative differences, then an adequate conclusion of the behavioral analysis process would be the set of transformation functions operating on the altered structural properties as well. Thus, as we proceed with this chapter, we shall have to distinguish which kind of process our generic system behavioral referents refer to, or if they are equally applicable to both the micro and macro level.

Going further, such problems have been considered in a somewhat similar way by other system scientists. Systems whose structural properties do not (or may be presumed not to) change through time are generally referred to as *stationary* systems, whereas those whose structural properties are susceptible to change through time are called *nonstationary* systems.[2] Thus, the macro level of behavioral analysis is properly associated with stationary-state systems, whereas the micro level must be employed when the system at hand is a nonstationary one. In the case of the former, outputs are assumed to alter only as inputs alter, with the mediating process assumed constant; in systems of the latter type, outputs (or concluding states) may be assumed to vary either as a function of variances in inputs, or as a function of structural changes that have taken place during the sampling interval.

As a final note, it should be clear that when we were speaking about the generation of maps of the structural dimension of systems in the previous chapter, we were basically concerned with developing devices of descriptive significance. Here, however, when we begin to be concerned with the behavior of systems, we are primarily concerned with the generation of devices which will serve the cause of system *prediction*. In short, the behavioral modalities we will be defining have utility for us in that they serve to summarize, in more or less abstract form, the way in which systems may be expected to behave in the future. This must be so, for the systems we encounter in the real-world will be assigned one or another of these modalities largely on the basis of any consistent behaviors they have exhibited in the past.

DETERMINISTIC SYSTEMS

Consonant with our major interest in being able to predict a system's behavior over some time interval, we shall first take a look at those systems that present the least problem in this respect. A deterministic system can be defined as one which for any given set of starting-state conditions, will generate only one concluding state that can be assigned any significant probability of occurrence.

This has implications for us at both the macro and micro levels. At the macro level, it means that a given set of inputs will always give rise to a specific output configuration, or that the output associated with a specific set of inputs is *predictable* with an extremely high level of confidence. At the micro level, it means that given the system's configuration at some time t, that which will exist at time $(t + 1)$ will be predictable with a high degree of confidence. Thus starting-state conditions (which would include input specifications) allow us to determine, with accuracy, the concluding-state after some interval.

Perhaps the most important aspect of the definition of deterministic systems is its equivocation. This equivocation is somewhat important for us, for philosophers have long been wont to point out that nothing in this world can be considered *inherently* deterministic . . . incapable of attaining anything except a single state. Their point is a good one. Consider something as simple as a common light switch. Each time we switch it up or down, there is some positive probability that it will misbehave (malfunction). However, for any reasonably well-engineered switch, that is not obviously old or weathered, etc., we can effectively ignore this probability, for it will be terribly small. Thus, most of us, under most circumstances, would tend to treat a light switch as an *effectively* deterministic system, though the fact that even an insignificant probability of malfunction exists prevents it from being an inherently deterministic entity.

Much the same thing may be said of some nonmechanical systems. Sociologists have recognized that a process known as *institutionalization* (a form of extended acculturation) can produce individuals who, within the context of a specific sociocultural system, behave effectively deterministically.[3] That is they, like certain machines, have one and only one significantly probable response to any given stimuli (e.g., any given set of starting-state conditions). So when we speak of effectively deterministic systems, it should by no means be suggested that we are speaking only of mechanical entities, a point we shall have to clarify further as we proceed.

We may now take a look at the two most prominent examples of deterministic-state systems, the steady-state and finite-state systems. The first we are already somewhat familiar with from the previous chapter; the second type will form an extremely important class of systems for a large number of disciplines or subdisciplines, among them behavioral psychology, traditional engineering, classical physics, etc. What should be kept in mind at this point is that when the ambition of our analyses is system prediction, these deterministic systems represent the simplest behavioral alternatives we are likely to encounter, and the most tractable entities.

3.1.1 The Steady-State System

Recall, from Section 2.3.1 that the steady-state system emerged as an agent of living (e.g., biological or social) systems, and seemed to contradict the suggestion that all systems will tend irrevocably to a situation of maximum entropy, maximal disorder. In short, the steady-state system is an *open* system in terms of the definition which von Bertalanffy earlier provided us. Katz and Kahn explain:

> The importation of energy to arrest entropy operates to maintain some constancy in energy exchange, so that open systems which survive are characterized by a steady state. A steady state is not a motionless or true equilibrium.

There is a continuous inflow of energy from the external environment and a continuous export of the products of the system, but the character of the system, the ratio of the energy exchanges and the relations between parts, remains the same.[4]

In this sense, steady-state systems are not only open systems, but are stationary as well, maintaining essentially the same structural configuration through time, and essentially the same input-output relationship. In terms of the predictive problem, then, a steady-state system is effectively deterministic, for we expect the same conditions to prevail through significant intervals of time, with a high confidence that our expectations in this regard will not be disappointed. In short, the state of the system that prevails at time t is expected to be *the* state of the system at time $(t + 1)$, etc.

A steady-state system is thus one that exhibits a stability through time, a property that appears to be much valued by systems of widely different superficial characteristics. However, we now need to distinguish between steady-state behavior at the macro and micro levels. The type of system described by Katz and Kahn is one which is steady state on both subdimensions. Neither the system configuration (e.g., the map) nor the input-output relationships alter significantly. A system that is able to accomplish this stability in the face of environmental changes (or exogenous perturbations) is generally referred to as a *homeostatic* system.[5] Homeostatic systems are all predicated on a closed-loop configuration that allows a constant feedback between system and environment (as in a thermostat or the mechanisms that regulate body temperature in animals). The ability to maintain the character of a system, much less its specific properties, in the face of adverse forces, is a much-valued one, and one that has been of considerable interest to system scientists since Cannon set out the descriptive principles of homeostasis during World War II.[6]

For Cannon, the human body constituted an open system engaged in continuous interchange with its environment, during the course of which conditions that act to disturb the body's integrity are constantly encountered. Yet, despite these perturbations, the body has the capability to maintain a constancy of things like blood sugar, alkalinity level, . . . and perhaps even of temperment. The maintenance of stable parameters in the face of unstable environmental conditions is made possible by the existence of mechanisms which can "read" changes occurring in the milieu, assimilate them, and dictate compensatory actions. When we engineer systems with such a capability, we call them *cybernetic* systems, a word with which we are all familiar, and a process which we shall treat in detail in Chapter 8.

Katz and Kahn, in their discussion of the concept of the steady state, bring to light an important equivocation on the treatment we have given thus far. They suggest that

 . . . the steady state which at the simple level is one of homeostasis over time, at more complex levels becomes one of preserving the character of the system through growth and expansion.[7]

This suggestion becomes especially important in light of the two evolutionary modalities we developed in the last chapter, segmentation and differentiation. It may immediately be seen that a homeostatic situation is maintained, *at the micro level,* in the replicative method of expansion employed by segmented systems. Obviously, the growth and expansion of a system via segmentation always involves changes in the absolute values of input and output variables, yet the basic ratio of inputs to outputs may be expected to hold rather constant over time. In fact, as we suggested in treating segmented systems, the relationships among components are linear and additive, which suggests that the addition of new units simply involves the extension rather than regeneration of the input-output relationship. In this sense, the fully-segmented system becomes an excellent example of a system that can grow—evolve, as it were—and still maintain homeostasis. It does not take too much imagination to realize that differentiated systems, by their very nature, are deprived of this opportunity, especially when differentiation appears on both the functional and structural dimension.

There are large number of natural systems (e.g., estuarial and beach complexes; geological phenomena; certain types of biosystems; some social systems) that are capable of maintaining a steady state on the macro dimension despite changes on the micro dimension. Individual components may change in character, may alter their interface conditions with other system components, yet the general character of the system remains the same, and its input-output configurations (and the face it shows to the outside world) remain roughly similar through time. Laszlo has characterized such systems as *dynamically stable.*

> Complex open systems which arise in the biosphere independently of conscious human planning include biological, social, cultural, as well as ecological systems. These systems have pattern-maintaining as well as pattern-evolving dynamics built into them without benefit of human engineering. In such dynamically stable systems deviation by any part is compensated by the corrective behavior of the rest.[8]

In such a system, a change in the basic configuration in one place is offset by a compensatory change made elsewhere. Consider, for example, that when certain portions of the human brain are destroyed through accident or disease, other portions automatically tend to absorb the functions that were performed by the lost components, such that the basic relationships between sensations received and responses inaugurated remains much the same despite a structural change. The appearance, from the outside, is that of a steady-state system; but, the ability to maintain functional integrity in the face of major structural changes is characteristic of a much more sophisticated system . . . the equifinal system discussed in the concluding pages of this chapter.

In some ecological and biological systems, dynamic stability is maintained simply by the constant provision of new components of the same order to replace those which have been eroded or destroyed . . . much as in geological systems, the constant decomposition of granitic materials tends to replace soil that has been washed away by erosion.

There are numerous attempts to build this dynamically-stable condition into man-made systems, presumably in the attempt to emulate nature.[9]

Two excellent examples are the fields of fiscal and monetary policy. These exist as instruments designed to compensate, on the macro level, for the myriad discontinuities, interruptions, and disturbances that occur on the micro level of economic systems. The ambition is to maintain a stability of price levels, interest rates, etc., not for themselves but for their affect on aggregated macro variables such as G.N.P. or inflation, etc. As such, actions taken at the macro level are designed to offset the adverse, aggregate affect of "locally-oriented" actions at the micro levels, such that the integrity of the system as a whole is maintained despite forces that are constantly trying to disrupt it. In another important sense, the dynamically-stable referent becomes important when we realize that many ecological and social systems will have constantly shifting components . . . different individuals or entities moving in and out of the system, all of which must be accommodated and employed to the interest of the system despite the different characters they bring with them. Obviously, such problems would be greater for a socioeconomic organization, for example, than for a coral colony or a beaver hutch, yet the importance of compensation and assimilation cannot be overstated. Another important aspect of the dynamically-stable system, as a representative of the class of steady-state systems on the macro level, is that they contain, at virtually all times, forces that act simultaneously for the dissolution or change of the system, and forces that act to consolidate the status quo. In such a situation, what is of interest to us is the dynamically-stable system's ability to maintain a constancy of the relationship between these antonymical forces, such that change occurs, but does so with the same rough quality and magnitude through long intervals of time.*

There is, of course, an adverse side to homeostasis as a system strategy. The attempt to maintain a given structural and/or input-output configuration—despite environmental or field changes—can often mean that a system is chronically suboptimal or secularly inefficient. When the system is "stubborn" enough in this respect, it can lead to obsolescence, atavism, and eventually to dissolution. As we shall later show, homeostatic systems as they exist in the natural world, and their artificial counterpart, the cybernetic system, both have only a limited capability for accommodating change . . . a highly constrained set of perturbations to which they can functionally react. Most steady-state systems, or most systems whose ambition is to maintain a steady state on either the macro or micro levels, are instances of *bounded adaptivity*; that is, they are resilient and

---

*To this extent, one of the characteristics of a dynamically stable system would be the maintenance of a rough constancy, through significant intervals of time, in the forces acting to dissolve or alter the system and those acting to conserve its character. By analogy, we would look then for a *stationary* function relating centrifugal to centripetal forces.

responsive only within a very limited range. A fully adaptive system, on the other hand, is one that constantly seeks to exploit new opportunities as they emerge, seeking always to maximize its efficiency rather than maintain its historical structure or preserve tradition. We shall treat such systems in the next section, only noting here that they appear to be explicable as instances of positive-feedback rather than the negative-feedback which characterizes homeostatic or cybernetic systems.

There is also one extremely dysfunctional homeostatic system, where the dysfunctionality emerges from the fact that it is really an *open-loop* system and only superficially homeostatic. This is the system whose ambition is to maintain a stable structure (e.g., stationarity on the micro level) despite the degradation this might cause to the input-output relationship on the macro level. This is the *structurally-homeostatic* system, where the preservation of a given structure or hierarchy becomes the prime and only ambition, ultimately at the expense of effectiveness.*

Encountering a steady-state system, on either or both the micro or macro levels, is always a happy experience for the system scientist concerned with system prediction. But a steady state is not always functional (i.e., positive or beneficial) for when maintained to an excess, it can lead to secular inefficiency or ecological ineffectiveness. In general, however, living and/or intelligent systems seek rightly to maintain the basic character of the system despite limited perturbations in the environment, or despite limited alterations in the character of their components. In such an instance, homeostasis or compensation become functional alternatives to adaption, which would find each incremental change in external conditions being accompanied by a roughly proportional alteration in system structure, or which might find the system altering either its basic input-output structures, or the relationship between them at the slightest provocation. In short, the steady-state system is always one that trades off the efficiency of differentiation for the expedience of the status quo, and may thus always be considered to be somewhat out of phase with the environment.

One of the prime considerations of modern science is the concept of the biological or *organic machine*, one that is capable of altering its structure and behavior in the face of the smallest changes in contextual conditions, and making such changes almost instantaneously. Such systems represent an adaptive ideal, but their rationale is exciting. The organic machine becomes an instance of a continuous-state, fully-differentiated system, one with the least rigidity, with the fewest structural constraints, and with the widest conceivable repertoire of behavioral states. We shall be exploring them somewhat later as ideal-types, mentioning here only that they are a conceptual nightmare for the predictive scientist.

---

*One need hardly suggest that a popular criticism of the bureaucracy is that it strives primarily to perpetuate itself, often long after its real function has become gratuitous.

A steady-state system, then, may be thought of as one that seeks to achieve, and in most part realizes, one of the following conditions:

(a) The maintenance of a structural status quo through an interval (steady state on the micro level).
(b) The maintenance of a given input-output relationship through an interval of time (steady state on the macro level).
(c) The maintenance of a steady state on *both* the macro and micro sub-dimensions through an interval.

Obviously, the accomplishment of the last condition, in the face of changes in the environment or milieu in which the system resides, is effectively impossible (e.g., counter-intuitive). On the other hand, the maintenance of a steady state on the macro level despite changes in the environment (or despite changes in the nature or relationship of system components calling for compensatory strategies) is something of an accomplishment. When we find physical or biological systems behaving this way, we may applaud the ingenuity of nature; when artificial or man-made systems exhibit this behavior, it may be taken as a tribute to the intelligence of the system architects.

As for the first of our conditions, it is laudable only when the environmental characteristics do not change, or where the effectiveness of the system is enhanced thereby (e.g., its survival value undiminished). A good example of this may be the suggestion by some social scientists that the Roman Catholic church would have done better to maintain some rigidity in the face of environmental perturbations rather than attempt to become adaptive. Their reasoning is interesting, for this institution may very well gain its basic significance and utility by being a constant in the face of inconstancy, such that the move we note toward an adaptive rather than steady-state posture may ultimately prove dysfunctional.*

A steady-state, again, may be defined on either the macro or micro dimension, or both. Systems that are able to maintain a given macro relationship (i.e., a given exchange rate between inputs and outputs) despite changes at the micro (structural) level, are called compensatory steady-state systems, and may usually be thought to demand both a differentiated structure and an element of "intelligence" at some level. Systems that seek simply to maintain structural stability in spite of environmental changes and in spite of any changes that this will cause in input-output ratios, are generally considered to be dysfunctional . . . excessively stubborn or conservative, as it were.

There is a final aspect of steady-state systems that we must discuss . . . one that has particular importance for the system scientist in his role as a predictor of system behavior. These are systems that have not yet obtained the deter-

---

*Indeed, there has been some comment that the ecumenical adjustment that the Catholic church has made during the last decade has actually accelerated the rate at which Catholics have "fallen away."

minacy associated with the steady state, but are only *converging* toward it. For when the convergence toward a rigid behavior is clear-cut, our statistical instruments will enable us to uncover such tendencies and make long-run or teleological assertions about relationships between starting- and concluding-state conditions. This is a rather important point. It suggests that when systems are converging toward a steady state, it may be possible to predict the terminal condition of the system at some time t, given a history of convergent behavior during some previous interval. Thus, while the relationship between closely proximate starting- and concluding-state conditions (e.g., short-run transformations) may not be deterministic or predictable with great accuracy, the state at some point in the relatively distant future will be determinable. It is in this sense that some political scientists make predictions about a long-run equilibrium state for Russia and the United States lying somewhere between capitalism and communism. In sum, both nations are seen to be converging, from different directions, on what appears to be a common set of properties that, when arrived at, are assumed maintainable.

In the same way, some geneticists argue that, in the long-run, we shall evolve toward a single phenotype through the gradual admixture of different races, which implies a convergence on a single set of human characteristics to replace the differential characteristics that now exist. While we cannot answer here for the validity of such predictions, they nevertheless serve to point out the existence of an interest in what might be described as teleodeterministic systems . . . those that in the short-run are behaviorally unpredictable, but that may be considered predictable in the long-run through the process of convergence.

With this introduction to the range of different steady-state systems we might expect to encounter, and with the defense of the proposition that such systems represent instances of effective identity between starting- and concluding-state conditions (on either or both the micro and macro dimensions), we now turn to the second class of effectively deterministic entities . . . the finite-state systems.

3.1.2 Finite-State Systems

The finite-state system differs from the steady-state system in one important respect. Here, a system will not exhibit a single state, (which remains invariant through time on either the micro or macro levels) but a number of alternative system states. That is, the system may take on different behavioral characteristics through time, but each starting-state condition will give us sufficient information to determine what the concluding-state condition will be. Thus a steady-state system is a very special case of the finite-state system, one where the number of alternative input-output (macro level) or configurational (micro level) states is reduced to one. This point was only implicit in the previous section, for what we did not stress was that a steady-state system will tend to exploit only a *single* resource or set of inputs, and produce only a *single* output or output set. In short, a steady-state system has found its "ecological niche," something that few phenomena can claim.

In this sense, then, the finite-state system offers considerably more possibilities than steady-state systems, and involves a somewhat enhanced level of complexity for the system scientist interested in behavioral prediction. With respect to finite-state systems, consider Figure 3.1. What occurs here is very simple. We have four starting-state alternatives (the X_i's) which may represent either structural configurations or maps at some time t, or a set of inputs existing at time t. These represent the rows of the matrix. The columns represent four alternative concluding states (Z_i's), which may represent either structural maps or output arrays at some time $(t + 1)$. The elements forming the major diagonal of the matrix are filled with probabilities, which in each case are valued at 1.0, with the remaining elements of the matrix being empty (implying a probability of occurrence valued at zero). For each unique starting-state condition, one and only one concluding-state condition will be assigned any significant probability of occurrence; this is one of the conditions for a system to be considered a finite-state one. As an example, consider finite-state *sequential* machines, where "states" are exercised in some predetermined order, such that the appearance of a preceding state automatically tells us to expect the subsequent state to follow.

In a sense, then, each of the rows of the matrix is a product of a function that relates successive structural states or input-output arrays (which become intelligible as vectors). Now, when any output or any concluding-state conditions exhausts the *transformation probabilities* by being valued at 1.0, no other output or concluding state is considered possible as a *consequence* of the input or starting state.

Now, as with steady-state systems, a system may be finite state on either of the two subdimensions of the behavioral dimension. If, for example, the starting-state conditions with which we are concerned are structural configurations existing at some time t (as represented by point-in-time maps), then the system is finite state on the micro level. In this case, a structural state existing

Array of alternative concluding-states

Array of starting-state conditions

	Z_1	Z_2	Z_3	Z_n
X_1	$P = 1.0$			
X_2		$P = 1.0$		
X_3			$P = 1.0$	
X_4				$P = 1.0$

Figure 3.1 The finite-state matrix.

at some present time is assumed to give rise inevitably to a predeterminable structural state at some future time. Many examples are found in nature. Thus the existence of certain structural properties in migratory fish, as evidenced by certain biochemical properties and flesh characteristics, can lead us to a conclusion that, within some usually well-defined interval, it will become a spawner (assuming, as it were, the spawning state). In the same way, medical diagnosticians evaluate an array of state characteristics in their patients at a point in time and reach an assertion about that concluding-state condition that appears most probable.

When a given set of starting-state conditions is deemed to be uniquely associated with a terminal, concluding-state condition, then the system is intelligible as a finite-state one. Thus, for example, redness of complexion, high blood pressure, and high cholesterol levels are taken as a sign, at some time t, that there is an extremely high probability a heart attack will occur prior to some time $(t + k)$. There are of course other conditions that might have to be considered, such as the fact that the fish might be caught prior to spawning, or that the afflicted patient will be killed in an automobile accident before the coronary can get him. Where such counter-alternatives are deemed highly improbable, or even gratuitous, the system may be deemed an effectively finite-state (e.g., deterministic) one. However, differences between deterministic-state and stochastic-state systems are often local, personal affairs, where two scientists considering the same system may assign it to different classes because of different contextual or evaluative criteria.

Essentially the same logic holds when we consider finite-state systems on the macro subdimension, where the starting-state conditions become identical to an input array and the concluding state becomes an array of associated outputs. In this case, all we are concerned about is that each unique input configuration give rise to a unique and predeterminable output or set of outputs. On the macro level, then, we may ignore the transformation functions by which such relationships are engined, as the analysis of the "process" aspect of systems does not really concern us on the macro level (e.g., the system is treated as a "black box"). Irrespective of any structural changes that might take place through time, a system may emerge as finite state on the macro level whenever strict functional correspondence is found between inputs and outputs. Most engineered systems are of this order, such that changes in input conditions give rise to roughly predictable changes in outputs.

Consider a processing system that is assigned the function of transforming a flow of raw materials into finished products. If the process is a finite-state one, then each variation in inputs will produce a unique variation in output properties, whether the process is one designed to produce fertilizer, steel stock, or whatever. In such cases we have to be concerned with both the qualitative and quantitative aspects of the process. In short, a quantitatively finite-state system will be one that produces a unique level of output of a given nature for each unique level of inputs of a given nature. When the changes are strictly proportional, such that a x% increase in inputs automatically gives rise to a y% increase in outputs, the system is said to be a *homogeneous* one.[10]

Where changes are not so neatly determined, but where they nevertheless are predictable and unique, the system is a finite-state one on the *macro-quantitative* dimension. A system may also be finite state on the *macro-qualitative* dimension, such that any changes in the quality of inputs will produce a unique (and predeterminable) qualitative alteration in outputs. Good examples of finite-state macro-quantitative systems are vehicle acceleration systems, where an increase in the flow of fuel is associated with a predeterminable increase in the speed of the vehicle, when all other factors may be assumed constant through an interval. As we shall see, most systems other than equifinal ones, are expectedly finite state on the macro-qualitative dimension, such that inputs of different quality do evoke predictably different outputs. Some biological exceptions come easily to mind however, namely those species that are capable of absorbing and transforming nourishments taken from many different sources into an eventually indistinguishable concluding state. Such systems are, in short, macro equifinal rather than finite state.

By far the largest representation in the finite-state category is that of mechanical or engineered systems, for finite-state behavior is a usually desirable property for the engineer to engender in his creations. In simpler machines, the structural (micro) characteristics of the system are steady state, such that they are designed to remain in a constant and fixed variation through long periods of operation. On the macro dimension, the systems should be finite state, such that every change in inputs produces a determinable change in outputs. Some machines are more complex, being designed to change their structure in response to input changes; but they are still finite state in that every change in inputs will give rise to one and only one structural state (unless there is a malfunction). An example of such a system would be a modern electric appliance that can "read" a power source and determine whether it is AC or DC, making the appropriate adjustment automatically. Even very complicated and sophisticated engineered systems, such as electromechanical servomechanisms, are designed such that a minute change in some input value will give rise to a predeterminable (via a deterministic transformation algorithm) alteration in system outputs (or attitude, behavior, etc.). In short, it is only when machines are ill-designed or ill-engineered that we expect them to behave stochastically . . . that is, in a way where starting-state conditions (or inputs) cannot be used to determine with a significantly high accuracy the concluding-state conditions or output.*

It is useful here to make a distinction which is too often neglected. This refers to the fundamentally different methods available to us for determining whether a particular system will be finite state, stochastic state, etc. There are basically

---

*With the exception of those machines which are deliberately designed to behave erratically or opportunistically . . . e.g., heuristic machines.

two methods we can employ, each of which is appropriate to a basically different sector. With mechanical, artificial, or engineered systems, we should be able to determine whether or not the system is a finite-state one by referring to the design criteria. For physical, biological, and most non-engineered social systems, it will be inferred to be finite state when its historical behavior, with negligible variation, has illustrated a strict correspondence between unique starting-state and concluding-state pairs (or between input and output configurations). In this instance, the system is said to be *statistically* finite state, whereas man-made systems would be said to be *designed* finite state.

Any system may be considered to be finite state if its behavioral properties may be reduced to the form given in the matrix of Figure 3.1, such that each unique starting state is expected, with great confidence, to lead to one and only one concluding state that is both unique and predefinable. In this case, a knowledge of the starting-state conditions or the input configuration is all the knowledge the system analyst needs to have in order to determine the state of the system at some future point in time, irrespective of whether the system is defined as discrete state or continuous state. In the case of the former, predictions are associated with points in time, whereas continuous-state transformations are treated as changes through some interval or as occurring just prior to some specific point in time.

There remain now two other points that must be noted before we proceed with our discussions of stochastic-state systems. The first is adding an "action" that will be imposed on the system to the array of starting-state conditions. In this sense, a finite-state process may be interpreted as one where, given a unique action we anticipate taking, one and only one outcome may be assigned any significant probability of occurrence. Here, our action, our interference as it were, becomes a component of the starting-state conditions, an input to the system we are seeking to change, alter, or somehow affect. A stochastic-state system, in this respect, would be one where we could not adequately predict the outcome associated with some interjection. This is the point where we notice the major difference between treating mechanical/artificial systems and natural/social systems, and the point at which the system scientist becomes something much more than a system *engineer*, per se. This leads us somewhat indirectly to the second point we want to consider, the distinction between an effectively finite-state system and an inherently finite-state system.

To be *effectively* finite state, we must have a great deal of knowledge about the input, output, starting- or concluding-state conditions, and also a knowledge of the mapping functions between associated (e.g., ordered) pairs. This implies, for mechanical or artificial systems, that we have at hand the design criteria or that we have the results of a set of empirical trials aimed at establishing indisputable data relative to system behavior. In the case of social, biological, or physical systems, it would imply only the latter, the concept of design criteria being gratuitous here. Thus, many systems that are *inherently* finite state may have to be treated at some point in time as stochastic, simply because the requisite information is not available to us. That is, it must be seen to be possible to gradually reduce, through scientific research and analysis, some effectively stochastic systems to effectively deterministic (e.g., finite-state) ones. However, as we shall now endeavor to point out, some systems are *inherently* stochastic in their behavior, and no amount of study or effort on our part will ever allow us to treat them, without penalty, as deterministic.

3.2 STOCHASTIC SYSTEMS

We may dispose of stochastic systems rather rapidly, recognizing that we are here concerned with inherently (rather than effectively) stochastic entities. On the behavioral dimension, stochastic systems are those where, given any set of starting-state conditions (e.g., input configurations or structural configurations), two or more concluding-state conditions must be assigned positive and significant probabilities of occurrence. An example is shown in Figure 3.2. The most

Array of Starting-State Conditions

	Array of Alternative Concluding-States			
	Z_1	Z_2	Z_3	Z_n
X_1	$P = 0.25$	$P = 0.25$	$P = 0.25$	$P = 0.25$
X_2	(All probabilities of occurrence valued at less than 1.0.)			
X_3	$P = 0.25$			$P = 0.25$
X_4		1.0		

Figure 3.2 The stochastic-state matrix.

obvious and critical difference between this illustration and the one used to introduce the finite-state system, Figure 3.1, is that here some elements of the matrix are valued at < 1.0. Particularly, for starting-state conditions $\{X_1, X_2$ and $X_3\}$, at least two Z_i's have been assigned positive probabilities of occurrence. However, were starting-state condition $\{X_4\}$ to occur, then Z_2 is the only outcome assigned a significant probability of occurrence. Thus, a system must be considered stochastic or deterministic with respect to some starting-state condition. And in the above example, the system is stochastic for $\forall X_i$, $i \neq 4$, only.

A stochastic system will thus become more or less analytically tractable (more or less predictable) depending on the number of outcomes (e.g., concluding-state events) for each starting-state condition that are assigned positive probabilities of occurrence, and on the nature of *morphology* of the probability distribution

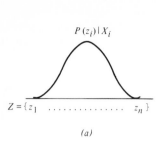
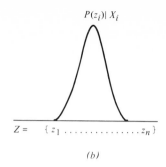

Figure 3.3 Event-probability distributions.

imposed on those events. In this respect, consider Figure 3.3. These are called event-probability distributions, and they will, beginning with the next chapter, form the major unit of operation for the remainder of this book. Here, however, we simply want to point out that the situation shown in 3.3 (a) is analytically less favorable than that in 3.3 (b). In other words, the system that gives rise to the distribution in (b) is *less stochastic* than that giving rise to (a). The reason for this is two-fold: first, fewer events have been assigned any probability of occurrence (given the starting-state condition, X_i) in the distribution in (b); secondly, of those events that are assigned positive probabilities of occurrence, there is a strong convergence on the event-range falling at the median of the distribution. In short, for those who remember their basic statistics, the event-probability distribution in (b) entails less *variance* (and hence less expected error) than that in (a).[11]

There is another aspect of stochastic-state systems which occasionally makes them very easy for the system analyst to deal with. This is *periodicity*, the process that finds essentially the same states being repeated with some regularity. The matter of regularity has long been of concern, for a completely random appearance of states—each of which is an element in a bounded or constrained set, such as the set of real numbers—gives rise to completely unpredictable systems, (e.g., the degeneration of certain radioactive materials or the trajectories of certain subatomic particles).[12] On the other hand, where the system is strictly periodic, such that the states appear in some ordered and invariant sequence, or always appear following the emergence of a particular condition (e.g., driven, as it were, by a regression variable), then system behavior becomes effectively deterministic, finite state in the most literal sense. Yet where the alternative states are known, and where they all belong to some finite (bounded) set, *and* where their probability of appearance is driven by a multinomial function with a proportionality operator relative to some point or interval in time, then the system becomes a periodic stochastic-state system.* By the same token, where the states appear in a fashion that prohibits any neat statistical

---

*e.g., a Bernoulli process.

probability distribution being imposed on their emergence, and where the states apparently are unique and unprecedented (e.g., elements of an apparently "open-ended" set), then we have an *aperiodic* stochastic-state system; one that promises to hold significant surprise for even the most cautious predictor.

As with finite-state systems, we must consider both the micro and macro dimension. A system that is stochastic on the micro level, such that its basic structure changes in unpredictable ways through time, is a *severely-stochastic system*. A system whose structure remains essentially invariant through time, however, with only quantitative changes taking place in outputs relative to some given input, is stochastic on the macro level only, and may be interpreted as being *moderately stochastic*. The use of the terms "severely" and "moderately" are not casual, for the difference between these two situations is a very important one for the system analyst. Systems where basic structural states may alter probabilistically through some interval become very difficult to work with. In fact, as we show in Chapter 5, they call for a completely different set of analytical instruments than do moderately-stochastic systems (e.g., the latter may usually be approached using tools of statistical inference and extrapolation, whereas severely-stochastic systems often demand more sophisticated instruments such as game-based analysis or simulation). These two categories of stochastic-state systems deserve more treatment.

3.2.1 Moderately-Stochastic Systems

Stochasticity on the macro level simply means that the relationship between input and outputs will alter in effectively unpredictable (and often unallegorizable) ways through some interval. This means, in effect, that a given input configuration does not completely determine the output configuration as was the case with the finite-state system. In dealing with the latter, we knew precisely what the unique output "event" would be on the basis of our reading of the input "event," such that a knowledge of the one was simultaneously a knowledge of the other; by the same token, the emergence of a particular output would allow us to infer, retrospectively, the nature of the input member of the ordered pair. In the finite-state case, then, the uniqueness of each input-output pair allows us to deterministically predict or reconstruct the macro behavior of the system. To borrow some terms from George Klir, the moderately-stochastic system would be one where ". . . the output quantities need not uniquely depend on the input quantities."[13]

In most cases, the emergence of a moderately-stochastic system, in such terms as we have used, would imply that we did not have a complete or accurate description of the process (e.g., the structural configuration on the micro level) which mediates between inputs and outputs. To this extent, most systems that we treat as moderately stochastic are only *effectively* so, suggesting that they would be inherently deterministic. In short, when input-output relationships vary through time, the presumption that the system is stationary on the micro dimension—structurally invariant through the interval in question—becomes a logical impossibility. Something has to alter the output configuration when the inputs remain stable, and that something would be a structural aspect of the system which is below the level of our comprehension. In this sense, many systems in the real-world are considered to be effectively moderately stochastic, though examples of inherently moderately-stochastic systems would be hard to come by.

In a moderately-stochastic system we are concerned mainly with quantitative changes on the macro dimension, with an input-output functional relationship that is different at different points in time. This means, in effect, that the efficiency of the system as a transformation process is constantly altering, but within some usually well-defined frame of reference. A more precise way of saying this is to suggest that systems become intelligible at the macro level in terms of the numerical coefficient(s) that relates a certain level and nature of inputs to a certain level and nature of outputs. To repeat some of the points made in Chapter 2, consider Figure 3.4. In it the structural aspects of the transforma-

Figure 3.4 The input-output model.

tion process (the structural properties of the system itself) remain invisible to us, for on the macro level all we really care about is the value of the transformation function, f. Now the definition of a moderately stochastic system may be stated quite precisely: . . . *a moderately stochastic system is one where the value of* $[f]$ *is expected to change through time, but where the alternatives values of* $[f]$ *to which we assign significant probabilities of occurrence are all members of the same qualitative set.*

That is, we will have to impose a probability distribution on $[f]$, through time, and that probability distribution will have to allow for two or more significantly probable values for the transformation function, as shown in Figure 3.5. All of the alternative values which the transformation function might assume at some

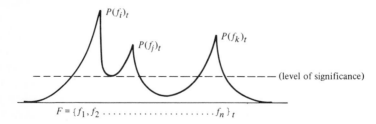

Figure 3.5 The moderately-stochastic model.

future point (time t) are arrayed as members of the set of all possible values, $[F]$; and three of these are considered significantly probable as the "event" for time t. In short, in trying to predict what the transformation function will actually be at some time t, at time $(t - 1)$ we can do no better than to suggest that one of three values may emerge as *the* actual value. This situation reflects the first of the definitional properties for a moderately-stochastic system . . . that, so far as our ability to predict the precise value for the transformation function through time, we expect only that it will change . . . even when the inputs are considered to remain constant through time. In contrast to a finite-state system considered on the macro dimension, the moderately-stochastic system has two or more "peaks" in the event-probability distribution, whereas the finite-state system would have only one (see Section 4.3).

The meaning of the second definitional property of the moderately-stochastic system should now be clear . . . all of the alternative values for the transformation function belong to a well bounded set, $[F]$, where $[F]$ must be defined as a set of elements all of which have a certain commonality as far as their qualitative properties are concerned. This is an artificial requirement, for sets may always be defined to include whatever properties we arbitrarily wish. But, artificial or not, the logic which is behind the constraint on the *universe* of values that the f's may assume has direct analytical implications for us . . . for it focuses our predictions on a *range* of alternatives all of which may be thought to reside on a single continuum. This means, in effect, that all the alternatives are valued on the same dimension, in terms of dollars, or calories, or horsepower, or amperes, etc. In short, the moderately-stochastic system gains its *stochasticity* largely in the fact that we must consider differently valued *quantitative* alternatives (f's) as being probable "events" on the macro dimension, where the f's all are members of a single *qualitative* set. What we are interested in, in dealing with a moderately-stochastic system, is the prediction of an output event, given a constant array of inputs, which will differ in *degree* from other alternatives, not in quality . . . and where changes in the structural dimension of the system during the interval in question are either ignored or considered negligible.[14]

There are many, many examples of such systems in the real-world, many systems where the function relating a fixed set of inputs to outputs varies within some well-defined range of essentially quantitative alternatives. What this means, in effect, is that such systems will tend to be seen as either more or less productive when evaluated at different points-in-time. This is also a definitional property, for the function relating inputs to outputs really values the *efficiency* of the transormations a system performs, which means simply the amount of output we receive for a given level of inputs. This pretty well sums up the usual situation with which most businessmen appear to have to deal, where the production processes *within* the firm, and the markets *outside* the firm, all tend to be treated (and indeed behave) as moderately-stochastic systems.* Even such a relatively "mechanical" entity as an assembly line tends to behave this way,

*At least for those products which are precedented or non-innovative.

with small but significant variations in productivity from day to day and even hour to hour . . . such that we have great success in predicting the range within which the tranformational values (e.g., productivity) will fall, but ill-success in determining any particular value, per se.

Another very common phenomenon that meets the criteria for moderately-stochastic systems is the automobile, when it is considered as a system that translates fuel (input) into mileage (output). The function measuring mileage seems to vary through time, such that at one time n gallons may take us 100 miles, and another time take us only 94 miles, etc. In trying to determine exactly how much gas to buy for a trip of given length, then, the driver would probably be wise to consider a *range* that incorporates the lowest and highest empirical mileage functions he has achieved in the past. If he is a statistician, he will develop a probability distribution (or frequency distribution) and gas up according to the expected value for the mileage function . . . where the expected value is the product of the probability of a certain mileage magnitude being the actual event calculated as a weighted average of all magnitudes multiplied by their probability of occurrence.[15] The frequency distribution might look like Figure 3.6. Now, without going into much detail, this distribution of discrete events—mileage actually achieved in past cases—may be thought of as being the probability distribution for the mileage function for the next period . . . assuming that no major structural changes have been made in the engine of the automobile (e.g., replacing a carburetor) or in its power/weight ratio, etc. In this case, the frequencies of occurrence of each of the actual mileage "values" are equivalent to their probability of occurrence, such that the expected value for mileage on the next trip or the next interval of driving is the weighted average of the previous experiences, which works out to be about 12.55 miles. Therefore, the best statistical estimate of how much gas to buy for a given trip would be the quotient of the number of miles to be traveled and the expected value of the mileage function (at 12.55 miles per gallon). Now, as suggested, the statistician

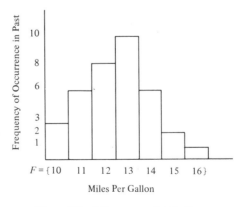

Figure 3.6 A frequency distribution.

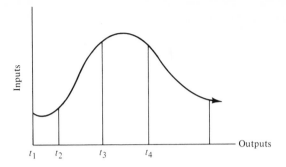

Figure 3.7 A natural growth model.

might formally calculate his purchase this way, but for most of us the safe purchase would be a non-statistical one . . . we might better use the lowest feasible
figure, 10 miles per gallon, even if this is a relatively improbable value to expect.
At any rate, we shall have much more to say about problems in decision-making
in Chapter 6, and might best continue here with another simple example of a
moderately-stochastic system or process.

A good area to consider is promotional elasticity, which is a function relating
the expenditure of advertising dollars in a market area (the inputs) to the incremental increase in sales associated with that expenditure (the outputs). Promotional elasticity is thus a measure of the productivity of advertising dollars. Now
it is a well known fact that the productivity of such expenditures follows what
might loosely be thought of as the natural growth curve, which prescribes a trajectory like that in Figure 3.7.

You may read the story of promotional elasticity (admittedly an oversimpli-
fied one as we present it here) from the nature of the curve in the figure. It
begins rather slowly, building a "threshold" amount of coverage . . . this is the
dipping and flat portion of the curve in the interval $[t_2 - t_1]$; next, it begins to
accelerate, such that the marginal productivity of our expenditures increases
(accelerates) in the interval $[t_3 - t_2]$; next, in the interval $[t_4 - t_3]$, it reaches a
stage of decreasing returns and eventually enters a steadily declining interval in
terms of the productivity of our expenditures $[t_n - t_4]$.

Such a process is clearly a moderately stochastic one. In basic terms, all of the
various values for the promotional elasticity function are positive, constituting a
sufficient condition here for membership in a single qualitative set. At any given
point-in-time, we may predict some magnitudinal range within which the value
for promotional elasticity might fall, i.e., $[f_k < f_i \leq f_j]$, and do so with a significantly high probability of accuracy. Yet the precise values of the function will
be difficult to predict, for the exact efficiency of the transformation process
must be thought to oscillate around this neat growth curve, as in Figure 3.8. We
can predict the gross direction in which we will probably be moving, and some

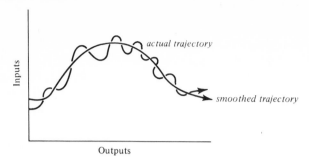

Figure 3.8 An oscillation model.

probable range, but not precise quantitative values for the promotional elasticity function.

This, then, has been a brief introduction to one of the most frequently encountered dynamic system "types," one whose characteristics on the macro level are of primary importance to us, and where the values assumed by the transformation function between inputs and outputs on that level are predictable within some *range*, housing (usually) quantitatively unique estimates of qualitatively similar events. We shall deal with such systems frequently in future chapters, leaving only the thought here that while moderately-stochastic systems are more difficult to predict on the behavioral dimension than finite-state systems, they are considerably more tractable than the type of system to which we now turn our attention.

3.2.2 Severely-Stochastic Systems

As was earlier suggested, severely-stochastic systems are those which exhibit significant structural change through time, such that we must deal with them on the more detailed and complex micro dimension and must be prepared to face considerably enhanced predictive problems regarding their behavior. There are two basic subcases in the class of severely-stochastic systems with which we shall be concerned here. The first is that case where structural changes *do* cause alterations in the input-output relationships . . . where changes on the micro level cause changes on the macro. The second, and more difficult (and somewhat rarer) case is where changes on the micro level *need not* cause changes in the input-output function of the system. Systems of this latter type represent instances of *equifinality*, and will be dealt with after we have briefly explored systems falling into the first category.

Severely stochastic systems are those where the basic structure of the system is expected to change, in fundamentally unpredictable ways, through time. They differ from the finite-state system, defined on the micro dimension, in the following way: whereas the appearance of a particular structural "state" (e.g., configuration or map) at time t was sufficient information to predict the state of the system as it would appear at some time $(t + 1)$ for the finite-state system, it is not sufficient for the prediction of the future state of a severely-stochastic system. In short, for the latter, concluding-state conditions are not determined solely by starting-state conditions. Thus a severely stochastic system may be defined as one where: *for any given structural state at some time t, there will be two or more structural states at time $(t + 1)$ which must be assigned significant probabilities of occurrence.*

And for nonequifinal systems, we must add that the value for the transformation function pertaining at time $(t + 1)$ is correspondingly unpredictable.

When we speak of a "structural state," we are really speaking again of the properties that constituted the *map* of a system on the structural dimension. These properties are: (a) the components of the system, (b) their distribution, and (c) the nature of the relationships among them. Recall that maps were made at moments in time, by taking "snapshots" of the system. Now if a severely-stochastic system is one where successive snapshots illustrate that structural changes have taken place, the primary unit of analysis for the severely-stochastic system is the function that has driven or engineered these changes. Thus, whereas with moderately-stochastic systems we were interested in the function that related inputs to outputs between intervals, we are here interested in the function that relates successive structural states . . . the function that contains, as it were, the *causes* for the state transformations.

In the most basic sense, then, the function for a severely-stochastic system will be isolated on the micro dimension and will, if properly constructed, be able to account for changes that have taken place in the structure of the system during some interval (or, for continuous-state systems, between two successive intervals). The function, in a word, captures the *dynamics* of the system. Whereas we shall later have much to say about our ability to model or allegorize system dynamics, here we shall simply be concerned with the properties of dynamic systems, per se. And the essential property is that they are *nonstationary* on both the macro and micro levels, the former being a usual consequence of the latter. As the reader may well imagine, we are not lacking for examples of severely-stochastic systems in the real-world.

In the obvious case, all evolutionary systems other than fully segmented ones (see again Section 2.2.1), are of the severely stochastic type. For successive generations or intervals bring differentiation, that on the structural dimension means that the state of the system at time t and the state of the system at time $(t + 1)$ are *qualitatively* different. If this qualitative difference is absent, then the process of change during the interval has been segmentation, such that only quantitative alterations have taken place (e.g., there are simply more components of a precedented type arrayed in an essentially constant set of relationships). In this case, we really need only be concerned about any changes that might take place on the macro dimension, so that at worst, segmented systems become moderately stochastic, and more usually simply steady state (e.g., deterministic).

But most systems that are properly evolutionary will involve a continuous change in structure, which generally assumes continuous change in function . . . or which serves as a motivation for change in function. But, again, in determining whether an evolving system should be treated as a severely stochastic one, the degree of differentiation that emerges through time is the critical factor; if this is sufficiently high, then the system is unlikely to be heading toward the kind of structurally-dynamic steady state which we assume for segmented systems.

Obviously, our ability to predict the character of future states of a system, on both the structural and input-output levels, will be largely determined by the severity of the structural changes that the system may potentially exhibit, and on the possibility of a periodicity in the transformation process. Severely-stochastic systems that are at least partially predictable as to state qualities are climatic or weather systems. That is, whereas day-to-day changes are generally unpredictable in great detail, gross state properties, through wider intervals, are reasonably predictable, due largely to the periodicity with which crudely defined qualitative states appear throughout successive years (e.g., the tendency for tornados to appear in early spring months in the southeast; the tendency for cold weather to appear in the central states in the middle of October). Climatic systems are thus severely stochastic, but at least partially predictable because of this periodicity, and because all the structural states that might emerge as alternatives are generally predefinable in at least gross terms . . . cold weather, hot weather, hurricane conditions, etc. There are other systems, however, that exhibit neither periodicity nor bounded alternative sets.

Examples of these less tractable, severely-stochastic systems are what the system scientist Magoroh Maruyama has called *deviation-amplifying* systems.

> Such systems are ubiquitous: accumulation of capital in industry, evolution of living organisms, the rise of cultures of various types, interpersonal processes which produce mental illness, international conflicts, and the processes that are loosely termed as "vicious circles" and "compound interests"; in short, all processes of mutual causal relationships that amplify an insignificant or accidental initial kick, build up deviation and diverge from the initial condition.[16]

The essential property of such systems will generally be our inability to accurately predict what new properties will enter into the system's structural map, either because of intrusion of unplanned exogenous forces, or because of the variations that appear in internal components and their relationships and may give rise to new system components interacting in effectively unprecedented ways according to new laws (as was the case, recall, with the neogenetic systems described in Section 2.4.1).

In all areas of the social and behavioral sciences, severely-stochastic systems become important references. In the field of group behavior, cliques come in and out of fashion in often unpredictable ways, and the interfaces among various members of the group often change rapidly, both in terms of the participants (who interacts with whom at a particular point-in-time) and the nature of the exchange (e.g., are the relationships amicable or unfriendly, positive or negative, synergistic or mutually detractive).

In the political world, new alliances and relationships come in and out of being with great rapidity, which considerably affects our ability to predict what political *maps* will look like at future points. In fact, most social, political, economic, and behavioral systems appear to belong to a special category within the broad range of severely-stochastic systems . . . those we might term *self organizing*. That is, they inhere the power, endogenously, to make structural alterations of many different kinds and on many different levels.

In general, then, the severely-stochastic system is one whose structure alters through time in qualitatively significant ways, such that some sort of differentiation process is at work. Where the system is a periodic one, the function describing state transformations will operate on a bounded set . . . that is, a collection of alternative states that, as an array, exhaust the possibilities we consider to be probable events. This, recall, was essentially the situation with climatic systems viewed in a gross way. In that case, no unexpected or unprecedented events are expected to occur, which means that we would assign an event-probability distribution that includes only predefinable events (predefinable either in terms of their empirical precedence or because of certain logical conditions being met).[17] A somewhat more difficult predictive case emerges in the deviation-amplifying case, where the events that might occur are likely to include at least some that have not appeared before . . . structural states that are effectively unprecedented or unamenable to deduction on logical principles.

At any rate, a point mentioned above needs a bit more amplification. Self-organizing systems, in which impetus for structural change can emerge from within the system itself, are usefully contrasted with another type of system, the *adaptive*. Adaptive systems, it will be recalled, were approached in the section dealing with finite state or deterministic systems, mainly in the context of *homeostasis*. Homeostatic systems were of two types: (a) those that acted to maintain a given input-output relationship in the face of external perturbations; and (b) those that acted to maintain a given structural configuration irrespective of what occurred on the efficiency dimension . . . e.g., irrespective of any changes that occurred in the input-output function. In either case, such systems tended to maintain a steady state on one or the other of the system levels, macro or micro. Now a fully-adaptive system may be defined as one where neither the micro or macro level remains stable in the face of environmental perturbations, but opportunities are constantly sought (though not always found) to increase the efficiency of the system either by altering inputs, altering outputs, or altering system structure . . . or altering all simultaneously. The adaptive system is one that couples the capability for internal change associated with self-organizing systems with the closed-loop, monitoring, and feedback capabilities associated with homeostatic systems of the first type. Using this latter capability to "read" environmental or exogenous properties, and the former capability to assimilate the information gathered there into predicates for reorganization on the structural dimension, such systems try to exploit continuously emerging opportunities for increasing the productivity of the system. In short, the adaptive system is consciously and intelligently opportunistic, whereas the homeostatic system, per se, merely seeks to maintain either a structural or productive status quo.

The important point here is that the magnitude of changes taking place in the environment or milieu—or in any exogenous entities that have a determination on the status of the system—will in large measure determine the magnitude of the structural changes that the system inaugurates. When the magnitude of the exogenous changes is significant, we can expect structural changes to follow suit, resulting in a system that must be approached as severely stochastic. On the other hand, where exogenous changes are of a minor order, the structural adjustments may often be ignored and we may legitimately treat the system as a moderately stochastic one, concerning ourselves solely with predictions of a range-type about system productivity (working only on the macro dimension). Thus, adaptive systems as we have defined them are inherently severely stochastic, or inhere the capability to be so, but are not always *effectively* severely stochastic. It is, however, often dangerous to ignore the inherent potential for producing surprises in terms of unprecedented system structures, a point we shall return to later. For the moment, simply consider the fully-adaptive system to be one that is potentially nonstationary on both the micro and macro levels, and where a change on the former is expected to give rise to changes on the latter.

The net result of severe stochasticity is the possibility, on the macro level, that a given set of inputs will give rise to qualitatively different outputs through time, a distinct definitional difference from the moderately-stochastic case (where outputs and inputs, through the interval in question, were elements of single qualitative sets). On the micro level, severely-stochastic systems produce structural changes that result in qualitatively different structural maps through time, where the impetus for such changes may be either exogenous or endogenous. At any rate, it is changes in structure which allows a system to take a given set of inputs and produce outputs that, at different times, inhere basically different qualities.

As the reader rightly might expect, very few artificial, man-made systems are designed to behave in this way. Indeed, one of the prime considerations in the design of mechanisms is their structural predictability through time, and the consequent predictability of outputs (both in terms of quantity and quality with respect to a given set of inputs). Apparently, however, Nature abhors determinism in her creations, leaving a majority of natural systems capable of behaving severely stochastically. This would include such systems as simple confrontations between two or several human beings, or systems as complex as large scale ecosystems, or the genetic process itself. Natural, cultural, or social systems appear to be always in a state of evolution, and the properties of the political world, at

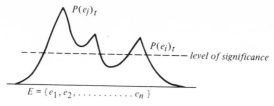

Figure 3.9   The severely stochastic case.

many different levels of organization or encompassment, seem to invite usually unpredictable structural change, if not through differentiation *qua* evolution, through revolution.

In summary, then, we may approach severely-stochastic systems through an event probability distribution with which we are already familiar, but with some essentially different interpretations. For example, look at Figure 3.9. The e's take on a broader interpretation than the f's associated with the illustration of moderate stochasticity given in Figure 3.5. In the first place, the e's here are all elements of a set $[E]$, but unlike the set $[F]$ of the moderately stochastic case, the $[E]$ set simply is a collection of events that share only a single property . . . all are considered events that have a positive probability of occurrence as structural or output states for the system at hand at time-t . . . they need not, as in the moderately stochastic case, be events belonging to a single qualitative class or set. In short, the e's in this distribution are the product of the relaxation of the constraint about qualitative similarity we associated with the moderately stochastic case, such that each of the e's will belong to different *primary* sets as well as to the secondary set $[E]$.

A brief example may help here to distinguish between a moderately- and severely-stochastic system. Suppose a businessman were considering making a change in wage levels for his employees. Looked at from one standpoint, the moderately stochastic, he would expect a reduction in wages to increase the efficiency of the firm as a transformation process . . . in this case transforming investments in wages into revenue achieved by the sales of products produced. A lowering of wages would automatically result in a favorable change in the input-output function for the firm if he ignores the possibility of state changes taking place on the micro (structural) level. Thus, from the strict standpoint of marginal economics, a reduction in wages, were all other factors held constant, would result in a positive change in the input-output ratio when reduced to dollar terms (the lowest common denominator). However, the reader will recognize from what he has read, seen, or can imagine, that treating the productive system of a firm (e.g., the man-machine subsystems through which products are produced) as a moderately stochastic one is a dangerous proposition . . . which becomes more dangerous the greater the reliance on labor and the lower the reliance on automated machines.

From the standpoint of the sociologist or behavioral scientist, the mere presence of human beings in a system is sufficient condition for structural changes to take place, structural changes that quickly move the system from moderate to severe stochasticity. Thus, for the businessman's problem, whereas the marginal economic viewpoint ignored the micro dimension, the sociobehavioral viewpoint could posit any one of several qualitatively distinct states that might emerge from a starting-state condition that consisted of a unilateral lowering of wages. Among those that are logically possible, and to which the businessman should assign positive probabilities of occurrence, would be the following: (a) lowering wages causes the formation of a union that in turn acts to raise wages and impose other conditions to constrain the autonomy of management; (b) lowering wages causes employees to work-to-rules, which considerably reduces productivity per man-hour; (c) lowering wages causes a strike, with the resultant loss of output; (d) lowering wages causes workers to engage in sabotage or destruction of company equipment; and (e) lowering wages causes workers to leave the firm and go elsewhere . . . and if there are indeed other openings available, this would mean that successively less well-qualified workers would have to be hired to take the place of those who left.

At any rate, and this is the critical point which we keep repeating, treating a system that inheres the capability for severely stochastic behavior as a moderately-stochastic system can result in serious repercussions and dysfunctions. In most cases then, the system scientist recommends that the expedience associated with assuming systems to be simpler or more predictable than they really are be avoided assiduously, despite the higher analytical costs associated with giving them their full due of complexity (a point we shall make much of in Chapter 5).

There remains one final topic to discuss before we finish with generic system referents and move onto other topics. This is the most interesting of behavioral system "types," the *equifinal* system. In the simplest terms, an equifinal system is one that inheres the capability to arrive at the same point by different paths, or to reach the same concluding state from different starting stages. The principle of equifinality was originally espoused in its present form by von Bertalanffy, and is a property unique to open systems. For, as von Bertalanffy explains,

> . . . in any closed system, the final state is unequivocally determined by the initial conditions: e.g., the motion in a planetary system where the positions of the planets at a time t are unequivocally determined by their position at a time t_0. Or in a chemical equilibrium, the final concentrations of the reactants naturally depend on the initial concentrations. If either the initial conditions or the process is altered, the final state will also be changed. This is not so in open systems. Here the same final state may be reached from different initial conditions, and in different ways. . . . The same final result, a normal individual of the sea urchin [family], can develop from a complete ovum, from each half of a divided ovum, or from the fusion product of two whole ova. The same applies to many other species, including man, where identical twins are the product of the splitting of one ovum.[18]

Without going into great detail, though we shall refer to this phenomenon again, the implications of equifinal behavior for the system scientist are these: (a) first, the one von Bertalanffy stated, that inputs or starting-state conditions do not necessarily determine output states or, specifically, that the same end may be reached with different means or the same output may result from different inputs; (b) a corollary is that the same means may produce different ends, or that the same inputs may produce different outputs (a point which the equifinal system shares with other instances of severe stochasticity); and (c) this has an implication for our ability to reconstruct the processes (e.g., develop a model of the function) by which a system moved from a given state at time t to a different state at time $(t + 1)$ ... if the system is an equifinal one, a knowledge of the concluding state is insufficient knowledge to retrodeduce or retroinduce the starting state, and insufficient for the purposes of reconstructing system dynamics; the same concluding state could have been arrived at by different causal trajectories. As we can see, however, the equifinal system is really just an extension of the severely stochastic case, where the relationship between inputs and outputs, or between starting and concluding structural states, is driven by a probabilistic rather than deterministic causal engine. What distinguishes them operationally is that the equifinal system is able (but may not always act) to reach the same concluding state from different starting-state conditions, whereas the severely-stochastic systems that we have dealt with (and which we shall deal with in later pages) are primarily distinguished by their ability to inaugurate structural changes that can cause a given input to ultimately give rise to two or more qualitively distinct outputs.

In summary of the behavioral dimension of systems, then, we are primarily concerned with our ability to predict their behavior. Deterministic systems were introduced as systems that could have future structural states and/or outputs predicted with great accuracy, given a knowledge of the starting-state conditions or the inputs. Stochastic-state systems were introduced as systems in which concluding states or outputs were not fully determined by inputs or starting-state conditions. Examples of the former were finite-state systems and steady-state systems; examples of the latter were adaptive, deviation-amplifying, and equifinal systems.

We are now at the point where we can consider (in the next chapter) integrated systems ... systems where the structural and behavioral properties are considered simultaneously rather than separately as we have done in this and the previous chapter.

3.3 NOTES AND REFERENCES

1. A macro-deterministic system is one that, as an integrated whole, is more predictable than its individual parts. The realization that many living systems, and perhaps basic physical systems, are macro-deterministic is a relatively recent achievement, and represents a significant aspect of the system sciences conceptual repertoire. Such an idea is, of course, quite alien to many

scientists, especially those adhering to the principles of classical physics, etc. for whom a system could be nothing more or less than a sum of its parts. The eminent biologist Paul Weiss takes explicit exception to the classical physics view: "Since experience has positively shown that such unequivocal macro relations do exist on various supra-molecular levels of the hierarchy of living processes in the absence of componential micro-determinacy, we evidently must let positive scientific insights prevail over sheer conjectures and preconceptions, however cherished and ingrained in our traditional thinking they may be." This is quoted from his paper, "The Living System: Determinism Stratified," in *Beyond Reductionism: New Perspectives in the Life Sciences*, ed. Koestler and Smithies (New York: Macmillan Publishing Company, 1969), pp. 3–55. For an interpretation of the importance of micro-determinacy for the methodological platform of the system sciences, see pages 42–45 of my *A General System Philosophy for the Social and Behavioral Sciences* (New York: George Braziller, 1973), or Section 4.1 of this book.

2. George Klir, *An Approach to General System Theory* (New York: Van Nostrand Reinhold Company, 1969), p. 171.

3. For those interested in the mechanisms available to societies for the transmission of values through acculturation, and the programming of behavior, see the classic by Edward Alsworth Ross, *Social Control: A Survey of the Foundations of Order* (Cleveland: Case Western Reserve University Press, 1969).

4. Klatz and Kahn, *The Social Psychology of Organizations* (New York: John Wiley & Sons, 1966), p. 23.

5. Good nontechnical references on the principle of homeostasis are found in Katz and Kahn, *op. cit.*, pp. 23–26, or in the late Kenneth Berrien's *General and Social Systems* (New Brunswick, N.J.: Rutgers University Press, 1968), pp. 37–39.

6. W. B. Cannon, "Organization for Physiological Homeostasis," *Physiological Review*, 9 (1929).

7. Katz and Kahn, *op. cit.*, p. 24.

8. Ervin Laszlo, "Uses and Misuses of World System Models," *The World System: Models, Norms, Variations*, ed. Laszlo (New York: George Braziller, 1973), p. 12.

9. On a basic engineering level, we find the principle of dynamic stability approached indirectly through cybernetic or servomechanical system construction. Although the analogy is an incomplete one between natural and engineered systems on this dimension, a good discussion of the principles of the servomechanism, and hence dynamic control, is given in Thaler and Brown's *Servomechanism Analysis* (New York: McGraw-Hill, 1953), and more recently in F. G. Shinskey's *Process Control Systems* (New York: McGraw-Hill, 1967).

10. For an interesting note on the homogeneity principle in economics, see William J. Baumol's *Economic Theory and Operations Analysis* (Englewood Cliffs: Prentice-Hall, 1965), p. 343f.

11. For a more thorough explanation of the importance of such statistical principles in information and decision theory, see my "Beyond Systems Engineering: The General System Theory Potential for Social Science System Analysis," *General Systems Yearbook*, XVIII (1973).

12. The principle of randomness postulatedly associated with basic particles of physical systems has, of course, been the driving force behind quantum physics as a replacement for deterministic classical physics. In this regard,

the concept of natural causal randomness becomes very important for the system scientist. For an explanation, see Warner Heisenberg's *The Physical Principles of Quantum Theory* (New York: Dover Publications, 1949).

13. Klir, *op. cit.*, p. 65.

14. As was suggested, the probabilistic nature of predictions about moderately stochastic systems really stems from the fact that our structural description is incomplete, rather than from any inherent stochasticity in the system itself. This approach is perhaps best expressed in modern econometrics, particularly in the "shock models" they employ. In this repsect, see Jacob Marschak's "Economic Measurements for Policy and Decision," *Studies in Econometric Methods*, ed. Hood and Koopmans (New Haven: Yale University Press, 1953).

15. For a rather complete analysis of expectation operators in formal statistics, see Hoel, Port, and Stone's *Introduction to Probability Theory* (Boston: Houghton Mifflin Company, 1971). An operational significance for expected value operations is given in de Neufville and Stanford's *Systems Analysis for Engineers and Managers* (New York: McGraw-Hill, 1971), pp. 120–125.

16. Magoroh Maruyama, "The Second Cybernetics: Deviation-Amplifying Mutual Causal Processes," *American Scientist*, 51 no. 2 (June 1963), pp. 164–179.

17. That is, there are some systems that will have only a limited number of alternative states available to them, states that are capable of being deduced. Hence, they exhaust the logical possibilities available to the system. Where we are employing logical "events" as alternatives in an event-probability distribution, we would then have to employ subjective probabilities, whereas objective probabilities may be used to reflect our expectations about the occurrence of empirically precedented events. For an explanation of the role subjective probabilities in system science, see my "Attacking Indeterminacy: The Case for the Hypothetico-Deductive Method and Consensus Statistics," *Technological Forecasting and Social Change*, 6 (1974).

18. Ludwig von Bertalanffy, *General System Theory* (New York: George Braziller, 1968), p. 40.

4

General System Theory and the Integrated System

4.0 INTRODUCTION

As was suggested in the Forward, this chapter will be a critical one. For it is here that we move into one of the most interesting and focal areas of the system sciences . . . *general system theory*. General system theorists feel that it is possible to develop meaningful constructs that will permit us to do for integrated systems (wholes) what our structural and behavioral system referents did for the static and dynamic aspects of systems. Chapters 2 and 3 presented abstract generic system referents pertinent to one dimension of a system, while the constructs developed here will be pertinent to systems on all three dimensions: (a) the *domain* (structural); (b) the *dynamic* (behavioral); and (c) the *ecological* (a dimension we have not yet considered specifically). We shall be replacing the isomorphisms of the previous chapters (e.g., linear and nonlinear referents; segmented and differentiated evolutionary modalities; finite-state and stochastic-state systems) with ideal-types. These ideal-types will be capable of encompassing more factors, in broader frameworks, than their isomorphic counterparts, and will be holistic in formulation and ambition. The price they pay for this is that they will be more general. However, the reader will hopefully agree that this is a relatively small price for the discipline and order the ideal-types can bring to our study of complex phenomena.

The process by which we develop these ideal-types is a particularly interesting one, for it lends us a chance to give a practical illustration of that analytical modality we discussed in Chapter 1, with which so many of us lack familiarity . . . the hypothetico-deductive method. The first step toward the generation of the ideal-types is strictly deductive. That is, we lay down some logical definitions that take the form of pseudo-axioms . . . definitions that depend only on a consistent deductive logic and not on any real-world experience or empirical predication. These pseudo-axioms will then lead to a definition of a system, per se; and some readers may suggest that it is about time we did this.

Given a definition of a system, it is then possible to generate the central constructs in modern system theory . . . an array of abstract, generalized system referents. These will be admittedly synthetic constructs (straw-men) which nevertheless carry an immensely important ambition: to serve as a set of referents against which all real-world, integrated systems we might encounter may be compared. The essential property of this array is that it is general, and therefore can be used as a referent for any system type (mechanical, organic, social, political, etc.).

Given these abstract general system referents, we may then take another critical deductive leap. We may introduce the general system iconograph, a construct that may serve to compare, both graphically and analytically, the most essential property of any system we might have to deal with. This essential property is simply its amenability to analytical treatment, the extent to which it permits accurate prediction, description, or causal reconstruction. What matters to the general system theorist is the nature of the system with respect to our abilities to analyze it. Beyond that one essential point, all other properties become superficial.

We now take something of a dramatic shift in tone. For we will abandon the efforts to encompass all systems, of whatever nature, and turn to an in-depth analysis of those which are of special concern to us . . . *socioeconomic systems.* Socioeconomic systems gain their social significance because they involve, in total or in part, human beings. The economic importance of the system stems from the fact that it exists or was formed to provide a service, attain an objective, or otherwise accomplish a *purpose.* As soon as we add this purposive element to a system, we automatically enter the domain of economics, for we must be concerned about things like efficiency and effectiveness.

If we then ask about the range of real-world systems that could be considered as socioeconomic systems given this definition, we find that we pretty well exhaust those that are of interest in the modern world. For the list would include all industrial concerns, governmental agencies and governments themselves, service agencies (e.g., social welfare systems), even military, religious, and educational systems. In short, socioeconomic systems are the major agents of action, change, and concern in the world in which we live. And considering the ultimate problem-orientation of this book, the socioeconomic system becomes the most appropriate target for our primary focus.

What we can do then is this: we can take our array of general system referents, the abstract ideal-types, and the general system iconograph, and put them to work in attacking the "universe" of socioeconomic systems, per se. This will lead us directly to a set of four ideal-types that carry direct empirical significance for the system scientist dealing with socioeconomic systems . . . that is, we shall take our abstract system referents, apply them to the real-world, and finally emerge with an array of ideal-types that, unlike the abstract set, are intended to provide substantive direction, insight, and discipline to the problem-solver, decision-maker, policy-maker, researcher, or system analyst. In short, what we finally accomplish here—the development of a set of integrated, empirically-supported ideal-type systems—is meant to be immediately *useful*.

4.1 ELEMENTS IN THE FORMAL DEFINITION OF A SYSTEM

What has been stressed thus far is the role of the system scientist as the purveyor of a new methodology. His job is to contribute to—and in some cases inaugurate—attempts to synthesize and unify science, or at least to bring together diverse and heretofore separated disciplines when the phenomenon at hand has variables that are the property of several different disciplines. In the most basic sense, this means that he must bring to scientists, analysts, and real-world decision- and policy-makers, instruments or concepts that will assist in unification.

Among the most powerful of these are abstract ideal-types against which all real-world systems may be compared . . . constructs that will serve as "masks" we can wear to bring some tentative, *a priori* order and structure to virtually all segments and entities of the world we live in. But not only should these ideal-types have substantive significance (pretending, as it were, to mirror reality), they must also serve to point directly to the analytical implications of phenomena. They should, in effect, suggest what instruments and what techniques should be used to treat systems approximating one or another of the ideal-types.

This is a particularly critical point, but also a rather subtle one. Works in general system theory *should* be of both substantive and methodological significance.[1] And the correlation between these two areas should work this way: the substantive contributions of the general system theorist should be those that make explicit the fact that while all real-world systems may be different in some respects, many will also be intelligible as members of certain classes, where "classes" are to be defined on methodological (or procedural) implications *only*. This can be done because, *when we raise our consideration of systems to a sufficiently high level of abstraction, real differences among subjects sorted into traditional disciplinary classification schemes often tend to disappear, and so the differences between the methodological procedures of the various fields often tend to become gratuitous.* This can lead directly to that efficiency of explanation we seek.[2]

Thus, it was initially thought that all that was necessary was an examination of already existing scientific constructs, not the creation of new ones. Yet it was rather quickly discovered that existing constructs were so deeply affected by parochialism and narrowness of application, that any attempt at generalization between fields was frustrated right from the start. So while many general system theorists still examine the academic structures of different disciplines in an attempt to find points of conceptual isomorphy (e.g., as when an aspect of a social system may be explained by a biological concept), others have seen the necessity to rebuild . . . to take a fresh, new look at the world.

The generic system referents in the two previous chapters were results of this latter process, as are the abstract system referents we shall be introducing here. For all serve, hopefully, the causes of unification of concept, efficiency of explanation, and exploitation of instances of isomorphism ... but not to the point where truly significant differences between phenomena are obscured in the enthusiasm of generalization. In short, the general system perspective is encompassing but not procrustean, Mendelian, but not Laplacian.[3] At any rate, the essence of the general system theory perspective is a formal definition of a system, an essentially deductive task at this point.

This formal definition of a system should allow us to isolate those properties that will serve to distinguish proper *systems* from other real-world phenomena we might encounter. Thus, for our purposes in this book, a proper system will be an entity that substantially meets the following criteria:

- A system must be in, or be capable of obtaining, a state of *integration* sufficient to separate it from its milieu. That is, looked at from without, a system constitutes an entity of determinable morphology.
- A system must encompass two or more morphologically determinable entities. That is, it must contain *multiple, differentiable subsystems* (where the differentiation may be either structural, functional, or spatial).
- A system must be capable of, or actually exercising, *constrained animation* among its subsystems, such that their behavior is not entirely autonomous. That is, at least a portion of the energy potentially available to subsystems must be co-opted by the system for the "larger" mission or for maintenance of the integrity of the whole.

These three criteria constituting a system give rise to what we want to consider as the three *dimensions* common to all systems. In meeting the criteria of integrity, a system exercises what we call an *ecological dimension*, this encompassing the "without" of systems. Here then, we treat its external configuration, the nature of its interchanges with its milieu (its immediate environment, housing its resources, etc.), and its relations with other systems which may somehow affect or be affected by it. Here also we must be concerned with analyzing or predicting the possible internal reactions that might result from external or exogenous forces. Thus the ecological dimension really considers the interface properties of the subject system and the inflow and outflow of forces which they regulate.

Every system also has a *domain dimension* within which its substantive properties reside. The domain is spatially equivalent to the territory bounded by the system's ecological perimeter. More specifically, the domain deals with the structural aspect of systems, treating their resource stocks and the broad, static patterns of internal behavior we might consider prevalent. To this extent, the domain is a proper subject for structural analysis via moment-in-time "shapshots."

Finally, the requirement for constrained animation is met by a third system dimension ... the *dynamic dimension*. This dimension is concerned with any alterations we might perceive between successive snapshots of the domain and, hence, attempts to capture the nonstatic, processual properties of the system at hand. We try here to explain or allegorize the origin and evolution of any structural changes that can be identified within the system (e.g., the nature of the work it does, combination and recombination of resources, and any significant alterations in patterns of interaction among the various components or between the components and the system as an integrated whole). To this extent, then, the dynamic dimension is the proper target for "functional analysis."

Now the domain and dynamic dimensions are already familiar to us. They, respectively, are the structural and behavioral aspects we have already discussed at length. As for the ecological dimension, it is already indirectly familiar to us through the work done in defining the difference between open and closed systems via von Bertalanffy's propositions in Section 2.3.1; and it will become more familiar shortly, as we explore it in detail in a subsequent section. So what is important here is not so much the formal properties of a system or the dimensional aspects, per se, but the extension of these bases into a classification scheme . . . one that is generalized but still capable of giving rise to useable analytical implications, etc. Fortunately, we already have at hand the basis for such a scheme.

4.2 THE ARRAY OF ABSTRACT SYSTEM REFERENTS

The classification scheme we need really evolves from the work that we did in the last chapter. The four generalized, abstract, integrated system referents we want are the following: (a) deterministic systems (those inhering the properties associated with the finite-state and steady-state systems of Section 3.1; (b) moderately-stochastic systems (or entities approximating the properties described in Section 3.2.1); (c) severely-stochastic systems (which inhere the capability for effectively unpredictable major state changes as did the cases discussed in Section 3.3.2); and (d) indeterminate systems (those that are really just extensions of the complexity associated with severely stochastic systems but that will nevertheless be assigned some effectively unique properties in subsequent pages). What is suggested here, then, is this: *a majority of real-world systems we may legitimately expect to encounter will have a tendency to sufficiently approximate one or another of the four abstract ideal-type systems.*

Exactly what we mean by "sufficiently" will be made clear in coming pages. What is important here is that because the elements in our classificatory scheme (e.g., the taxonomy of ideal-type abstracts) are already familiar to us, so too will be the method of their presentation. Particularly, the concept of the *event-probability distribution*, introduced in the previous chapter, can be reemployed here.

The four ideal-type systems, the deterministic, moderately stochastic, severely stochastic, and indeterminate, all become comprehensible in terms of the event-probability distributions that we may impose on them. The events in question may refer to anything: output configurations (in terms of either magnitude or quality); states of the world; specific structural system states (maps); etc. They may be determined qualitatively, numerically, or as complex entities (a combination of quantitative and qualitative properties). They may be empirical (real or actual events) or imaginary. In any case, the four event-probability distributions displayed in Figure 4.1 constitute the array of analytical ideal-types that become the central vehicles for general system theory.

As the reader will note, all four of the definitions in Figure 4.1 really refer directly to our ability to predict the behavior of these systems with respect to some set of starting-state conditions. A starting-state condition, as used here, may comprise any or all of the following:

(a) The appearance of a stream of inputs of a specific configuration.
(b) The structural state (e.g., configuration; map) of a system as it pertains at some particular point-in-time.
(c) A more complicated but very frequently encountered starting-state condition would also be where there is some system on which we wish to act. In this case, an element of the starting-state condition is the nature of the action we plan.

In any case, the analytical ideal-types defined in Figure 4.1 are references against which we measure our ability to predict system structure or behavior in the face of a set of initial conditions, and are hence broad enough to apply to almost any type of real-world system.

In this sense, then, the four analytical ideal-types are simply very broad, context-independent "masks" we can wear in approaching the systems with which we are forced to deal. The four cases represent idealized "states" that real-world systems, entities, or processes will tend to approximate, more or less fully. In other words, when first studying a system, an initial effort should be made to determine which of these abstract (and synthetic) event-probability distributions best reflects our knowledge or expectations about the behavior of the system at hand. Assignments of real-world systems to one or another of these abstract categories may take place in either of two ways. First, there is the *deductive* or *a priori* modality. Here we simply try to build the event-array through intuitive, logical, or analogic means (this latter is appropriate to the extent that an analogy can be drawn between the current problem and one with which we have had prior association). Under this deductive modality, the probabilities, which are assigned the various alternative events we deduced, are themselves products of intuition, logic, or speculation . . . that is, they represent subjective rather than objective (i.e., statistically determined) values.

Obviously, this approach would be employed only where we had no adequate empirical base associated with the system at hand . . . no history of its behavior from which to draw inferences about future behaviors. For when an empirical record or history does exist, we can analyze it for clues as to the proper as-

I. DETERMINISTIC	Where, for any given set of starting-state conditions, there is one and only one event which may be assigned a significant probability of occurrence (i.e., as with the finite-state automata).	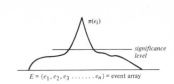

II. MODERATELY STOCHASTIC	Where, for any given set of starting-state conditions, a limited number of qualitatively similar events must be assigned significant probabilities of occurrence (as with the problem of trying to estimate next period sales levels for a well-precedented product).	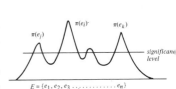
III. SEVERELY STOCHASTIC	Where, for any given set of starting-state conditions, a large number of qualitatively different events must be assigned significantly high probabilities of occurrence (as in the area of conflict behavior or game-based analysis).	

IV. INDETERMINATE	Where, for any given set of starting-state conditions, there is *no* event which can be assigned a significant probability of occurrence; thus the high probability that some outcome we have not been able to prespecify will occur (as in extremely long-range forecasting problems).	

Figure 4.1 The array of analytical ideal-types.[*]

[*]Note that these are synthetic probability distributions in that they treat what are essentially discrete-state systems as continuous ones. This is done for expository purposes only, and a simple frequency distribution could be employed for discrete systems without countermanding the logical implications of the constructs.

signment. Hence the *empirical* modality is usually a great deal more accurate than the deductive. We can arrive at empirically-predicated indications of the analytical category to which a system belongs (or which a system approximates) by examining something of the history of its past behavior. A deterministic system, in this sense, would be one that exhibits no major structural alterations through time on the micro level, and great stability of input-output relationships on the macro. In a similar way, a moderately-stochastic system would be one that is historically stationary on the micro level, but exhibited some variation in input-output conditions on the macro (in terms of the function relating inputs to outputs).

A severely-stochastic system would be defined as one exhibiting significant but limited structural changes, such that the system becomes probabilistic on both the micro and macro levels (e.g., the stochastic-state phenomena of the previous chapter). The important thing that distinguishes the severely stochastic entity from an indeterminate one is in the use of the term "limited" with respect to the state alternatives. Thus, a severely-stochastic system is one where we can expect that some manageable number of pre-definable system states will constitute the array of alternatives that must be assigned significant probabilities of occurrence, with these states representing qualitatively different events (whereas those of the moderately-stochastic system were different in degree only). The indeterminate system, on the other hand, is one where the alternative event array is unbounded and incapable of being predefined in full . . . a product of a system with a long history of immensely wide variation in behavior and structure. The indeterminate system thus represents the worst of all possible worlds from the standpoint of the system analyst.

With these as yet ill-structured and ill-explained definitions in mind, it should still be clear that any system as a whole, any subsystem, or any dimension of a system will tend to approximate one or another of these categories. For what we are really asking is this: how well-behaved, how predictable is the phenomenon at hand?; how analytically tractable will the entity be when we begin to try to study, understand, or manipulate it? Thus, these four analytical categories have more immediate meaning for us when they are collapsed onto a continuum, as in Figure 4.2.

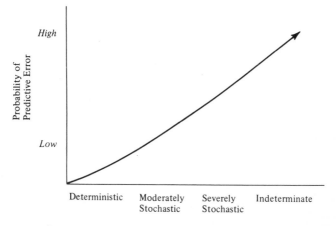

Figure 4.2 The continuum of analytical tractability.

For our purposes here, we can think of analytical tractability as reflecting the degree to which a system under investigation or treatment allows the development of models that accurately and completely capture its properties, models that are both causally and predictively sensitive, where:

- The *causal sensitivity* of a model is reflected in its ability to account for the behavior of a system, such that there is a strong morphological correlation between the allegory itself and the real-world concatenation of events that determined the system's successive states during any given interval.
- The *predictive sensitivity* of a model, on the other hand, is highest when the variance between events predicted by the model and real-world events is lowest; to the extent that elements of the predicted and actual event-sets diverge, the model is predictively insensitive.

The essentially deterministic entity, therefore, is most amenable to the development of causally and predictively sensitive models. Indeterminate entities are ill-behaved, causally complex, and effectively unallegorizable, and therefore analytically intractable ... unamenable to either prediction or causal reconstruction.

4.3 THE GENERAL SYSTEM ICONOGRAPH AND ITS IMPLICATIONS

A system is assigned to one or another of the four analytical states on the basis of its integrated behavior ... some function of the behavior it exhibits on its individual dimensions. Suppose, for the moment, we consider only two collapsed states, *tractability* and *intractability*, polar opposites on the continuum of analytical tractability. We may then move directly to the General System Iconograph (Figure 4.3).

Any system may be assigned some specific position within the iconograph depending on the properties it exhibits on its several dimensions. Thus, each of the three legs of the iconograph represents a continuum of analytical tractability, one for each of the three major dimensions of general systems.

The location of the gestalt suggests that it is the least tractable of all system types we might encounter, having a high degree of indeterminacy on all three of its dimensions. The mechanism, on the other hand, sits close to the origin of the iconograph, indicating that it is essentially tractable on all three dimensions. Thus, the *mechanism* and the *gestalt* represent theoretical "limiting" cases, which real-world systems will tend to approach to a lesser or greater extent.

As a general rule then: the greater the distance from the origin to the central point on a plane defined by a specific system, the greater the expected analytical intractability of that system. In the *a priori* stage (that is, prior to the inauguration of formal, empirical investigation of some subject system), this distance is determined subjectively. But once analytical investigations have begun and we have empirical records of the system's behavior (during the *a posteriori* stage),

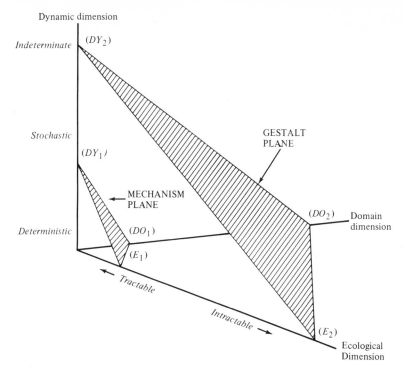

Figure 4.3   The general system iconograph.

we can locate it on a plane where the dimensional points have been objectively and more precisely obtained. In this latter case, we replace "expected" analytical tractability with "calculated" analytical tractability.

The three dimensional points for any given system need not be equidistant from the origin (which would suggest a perfect correlation between degree of analytical tractability for all three system dimensions). We can specify intermediate cases between the extremes defined by the essential gestalt and mechanism. The number of the unique cases we can handle depends on the precision with which we can scale the various dimensions—on the *narrowness* of the intervals we can accommodate—and this number will generally increase as we move further into the *a posteriori* stage and thereby learn more about the properties of any phenomenon we are treating.

Here, however, just to give some idea of the versatility of the iconograph, we use only two basic analytical categories for each dimension and thereby explicate eight (i.e., 2^3) different cases. On each of the three dimensions of the iconograph we have placed two points: $DO_1, DO_2; DY_1, DY_2; E_1, E_2$, respectively. The points subscripted with a "1" represent cases of greater analytical tractability, approaching the limits set by the points associated with the essential *mechanism*;

those subscripted with a "2" suggest a tendency toward greater analytical intractability, being coexistent with the dimensional points of the essential *gestalt*. Hence, the following interpretations of the six new cases.

DOMAIN
DO_1 The domain of the system is highly constrained, homogeneous or otherwise amenable to accurate "mapping" (e.g., a segmented system).

DO_2 The domain is likely to be at least partially empirically inaccessible, heterogenous, or ill-structured (e.g., a differentiated system).

DYNAMIC
DY_1 The processual properties of the system are likely to be highly stationary or consistent (replicative) through time (e.g., a steady-state system).

DY_2 The dynamics of the system are likely to be inherently complex with significant variation through time (e.g., an equifinal or stochastic-state system).

ECOLOGICAL
E_1 The system's interrelationships with its environment are likely to be highly programmatic and constrained and the environment itself will be likely quite simple (e.g., an effectively closed system).

E_2 The system is likely to be sensitive to a protean and complex environment, such that exogenous factors of a potentially very complex nature act as effective determinates of the system itself (e.g., an open system).

Given these six as yet ill-defined points, we can consider that we really have eight specific analytical states into which real-world systems might fall . . . all the possible combinations generated by classifying systems as essentially tractable or intractable on each of the three dimensions.

Hence we have Figure 4.4, representing the general system typology for the (2^3) cases; including the essential *gestalt* and the essential *mechanism*, and six intermediate system types.

As may easily be seen, the cells (elements) of the typology are occupied by miniatures of the iconograph, with the various planes used to illustrate varying degrees of analytical tractability. It is difficult to say at this point, but it may be that eight cases might just about exhaust our precision in assigning complex phenomena to analytical or ideal-type categories. The essential reason for this is the unamenability of most socioeconomic system properties to accurate quantification. In dealing with engineered phenomena or with many physical systems, we are able to think of critical variables approaching explicit values from a continuous distribution of values. But when first approaching most socioeconomic phenomena, we will have to be content with broad categorical values and with highly disparate events set on highly discrete continuua.

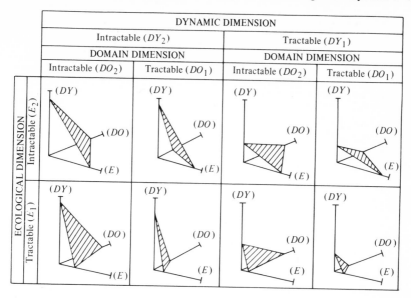

Figure 4.4 The 2^3 general system typology.

In other words, whenever we try to perform a categorization operation, the inherent simplicity or complexity of the phenomenon at hand will determine the width of the intervals employed, and the definitude of the boundaries of the categories. So most ideal-type categories we try to construct in the socio-behavioral or administrative sciences are likely to be much cruder than those that can be constructed in the physical, biological, or engineering sciences. Indeed, much of the work in later sections of this book will be devoted to making this assertion a working axiom of the nascent social system analyst.

Despite the fact that we currently lack some of the tools necessary to translate the abstract general system typology into an empiricalized one, we can nevertheless take a rough cut at the problem. In this respect, consider Figure 4.5. In each of the eight cells of the typology we have placed a real-world (empirical) system from each of two broadly different socioeconomic sectors. The first entry in each cell represents a political system that, in the author's opinion, exhibits the properties appropriate to such placement on its domain, dynamic, and ecological dimensions.

Thus, for example, Israel is assigned to Cell 1, 2. The reasons for this assignment are essentially these. So far as its domain dimension is concerned, Israel is a tractable system because of its great homogeneity (there are only a few, clearly distinct subclasses we need consider, e.g., oriental and European Jews; doves and hawks). The dynamic dimension, however, is intractable, because there are internal struggles among these groups for control of the system, and the resolution of these struggles is not predictable (deterministic) at this point.

	DYNAMIC DIMENSION			
	Intractable		Tractable	
ECOLOGICAL DIMENSION	DOMAIN DIMENSION		DOMAIN DIMENSION	
	Intractable	Tractable	Intractable	Tractable
Intractable	(a) East Pakistan (b) Corporate conglomerate	(a) Israel (b) Professional organization	(a) Mainland China (b) Criminal or guerrilla organization	(a) Taiwan (b) Army Unit
Tractable	(a) Argentina (b) Research or creative agency	(a) Northern Ireland (b) Institutional system (e.g., prison)	(a) Canada (b) Bureaucratic system (with an informal organizational network)	(a) Chad (b) Subsistence agricultural system

Figure 4.5 Empiricalizing the 2^3 typology.

As for the ecological dimension, the intractability there reflects the widely ramifying problems with the Arab world.

Canada, on the other hand, was placed in Cell 2, 3 for the following reasons. On the domain dimension, it is an essentially broad, diverse, eminently heterogeneous nation, exceedingly difficult to "map" with any precision. On the dynamic dimension, however, it is a relatively stable country internally, despite occasional flareups between French and English Canadians, and some tension between Ontario and the Western Provinces. And its ecological dimension is essentially tractable as well, as Canada takes great pains to remove herself from frenetic power politics or binding alliances. At any rate, it is hoped that a similar analysis of the other typology examples would make clear the basic (if somewhat arbitrary) assignment logic employed in this example.

4.4 DIMENSIONAL IDEAL-TYPES

We must now face the focal problem for the practicing system analyst, the problem of determining, in a relatively precise way, exactly what analytical category (e.g., deterministic, moderately stochastic, etc.) a specific real-world system best approximates. We know already that this will have to be some function of the properties that the system exhibits on its several dimensions—the ecological, domain, and dynamic. We also know that once a determination of the relative tractability or intractability of the several dimensions has been made, the system will be made to occupy a specific positional plane in the general system icono-

DIMENSIONAL VARIABLES	VALUE ASSIGNMENTS	
	Tractable	Intractable
ECOLOGICAL		
a. The mode in which the system's ecological properties are determined.	Endogenously	Exogenously
b. The nature of the system's ecological interfaces.	Selective	Universalistic
c. The relative complexity of the environment in which the system resides.[4]	Well-behaved or placid	Turbulent or protean
DOMAIN		
a. The porportion of the domain which is empirically accessible.	High	Low
b. The degree of homogeneity among structural properties.	High	Low
c. The degree of symmetry in their distribution.	High	Low
d. The absolute size of the domain.	Small	Large
e. The density of property distributions.	Low	High
DYNAMIC		
a. The range of behavioral alternatives (roles) available to each system component.	Few	Many
b. The range of different interfaces in which each part may engage.	Few	Many
c. Nature of relationship between parts and whole.	Dependent	Semiautonomous
d. The range of different processual "states" the entity may employ in the face of any given set of inputs or any given output demand.[5]	One	Several or many

Figure 4.6   Table of polar dimensional properties.

graph. Thus we must first learn how to recognize conditions of tractability or intractability with respect to dimensional properties, a task that Figure 4.6 should ease.

The elements in this figure must now be elaborated and defended. Our discussions will, however, be directly pointed at the implications of these terms for socioeconomic systems; an essentially different set of defenses would have to be constructed were we concerned with mechanical or biological phenomena, etc. At any rate, it is best to begin with an treatment of ecological properties for, as we shall later show, it is these that more than any other factor appear to decide the character of systems.

4.4.1 Ecological Cases

In reiteration, our concern on the ecological dimension is with the "outside" of systems. There are three foci of interest:

- The nature of the system's interfaces with its milieu (e.g., the extent to which its boundaries are open or closed).
- The nature of the input-output flows between the subject system and its milieu.
- The nature of the relationships between the subject system and other systems resident in the environment . . . its ecological "posture."

We can now suggest that the analytical amenability or tractability associated with the ecological dimension of any entity will depend on several factors. First, amenability depends on the extent to which the system itself determines the ecological posture it will employ (that is, the extent to which it is the "master" of its own behaviors). A system whose external relationships are determined largely endogenously can have its ecological behavior predicted to the extent that we have access to the algorithms it employs; thus, the foreign policy of the Third Reich was *a priori* predictable in that it was preprogrammed in great detail in Hitler's *Mein Kampf* . . . when he succeeded to the chancellorship, the program became the real-world event-set.[6] A system whose ecological conditions depend primarily on outside or exogenous forces is, on the other hand, more difficult to analyze or predict. This is because we not only have to gain access to *its* intentions or policies, but those of the "dominant" forces in the environment as well (thus, the ecological future of Canada depends in large measure on the policies followed by its "dominant" neighbor, the United States).

Secondly, analytical tractability will depend on the extent to which interfaces are constrained, such that the qualitative and/or quantitative range of intrusive forces is severely constrained . . . they thus become more amenable to observation, measurement, and manipulation. So we would find it generally a simpler analytical task to allegorize and predict the input-output flows of, say, a major defense installation than a nonselective institution like an urban university. In the same way, the highly constrained interfaces of a machine, essentially sealing it from unanticipated environmental effects, make such entities relatively deterministic on the ecological dimension, whereas the *openness* of most non-insular biosocial systems promises some analytical indeterminacy.

The obvious third factor in analytical amenability is the relative simplicity or complexity of the system's environment itself . . . the nature of the "field effects" as it were. A "placid" environment (borrowing this term from Eric Trist and Fred Emery) is one that is characterized by temporal and spatial simplicity or consistency, such that its future states are unlikely to depart significantly from historical states, etc. Thus, no matter how "open" a system is to this type of environment, its ecological properties will be quite amenable to allegorization and prediction. The turbulent environment, the most complex of Trist and Emery's field types,[4] is characterized by great indeterminacy, such that no system forced to operate in this context will be ecologically simple, despite the degree of insularity or selectivity it tries to maintain. Thus, so far as ecological properties are concerned, we have the following simple dichotomies:

Properties of an Ecologically Tractable System	Properties of an Ecologically Intractable System
• Behavior determined endogenously. • Interfaces highly selective. • Resident within an essentially placid, simple environment	• Behavior determined primarily by exogenous factors. • System boundaries open and non-selective. • Resident within a protean, rapidly changing environment (e.g., a turbulent field).

Basically, the relative complexity or simplicity of any environment is dependent upon three things: first, on the way in which resources are distributed across the milieu (the nature of the distribution function); secondly, on the rate of change in this distribution from one point in time to another (the time-dependent variance); and finally, on the nature of the interrelationships which prevail among the systems that are sharing that environment. So thanks largely again to the work of Trist and Emery on types of organizational environments, we can make some rather specific suggestions, as shown in Figure 4.7.

FIELD TYPES[4]	RESOURCE DISTRIBUTION FUNCTION	EXPECTED VARIANCE $[t - (t + 1)]$	NATURE OF SYSTEM INTERACTIONS	GENERIC EXAMPLES
I. Placid-Random	Symmetrical (or simple-random)	None (at least in the short-run)	None (usually only one resident system)	Subsistence Agricultural System
II. Placid-Clustered	Clusters of differentiable resources	Low	Positive-sum game . . . high interdependence	Prototypical ecosystem
III. Disturbed-Reactive	Stratified	Moderate	Zero-sum game	Competitive market system
IV. Turbulent	Nonalgorithmic	High	Indeterminate	Developing or adolescent systems (e.g., Post-Industrial societies)

Figure 4.7 Table of ecological implications.

The detailed aspects of Figure 4.7 will be treated in Section 4.6, where we concern ourselves specifically with the concept of the "field" in the system sciences. Yet a brief analysis of its implications will be useful here. First, in the Type-I field, what few, essentially homogeneous resources there are, are distributed more or less symmetrically (e.g., simple random distribution) across the milieu and this distribution does not alter significantly through time. Usually there is only one socioeconomic system associated with such a field because of the scarcity and homogeneity of the resources, obviating opportunities for interaction with other systems. Systems occupying such fields then tend to become somewhat insular or *autarchic* (as with subsistence agricultural societies and other essentially primitive, mystery-ridden systems).

With the Type-II field, we consider the prototypical ecosystem, with the field containing clusters of differentiable resources, each cluster being controlled primarily by one or another of the resident systems. In this field, the systems enter into a well-defined *symbiotic* relationship, such that the surplus resources or output of one system may become a primary input for another, etc. The growth of any one resident system then is dependent to a considerable extent on the growth of the others; hence the origin of the positive-sum game (e.g., the traditional models of economic and regional growth make explicit the "ratchet" process by which agricultural, hunting, and bourgeousie segments in an area develop an interchange of surpluses, the coefficients of which set a ceiling on the relative growth of any one segment).

In moving to the Type-III field, we find two or more systems competing for a single resource (or resource set), such that resources are stratified rather than clustered, with each resident system containing or controlling some proportion of the total. Hence, they play a competitive zero-sum game, with any incremental resource accummulations made by one system being perceived as directly related to a corresponding reduction in the resource proportions held by the other system(s) in the milieu. These proportional changes account for most of the "variance" in the field.

Finally, in the Type-IV field, there is no simple statistical algorithm expressing the distribution of resources, largely because there may be a large number of trade offs which any system may make among the various resource classes present in the environment . . . with the nature of these trade offs not stabilized. Thus the systems keep getting in each other's way, with often indeterminate outcomes, and with the aggregate behavior of the systems altering the nature of the field itself in ways which are *a priori* unpredictable. Hence, the environment itself is in flux, with the systems more or less *dependent* on field changes which they can neither control nor predict.

Now, there should be unique ecological strategies and postures associated with systems resident within one or another of these environmental states, as they must adopt positions congruent with the nature of the context in which they reside. (See Figure 4.8.)

CORRELATIVES

Environmental Type	Ecological Strategy	Ecological Objective	Ecological Posture	Real-World Counterparts
I	Homeostasis	Conservation	Autarchic	Institutionalized systems
II	Specialization	Compromise	Symbiont	Bureaucratic system
III	Accretion	Exploitation	Dominant	Competitive system
IV	Adaptivity	Responsiveness (plasticity)	Dependent	Emergent or professional system

Figure 4.8 Table of ecological behaviors.

Looking at the elements of the figure, we note that the *autarchic* system, resident as it is in a simple and essentially invariant environment, seeks to maintain a structural, functional status-quo through time, with homeostatic properties usually being fostered via "institutionalizing" processes (thus, among primitive systems, virtually every aspect of existence is tightly determined by some kind of ritualistic algorithm). Naturally, such rigid systems remain viable only to the extent that conditions affecting the system remain within rather narrow bounds.

The *symbiont* system, on the other hand, seeks viability by ever greater specialization, accompanied by increasingly effective (e.g., profitable) compromises with its partners, such that it gradually gains greater control over some valued resource or survival function. Thus, bureaucratic agencies grow by extending their power over some highly specific resource or function, but only to the extent that this resource or service is demanded by other systems . . . or may be imposed on them. Similarly, the oligarchist survives so long as he can maintain a mutually effective compromise with his symbiotic partners within the industrial sector concerned, dividing total resources or markets among themselves according to some well-defined algorithm (which is adhered to under pain of a competitive "war" which might adversely affect all parties). Thus, competition is anathema to the symbiont system, and "division of labor" is the ecological *sine qua non*.

The *dominant* system, by contrast, actively seeks to drive competitors from the field by pursuing an exploitative, accretative policy (accummulating ever more of a resource on which all resident systems are more or less dependent). This is a posture followed (at least ostensibly) by most modern commercial corporations and other systems where the aggregate resource level is sufficient to simultaneously support a limited number of similarly directed systems. At any rate, the zero-sum game assumption underlying this environmental state means that the system that does not actively pursue dominance is likely to quickly become subsumated.

Clearly, the dependent system, forced to operate in an indeterminate, non-algorithmic situation, can only survive to the extent that it is versatile . . . prepared to alter its posture and/or resource requirements as the environmental state alters. Here then, a premium is placed on responsiveness as opposed to conservatism, on adaptivity as opposed to institutionalization or functional/ structural rigidity. Thus long-run survival depends on the ability to make rapid adjustments and accommodations, avoiding the temptation to seek short-run efficiencies by mechanization. Hence, the *dependent* posture is one most closely associated, for example, with various professional or creative agencies who must learn-while-doing, proceeding more heuristically than algorithmically, and with a wide range of other "emergent" phenomena, per se.

The pertinence of these four conceptual referents (e.g., ecological ideal-types) is found in our ability to make assertions about the analytical category into which each will fall, however gross may be the approximation at this point. So, when we tabularize the unique properties associated with each of these ecological ideal-types along the subdimensions pertinent to the ecological dimension of systems, (nature of environment in which the system is resident, the nature of the interfaces the system has with other systems that may be resident in its environment, and the modality by which its ecological posture is determined), we arrive at a construct like that of Figure 4.9.

Thus, as the nature of a system's environment goes from placid to turbulent, as the system's interfaces become gradually less selective, and as the point-in-time behavior of the subject system becomes more and more dependent on the attitude of other systems, the degree of predictivity associated with that system declines, as does the probability of our being able to accurately reconstruct the

ECOLOGICAL TYPE	NATURE OF ENVIRONMENT	NATURE OF INTERFACES	ECOLOGICAL BEHAVIOR DETERMINED	ASSOCIATED ANALYTICAL CATEGORY
Autarchic	Very simple	Essentially "closed"	Endogenously	Deterministic
Symbiont	Highly programmable	Highly selective	Predominately endogenously	Moderately Stochastic
Dominant	Severely stochastic	Moderately "open"	Predominately exogenously	Severely Stochastic
Dependent	Highly complex (indeterminate)	Wide "open"	Exogenously	Indeterminate

Figure 4.9 Typology of ecological ideal-types.

causal record of that system on the ecological dimension. As rough as they are, though, our deductions lead to the expectation that institutionalized and primitive systems will be the most ecologically tractable, bureaucratic or oligarchistic systems moderately tractable, most competitive entities relatively intractable, and finally, most professional, creative, or emergent systems least tractable . . . contentions we shall elaborate on in Section 4.6.

With the ecological dimension thus "typed," we can now turn to a consideration of the domain dimension, still in the effort to discipline (however grossly at this stage) our categorization of various real-world systems we might encounter.

4.4.2 Domain Cases

As was earlier noted, on the domain dimension we are concerned with our ability to capture and allegorize the static or structural properties of a system . . . its "within." Generally this involves the development of an *inventory* of system-owned resources and subsystems, along with the development of a force-field type *map* of the essentially static interrelationships prevailing among the various system components . . . the essentially invariant or semipermanent paths of causality and interaction. In most cases, this map of basic functional relationships will show the normative patterns of influence within the system—the sequential and directional aspects—without attempting to capture precise processual details (this being the task done on the dynamic dimension). And as we earlier suggested, domain analysis is usually performed via the device of taking moment-in-time "snap shots" of the system's substance.

But what if our lens is not capable of reflecting the entire domain of a system at a given point in time; or if there is no feasible perspective that allows the inclusion of all territory within the system's ecological perimeter? That portion of the system's domain that cannot be observed—that which is empirically inaccessible to us for some reason—must be *inferred* to be some function of the observed or empirically accessible portion. Accordingly, there is a positive relationship presumed between the attributes of that portion of the domain that is observable and that which escapes observation.

Normatively, we expect the potential error of a structural inference to vary inversely with the *proportion of the domain actually sampled*: the greater this proportion, the lower will be the expected variance between the analytical estimation and the actual state of the system's domain. This proportion, then, becomes the first of the factors by which we attempt to classify system structures (see Figure 4.10). But there are other factors which also influence the probable accuracy of any domain or structural-analysis exercise (for any given proportion of the domain actually sampled), with the probability of inductive or inferential error decreasing as: (a) the degree of *homogeneity* of objects in the domain increases; and (b) the *symmetry* of their distribution increases.

Accordingly, a domain which has essentially similar properties (homogeneous resources or components, etc.) and these symmetrically distributed, needs a lower proportion subjected to empirical analysis to produce inferences at any given level-of-confidence than a domain whose properties are highly heterogeneous and whose distribution pattern is confused (asymmetrical or clustered, for example).

Another factor is the *absolute size* of the domain which must be investigated, with analytical intractability increasing (given all other considerations constant) as the space to be sampled increases. A final factor is also of concern to us here: the *density* with which properties are distributed across the domain, with a low density usually increasing the visibility and isolability of relevant interaction patterns and decreasing the probability of structural/functional confoundations.

Considering these subdimensional categories in what might be the broadest sense, systems whose domains are totally empirically accessible to us, whose properties (components) are homogeneous, whose distribution of properties is symmetrical, whose size is constrained to manageable proportions, and whose properties are distributed with low density, will represent considerably more tractable systems than those that exhibit antonymical properties. But the *statistical* significance of our classifications comes in at the point where we consider any system whose domain is not totally empirically accessible, such that a "map" of that system would have to include some inferences or projections about the properties of unobserved portions of the domain. It should easily be seen that homogeneity, symmetry, small size, and low density directly contribute to both the efficiency and accuracy of such structural projections. The efficiency emerges from the consideration that any unit of information pertinent to the unobserved—or unobservable—portions of the domain would be obtained at lower cost (in terms of either analytical resources or time) the more completely these criteria are met. On the other hand, heterogeneity, asymmetry, large size, and high density would make such statistical projections available at higher cost per unit of information and ultimately probably make us less confident in their accuracy as well. At any rate, to lend these criteria some empirical substance, consider Figure 4.10.

From a broader perspective, we can restate the proposition that real-world systems tend to evolve along one of two basic trajectories, each leading to an effectively polarized situation so far as structural or domain properties are concerned. The first trajectory is *segmentation*, where the system's components tend to be both functionally and structually identical (all look alike and all seek a similar functional objective in a similar way). The second path is *differentiation*, where each of the components of the system evolves effectively unique structural and functional properties.*

Structural and functional differentiation is carried to its operational limits by the modern industrial corporation, where each differentiable function is per-

*See, again, Section 2.2.

SAMPLE ENTITIES

Critical Analytical Variables	Tractable	Intractable
1. The *proportion* of the domain which is accessible empirically.	High: An elementary school	Low: A guerrilla group
2. The degree of *homogeneity* among structural properties.	High: Newport, R. I.	Low: New York City
3. The degree of *symmetry* in the distribution of system components or properties of interest.	High: A military unit	Low: A multi-national corporation
4. The *absolute size* of the domain.	Low: Disneyland	High: Sahara Desert
5. The *density* with which properties of interest are distributed.	Low: Sahara Desert	High: Disneyland

Figure 4.10   Table of polar domain properties.

formed by a differently configured subsystem or component . . . the socioeconomic equivalent of the engineer's optimally efficient "machine." In the same way, more modern, technologically advanced societies have historically been marked by their greater specialization of both structural and functional attributes . . . in effect, by the intensity and breadth of their division of labor. Generally speaking, we find only two types of essentially segmented systems existing in the real-world. First, there is the *primitive* system, where a single individual, or single group of individuals, inheres within itself the capability to perform many different functions at different points-in-time (as, for example, in the small business, where a single man may be part accountant, part executive, part personnel manager, and part laborer, etc., or in the archaic social system, where the same tribal members are expected to play many different roles as the situation demands: warrior, fisherman, hunter, farmer, shaman, etc.). Secondly, there is what we might call the *replicative* system where virtually all subsystems are indistinguishable, except that they occupy a unique point in space (as, for example, with political and charitable organizations, where one "cell" is a structural/functional replicate of all others, uniquely identifiable only in that it occupies an exclusive territory).

Not all the real-world systems we encounter will, however, belong to either the fully-differentiated or fully-segmented category. Some may fall under one of two intermediate cases:

(a) *Structurally segmented/functionally differentiated:* where morphologically similar subsystems or components are used to perform essentially different functions (as, for example, in the case of the bureaucratic system or military organization, where "departmentalization" or "platoonization" finds structurally indistinguishable units performing very different tasks).

(b) *Structurally differentiated/functionally segmented*; in this least common of all cases, we find the same functional objective being pursued via different organizational substructures. For example, a university may permit its professors to teach the same subject under substantially different structural conditions (e.g., a basic computer programming course may be taught by a lecture, by a tutorial, by an informal practicum, or individualized learning mode). In the same way, a psychology clinic may permit many different structures in trying to reach any given objective (for example, the same effect may be sought via group counseling, psychopharmacology, or behavioral or gestalt therapy, etc.).

At any rate, as should have been clear from Chapter 2, segmented and differentiated system structures are extremely important system referents. For the segmented system, by definition, will inhere greater degrees of homogeneity and symmetry than differentiated systems . . . such that the greater the degree of segmentation in a system, the more tractable that system in terms of our ability to generate structural "maps." As for the other subdimensions—size of system, density of property distribution, and empirical accessibility—these are straightforward enough, and really independent of whatever other properties a system may possess in terms of domain characteristics. Thus, the most authoritative classificatory scheme for systems' domain dimensions would be predicated on the segmentation-differentiation dichotomy, as shown in Figure 4.11.

Segmentation serves to make any system more structurally tractable, *to increase the probability that empirically unobserved portions of the domain will be some calculable function of the observed.* Just as obviously, tendencies toward functional/structural differentiation tend to decrease this probability in all instances. Thus, for the fully-segmented system, we need only observe a

FUNCTIONAL DIMENSION	STRUCTURAL DIMENSION	
	Segmented	Differentiated
Segmented	TYPE-I: the primitive society; the political or charitable organization.	TYPE-IV: client-oriented systems; research and development groups; professional organizations; emergent systems.
Differentiated	TYPE-II: the army or religious order; the bureaucracy.	TYPE-III: the modern industrial organization or advanced socioeconomic system.

Figure 4.11 Typology of domain ideal-types.

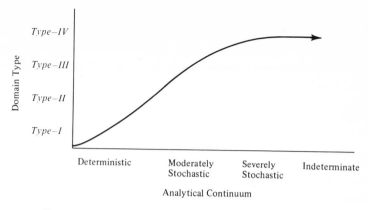

Figure 4.12   The domain continuum of analytical tractability.

relatively small portion of the total to make expectedly accurate projections about the basic substantive properties associated with the unobserved portion.

In this sense, the Type-I system emerges as most tractable, with higher number system-types becoming progressively more difficult to analyze structurally, yielding a continuum of tractability for the domain dimension like that shown in Figure 4.12.

4.4.3 Dynamic Cases

On the dynamic dimension we must try to explain any changes that have been noted between successive domain analyses, between successive "snapshots" . . . even if the origin of such changes rests in the system's environment. Changes of interest might be any of the following:

- Changes in the composition and/or level of resource stocks held by the system.
- Changes in the quality and/or quantity of system components (e.g., subsystems).
- Changes in the causal patterns or interaction sequences prevalent among these components.

We may also be concerned about space-dependent changes, as when the same task is performed differently in different parts of the system, a function which usually reflects the degree of autonomy allowed the subsystems, etc.

Basically then, dynamic analysis involves the articulation of transformation functions that explain the way in which a given system state at time t was translated into a different system state at time $t + 1$, using the resources, components, and interaction patterns of the system as the major foci of analysis. The greater the change exhibited in these three areas in any interval, the more important is the dynamic dimension of the system . . . and the more complex its functional properties. Thus, the most analytically tractable entity on the dynamic dimension is that which exhibits the least amount of structural change in a given time period. When structural changes are widespread and highly rapid in occurrence, we may not be able to develop any calculable, rigorous transformation functions explaining them. This may be because of the limited frequency with which we can make successive structural analyses (e.g., take successive snapshots); but it may also be because the causal factors are simply too complex, transparent, or protean to allow the derivation of dynamic algorithms from successive structural snapshots. In this latter case, we emerge with a discontinuous or incomplete dynamic record, such that our system models or allegories become products of *causal inference*, as we may have to fill in gaps and bridge discontinuities analytically rather than empirically.

As a rule, dynamic properties are easier to isolate and allegorize the more tractable the domain. But the dynamic dimension has a life apart from the structural, with its analytical tractability increasing as:

1. The behavioral repertoire of the system's components decreases, such that each can assume only fewer alternative behavioral states.
2. The range of possible interfaces that can exist among the components becomes successively more constrained or proscribed (that is, where the number of other components with which a given system component can interface decreases).
3. The nature of the relationship between individual parts and the system as a whole becomes successively more constrained and mechanical (such that the autonomy of the parts decreases).
4. The nature of the processing the system must do becomes successively more mechanical rather than "strategic" or opportunistic (heuristic) in nature, such that the number of different functional states the system can assume declines.

A system becomes dynamically tractable then to the extent that it contains parts that are functionally specific, highly dependent (non-autonomous), and capable of assuming only a limited number of preordained interfaces with other parts . . . with the entire system existing within an essentially closed or highly selective ecological envelope.

The *inherent complexity* of a system's dynamic dimension involves the different "values" which might be assigned it with respect to the factors given in Figure 4.13. These values reflect the ease or difficulty we can expect to encounter in constructing accurate processual or causal allegories for the system at hand.

The differences between the values assigned to the three subdimensions of Figure 4.13 may be thought of as those we would expect to be associated with, for example, a mechanical system at the deterministic extreme and, at the other, a non-institutionalized social system populated by opportunistic, role-independent human beings. Thus, the former is expected to lend itself more fully to any

| | VALUES LEADING TO | |
ANALYTICAL FACTORS	Low Inherent Complexity	High Inherent Complexity
1. Number of roles parts can play.	Only one	Many
2. Different processual interfaces available to the part.	Only one	Many
3. Degree of autonomy enjoyed by the parts.	None	Much

Figure 4.13 Table of dynamic subdimensions.

effort we might make to describe or allegorize the way in which it operates or to capture its processual/dynamic properties.

But there is a fourth dynamic subdimensions to which we now want to turn our attention, for this concerns not only our ability to allegorize the processual/ causal properties of a system or subsystem, but our ability to *predict* its processual behavior. So, in addition to the inherent complexity of a system, we are concerned also with its *acceleration* . . . the range of different processual "states" a system might enact in the pursuit of any elected or assigned objective.* Our concept of acceleration, then, is intimately tied to the phenomenon of *equifinality* in a system or subsystem. This factor reflects the ability to achieve the same set of objectives via essentially different causal/processual trajectories. With an equifinal system, simply being informed of the objective assigned the system or subsystem does not permit us to make any strict determination as to the processual or causal sequence that it might employ. Even *after* the occurrence of some event, an equifinal entity forces us to operate probabilistically, for we cannot be certain (even in retrospect) of the precise means that were employed to achieve that event unless we have a complete causal record at hand. In contrast, the nonequifinal system will have one and only one processual state associated with any outcome, such that a knowledge of the one introduces a significantly high probability of the other . . . a very desirable analytical property indeed. Obviously then, a light-switch with its binary on/off capabilities would be more dynamically tractable than a system in which any given situation may be met in any of several, possible *a priori* undefinable ways. This latter type system (high-acceleration) represents the worst of all possible worlds on the dynamic dimension for the analyst and/or administrator.

This concept of acceleration is not, of course, new to us. We dealt with it indirectly, and at length, in the preceeding chapter. For acceleration, as used here, is entirely reminiscent of the concept of *state stationarity* on the micro level . . . the extent to which processual conditions—basic operational algorithms,

*Within some finite interval.

processes and relations—remain stable or invariant through time. In that respect, the steady state, finite state, moderately stochastic, severely stochastic, and equifinal systems emerged as successively *less tractable* entities. Much the same logic holds now, where acceleration on the dynamic dimension equates very nicely with non-stationarity on what we previously called the micro level (see, again, Section 3.1).

At any rate, we may use inherent complexity of the processual states (in terms of their structure) and the degree of acceleration a system exhibits to develop a typology of dynamic ideal-types, as in Figure 4.14.

An example of the intermediate case (Type-III entities) is the modern competitive organizations who ensure their survival by the search for ways to lower input-output ratios for all processing foci, through a constant exchange of less efficient for more efficient processing state-alternatives. But the purposive and disciplined nature of commercial or industrial processes means that these "states" will be algorithmic or orderly in nature, such that causal allegorization is possible only if we can gain access to them. However, the competitive advantage of business firms lies primarily in their ability to keep favorable processual innovations a secret from competitors (or to restrict the knowledge of them as highly as possible). Thus, we as analysts may often labor under a disadvantage shared with potential competitors . . . the inability to predict what form the processing "state" will assume, even though that "state" would be amenable to precise modeling upon access. Such a situation is even more obvious in military and athletic contexts than in the commercial, and might be thought of as an operational problem associated with any effort to analyze "dominant" systems.

The electronic computer system shares a cell in the figure with the modern, commercial corporation, but for an entirely different set of reasons. Particularly, the computer system is capable of using many different combinations of resources and functional algorithms in attacking any given job at any given moment, the precise "state" being selected in effective "real-time" with respect to the current distribution (and availability) of processing resources and the pro-

INHERENT COMPLEXITY OF PROCESSUAL STATE(S)	DEGREE OF ACCELERATION	
	Low	High
Low	*TYPE-I* • Finite-state automata • Ritualized (institutionalized) sociocultural systems	*TYPE-III* • Electronic computer systems (with executive software) • Modern competitive (technocratic) enterprises
High	*TYPE-II* • Genetic processes • Bureaucratic agencies (with informal organizational component)	*TYPE-IV* • Complex "organic" socioeconomic systems • Heuristic machines

Figure 4.14 Typology of dynamic ideal-types.

cessing or resource demands being made by incoming jobs. The computer attempts to optimize its input-output and resource-production ratios by selecting, from among a continuous array of potential processual states, that which promises to make most efficient use of available capabilities relative to impending processing demands. This is, in essence, the task of the sophisticated executive programs that accompany the installation of most third-generation computer systems. What this means is that we are effectively unable to predict exactly the causal sequence which will be followed in the processing of any particular job (though by continuously tracing circuitry employed we may be able to reconstruct the sequence of operations). In the broadest sense then, the electronic computer and modern industrial organization represent cases where the processual states which will be employed may be unpredictable but will usually be amenable to causal reconstruction (hence the utility of patent laws, etc.).

The unlikely pair of examples of Type-II entities (the low acceleration, high inherent-complexity case) share the following properties:

- When we can specify the starting-state conditions associated with a simple genetic process, we can predict the nature of the outcome with a fair degree of probability; similarly, when we subject a bureaucratic entity to a given array of processing demands, we can estimate fairly well the resultant input-output ratio or productivity indices which will result.
- However, in neither case can we (even in retrospect) allegorize the precise causal/processual state that led to that output event or input-output ratio . . . genetic transforms remain a causal mystery to us even after years of analysis and experimentation; similarly, the sub rosa processing networks through which bureaucratic systems get the work done represent phenomena that have for long escaped precise empirical capture.*

In other words, we are fairly certain that these cases are nonequifinal with low acceleration on the dynamic dimension, yet the precise nature of the processual state which is employed remains below the level of empirical accessibility. Overall then, the consistency between input and output events that has been noted empirically (historically) with respect to both genetic and bureaucratic entities argues for some deep-seated, relatively invariant, complex causal algorithms.

What we lack here is a deductive "mask" out of which the presumed order in genetic processes may be derived, an order that is now available to us only by inference and surrogation. In the same way, we indirectly "infer" the critical nature of informal bureaucratic networks by observing what happens when bureaucratic agencies "work to rules." What happens is that productivity

---

*It is thought that these "informal" organizations are relatively invariant and fixed, and would be allegorizable as finite-state subsystems if only we had empirical access to them.

plummets. But hard as we may try, the sub rosa processing algorithms inherent in bureaucratic agencies are often too complex to abstract.

Thus the genetic process and the bureaucracy differ from the electronic computer in that the formers' processual properties inhere less acceleration, but greater inherent complexity . . . i.e., the genetic process is less amenable to causal allegorization or analytical reconstruction.

We may summarize these discussions by developing an array of dynamic ideal-types to stand beside the domain and ecological we have already developed. The properties determining this array are summarized in Figure 4.15. The conclusions to be drawn from this figure are rather straightforward. A system exhibiting Type-I (mechanical) properties on its dynamic dimension should permit us to make effectively optimal resource allocations, to control processual parameters at virtually all points, and to assume that the system will fully and immediately carry out whatever control commands are issued it (and these criteria, in the broad sense, may serve as an operational definition of the engineer's concept of finite-state automata). On the other hand, the system that exhibits Type-IV (heuristic) properties on its dynamic dimension must be approached with great caution. For it inheres the potential to react opportunistically and strategically, having, as it were, a mind of its own. Hence, neither its processual parameters nor its mode of operation will be entirely amenable to prediction (or even causal reconstruction). When we broach the subject of system control in the next chapter, these attributes will become both more clear and more compelling.

The net result of all this is, so far as dynamic ideal-types are concerned, the heuristic emerges as the least predictable, the hardest to control, the most intractable to analyze, and the most difficult to administer; the mechanical system, of course, represents the best of all possible worlds on the dynamic dimension. (We may rely on Chapter 8 to amplify these points even further, as it will begin where we leave off here.) Let us now turn to the last of our deductive constructions for this chapter . . . the array of empirically-predicated ideal-type *integrated* systems.

4.5 THE ARRAY OF INTEGRATED IDEAL-TYPES

We have now reached the point where we may talk about a set of empirically-predicated integrated ideal-types against which real-world socioeconomic systems may be compared. The road has been a long one, but we have finally reached the point where we have identified four ideal-types under each of the three major system dimensions, with the ideal-types reflecting the properties of one or another of our basic analytical abstracts: (a) deterministic, (b) moderately stochastic, (c) severely stochastic, and (d) indeterminate. These dimensional ideal-types could serve as a reference against which the individual dimensions of systems could be compared, which would then allow us to define a plane for that system on the general system iconograph. As explained earlier, the gross

ANALYTICAL FACTORS	DYNAMIC IDEAL-TYPE			
	Type-I	Type-II	Type-III	Type-IV
1. Number of different functional or processual states the entity might invoke to achieve some elected or imposed "end".	One	Constrained (on the formal level).	Few	Potentially many
2. Predictability of processual parameters (e.g., input-output ratios).	Deterministic	Moderately stochastic	Severely stochastic	Indeterminate
3. Responsiveness of the entity to processual control (e.g., amenability to process control algorithms).	Highest	Relatively high	Relatively low	Lowest
4. Amenability of the dynamic dimension to causal reconstruction.	Highest	Low (where an informal organization exists).	Moderately high	Lowest
TYPE DESIGNATION	MECHANICAL	NONEQUIFINAL	EQUIFINAL	HEURISTIC

Figure 4.15 Properties of dynamic ideal-types.

analytical tractability of the system would then be indicated roughly by the distance from the origin of the iconograph to the central point on the plane . . . and we would have a graphic scheme within which virtually all systems could be compared, one against the other, in terms of an abstract set of references that are context-independent.

In other words, it is now possible to compare different systems, from very different sectors, in terms of their analytical tractability, which is an attribute far more important to the system scientist than any superficial properties that systems may exhibit. Thus, at this level of abstraction, biological and social and mechanical and political and behavioral systems, etc., all become intelligible in essentially the same terms. Stretching a point, perhaps, it is in such a way that we can begin to compare the proverbial apples and oranges, not in terms of color or other such properties but in terms of more abstract properties such as symmetry, homogeneity, geometric, or topological qualities, etc.

It is thus possible for us to consider socioeconomic systems as amalgams of their dimensions, which in turn may be seen as approximate to one or another of the dimensional ideal-types we developed. In a sense, this is what we did when we took the general system iconograph and translated it into the general system typology, giving us eight unique system referents (which were then lent some empirical substance when we replaced the abstractions with real-world systems, in Figure 4.5). At any rate, considering that we have three basic system dimensions, and can have a system occupy any of four basic analytical positions on each dimension, we can now potentially define $[3^4]$ cases, or 81 unique system-types within the socioeconomic system sector. This, obviously, would be far too many system referents to keep in mind.

There is another reason why we do not really need this large number in order to pretty well cover the range of real-world socioeconomic systems we might encounter. This reason is embodied in the recognition that some combinations of the various dimensional ideal-types will be highly probable, whereas others that might theoretically be formed will be highly improbable. Thus, for example, we would not expect to find an ecologically autarchic system having a fully-differentiated structure or being heuristic in terms of its dynamics. By the same token, a fully-segmented system on the domain dimension would hardly be expected to exhibit equifinal behavior on the dynamic dimension, or be involved in competitive relationships on the ecological dimension. Such combinations would be *incongruent*, and therefore highly improbable in the real-world.

In reviewing the various dimensional ideal-types, then, we find that there are some associations which are more logically appealing and more probably congruent than others. Indeed, by going through such a process, it is possible to develop what we have referred to as the array of integrated system ideal-types . . . a set of four systems, viewed as wholes, which are comprised of those dimensional ideal-types that appear to be most congruent. These would be those systems where the dimensional ideal-types employed are *most complementary*, most positively correlated in terms of function, structure, and ecological mission. By isolating these collections of dimensional ideal-types, we should be assured of coming up with *the* taxonomy of integrated ideal-types that, as a set, will have the highest probability of exhausting the largest number of empirical socioeconomic systems we might find operating in the real-world.

We have attempted to develop such a set here. They are the four generic systems of Figure 4.16. The process by which they were evolved is a long and difficult one, but the logic may be summed up quickly. First, a system's basic effectiveness will be found in its ability to develop a system structure (a set of domain properties) that most facilitates meeting the ecological mission the system is forced, or has elected, to pursue. This, in a sense, would be that particular system structure which is most congruent with the ecological posture the system exhibits. Given this association, there will be high correlation between ecological and domain attributes and the dynamic properties the system exhibits, with the raw complexity of the dynamic dimension generally increasing in proportion to the "sophistication" of the system's ecological posture (reflecting the complexity of the field in which it operates) and the complexity of its domain, etc. In this sense, then, there are distinct theoretical patterns of dimensional ideal-types that become congruent, probable, and that therefore are most frequently expected in the real-world. It is this set of patterns that our collection of integrated ideal-type systems is meant to represent.

But with respect to the array of integrated ideal-types set out in Figure 4.16, not all readers may agree with the logic in making these collections, nor do we suggest that *all* real-world socioeconomic systems will fall neatly into these four categories. As for the first, the readers may return to the dimensional ideal-types and generate their own arrays according to whatever criteria appeals to them, or perhaps according to experiences they have had which dictate different patterns as most appropriate. As for the second argument, some real-world systems will fall through the interstices between these four cases, but this is the price one pays for generalization, and is a problem that the reader may repair by developing more precise and detailed arrays.

That there is some reason for faith in these particular generic system referents, however, is illustrated in Figure 4.17, where we give a rather exhaustive list of social, political, and economic systems that appear to approximate—sufficiently if not completely—one or another of the integrated system ideal-types just set out.

The logical jump from the dimensional properties we discussed to the ostensibly empirically-relevant integrated system ideal-types is a difficult one . . . it will no doubt require much reading and rereading, much comparison and study, before the essential correlations become clear. Yet we must, as system scientists, now go one step further . . . for the organizational ideal-types we have set out are not really the most appropriate units of analysis for us. There is another, still more broadly defined entity than the integrated ideal-type. This is the *field*.

GENERIC SYSTEM TYPE	Ecological Type	Domain Type	Dynamic Type	ASSOCIATED ANALYTICAL REFERENCE
I	Autarchic	Fully segmented	Mechanical	Deterministic
II	Symbiont	Structurally segmented/ functionally differentiated	Nonequifinal	Moderately stochastic
III	Dominant	Fully differentiated	Equifinal	Severely stochastic
IV	Dependent	Structurally differentiated/ functionally segmented	Heuristic	Indeterminate

Figure 4.16 The array of integrated ideal-type systems.

APPLICATIONS	PHENOMENAL IDEAL-TYPES			
	Type-I	Type-II	Type-III	Type-IV
Economic Modalities	Agrarian/subsistence systems	Industrial/secondary	Technocratic/innovative	Post-Industrial (tertiary and welfare)
Social Modalities	Ritualistic systems	Coercive systems*	Instrumentalistic/purposive	Volunteeristic/affective
Political Modalities	Theocratic/strict monarchic	Totalitarian/nationalistic	Democratic/parliamentary	Anarchistic
Organizational Modalities	Institutionalistic/ascriptive	Bureaucratic/centralistic	Decentralistic	Adhocratic[7]
Behavioral Modalities	Dogmatic	Algorithmic	Utilitarian/rationalistic	Opportunistic/idiographic

*Generally designed to serve some "critical" mission (e.g., national defense).

Figure 4.17   Table of empiricalizations.

The field is actually a unit of analysis that simultaneously considers both the environment (e.g., ecological milieu) and the system or systems contained within it. And as we shall now see, the integrated ideal-types are the central foci of the field concept, and during its development, we shall be offering a further elaboration of the relevance of the four system ideal-types just developed.

4.6 THE CONCEPT OF THE FIELD

What we shall be suggesting in the pages to come is this: each of the four integrated ideal-type systems (which we may now refer to as organizational ideal-types) will tend to be congruent with one of four environmental ideal-types. We further propose that the correlation between the existence of a specific environment and the existence of an organization inhering properties of one or another ideal-type will be quite strong . . . such that there will be certain *generic* interface conditions between organizations and environments that prevent our having to treat each organizational/environment interface as a unique "event." We arrive at this proposition through what basically is an extension of the ideal-types earlier introduced in the section dealing with the ecological aspects of systems, those used us by Emery and Trist. The logic of this extension is given in Figure 4.18. Let us now examine each of the field types in some detail.

4.6.1 The Autarchic Field and the Type-I Organization

The *placid-random* environmental ideal-type is the simplest of the cases defined by Emery and Trist,[4] and hence gives rise to the simplest (e.g., most primitive) organizational response. For in a placid-random environment, we have a relatively stable, more or less symmetrical distribution of essentially homogeneous resources (where noxients, nutrients, or other pertinent properties are distributed randomly and invariantly across the organization's milieu).

Faced with such an environment, the organization tends to adopt an ecological behavioral modality such as that employed in running a maze . . . experiential trial-and-error.* The placid-random environment, indeed, tends to reduce the utility of cognitive or strategic modalities, for there is no order in which properties "hang together," no meaningful correlations on which the organization may rely that would enable it to employ statistical or probabilistic instruments (e.g., regressions of property x against property y; inferences about unobserved portions of the milieu derived from empirically observed portions). Thus, when faced with a placid-random domain, as Emery and Trist have so correctly pointed out, strategy becomes indistinguishable from tactics, and the cognitive component of organizational behavior is reduced to an effective minimum.

An inescapable corollary of the placid-random environment is ritualization

---

*Lord Russell once pointed out that not even Isaac Newton himself could have devised a more efficient method for running mazes than trial-and-error.

FIELD TYPE	ENVIRONMENTAL IDEAL-TYPE (via Emery and Trist[4])	ENVIRONMENTAL PROPERTIES			ORGANIZATIONAL PROPERTIES	
		Resource Distribution Function	Resource Transformation Function	Nature of System Interactions	Congruent Ecological Posture	Behavioral Characteristics and Ecological Objectives
Autarchic	Placid-Random	Random or symmetrical distribution of homogeneous properties.	A steady-state is maintained as the norm.	Usually only one system per field.	Conservation	The system tends to seek homeostasis and automaticity in the face of essentially invariant environmental properties.
Symbiont	Placid-Clustered	Differentiated resources are clustered.	Clusteration tends to intensify through time.	Systems play a positive-sum game.	Compromise (cooperation)	Systems try to increase control over a relevant cluster through increased specialization and programmation.
Competitive	Disturbed-Reactive	Demand for resources (or resources themselves) are stratified.	Changes in the stratification coefficients occur via systems' strategic actions.	Systems play a zero-sum game.	Exploitation	Systems seek to gain a larger share of some scarce resource by remaining responsive to emerging opportunities for exploitation of markets, resource stocks, or other units.
Emergent	Turbulent	Resources are distributed non-algorithmically.	Alterations are often autochthonous and non-allegorizable.	Usually opportunistic, serendipitous, or otherwise *a priori* indeterminate.	Heuristicity	Organizations remain viable to the extent that they can create and rapidly implement original responses to a succession of unprecedented situations.

Figure 4.18   Table of ideal-type field properties.

and automaticity of the organization's activities. When faced with environmental consistency through time, organizations have the opportunity to translate historically favorable responses into automatic reactions. Generally, this programmation of virtually all aspects of organizational life proceeds through the mechanism of ritualization, which is the irrational counterpart of institutionalization. Members of organizations faced with the placid-random environment tend, then, to become the social counterparts of the engineer's finite-state automata. For, given information about the stimulus at hand (e.g., the starting-state conditions), the reaction of the individual and the system as a whole is *a priori* determinable with an insignificant probability of error. In short, environmental simplicity and invariance places little if any emphasis on innovation, creativity, or departure from precedent.

The finite state quality of systems facing placid-random environments tends to mark them as *primitive* (as opposed to the equifinal potential which characterizes more complex systems). The primitive aspect of such systems takes on added significance when we note that little benefit is to be gained from structural or functional differentiation. In the primitive system, where environmental properties are both entirely predictable and largely heterogeneous, components of the organization will tend to be structural-functional replicates of one another. Such systems tend to be fully segmented,* such that all organizational components both look alike in terms of morphology and perform essentially the same tasks. Division of labor, or specialization, is thus minimized . . . all individuals, tribes, or clans, for example, tend to automatically shift roles as aspects of the environment dictate. They will be equally at home as farmers, warriors, priests, gatherers, etc. And as we have already implied, the ritualization permissible in the face of the placid-random environment promotes an acculturation process that, for all generations, programs individuals for these roles and argues against any attempt to evolve structurally unprecedented groupings or innovative responses.

The strength of fully-segmented, ritualized systems tends to be found in their ability to instantly focus the entire organization (with extremely low probabilities of error or dysfunction or departure from programmaticity) on the very few iterative or invariant opportunities that the placid-random environment offers. Naturally, such organizations tend to achieve this automaticity and predictability only by paying a compensatory price, particularly in the form of organizational resilience or adaptivity; for the placid-random environment holds no motivation for the development of mechanisms for managing perturbations, or accommodating changes.

Thus, the primitive system remains viable only so long as the environment remains essentially consistent in terms of properties, their distribution, or transformations. As such, these systems will tend to develop and implement an essentially *conservative* ecological posture, both toward the resources present in

*See, again, Section 2.2.1.

the milieu, and toward whatever other primitive systems might be present in a field. Depending so fully on the consistency of exogenous factors, such systems may even tend to adopt a pantheistic or naturalistic association with the natural environment, such that exploitation of resources is viewed as an unsanctionable sacrilege.

By the same token, the homogeneity of the resources in the milieu (a property we note particularly in large segments of the tropics and the Asian-African deserts) and the emphasis on the status quo tends to discourage interchange with other systems which might be present in the milieu. In fact, one of the characteristics we associate most frequently with primitive systems is their essential self-sufficiency on all dimensions . . . political, social, economic, and religious. The lack of differentiation of resources in the milieu inhibits the formation of a concept of specialization, which in turn is the prerequisite for trade among systems. This lack of specialization, in turn, inhibits moves toward social and economic differentiation, which in turn dampens the motivation for political units more complex and more encompassing than the simple extended family or clan (each of which will tend to be geographically isolated, generally because of the inability of the low-fertility regions occupied by primitive systems to support anything but widely distributed, small groups).

Hence, the *autarchic field* emerges as the unit which finds a placid-random environment occupied by essentially isolated, self-sufficient, primitive socio-economic systems . . . with little or no mechanism for innovation, intersystem exchange or differentiation. Today, we tend to find such groups only in the least fertile and least desireable areas of the globe, possibly because it is only there they have been able to avoid the confrontation with expanding, more sophisticated systems which provide perturbations against which the rigid, insular, primitive system cannot stand.

4.6.2 The Symbiont Field and the Type-II System

The second of Emery and Trist's environmental ideal-types, the *placid-clustered* case, is slightly more complex than the placid-random and therefore gives rise to a slightly more complex type of organizational response. Particularly, in the placid-clustered environment, we find essentially differentiated (e.g., hetero-geneous) properties or resources organized into clusters, where each cluster contains an essentially unique resource or property . . . such that inter-cluster variance is effectively maximized. Both the placid-random and placid-clustered cases tend to have empirical counterparts. Whereas the former tends to reflect the sparse and relatively symmetrical distribution of a single, relevant resource or property (such as seals in the Eskimo lands, reindeer in Northern Europe, or certain families of roots and berries in the tropical stretches), the placid-clustered case represents both a more usual and a richer situation. Here, in topographical terms, different points would tend to be associated with concentrations of es-sentially different resources; fish near the coast or along estuaries; grazing animals on the inland plains; fur-bearing animals in the mountains; natural grains in the river valleys of lower plateaus, etc.

When faced with a placid-clustered environment, then, the normative and apparently "natural" organizational response is *specialization*, such that systems tend to be located in a way that emphasizes their control over, or reliance on, one or another cluster among the several that comprise the milieu. In the social world, specialization is historically accompanied by exchange or trade among systems, such that the excess of a unique resource enjoyed by one system is exchanged for the excesses of other monopolized resources controlled by other systems in the field.

This type of process is reflected in the prototypical ecosystem found in the biosphere, for ethologists and ecologists have long noted the depth of specialization and interdependence found in natural contexts. In the prototypical ecosystem, each species or resident system tends to rely primarily on a single resource, which it then maximally exploits. In the process of exploitation, the system produces an output that, in turn, becomes an essential input to some other system, and so forth. A variation on this is the long and amazingly elaborate food-chains which find ecosystems organized into reticulations, such that the excess population of one system becomes the primary input for another system, etc.

The conditions of the placid-clustered milieu, accompanied by its corollaries of surplus and exchange, lend us the basis for the *symbiont field*. The essential properties of the symbiont field are that it will be occupied by as many unique systems as there are unique resource clusters, and that the welfare of the resident systems will be codeterminate. Particularly, this means that the socioeconomic system engaged in a symbiont field, like the natural system or species involved in a prototypical ecosystem, will have its growth at least partially determined by the growth of the other systems that either demand its excess output or that supply the resources requisite for its growth and development . . . in short, the congruent response to the placid-clustered environment is a set of specialized systems maintaining an essentially symbiotic relationship among each other.

The intensity of the symbiosis in such a field depends jointly on several factors:

- The degree of differentiation among clusters, with greater differentiation normally indicating greater interdependency among systems.
- The degree of specialization among the systems (or, conversely, the lack of autarchic characteristics), with greater specialization usually accompanied by greater reliance among the systems for each others' specialized outputs.
- The distance between clusters, with greater distance generally acting to discourage attempts at diversification by any one system in the symbiont field.
- The degree to which inelasticities of demand for clustered resources are present among the members of the field.*

---

*Which may be extended to mean the extent to which suitable substitutes are available for the several systems' resources or outputs.

When any or all of the conditions are present to some degree, we tend to find systems playing a positive-sum game among each other, where there is the recognition that what is good for one can, potentially, be good for all. Particularly, the wealthier, healthier, larger, and more efficient the other members of the symbiont field (or the other species present in an ecosystem), the higher will be the minimum welfare (or minimum population) any one member can achieve.

Thus, each member will be encouraged to increase the efficiency with which it exploits the particular resource it controls, or the efficiency of the processes by which it produces the output demanded by the other members. When we extend the definition of monopolized resource or output to include some specialized function, we have here the basis for the association of the bureaucratic organizational ideal-type with the placid-clustered environment, and hence our assertion that the symbiont field will tend to be comprised of systems that are effectively bureaucratic in structure and behavior.

The bureaucratic organization tends to specialize in the production of a particular output or the provision of a specific service, and may expect to grow only to the extent that that output or service is valued by other members of the field in which it operates. Efficiency is obtained by the bureaucracy to the extent that the functions associated with the organization can be mechanized, either through automation or by the provision of "rules" and algorithms which dictate precise and compartmentalized performances by individuals in those areas where machines cannot be used. In short, the bureaucracy is the organizational modality best designed to deal with a set of iterative, largely predictable environmental stimuli or demands for service or output. Many of its aspects serve this ambition directly: the emphasis on programmation and reduction of tasks to algorithmic processes; the reliance on seniority as the basis for promotion; the tendency to insulate system members from outside influences; the careful compartmentalization of authorities and responsibilities, and the sanctions against exceeding them; the rigid lines of communication and command . . . all serve to make the bureaucracy as well-behaved and predictable as the environment to which it responds. Innovation, assiduity, individuation, and experimentation are actively legislated against, especially where the output or mission of the organization is an especially critical one (as with, for example, national defense units).

Thus, in the symbiont field, systems tend to respond to the natural or contrived clusteration of different resources or prerogatives by emphasizing specialization, a cause well-served by maximizing the mechanistic (or algorithmic) properties of the organization. Where clusteration is distinct and complete, competition tends to be ignored in favor of cooperation, an ecological posture that recognizes the interdependency among systems in a symbiont field. Organizations tend to adopt a bureaucratic posture that serves to direct their energies and resources toward a highly specialized, precedented set of tasks, with the major cognitive aspects of organizational behavior being those statistical exercises aimed at forecasting demands of other systems for the particular resource, function, or output in which the system specializes. Strategic decisions, then, will be directed largely at avoiding the penalities of either over or under production, and toward avoiding political, social, or ideological conflicts that might imperil exchanges on the economic dimension. In short, the organizational response to the placid-random environment is specialization, and the ecological posture congruent with the symbiont field is compromise. In dynamic terms, what we expect to see when we look at a symbiont field through time, is a gradual (Bayesian-type) convergence on a steady state, where relations among systems are more or less stable within a relatively narrow range of input-output parameters.

In summary, then, the symbiont field is not only a relatively pleasant concept, but one that has strong biological and some historical socioeconomic precedence . . . and one that is relatively analytically tractable from the standpoint of the system analyst or social scientist. But, as we are all aware, it is also a relatively precarious entity, too easily transformed into the competitive field that we will now discuss.

4.6.3 The Competitive Field and the Type-III System

The third field is that associated with Emery and Trist's *disturbed-reactive* environment, that which occurs, according to them, when there is more than one organization of a given type operating in a bounded milieu. We may extend this to mean that there are two or more organizations each interested in controlling as large a share as possible of some scarce environmental property (e.g., a particular resource stock, a market for products or services). In such a case, control over the pertinent property tends to be *stratified*, such that each of the essentially similarly directed organizations owns some proportion of the available stock.

In the natural or biological world, we have counterparts of the disturbed-reactive environment when a particular resource is distributed rather than clustered, such that several different species (or socioeconomic systems) have their welfare and growth limits dependent upon the proportion of the resource that they can exploit over a particular interval. At any rate, when either resources themselves or interest or dependence on the resources are *stratified*, systems tend to play a zero-sum game, such that whatever gains one system makes in proportional control are perceived to be at the direct expense of the other systems. Hence the basis for the *competitive field*, where the insularity of autarchy or the compromise of symbionce is displaced by ecological exploitation . . . for each system knows that that proportion of the resource or property that it does not exploit will quickly be exploited by others.

In the competitive field, that system which does not actively seek dominance is soon dominated, and from there is either absorbed or dissolved. Thus, the system here has little recourse except to adopt the zero-sum game approach to ecological behavior, which finds it either trying to devise strategies that will advance its cause and inhibit opponents, or trying to predict inhibiting moves that opponents will inaugurate, so that adequate contingency moves or even pre-emptive actions may be developed. Here, then, the cognitive component of ecological behavior is both imperative and constant.

Organizations that have elected or have been forced to operate in a competitive field will tend to carry both structural and functional differentiation to their feasible limits. Thus, for example, modern commercial corporations tend to have each unique function performed by a morphologically unique subsystem, whereas in the bureaucratic structures associated with the symbiont field, different functions were all performed by units which looked alike (e.g., all predicated on platoonization or departmentalization). On another dimension, competitive organizations will generally tend to foster internal competition—for position, status, or rewards—in the belief that such an approach will yield an organization that is best prepared for external competition at all points. Here, also, we will tend to find expertise or objectively-audited ability displacing seniority as the criterion for promotion, and innovation, assiduity, and originality displacing the emphasis on obedience and complete predictability we associated with the bureaucratic ideal-type. This occurs because the mechanisticity and tractability valued in the symbiont field become handicaps here, where the emphasis is properly on the ability to move quickly, recover rapidly, or implement strategic moves or countermoves unlikely to have been considered by one's opponent(s). Rather than rigidity of structure, then, the competitive organization demands versatility and resilience; rather than being driven by precedent, the competitive organization will constantly be searching for new ways to exploit existing opportunities, or for techniques and individuals who can identify emergent opportunities for exploitation more quickly than others.

In short, then, if the bureaucracy is the normative resident in the symbiont field, the *technocracy* is the organizational ideal-type most apparently congruent with the competitive field. In the technocracy, system responsiveness is fostered by decentralization, system preparedness by internal competition; monopoly profits are sought by constant attention to innovation and by ensuring that the subject system can adjust to a new exploitative posture more rapidly than other systems; the lack of preprogrammation of tasks reflects the implausability of controlling or dictating the originality required of both system members and competitive systems themselves. Much in the spirit of these ideas we have seen the gradual differentiation of athletics, some government services, and the "liberalization" of many military and religious units. In all cases, the distinction between line and staff operations becomes more pronounced, differential penalty-reward schemes become more common and operations determined by "the book" less feasible.

By the same token, with the exception of such essentially collusive fabrications as oligopolistic systems or cartels, competition necessarily tends to become more intense, especially as the available stock of the pertinent resource or property declines in absolute terms. Positions in industry become less secure, the fun goes out of sports, competition tends to degenerate into conflict; and the rate at which resources and/or opportunities are exhausted apparently tends to accelerate.

In summary, then, the competitive field is characterized structurally by several systems all competing for control over a scarce property, and in the process adopting an exploitative posture with respect to both the other systems and to the property itself. On the dynamic dimension, changes in the field tend to become intelligible in terms of the changes in the coefficients of stratification (e.g., market shares and proportions of total resource stock distributed to various systems) and also in terms of perceived or real changes in the total available stock of the pertinent property.* At any rate, the behavior of the field as a whole is a function of the concatenation of strategic and counterstrategic moves made by the system residents in the spirit of the zero-sum game. In contrast to the symbiont field, where we proposed that there would be a secular convergence on some steady state, reflecting limiting values for the exchanges among member systems, no such simple concept is available to us here. In the competitive field, system analysts or organization theorists must be primarily interested in the probabilities of transition from one state to another, where these transition probabilities are estimable only in a complex game-based context with a strong deductive element. In sum, then, the competitive field represents a source of unpredictability to the member systems, and also to those who seek to understand them from outside. But as we shall now attempt to show, the competitive field does not represent the upper limit of analytical intractability . . . this title belongs to the fourth of our ideal-type constructs.

4.6.4 The Heuristic Field and the Type-IV System

The last of our ideal-type fields is that predicated upon the fourth and most complex of Emery and Trist's environmental cases, the *turbulent*. In the turbulent field, they suggest that ". . . dynamic properties arise not simply from the interactions of the component organizations, but also from the field itself."[4] From this we gather that the turbulent environment carries the potential for autochthonous change, that it is inherently indeterminate from the standpoint of the organizations operating there.

In our terms, the turbulent environment would arise from the following factors: (a) properties in the milieu are heterogeneous (e.g., protean); (b) they are distributed asymmetrically and non-algorithmically; and (c) the transformation functions driving state-changes from one period to the next are continuous, complex, and largely non-allegorizable. When faced with such an environment,

---

*Note that a perception of fixed limits on resources or properties of interest is a requisite for competitive behavior and that the symbiont field quickly becomes transformed into a competitive one when one of the members perceives an approaching limit on its specialty.

organizations are deprived of adopting a single, invariant ecological posture, or from concentrating on any single resource or set of resources. The turbulent environment must appear to organizations as engining a concatenation of unprecedented situations, such that yesterday's optimal strategy is tomorrow's anachronism.

With the properties of the environment itself in flux, and with the organizations consequently unable to rigidify or mechanize any particular ecological posture, the situation is one where the field in which these entities are united is constantly in a state of "becomming"; nothing is fixed or final. The personality and the ultimate morphology of both environment and resident organizations has yet to be determined. It is, in short, a confrontation between adolescents. Consequently, the *emergent field* is one characterized by almost equal measures of anxiety and opportunity.

The anxiety stems from the indeterminacy that pervades the emergent field. Particularly, organizations cannot presume that future states of the environment (much less of the field itself) will be calculable functions of past states; in fact the usual presumption will be, as we suggested, that successive states will be successively unprecedented. Secondly, the organizations cannot make any inferences about unseen portions of the environment on the basis of those portions that have been empirically observed and mapped; indeed, the assumption must be that properties are not distributed symmetrically, such that each new unit of space holds potentially the same surprises as each new unit of time.

But the opportunities stem from essentially the same factors, for the adolescent quality of the emergent field means that there are causal discontinuities at any given point-in-time, structural lacunae, which the alert organization can fill and exploit, however ephemerally. Most especially, however, organizations operating here have the ability to exercise trade offs that are really not available to systems resident in the other three environments. The protean and rapidly changing resource characteristics of the turbulent environment mean, for example, that the organization can substitute one resource for another during various intervals; similarly, the organization can temporarily displace one ecological posture for another that seems locally or immediately more appropriate. In short, the turbulent environment poses the fewest *a priori* constraints on the organization. In this sense, then, indeterminacy, while it may horrify the system analyst or organization theorist, offers great freedom of operation. Simply, the inchoate and metamorphical character of the turbulent environment, and hence of the emergent field itself, means that organizations need not irrevocably commit themselves to any particular resource, to any particular attitude toward other systems, or to any particular action. Alliances may come and go as local circumstances or emerging (if temporal) opportunities are recognized; systems may even be allies on one dimension (e.g., the ideological or political) and opponents on another (e.g., economic). And, finally, if success is fleeting, failure need not be complete, utter, and irreparable.

The turbulent environment carries, of course, great perils, due largely to the pervasiveness of surprises, and the inability of any single organization to pre-account for all the ramifications (e.g., second- and third-order effects) of its actions, strategies, or resource or behavioral elections. The future in the turbulent environment is abjectly indeterminate; the past is fraught with causal discontinuities or characterized by such great variance that precedent and experience become gratuitous. The wealth of situations that might occur in the turbulent environment, and the consequently wide range of strategic and tactical options open to all resident systems, makes simple game-based behavior precarious . . . largely because the range of alternative events or system-moves is too large to be manageable. All these thrusts and parries, the array of opportunities created, accepted, or foregone, all the reactions and actions with indeterminate ultimate consequences will cause the field to *undulate*, to appear to have a complex life of its own in the parade of temporal gestalten it presents. In short, the complexity of the interchanges among systems, and between systems and environment, will resonate with such range and power that the basic character of the field itself will alter . . . in consequence if not in sympathy.

Quite obviously, when faced with such a situation, the congruent organization will be one that attempts to wind its way through this *a priori* unallegorizable (and therefore unpredictable) domain in such a way that will minimize the probability of inescapable analytical errors (e.g., errors in prediction, forecasting, or expectations) becoming translated into dysfunctional actions. The paradigm that seems to serve this cause is the *heuristic* modality which finds the system operating through disciplined trial and error, with the discipline being in the form of artificial yet formal rules for determining which path among all alternatives should be taken at some point-in-time . . . and rules that allow us to distinguish good from bad moves. In short, organizational decision- and policy-making in the emergent field becomes an exercise in the hypothetico-deductive method, as the properties of the turbulent environment make inductive inference a precarious engine for operation. The heuristic system will be one that relies more on real-time feedback, control, and modification processes than on any pre-established plans or performance criteria; it will be one whose structure is more reflective of the *adhocratic* ideal-type proposed by Toffler[8] than of the bureaucracy, whose limitations are well articulated by, among many others, Warren Bennis;[9] it will be one that acts to delay irrevocable committments of resources and/or action until the last possible moment; it will be one whose activities, in aggregate, are housed within a disciplined "learning" context, such that to the extent possible, *a priori* indeterminate phenomena in the field may gradually be transformed into *a posteriori* deterministic ones.*

---

*These properties, essentially, will form the basis for the "heuristic" administrative modality discussed in some detail in Chapter 8.

In summary, then, the heuristic behavioral modality is entirely congruent with the ill-structured, protean, and metamorphical turbulent environment, and especially well-suited to the generation of original (creative) responses to the flow of unprecedented circumstances which there present themselves. An organization operating here would, therefore, reflect scientific, professional, or creative enterprises rather more than the automatic (ritualistic), bureaucratic (mechanistic), or technocratic organizations that populated the other fields.

Finally, in the real-world, there is a tendency to suggest that the emergent field is the proper reference for post-industrial society, with its organismic concept of the *global village* in which each system affects every other in generally unpredictable, unallegorized ways (if not directly, then through the sympathetic alterations of the field itself). And, indeed, there are some factors today that tend to move us toward the kind of complexity associated with the emergent field, among them: (a) the multi-national corporations displacing local actors on the economic dimension; (b) the increasing interdependency of economic and political factors, such that determinants tend to evolve from the historically singular to the currently plural; (c) the growing strength of ideological-politico blocs as opposed to nation-states; (d) the international aspects of finance, science, and reformation; (e) the secularization that makes the axiological predicates of individual and social behavior more elusive and empirically inaccessible, and that disables some of our ability to develop classes of post-industrial actors; and (f) the regressive tendency to replace principle with opportunism and *ad hoc* justification of actions, both individually and collectively (which means that predictability of behavior becomes more difficult).

Thus we conceive of the emergent field as the most complex and analytically intractable of our ideal-types, born as it is in the interstices between heuristically-driven organizations and the turbulent environment. But it is here that we must look for the great deflection points in history, for this is the domain of change, the field of flux. Here, as in no other defined field, both the environment and the resident systems are free to change in non-algorithmic ways, at their own volition or in sympathetic response to resonations of indeterminate origin. There is, naturally, some anxiety associated with residence in an ill-structured, emergent milieu. But there is also an opportunity that is not available in any other field-type . . . the opportunity to take advantage of the lack of structure and stability, and to create, however fleetingly, one's *own* environment.

In summary, in this chapter we have emerged with four organizational ideal-types, four environmental ideal-types, and four fields (which are "ordered" pairs of organizational- and environmental-types). We are pretty well finished with our definition of phenomena that system scientists might legitimately expect to encounter, yet these organizational, environmental, and field taxonomies will provide the basic units of analyses for all the work which is to follow.

Particularly in the next chapter, as we begin to discuss the analytical instruments available to the system scientist, we shall show that the four ideal-type

SYSTEM TYPE

	I. Deterministic	II. Moderately Stochastic	III. Severely Stochastic	IV. Indeterminate
CHARACTERISTIC:	Certainty	Probabilisticity	Risk	Meta-risk
ASSOCIATED INSTRUMENT CLASS:	Optimization	Extrapolative	Game-based; simulative	Heuristic; learning
ANALYTICAL BASE:	Positivistic	Inductivistic	Deductivistic	Meta-theoretical
RELATIVE CON-TRIBUTION OF:				
(a) Factual or Data Component	Highest	High	Low	Lowest
(b) Judgmental or Model Component	Lowest	Low	High	Highest

Figure 4.19 Table of system analysis logic.

systems (and analytical ideal-types) have direct relevance for us; for each will be the target of a specific subset of the analytical instruments. That is, if we take the entire arsenal of quantitative and qualitative analysis tools and techniques, we can neatly partition it into categories that are "congruent" with one or another of our ideal-type systems, as is shown in Figure 4.19.

4.7 NOTES AND REFERENCES

1. See, in this respect, my review of George Klir's "An Approach to General System Theory," in *The International Journal of General Systems*, 1 no. 1 (1974), pp. 76–78.
2. Many of the suggestions about the efficiency of science used in this book emerged rather directly or indirectly from a reading of James B. Conant's brilliant book, *Modern Science and Modern Man* (New York: Doubleday-Anchor, 1952), *passim*.
3. An excellent discussion of these two approaches to phenomenal explanation is given in Herbert Simon's "The Organization of Complex Systems," *Hierarchy Theory*, ed. Howard H. Pattee (New York: George Braziller, 1973), pp. 3–27.
4. The vehicle on which we rely for most of our theoretical treatment or organizational environments is that provided by Emery and Trist in their now rather famous paper, "The Causal Texture of the Environment," *Human Relations*, 18 (1965), pp. 21–32. In this work they define four ideal-type environmental "states" the simplest of which is the *placid* and the most complex of which they term the *turbulent* environment. Basically, their field types are defined in terms of the nature of the distribution of resources,

on the complexity of the interchange between the resident systems, and on the possibility of the fields themselves exerting some determining force on the character and behavior of the systems. Here, however, we introduce the implications of the field types largely by inference, leaving the paper itself as the essential source for readers wishing to know more about Emery and Trist's work with environmental textures.

5. The last aspect of the dynamic dimension refers to the very important phenomenon of *equifinality*, where an equifinal system is one that may product the same outcome from any of several different starting-states. For an analysis of the theoretical implications of this property, see G. H. Waddington's "The Theory of Evolution Today," *Beyond Reductionism: New Perspectives in the Life Science* ed. Koestler and Smithies, (New York: Macmillan Publishing Company, 1969).

6. In this respect, see William Shirer's *The Rise and Fall of the Third Reich* (New York: Simon and Shuster, 1959), p. 81.

7. We are thinking here, particularly, of the type of system that Alvin Toffler so aptly described as *adhocracies* (as compared with bureaucracies) . . . more or less temporary organizations that come in and out of being to solve especially complex problems as they arise. For a full description of their properties, see Toffler's *Future Shock* (New York: Random House, 1974), Chapter 7. Toffler himself credits Warren Bennis with the seminal idea for the adhocracy, and cites Bennis's "Beyond Bureaucracy," *Transaction* (July–August 1965), pp. 31–35, as a prime source.

8. Toffler, *op. cit.*, p. 112–135.

9. See, especially, Warren Bennis's *Changing Organizations* (New York: McGraw-Hill, 1966).

PART II
INSTRUMENTS AND METHODS

In this second part of the book, we turn to a discussion of the instrumental and methodological bases of the system sciences. In short, we shall be concerned with operations and procedures in the final four chapters. Thus, Chapter 5 introduces the logic of system analysis and the analytical instruments that constitute the system science's arsenal. There we introduce the single most important concept relative to analytical operations . . . the concept of *congruence*. In essence, congruence demands that systems be attacked using that particular analytical modality—and that particular subset of instruments—which promises to be most effective and efficient, given the properties of the problem at hand. Chapter 6 then turns to a discussion of *general problem-solving*, significantly extending the logic of system analysis. Particularly, we there introduce a broad procedural algorithm known as the system architecture paradigm . . . a platform for the disciplined, systematic solution of problems, with facilities for handling the most complex as well as the simplest phenomena. It is there, then, that we have a chance to become familiar with the "technology" of system analysis and design. While Chapter 6 concentrates on procedures for the design of problem-solving systems, Chapter 7 begins to attack two major applications of system analysis: (a) policy-setting and (b) decision-making. We shall see that the establishment of rational policies is roughly the equivalent to the design of *normative* systems . . . that is, systems that inhere desired properties, and hence serve as the setting in which "utopian" or favorable futures may be realized. The procedure set out in the first part of the seventh chapter thus also serves as an introduction to the technology of *large-scale system design*. The second part of the seventh chapter deals with the procedures for normal decision-making, and for extending the bounds of decision rationality in a systematic way. The eighth and final chapter then attempts to integrate the work of the seven previous chapters, outlining a system approach to *organization, administration, and control.* It is there that the immediate impact of the system sciences may be felt most keenly, and there that we find the appropriate point for concluding this present study of system science concepts.

5
The Logic of System Analysis

5.0 INTRODUCTION

We emerged from Part I equipped with an array of integrated ideal-types, that is, the four final constructs in Figure 4.16. We arrived at these by looking for certain predominant "patterns" of association between the various dimensional ideal-types we defined, suggesting that some patterns would tend to reflect conditions of congruence, and therefore be more probable than others we might have established. The logic that led us to this conclusion was that certain ecological postures would be the congruent responses to certain environmental conditions, and would in turn lead to the establishment of certain domain or structural properties; these, in their turn, would in large part determine the dynamic or behavioral aspects of a system, marking its overall behavior as approximate to one or another of our analytical ideal-types: the deterministic, moderately stochastic, severely stochastic, or indeterminate referents of Section 4.2. What we only obliquely suggested was that there were also definite analytical and administrative implications associated with a system being approximate to one or another of these analytical ideal-types, an assertion which we make explicit with Figure 5.1.

It is in this chapter that we want to examine the *analytical* implications of a system being deterministic, moderately stochastic, severely stochastic, or indeterminate, whereas Chapter 8 will examine the *administrative* implications of the various analytical states a system might approximate. In short, what we want to accomplish here is an explanation of the concept of analytical *congruence* . . . the condition that finds us employing the right scientific instrument, in the right way, at the right time.

The importance of analytical congruence cannot be overstated. For, as we suggested in the Foreword, there is a strong and debilitating tendency for the social, behavioral, and administrative sciences to be polarized on the methodological dimension. Polarization finds disciplines split into distinct camps, where one suggests that *the* way to comprehend the phenomena of interest is to approach

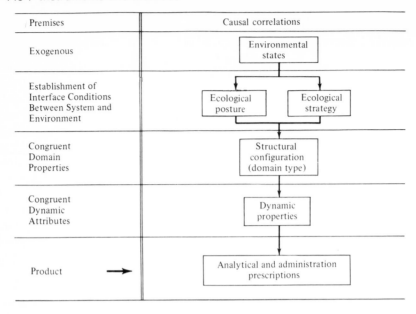

Premises	Causal correlations
Exogenous	Environmental states
Establishment of Interface Conditions Between System and Environment	Ecological posture Ecological strategy
Congruent Domain Properties	Structural configuration (domain type)
Congruent Dynamic Attributes	Dynamic properties
Product →	Analytical and administration prescriptions

Figure 5.1 Strategic correlations.

them qualitatively, while the other camp employs the various guises of empiricism: reductionism, formal analysis, generation of "localized" hypotheses, controlled experimentation, and finally some limited attempt at development of constrained generalizations via inductive inference.

The output of the former camp generally evinces a semi-evangelistic, usually imprecise, and somewhat idiographic quality . . . these are the paradigms, models, and deductive systems spawned by the "grand theory builders," amazing in their scope, usually highly productive of ideas and argumentation, but often a bit weak in terms of real explanatory power or in terms of their ability to generate operational prescriptions with respect to specific real-world problems. And sometimes, like the Ptolemaic thesis in astronomy, they are downright wrong. But if the products of the "rhetorical" camp have these faults, those of the other camp—the positivist-inductivist—have a distinct tendency to be trivial, glorying in their precision often at the expense of any significance.[2]

As we also explained in the introduction, these camps tend to be founded on what are largely *a prioristic*, fact-independent biases. But, as we also explained there, there is absolutely no methodological approach that may be *rationally* supported independent of the properties of the problem at hand. This proposition is the cornerstone of the methodological significance of the system sciences, and harks back to that Aristotelian dictate from his *Nichomachean Ethics* which we earlier quoted,

It is the mark of an educated man to look for precision in each class of thing just so far as the nature of the subject admits. It is evidently equally as foolish to accept probabilistic reasoning from a mathematician as to expect from a rhetorician rigorous proofs.

What this means for us, in practice, is that there will be a potentially unique approach to each unique problem we encounter—as emerging properties dictate. But because problems tend to naturally approximate one or another of our analytical ideal-types, we will have to consider four basic (generic) system approaches . . . one for each category: deterministic, moderately stochastic, severely stochastic, and indeterminate. Fortunately, the analytical instruments available to the modern sciences break down rather neatly into subcategories that are especially congruent with one or another of these analytical categories. This correlative tendency will be the major focus of our work in this chapter.

The by-product of our discussions here will hopefully be the *empiricalization* of some of the methodological (epistemological) issues that, in the absence of the kind of perspective the system scientist can provide, tend to remain largely rhetorical. And, here, we have an opportunity to briefly introduce the reader to the major instruments of analysis in the system science's arsenal, an introduction that is perhaps somewhat overdue. Before we can appreciate the specific properties of the various system analysis procedures we shall be introducing, it is well to take a brief look at system analysis as a phenomenon in its own right.

5.1 INFORMATION STATES AND LEVELS OF ANALYSIS

The applied scientist is primarily a model-builder. The models he builds are intended to capture the properties of real-world phenomena that he wishes to describe, predict, or reconstruct. These models may, moreover, take several different forms: mathematical, statistical, metaphorical, physical (i.e., simulative), or some combination of these modalities. The substance that drives models, and provides their structure, is *information* . . . and information is the output from an analysis exercise. In short, the scientist engages in research and analysis in order to generate the information necessary for the construction of accurate models of predictive or descriptive significance.

In this chapter, we shall be concerned with information in three guises:

(a) There is the stock of *a priori* information. This is the knowledge we possess or think we possess (about a system) that exists prior to the inauguration of a formal, dedicated analysis process. That is, it is knowledge whose roots are to be found in theory, intuition, or other non-empirical predications. Thus, were we to set the analysis process in a time frame-work, the *a priori* stock of information would be that which we possess at time t_0. That is, it is information we have obtained without any current analytical expenditures or empirical observations on the subject immediately at hand.

(b) There is the succession of *a posteriori* information stocks. These are the aggregations of information which have been acquired by iterations of analyses aimed at empirically capturing (and inductively ordering) the emerging properties of the system at hand. More generally, these information stocks are the products of incremental expenditures of analytical resources. Thus, if the *a priori* information stock exists at time t_0 in the analysis process, the *a posteriori* stocks are those that exist at times $t_1 \ldots t_n$; and each has a direct expenditure of analytical resources associated with its generation.

(c) There is an information stock that we will call the *real*. This is an abstraction that both the *a priori* and *a posteriori* stocks seek to approximate, for it houses our expectations about the "limits" of information available about the entity under investigation. That is, it serves as a reference point against which we can measure the relative quality of the *a priori* and *a posteriori* information stocks at any point in the analysis process. The limiting state of information available about some entity may have several origins:

- It may result from past experience with the same or similar problems.
- It may be a product of intuition or some other idiographic mechanism.
- It may be a product of deductive inference—disciplined judgement— such that the properties of the real state are derived from some theoretical platform.

At any rate, the real information stock represents our expectations about what can be achieved by the analysis process in its role as a producer of model-oriented information.*

The analysis process, then, is the vehicle by which we attempt to move from a less favorable *a priori* informational state at time t_0 to more favorable ones at times $t_1 \ldots t_n$. Time t_n may, for the moment, be thought of as the point where we feel that the currently existing *a posteriori* information stock has adequately exhausted the postulated properties of the real information stock. Graphically, the process looks like that shown in Figure 5.2.

This curve is what we shall refer to as the *normative learning curve*. It shows that increased expenditures of analytical resources (time, energy, computational cost, man-hours, etc.) are expected to result in a more accurate model in either of two ways:

- If the model we are building is predictive (or if we are trying to causally reconstruct some historical event), then a reduction in error is realized when events predicted by the model and events that actually occur are identical . . . or to the extent that the *variance* between predicted and actual events declines.

*Chapter 6 will undertake a more exhaustive treatment of the various information stocks and their operational implications.

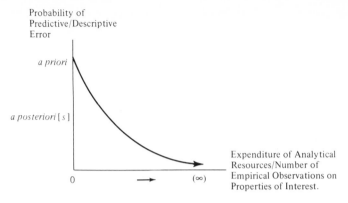

Figure 5.2   The normative learning curve.

- If the model we are building is intended to serve as a descriptive allegory, then error declines to the extent that we realize a *morphological correlation* between the real-world entity and the properties of the model.

If, then, we were to establish some sort of generic objective function for the system analyst *qua* model-builder, it would be that he should act in ways that will minimize the error component of the predictive/descriptive constructs he builds. What this means, in essence, is that his models will then be more representative of reality, his allegories more valuable. There is, however, an equivocation we must enter, for there are some phenomena which simply do not warrant much expenditure of effort or energy—e.g., those that, even if we are wrong about them, carry very little penalty for us in terms of expected loss or cost.

Thus we must insert the concept of economic marginality, asking that the system analyst seek to acquire information that will minimize the error component of the models he builds up to the point where expenditures for the acquisition of information are equal to (or just slightly less than) the expected value of the information. We shall, shortly, define the expected value of information in a more formal way, simply noting here that this rule is the equivalent of the micro-economic law that asks that firms produce up to the point where marginal revenue equals marginal cost.*

This dictate brings us squarely to the most difficult problem we shall face in this chapter ... the problem of assessing the value of information during an analysis process. For our ability to accomplish this is the key factor in determining when to stop information collection and analysis, and inaugurate some action. There are two basic modalities at our disposal for making the decision to conclude analysis: the empirical and the deductive. The empirical

*On a natural growth curve, of the type we shall employ in Chapter 7, this would be the point where the second derivative of the input/output (cost/revenue) function reaches unity.

modality is available to us when the problem at hand (or the system we are trying to analyze) is a precedented one, such that we have some historical experience with it or with the class to which it belongs. In this case, statistical or inductive criteria will dictate when we have acquired sufficient information ... when we have, in effect, attained an *a posteriori* information stock that adequately exhausts the *real*. When such an experiential base is denied us—where the problem at hand is an unprecedented one or where we have not kept an audit of our previous problem-solving exercises—we are forced to use the deductive modality. This latter modality is of most interest to us here.

The first step is to consider that any real-world phenomenon we encounter will be amenable to modeling on any or all of four dimensions or *levels* of analysis:

(a) The *state-variable* level. Here we try to identify the major structural or qualitative aspects of the entity at hand—the determinants of the system.

(b) The *parametric* level. This involves the assignment of specific numerical (or precise qualitative) values to the state-variables for specific points in time or space.

(c) The *relational* level. This involves establishing the nature of the relationships among the state-variables (i.e., the array of interfaces and the major directions in influence).

(d) The *coefficient* level. Here we assign specific numerical or magnitudinal values to the interfaces among state-variables.

In a sense, we are already somewhat familiar with these terms and their implications. First of all, the concept of a state-variable is the direct equivalent of the concept of a system component in our discussions of "mapping" on the structural dimension of systems. In other words, state-variables are the components of a system. They may refer to structural (configurational) entities such as the individuals comprising a group, the machines comprising a manufacturing process, the subsystems comprising some macrosystem, the inputs to a transformation process or any other factor which would fall within the *domain* of a system. But an array of state-variables for a system would also have to include those exogenous factors that in some way determine the system's condition, those environmental entities or properties to which the system responds (or which it affects). Thus the array of state-variables pertinent to a system should exhaust the relevant components of both system and milieu. They are "state" variables, therefore, because they determine the system's condition and contribute to its identity; they are "variables" because they are assigned specific values (quantitative or qualitative) at specific points in time or space (or, for continuous systems, over specific intervals). The point or interval values that they are assigned are the system *parameters*. In formal mathematical terms, parameters always are assumed to receive a value exogenously, yet here we will relax this assumption, suggesting that the values may be determined either exogenously or endogenously. At any rate, as was suggested, the parametric values that are assigned state-variables may be either numerical values or qualitative values, these latter being rather precisely defined but basically "fuzzy" terms (e.g., high, low, intermediate, black, white, red, deterministic, stochastic, indeterminate, bureacratic, adhocratic, technocratic, segmented, differentiated, mixed, etc.).[3]

Considering systems on their relational level, we again have a parallel. For the relational components of a system are the prevailing relationships among system components, which constituted another of the major targets of "mapping" on the structural dimension. It was the nature of the relationships among components that, for example, determined whether a system was linear or nonlinear; it was the nature of the relationships among components that determined whether a system was additive or synergistic, etc. Basically, then, on the relational level, we are intrested in allegorizing the nature of the interface conditions that prevail among all state-variables, and particularly whether they are related linearly or nonlinearly, positively or negatively, and where causality lies (e.g., are the state-variables capable of codeterminacy as in a network or is causality assumed to be unidirectional as in the strict hierarchy).[*]

The point here is that, on the relational level, we establish the basic nature and direction of relationships among system components (both endogenous and exogenous), relying on the coefficient level to assign specific point or interval values to these interfaces. Thus, for example, it may be enough on the relational level to suggest that two state-variables tend to be related positively, such that an increase in the one is followed by an increase in the other. But on the coefficient level, we must assign a specific *magnitude* to this relationship (e.g., suggesting, for example, that as x increases, y increases by k, where k is a specific numerical value). Thus, in a sense, the coefficient level does for the relational aspects of a system what the parametric level did for the state-variables ... it provides more specificity. In this sense, then, relationships among system components are also considered to be variables, variables that must be assigned specific values in order to complete the model of a system. As with the parametric level, the values that are assigned relational variables may be either quantitative or qualitative. Thus, where we were not able to determine the numerical association between x and y, our coefficient could have been phrased in a "fuzzy" way (e.g., x and y are "strongly" related).

Through these four levels of analysis, virtually any phenomenon becomes susceptible to modeling. The state-variable and the relational levels provide the essential ingredients for a structural "map" of the system that is expected to maintain itself through some significant interval in time, whereas the specification of the parametric and coefficient levels, expectedly more ephemeral, adds precision and detail to our system description (model). The *precision* of a system model will therefore be determined by the extent to which parametric

---

[*]See, again, Section 2.4.

and coefficient values are numericalized (and, carrying this a step further, by the number of significant digits to which we take them). Its accuracy will have to be determined in ways we already mentioned, with predictive models being evaluated in terms of the variance between predicted and actual events, and with descriptive models being evaluated in terms of the morphological correlation between actual system configurations and the substance of the allegory or model itself.

There is one more thing to be mentioned, something that should be obvious to all those readers with a mathematical background ... these four levels correspond directly to the levels we employ whenever we write a mathematical equation or system of equations. In this respect, consider the following:

$$y = \frac{x + zx^n}{w}$$

The state-variables in this equation are x, z, and w; the relational components are: the "+" operator between the two terms in the numerator, the implicit multiplier between z and x, the division operator between the numerator and denominator, and the exponential operator assigned to x in the second term of the numerator. In order to determine a value for y (pertinent to some specific point-in-time), we now have to move to the parametric and coefficient levels. For the former, we would have to assign specific values to the state-variables, x, z, and w; on the coefficient level, we would have to assign some specific value to n. At that point, the value for y would be determined. This logic would apply irrespective of the complexity of the equation or equational system with which we are working. And the logic also applies to models other than those that are mathematical in nature ... for physical, verbal, metaphorical, simulative, or any other type of predictive or descriptive model still would require attention to all four levels of analysis, such that the concept of a model becomes intelligible in the same terms despite any superficial differences as to precision or form of terms, etc.*

Having these four levels of analysis at hand, we may reconsider our basic analytical ideal-types. In a somewhat constrained sense, deterministic systems now become those where all but the parametric level are assumed fixed. That is, we anticipate no alterations in the state-variables, the relational components or the coefficients comprising the system. Moreover, whatever changes are allowed on the parametric level must involve a very special property ... the determination of a value for any one state-variable must automatically set the values for all others that are related to the first state-variable. In short, the only things that we expect to change are the parametric values assigned the system at

---

*That is, even if the model we are building is a strictly qualitative (e.g., verbal) one, a proper and complete system allegory would have to contain information pertinent to all four levels. In this case, rather than having numerical parametric and coefficient values, we would have "fuzzy" or qualitative values.

specific points-in-time (or during specific intervals), and these must change in an entirely predictable way. The moderately stochastic system now becomes intelligible as one where coefficients and parameters may change, but where state-variables and relationships remain constant. This is entirely consistent with the definition of the moderately-stochastic system given in Chapter 3, as only the magnitudes of the functional relationships between inputs and outputs from singular sets were allowed to fluctuate within some range. The severely-stochastic system now becomes one where basic relationships among state-variables are allowed to change, which in turn means that changes will occur in coefficient and parametric values. The worst of all possible worlds, then, would be that where the basic components of which the system is comprised—the state-variables—are inconsistant, such that the basic substance and nature of the system may change through time. These points are summarized in Figure 5.3.

These definitions do not replace those that we gave for the analytical ideal-types in Section 4.1; they complement them.* And they serve a very definite purpose for us, for we can make empirically-predicated assignments of real-world systems to one or another of these abstract categories on the basis of the nature of the historical alterations that system has exhibited through time . . . assuming the system at hand has a history (if not, then we are left to the deductive techniques outlined in the previous chapter). At any rate, the logic here is simple enough . . . systems that have the capability of altering their basic components (Type-IV systems) will be potentially the most difficult to predict, and possibly the most difficult to "map" as well, as the properties on the structural dimension may be altering more rapidly than we can sample. By the same token, where only the values assigned parameters can change, the prediction and description problems are considerably simplified.

This point becomes especially important when we consider the situation where we have previously made a model of the system at hand. In the case of the deterministic system, to up-date that model requires only the addition of new values for parameters, whereas the up-dating of the models associated with the other system types will all require more major revisions . . . and perhaps complete and perhaps rather frequent redefinition when the system with which we are concerned approximates the indeterminate ideal-type. In those cases where we are approaching a system for the first time—where the model is an un-precedented one—we will have some rather specific points to make . . . as the category to which a system belongs will have considerable impact on the methods, efficiency, and ultimate accuracy of any modeling exercises we undertake. (These differences are the subject of the third section of this chapter.)

*That the two sets of definitions are not strictly substitutes is easily seen. For example, the definitions given in Section 4.1 for the analytical ideal-types, per se, simply asks about the predictability of a system on any dimension. In this respect, a system could have variances more widely distributed than those simply on the parametric level, and still be deterministic. In general, however, a *majority* of deterministic systems we encounter will be those with only a capability for parametric change, a point that will be made clearer in subsequent chapters.

SYSTEM-TYPE	PERFORMANCE CHARACTERISTICS	SUBSTANTIVE EXAMPLES
I. Deterministic	Only parametric changes through time, where relationships among parametric values are highly programmed.	Finite-state automata; mechanical (automated) production processes; highly institutionalized social systems; steady-state systems.
II. Moderately Stochastic	Possibility of some fluctuations at the coefficient level, leading to parametric changes within some "range" (e.g., changes at the macro level only).	Promotional elasticities; genetic processes; demand parameters for established products; market shares for oligopolistic industries; input-output functions for man-machine systems; automobile mileage.
III. Severely Stochastic	Some changes in basic relationships among factors, leading to coefficient and parametric alterations . . . state-variables fixed through the interval in question.	Stochastic-state machines; political elections between established parties; athletic contests; meteorological phenomena; relationships between human beings or interest groups; military "games."
IV. Indeterminate	Changes in the basic components of the system (e.g., fluctuation in basic state-variables) that yields potential changes on all other levels.	Political alliances and "blocs" at the international level; the fashion industry's market; impaired (e.g., psychotic) behavioral systems; heuristic machines; properties of post-industrial society; axiological systems.

Figure 5.3 System properties and levels of analysis.

Here, however, we may move ahead by mentioning an obvious corollary to these discussions. If we make an error in our modeling exercises, the *seriousness* of that error will be largely determined by the level at which it is made. In most cases, and we will not attempt to qualify this here, the neglect of a critical state-variable or the addition of a state-variable that is not actually involved in the system will lead to the highest levels of predictive or descriptive error. Next most-serious is to misrepresent the nature or direction of the relationship among state-variables (e.g., to enter a positive relationship where the relationship is negative, or to assume a relationship to be additive when it is really nonlinear). The results of such an error will resonate throughout the model, producing predictions or descriptions that may be way out of line. Less serious is to misread a coefficient, to make an error in the magnitude of the relationship between state-variables. While this will still cause the predictions to be in error, it does not affect the basic description of the system's structure at the fundamental levels, and will yield only magnitudinal predictive errors (e.g., errors that are matters of degree rather than of quality). The same thing may be said of parametric errors; they also will affect predictions, but will result in less gross misreadings than errors made at the other levels. The substantiation of this proposition about higher-level errors resulting in more serious mispredictions or misdescriptions is not simply an intuitive one . . . the reader can check it by actually introducing errors at the various levels into existing models, or by examining historical instances of error.

For example, in an earlier section we raised the decision to fight inflation by the imposition of a surtax.* In terms available to us now, we see that there was a serious mistake made on the very highest level—the state-variable level—in the neglect of expectations as determinates of economic behavior. At the relational level, there was the basic error in assuming the surtax and spending to be negatively related (when, in fact, an increase in the surtax caused an increase in spending). Obviously, with errors at these levels, the entire model of the economic process used as the premise for the surtax decision was a most profoundly inappropriate one.

In summary, then, the information acquired during a system analysis process (whose properties we have barely begun to explore) will be directed toward the completion of models on one or more of the four levels: state-variable, relational, coefficient, and parametric. There are certain special cases, however, that should be mentioned. In dealing with the behavioral dimension of systems in Chapter 3, we suggested that we might work at either the micro or macro level. In the case of the latter, all we are really concerned about are the parametric values that are assumed by the system, the relationship between inputs and outputs yielding a function at the coefficient level. In micro analysis, we are not really concerned about the parametric and coefficient levels, but simply about the state-variables and their relationships modeled in gross terms (e.g., directional influences). There will be other cases where we simply do not need a complete system description, being content to treat structural aspects as a "black box," or ignoring certain levels. In general, however, when we speak of model-building in the pages to come, we are speaking of the process of developing *exhaustive allegories*, those that are developed on all four levels of analysis and that have pretentions to being complete system descriptions or effectively "optimal" predictive vehicles. With this in mind, we may now return to a problem we left a while ago . . . the problem of arriving at a value for information acquired as a result of analysis.

5.2 IMPUTING A VALUE TO INFORMATION

We are already familiar with the concept of the event-probability distribution from earlier sections. It may serve us rather well again within the present context. Consider, for example, that at each level of analysis, the process of model-building involves the determination of the "best" components to include in the model . . . those that promise to best serve the causes of prediction or description. Obviously, the first decision we must make refers to the selection of that particular array of state-variables which promises to most fully exhaust the real structural determinants of the system. That is, from among the universe of factors available to us, we must select that subset which, in our best estimation, represents the complete set of state-variables. The second level decision refers

*This example was given in Section 1.4.

to the problem of establishing the relationships among these state-variables; again, this is accomplished by assigning each pair of interacting state-variables that particular interface alternative, from among the entire array of alternatives available to us, that most closely approximates or mirrors reality. The same thing is true in deciding on a particular coefficient value for each interface or a particular point value for each state-variable. Thus, *a model-building exercise is a sequence of decisions* . . . decisions that find us isolating, at each point in the model, that component expected to be most accurate or useful from among all others we could have selected. Thus, each point in a model may be conceived of as having an event-probability distribution imposed on it, where the "events" could be any of the following:

- The set of alternative parametric values that a specific state-variable may assume.
- The set of alternative coefficient values that a particular interface (i.e., set of state-variables) may assume . . . that is, a specific magnitude of inter-relationship.
- The array of alternative sets of state-variables we might employ to establish the structural aspects of an entity . . . alternative sets of determinants proposed as fully exhausting the structural properties of the phenomenon we are treating.
- The array of alternative relational conditions that a specific set of purportedly interrelated state-variables might evoke at a specific point in time (or space).

Clearly, now, some event-probability distributions will be more favorable than others, reflecting as it were, greater degrees of confidence in our knowledge about a problem or some system we are trying to predict or describe. And considering the normative learning curve introduced in Figure 5.2, we would expect that *a posteriori* event-probability distributions would be more favorable than *a priori* . . . that the increase in information obtained between these states would be reflected in more highly-disciplined, lower-variance probability curves. In short, the utility of analysis—and hence of the information the analysis process generates—is found in its ability to cause favorable transformations in event-probability distributions surrounding each component of a model we are building. And if the "normative" learning curve holds sway, we should be able to note transformations something like that illustrated in Figure 5.4.

The main point of the figure is that the *a posteriori* event-probability distribution represents a more favorable informational condition than the *a priori* because: (a) the more outlying events which were assigned positive probabilities of occurrence in the *a priori* phase have been eliminated from consideration in the *a posteriori*, and (b) there is a more constrained (or localized) density of probabilities for those events remaining in the *a posteriori* distribution. In short, the *a posteriori* distribution entails much less *variance* than the *a priori*,

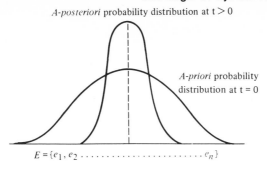

Figure 5.4 The transformation function.

and therefore represents a situation of greater certainty about the event that will occur. As a result, the expected value of an error with the model of some real-world system is lower in the *a posteriori* than the *a priori* case.

By way of illustration, suppose that we faced, at some point-in-time, the problem of estimating the magnitude of the relationship between two state-variables (determinants) of a system. In the *a priori* phase, before the start of empirical observations, let us say that we have only the vaguest notion of the value that might be assumed. More specifically, we know with assurity only this: the value that the coefficient may assume may not be lower than some x nor greater than some y. Thus the *a priori* event-probability distribution we will establish will be similar to that of the diagram . . . x and y are assigned the lowest positive probabilities of occurrence and, therefore, rest at the tails of a probably normal distribution. Once we begin observations on the empirical relationship between the state-variables, we will expect the *a priori* distribution (wide and flat) to gradually be transformed into one which converges on some specific value.

When the event-probability distribution spawned by successive observations begins to find a "limit" at some value, and when successive observations do not yield significantly different estimates, we can assume that we have pretty well exhausted the informational potential associated with this particular aspect of the system we are modeling. In short, the value that we will then enter into our emerging model for the particular interface under investigation is that coefficient estimator converged on by the successive *a posteriori* distributions. In the case of the diagram we have used, this turns out to be the central estimate, the mid-point between x and y. We did this not by coincidence but to make a critical point: even if the most likely estimates yielded by the *a priori* and *a posteriori* probability distributions are the same, the *a posteriori* is still more favorable for we are *more certain* about its prescriptions than we are with the *a priori*. So, was the expenditure of time, dollars, and effort required to produce the *a posteriori* distribution wasted? Not from the standpoint of the information theorist. To him, the "value" of information is directly related to its ability to cause just such a convergence, which in turn forces a reduction in the potential variance or error associated with an estimator to be entered into a model purporting to predict and/or describe some real-world entity.

This point may not be immediately clear, but it is critical in terms of the perspective it lends us. First, if a model is comprised of many such estimation processes, each estimator carrying with it a specific index-of-accuracy (or conversely, a probability of error), then the aggregate index-of-expected-error we would associate with the model as a whole would be some product of the error estimates associated with its components. Thus, by acting to minimize the expected error associated with each component of the model, we also act to decrease the variance or error we expect to find with the model as a whole (and this becomes especially critical when we recognize that errors in an integrated model tend to behave concatenatively, not simply additively).

We now have one more step to take before approaching the problem of estimating the value of information within the confines of the systems analysis process. It consists, basically, of formally defining the concept of the *expected value of an error*. This is a bivariate function, the product of the following factors:

- The probability of an error of a given magnitude occurring.
- The absolute cost (or loss) expected should that magnitude of error be realized.

Now although there are other units we might use under special circumstances, we will usually try to estimate the cost or loss associated with errors we might make in terms of some standard unit, like dollars.* Thus, were we, for example, building a model to predict demand levels for some product we are marketing, or trying to develop a model that would estimate the number of case workers we should hire and train, the relationship between errors of estimation in the entering of the model's components and the cost of those errors is direct ... either under- or over-supply might result in both actual and potential (opportunity) costs. The normative construct we would impose, then, is given in Figure 5.5.

As the best estimator for some event we are trying to predict is increasingly inaccurate, we must expect to incur successively greater losses *if* we act on that estimate. Generally speaking, then, greater magnitudes of error carry with them greater absolute costs.

Thus it is more costly to oversupply a product by 1,000 units than by 100. Similarly, it is more costly to have overestimated the demand for caseworkers by 10 than by 3, etc. As for the second factor—the probability of incurring an error of a given magnitude—we have already suggested that we want it to decrease with informational acquisitions. That is, information has its direct

---

*e.g., in Section 7.1, we show that we can deal, in a relatively disciplined way, with qualitative or "fuzzy" variables as well as with quantitative values. Thus, the expected value of a loss might be measured with respect to the qualitative difference between two "fuzzy" sets representing alternative events.

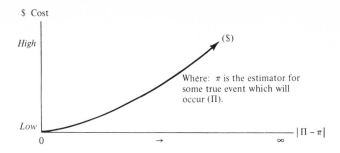

Figure 5.5   The absolute cost of error curve.

value in accomplishing the situation described in Figures 5.6 and 5.7 . . . where the favorable transformation of the event-probability distributions in Figure 5.6 directly translates into the more favorable error situation in Figure 5.7.

And.we can now suggest that, because expected loss is jointly a function of the absolute cost of errors of certain magnitudes and the probability of incurring errors of those magnitudes, a reduction in the latter factor results in a direct reduction in the expected value of errors associated with a prediction or description problem.   More explicitly: *the value of information generated via analysis process is imputed equal to the reduction in the expected cost of errors associated with its generation.*

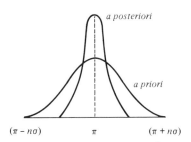

Figure 5.6   Probability transformation model.

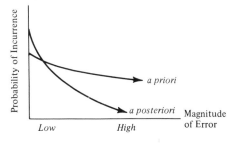

Figure 5.7   Expected error model.

Now none of this says anything about the "actual" value of the information generated during an analysis process, i.e., how much was actually saved by conducting formal research, etc. The reason is a simple one: we cannot ever arrive at this value except after the event of interest has already occurred (such that it is now an historical phenomenon rather than a target for analysis, per se). Thus, in a prediction exercise, our best estimators of what some true parameter will be, our best estimates of the nature of the relationship between two variables, etc., are simply that: *estimates*. And although we may have assigned our particular estimators overwhelmingly significant probabilities of occurrence relative to all other alternatives we considered, our probability constructs do not drive the real world, they simply attempt to approximate it. Thus, when considering the value of information, we are forced to operate with expectations, and use the abstract event-probability distributions to discipline our decisions about when to continue or when to discontinue analysis and finalize the model at hand. In other words, we expend resources for analysis in the expectation that the marginal product of the information generated will be positive . . . positive, that is, in terms of the reduction in the expected value of error exceeding the cost of obtaining the information which led to the reduction.

In summary then, the applied scientist exercises himself in the generation of models which have their "purpose" in the treatment of a real-world phenomenon in terms of prediction, description, or causal reconstruction. The models are predicated on information that may be either *a priori* or *a posteriori* in generation, and that may be directed toward the completion of the model on any of four levels (state-variable, parametric, relational, or coefficient). The information generated—at positive expenditure of time, effort, dollars, or other analytical resources—finds its utility in the ability to produce more favorable *a posteriori* informational states from less favorable *a priori* ones, where the quality of the informational states is determined indirectly by the morphology of the event probability distributions associated with them. Hence, every model we build, and every component of the model generated during a system analysis process, may be indexed with some probability of accuracy, where this refers to our confidence that the "event" we have elected to enter into the model will be identical with the real-world event as yet to occur (or, in the case of causal reconstruction, that occurred). The imputed value of information is found in the reduction in the expected value of error associated with its acquisition; thus, the transformation of the event probability distributions driven by successive increments of information has a directly utilitarian significance for us, and the fundamental concepts of marginal economics may be called into play (however grossly they must be applied initially). And, so long as the marginal product of increments of information may be calculated as expectedly positive, analysis processes will be iterated and the finalization of the model delayed.

In Chapter 6 we shall carry these discussions a great deal further, developing a normative model of the analysis process itself and incorporating more formal discussions of the logic and mechanisms of decision-making. Now, however, it is time to return to a point we left behind . . . the extent to which the nature of the problem at hand—in the form of one or another of our four analytical ideal-types—will determine the kind of analysis process we go through, and particularly the rate at which information is acquired and the ultimate error levels we might legitimately expect to arrive at for the models we build.

5.3 THE DETERMINACY OF THE IDEAL-TYPES

Recalling the ideal-types we built in Chapter 4, we can see that as soon as the system we are trying to predict or describe begins to depart from the criteria laid down for determinism (e.g., the mechanical ideal-type or the Type-I system of Figures 4.16 or 5.3), our model-building tasks will become more difficult. Particularly, as the system at hand begins to approach the properties associated with indeterminacy, the model-building process will begin to be characterized by the following:

1. *The array of problem determinants identified will probably be incomplete* because complex (open; indeterminate) systems cannot be isolated from the environment in which they occur. They are, rather, caused by external factors that may be spatially or temporally far removed and therefore not identifiable at a specific point-in-time. For example, an individual whose economic performance is poor may have been subjected to early diet deprivations, adverse social or cultural experiences, a religious belief which countermands material acquisition, etc. A system designed to treat poverty would, therefore, have to consider all these and many similarly analytically amorphous factors for which no models currently exist, except those of the most speculative kind. Simply, *all* the structural factors comprising a problem are unlikely to be empirically accessible to the analyst during the formative stages of analysis.
2. *The behavior of problem determinants may often be accounted for only approximately.* We may not, for example, know the precise nature of the interrelationship between state-variables in organic or complex systems. Therefore, any causal inference correlation we use is likely to have some significant probability of being wrong (either in magnitude or, more seriously, in direction). This reflects not only the inherent behavioral complexity of organic systems themselves, but the analytical transparency— the empirical inaccessibility—of the forces driving them. Moreover, their components, unlike mechanical, can alter their behavior endogenously, in response to localized changes, suggesting that an accurate dynamic allegory at one point in time may be highly inaccurate a short time later.
3. *The allegory or model we develop must generally be treated as probabilistic rather than deterministic.* The major reason (along with the two-points

mentioned above) is that the determinants of an organic system may interact with each other in unpredictable, unspecified ways. Whereas, for example, the combined effects of gravity, friction, and atmospheric density on a space vehicle of a certain configuration become calculable in terms of known, resolvable interaction models (e.g., force vectors), the same can hardly be said for properties of most human or socioeconomic systems. This is largely due to the pervasiveness of the equifinal potential we earlier discussed.

In total, these three conditions simply reflect the fact that complex systems are very "open" rather than closed, and that organic system components, do not have the casually, spatially, or processually constrained behavioral repertoires expected of physical, noncognitive, or engineered systems. Indeed, if we were able to "map" properties of many Type-III and Type-IV systems, we would emerge with incredibly complex, reflexive, and equifinal networks that all but defy mathematical representation or physical reproduction because of the analytical discontinuities we are forced to accommodate.

In summary then, the systemic ideal-type which the entity at hand approximates will have a direct determinacy on the nature of the resultant system analysis process. Specifically, with the defining properties of the four phenomenological ideal-types firmly in mind from our earlier work, the rationale behind the following propositions should be clear:

- The greater the inherent complexity of any entity whose behavior we are trying to describe and/or predict (i.e., the greater its approximation to the indeterminate or organic ideal-type), the more "expensive" will be each increment of information in the *a priori/a posteriori* transformation.
- The greater the inherent complexity of any entity we are attempting to treat analytically, the greater will be the minimum expected loss we can legitimately expect to incur. That is, there will be some significant "floor" level of expected error below which we cannot force the model we are building. This is irrespective of the level of analytical resources expended or the number of empirical observations made on properties of interest.

These two contentions are combined in the disparate learning curves of Figure 5.8. As is clear from the figure, the learning curves associated with the various analytical ideal-types show marked differences in two aspects:

(a) The rate of decline in error relative to a given *a priori* base.
(b) The limiting values of the asymptotes.

The deterministic entity must be taken as the purest embodiment of the properties earlier associated with the mechanical plane of the *General System Iconograph* (Figure 4.3), and normatively we expect its learning curve to drop most rapidly and intercept the zero-error point after the least number of empirical

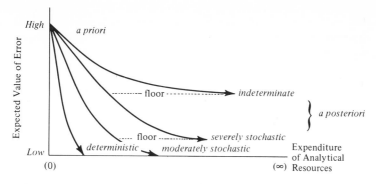

Figure 5.8 Disparate learning curves (normative).

observations (or at the lowest expenditure of resources). In the case of the essentially indeterminate system, the surrogate for the gestalt of the iconograph, we notice the least decline per unit of expenditure, and postulate that there will still remain a significantly positive probability of descriptive or predictive error even if infinite resources were expended (or if an infinite number of empirical observations were made on the properties of interest).

The learning curves bring us to another interesting point—the probability of ever reaching a zero-error level (irrespective of the amount of analytical resources expended or the number of observations made on the system) declines rapidly as the system at hand departs from the criteria for determinism. But here, again, we must distinguish between *effective* and *inherent* states. A system may be effectively indeterminate or stochastic at any point in the analysis process, but if it is inherently deterministic, we will eventually be able to eliminate the error associated with models of that system. Obviously, inherently stochastic or inherently indeterminate systems make this ambition impossible to achieve. Thus, the following formulation, central to mathematical learning theory,[4] will hold only for inherently deterministic systems.

$$\lim_{n \to \infty} E\left(\hat{X}_n \| Q_n\right) \to X$$

where: X_n is the most likely estimate for the true value X of an event, generated by the n'th *a posteriori* probability distribution in a Bayesian type successive approximation process Q_n; and $\|$ indicates a contingency condition (e.g., $\hat{X}_n$ given Q_n).

For inherently indeterminate systems, however, we cannot expect that the limiting value of our estimator of an event (e.g., a specific parameter, coefficient, relational or state-variable specification) will approach the true value; even as (n), here representing expenditure of analytical resources or number of observations, approaches infinity. Rather, we must provide another construct for the indeterminate or Type-IV system.

$$\lim_{\eta \to \infty} P\ (X_n \| Q_n = X \| F) \ll 1,$$

where: F is the true stochastic distribution for the parameter in question, and X is the most likely value of that parameter, given F. Because:

$$\lim_{\eta \to \infty} P\ (Q = F) \ll 1.$$

In other words, we normatively expect our estimates of gestalt-like or "organic" properties to be indexed with a significant probability of error, despite the extent of our analytical efforts (both for event-values themselves and for the successive *a posteriori* probability distributions purporting to reflect the true stochastic distribution). Indeed, it is possible that some essentially extremely-complex socioeconomic entities might give rise to the (*ergodic*) paradox of increasing information entropy, because their potential for change consistently exceeds the resolution power of our analytical instruments. Simply, we must assume that our predictive models will always be somewhat out of phase when working with subjects approximating the indeterminate analytical ideal-type.

To bring the concept of the learning curve into operational perspective, we can replace the error variable with which we have been working with another factor. This factor is the first differences in stocks of information acquired during a systems analysis process; the difference between the stock of information which existed at some time t and that which exists at some time $(t + 1)$.* The interval between time t and time $(t + 1)$ is the time during which another iteration of the analysis process (e.g., another empirical observation on the properties of interest) was conducted. Let's employ three generally familiar, abstract ideal-types and set out normative learning curves for them, as in Figure 5.9. These curves describe the following function, where the (B's) are limits.

$$\lim_{\eta \to \infty} E\ (\hat{X}_n - \hat{X}_{n-1}) \to B$$

where: X_n is the value of the n'th observation of the parameter X taken in a disciplined learning exercise.

Quite obviously, the concepts of the "limiting value for the learning curve" and the "residual probability of error" are closely related, for when the asymptotic value of (B) declines—as successive observations bring us less and less new quantitative or qualitative information—we can suggest that:

$$\lim_{B \to 0} P\ (\hat{X}_n = X) \to 1$$

where: X_n is the value of the n'th observation on the value of a parameter, and X is the true value. Conversely, for nondeterministic entities:

$$\lim_{B \to \infty} P\ (\hat{X}_n \neq X) \to 1$$

So, letting (R) stand for the residual probability of error associated with the

---

*Again, these differences may be determined either quantitatively or qualitatively.

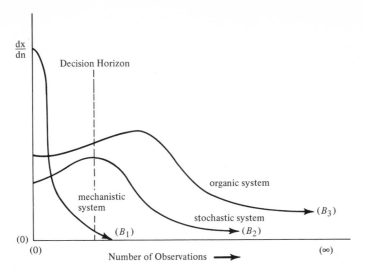

Figure 5.9 Normative learning curves.

given level of (B), and setting 1, 2, and 3 as indices representing the mechanical, man-machine, and organic system types, respectively, we propose:

$$\lim_{\eta \to \infty} P\,(R_1 \| B_1 < R_2 \| B_2 < R_3 \| B_3) \to 1.$$

and

$$\lim_{\eta \to \infty} P\,(R_1 = B_1 = 0) = 1.$$

Simply, as the number of observations on a system increases toward infinity, the residual probability of error associated with the limiting value for the learning curve will be least for the *mechanical* entity, greatest for the organic *system* and intermediate for the stochastic type system. However, we need not consider only limiting values, for the inclusion of a *decision horizon* in Figure 5.9 (which reflects the point-in-time where a decision must be made, irrespective of the current error level) indicates that: (a) for any given level of resource expenditures or for any given number of observations, the residual probability of error and the first-difference between successive observations will be highest for the gestalt-like organic system; and (b) therefore, our associated predictive models will be least accurate.

We can extend this analysis somewhat to include some brief comments on administrative decision-making.* For we may note that the concepts of *probability of error* and the *absolute cost of errors* combine to give us the central variable in decision analysis: the expected value (E.V.) of a decision error (dysfunction).

*Elements of Chapters 7 and 8 will deal with this subject more thoroughly.

It may be computed as follows:

$$E.V. = \frac{\sum (p_i x_i)}{n}$$

where:

> p_i = the probability of occurrence assigned any (x_i).
>
> x_i = any considered error value ($) for each unique $|\pi - e_i|$, and (π) indicates the central (or best) estimate of some true value (II) not known beforehand . . . the event *qua* decision (action) premise.
>
> n = the number of discrete events considered . . . the number of alternatives (the set of e_i's).

We are postulating a normative decision-rule that asks us to minimize, to the extent possible, the E.V. associated with a decision, though other rules might be formulated (such as the loss minimization rule that suggests operating to reduce the highest $(p_i x_i)$ pair to the lowest possible value, even at the expense of incurring a relatively higher overall weighted-average). We select the E.V. minimization rule, however, because it usually involves (or results in) an operational realization of the strategies suggested by most other, more specific decision-rules we find in decision theory literature.

In a normative vein, we can suggest that the absolute cost or loss associated with any decision or policy we elect to implement will be directly related to the variance between the estimator we use as a decision or policy premise and the *real* "event" to which it pertains. This is illustrated in Figure 5.10).

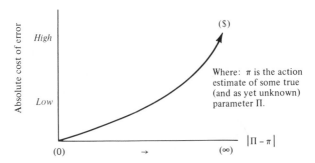

Figure 5.10 Generic absolute cost model.

On the other hand, the probability of incurring an error of a given magnitude is inversely related to the variance between estimators and real events. The reasoning behind this latter proposition is logical rather than empirical. We suspect that, as a system analysis exercise proceeds, the more extreme departures from the true "event" gradually become eliminated from probabilistic consideration. Hence, the curve in Figure 5.11.

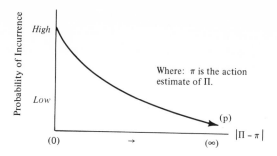

Figure 5.11 Error occurrence model.

In a sense then, these two factors act to produce normally *compromisive* values for the expected value variable, with the absolute cost associated with larger estimator departures being off-set to some extent by the lower probability of incurrence associated with them in their role as potential decision or policy premises.

Directly then, the "quality" of a decision-maker must be reflected in the nature of the changes that take place in the event-probability distributions associated with the processes or systems he is treating. The effective decision-maker will be one who, considering the inherent complexity of the problem with which he is asked to deal, arrives at the most favorable *a posteriori* event-probability distribution, where "favorable" refers to the distribution's morphology, as in the now familiar Figure 5.12.

Reiterating then, in the figure the *b* curve is the more favorable because there is less variance to the distribution. This curve implies a greater *convergence* on a single estimator because of the mathematical properties of probability density functions. Thus, the expected value of decision error (or loss) must be lower than that associated with the *a* curve, as may be seen by glancing again at the computational algorithm given earlier. It is not relevant at this time to consider that the action estimator (π) may not in fact reflect the true state or parametric event that will occur, for decisions or policies take place always before the fact,

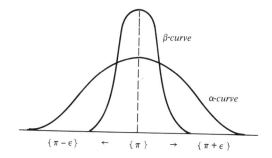

Figure 5.12 Generic event-probability distributions.

and thus a mechanism for judging the relative quality of a given decision process or decision-maker must also operate before an event or process has occurred. The quality of a decision-maker is empirically accessible, before the fact, only through an analysis of the morphology of the event-probability distributions on which he predicates his decision or policy actions.

As a final note, the *inherent* complexity of the decision at hand (reflecting the *inherent* complexity of the entity being treated) will, of course, have an effect on the rate at which an unfavorable *a priori* event-probability distribution may be transformed into a more favorable one, and ultimately on the morphology of the limiting *a posteriori* distribution. Without going into great detail here, we can only suggest that the nature of the "best" *a posteriori* distribution one can legitimately expect to arrive at will reflect the nature of the ideal-type which the entity at hand approximates. In this regard, it *should* reflect the morphology of the abstract event-probability distributions we associated with the basic analytical ideal-types at the outset of Chapter 4; i.e., the deterministic, moderately stochastic, severely stochastic, and indeterminate cases.

5.4 THE ARSENAL OF ANALYTICAL INSTRUMENTS

Now, just as we can translate populations of phenomena into categorical ideal-types, we can also think of taking the entire arsenal of scientific instruments available to us and partitioning it into meaningful categories. Moreover, we may use our analytical ideal-types to engineer this partitioning.

Hence, Figure 5.13, which associates each of our analytical ideal-types with the most appropriate subset of scientific tools and techniques.

Those who are not familiar with the nature and operations of the specific instruments employed in the table will find no lack of literature treating them . . . until one begins to study the instruments associated with the indeterminate analytical type. For it is here that the techniques of mathematics and statistics, even when coupled with computer, tend largely to fail us; it is here that the idiosyncratic imagination and *logical* capabilities of the system analyst are called into play. And because this (of all the instrumental categories) is least well-treated in existing literature, we will devote a significant portion of subsequent chapters to the explication of a *heuristic* modality especially designed to treat effectively indeterminate, gestalt-like phenomena.

In the meantime, however, the reader who is awed at the prospect of having to learn the detailed properties of the various instruments may take heart, for all we are interested in doing here is lending him some broad conceptual or intuitive appreciation for their application and limits. In this way, he may know *what* should be done to various system types at various points in an analysis process, if not precisely *how* it should be done. The essential point we wish to make is simply this: instrumental congruence is obtained when the system analyst applies an instrument that, given the point-in-time properties of the phenomenon at hand, promises to yield a desired (or maximum) amount of information with the lowest expenditure of analytical resources and/or time. The assignments made in

ANALYTICAL IDEAL-TYPE	RATIONALE	ASSOCIATED ANALYTICAL INSTRUMENTS
Deterministic . . . data bases and causal relationships are highly specific and accurate with respect to the phenomenon at hand.	There is expected to be one and only one "probable" event. Hence, we search for one-answer functions which "fit" the temporal and/or cross-sectional data available to us.	• Finite-state system analysis techniques • Linear programming and maximization-minimization algorithms • Optimization models
Moderate Stochastic . . . basic causal relationships are probably *a priori* known (and accurate), but data bases incomplete; hence the parametric uncertainty.	Here we are concerned with the possibility of an event assuming some *value* within a prespecified, manageable range. Hence, the probability of any specific value occurring is *a priori* less than unity, but the structure of our formulations is essentially deterministic, only with error treated endogenously. In any case, the domain of the function is highly constrained and the event-alternatives *a priori* well-specified.	• Markov processes • Statistical inference processes. • Bayesian estimation processes • Range estimation techniques (e.g., probabilistic projection models) • Numerical approximation techniques (e.g., Taylor functions) • Simple simulation techniques. • Shock models. • Regression, correlation, time-series or harmonic analysis techniques.
Severely Stochastic . . . data bases might be fairly good, but causal models are ill-defined or entity is inherently capable of assuming any one of several predefinable states.	Here we must consider a wide range of significantly qualitatively different events which might occur, each of which will lead to highly differentiated "futures." We will have to handle multiple "state" variables and, at some points, must postulate alternative causal chains (action/reaction sequences) that might be generated by the hetermorphic alternatives assigned significant probabilities of occurrence. In any case, empirical investigation will be used to "converge" on one or another state-alternative in the *a posteriori* stage.	• Game-based models • Stochastic-state system analysis techniques • Adaptive or dynamic (usually Bayesian-based) programming algorithms • Network (e.g., neural) formulations • Stochastic simulation techniques • Analogic models
*Indeterminate** . . . there are no relevant empirical data bases and the inherent causal relationships for the phenomenon at hand are *a priori* unallegorizable.	Here, lacking prespecified alternative outcomes, futures must be deduced by reference to any generalized, empirically-unvalidated theoretical constructs that might exist. *A priori* then, this situation is unactionable except to designate those phenomenological foci that are expected to be most fruitful targets for subsequent "learning" exercises. The usual strategy is to gradually narrow the range of alternatives so that the indeterminate *a priori* state may gradually be transformed into a more actionable stochastic situation, etc.	• Deductive analysis leading to the generation of broadly defined, logically-possible alternatives • Heuristic programming or "learning" algorithms (usually just to discipline empirical investigations) • Axiological tools (e.g., Delphi; defactualization) • Scenario-building • Normative system analysis

*Because literature on the category of instruments designed to deal with phenomenal indeterminacy is scarce, and also somewhat confusing, we shall treat such instruments briefly in Chapter 7.

Figure 5.13. Elements of the system analysis instrument array.

Figure 5.13 between the various instrument subsets and the several analytical ideal-types were designed to guide the analyst toward just such an outcome.

Taking just one of the instrumental categories and treating it in some detail might help make this clear. The example we can work with is the statistical instruments of (linear) econometric methods, designated to be used in the face of moderately stochastic problems. Whenever we are concerned with the forecasting or the prediction of factors pertinent to our operations, and whenever we can legitimately assume that future values of those factors will be a product of their historical behaviors, we enter the domain of econometric competence. Econometrics is basically just a collection of statistical devices which are appropriate for dealing with problems that may be approached primarily using regression analysis. The central model of econometrics is the straight line equation ($Y_t = a + bX_t + U_t$), where a indicates an intercept for the line on the Y-axis of a graph, b indicates the slope of the line acting as a surrogate measurement for the relationship between X and Y, and U represents the "shock" factor . . . an unspecific, presumably randomly-distributed error factor.

The aim of econometric studies employing this model is to produce predictions which are *BLUE* (*B*est *L*inear *U*nbiased *E*stimators). The assumption underlying the model is that X and Y are factors that are, in reality, linearly related (with X being a direct or effective cause of Y).* The primary assumption is that we can isolate real-world phenomena that are linear in design, and whose *state* at some future time is very likely to be a product of its past states. In short then, the fundamental model of econometrics is entirely appropriate to those problems or processes that meet the criteria we set out for moderately stochastic phenomena.

The problems with the econometric approach are many. For example, the major instrumental facility of econometricians is with linear models, and with models where there may be presumed to be no codeterminacy among the state-variables leading to a particular system state. But, in reality, phenomena meeting these assumptions will be only rarely encountered. As such, estimates of future events (e.g., parametric demand values, next-period interest rates, commodity flows, or raw material yields) that are made by projecting values driven by *least-squares* analysis are likely to be in error. We can, however, gain some (statistical) idea of the probable accuracy of our projections by analyzing the degree of variance exhibited in the historical data record from which the projections were made, and also by trying to retro-apply our model to produce an array of model-driven estimates to be compared to historical event values (curve fitting). When unexplained variance is too high, we might want to shift to another instrument entirely (e.g., harmonic analysis when our process is one that exhibits sinusoidal properties). We may also move into the domain of formal time-series analysis and try to obtain the function which best "fits" the historical data

---

*Essentially the same logic holds for multivariable formulations, where x represents a set of variables $\{x_i\}$ rather than a single factor.

record irrespective of that function's complexity. When we do this, of course, both expense of analysis and cost of computation rise rapidly.

At any rate, despite operational problems of nonlinearity, codeterminacy and the possible nonrandomness of the error variable U, the econometric method is appropriate in the face of problems that have an adequate historical (empirical) data record associated with them, and where the record does not house significant variance that the regression models cannot explain. And fortunately for both us and the econometricians, within most socioeconomic systems there will be some instances of processess or phenomena that more or less meet these criteria. As such, the potential contribution of the econometric approach is very great, and it is only when we move from short to long-range forecasting—or from precedented to unprecedented problems—that we must employ a modality of more resolution power (e.g., the game theoretical or contingency programming instruments associated with severely stochastic phenomena).

The econometrician's linear regression model, then, is used to develop estimates of future events that are statistically most likely, *given* an empirical record of past events. In a somewhat broader view, whenever we can assume that one factor is largely determined by another, and when we have historical records of these factors (and we can apply this logic and operation to more than just two factors) the econometric approach is appropriate. However, it is most appropriate when another assumption can be legitimately entered: the assumption that there is no special weight that should be attached to any particular segment of the empirical data record. In short, econometric models usually lend equal determinacy to the entire record of actual events. Where this assumption clearly does not hold, we must make adjustments. The adjustment that permits us to remain within the econometric envelope is the elimination of selected historical values from the data record. In other words, by manipulating the empirical event-set used to generate predictions, we can force alterations in our future estimates that reflect the different weights we want to assign to selected past events. In another mode entirely, when it may be assumed that only the latest events have a determinacy on the next period's estimates, we may employ the Markov technique and its variations. Similarly, when we wish to take account of secular, seasonal, or specific "shock" factors, we can use certain techniques of time-series analysis which allow us to isolate such effects (e.g., pre-whitening the data base to eliminate trend).

Again, however, the prerequisite for the legitimate use of econometric methods is a solid empirical data base which becomes the source of whatever temporal (or cross-sectional) *inferences* we make as system analysts. Thus these techniques allow us to escape from determinism through their ampliative capabilities and their provision of some probabilistically determined *range* of events which might occur (whereas finite state or optimization models yield only single, unique answers in the face of any given set of premises or starting-state conditions). Moreover, we are able to give a statistical estimate of our *confidence* that the true event will actually fall within this range.

Now the cynic may suggest that all such instruments are simply expedients, hedges against bets on the future. For whenever we must introduce a *range* of possible alternative events we are really suggesting that we simply do not know as much as we should about the nature of the phenomenon being treated (e.g., we do not know all the state-variables or the relationships among them, or we cannot isolate singularly significant coefficient or parameter values). In actuality, however, many real-world phenomena are *inherently* stochastic, and in many other cases the incrementally greater expense which would be required to yield deterministic estimates (where they could conceivably be isolated) is simply not worth it in terms of the marginality concepts we introduced under the previous discussions of information economics. So the majority of the models that are used to discipline short-to-intermediate range forecasting efforts will be of the "shock" type. These are models that yield probabilistic sets of alternatives to be used as decision premises. If the real-world event which actually occurs falls somewhere within the range of alternatives supplied, we may consider our analysis process a success. But the operational limitation on this approach is that we, as analysts, can always be right by setting the range of statistically probable events wide enough. However, when the number of event-alternatives is too great, or where the difference among the beginning and ending events in the range is very broad, the method loses its utility. In short, the informational output in this case simply becomes unactionable.

Now in order to return to the elaboration of the normative learning curves we introduced in Section 5.3 (see again Figure 5.8), we have to take a closer look at the characteristics of these components of the aggregate model base, and in the process look for reasons why analytical efforts aimed at deterministic phenomena result in learning curves that rapidly drop to an asymptote of zero-error, etc. We find the reasons in the morphological parallel between the various analytical ideal-type categories and the instrumental subarsenals.

Essentially then, as we move from determinate toward indeterminate phenomena, the empirically-validated component in the models declines in favor of judgmental or "deductive" factors, with a corresponding decrease in the morphological correlation between the entity under study and the allegory purporting to describe or predict it. Quite simply, we begin to displace fact with opinion and, in the process, incur ever greater levels of expected predictive or causal error. Hence, the empirical predication of deterministic models is expected to yield (normatively) a lower variance between "predicted" and "real" events than a statistical inference-based model; the statistical-inference model is, in turn, expected to be more reliable in its predictive or causal allegories than the deductive inferences underlying severely stochastic models; and, at the indeterminate extreme, the strong intuitive or deliberately fabricative (defactualized) component argues that we expect significant divergence between predicted or allegory-driven events and those that actually occur in the real-world.

So the instrumental categories differ as greatly in their properties as do the analytical ideal-types themselves, as is summarized in Figure 5.14. As that table

INSTRUMENTAL CLASS	GIVEN THE FOLLOWING IDEAL-TYPE	ANALYTICAL BASE*	NATURE OF INFORMATIONAL OUTPUT	QUALITY OF OUTPUT	EXPECTED PROBABILITY OF ERROR
Optimization	Deterministic	Positivistic (i.e., hypothesis or assumption-free analysis)	Generates a single solution for any given set of predicates within a closed-system context (i.e., as linear programming models).	High degree of precision . . . results depend directly on contents of an empirical data base with minimal judgmental intervention.	Extremely low (as there is no attempt to generate conclusions not directly obtainable from the data base).
Extrapolative/projective	Moderately stochastic	Inductive (or statistical) inference	Generates a "range" of possible solutions or a probabilistic estimate assigned some index of confidence . . . where alternative events are derived from an empirical (historical) data base.	Prescriptiveness of output depends on the "width" of the range of event-alternatives; precision on data base quality.	Depends on the "quality" of the data base as a source of inferences . . . objectively determined.
Game-based (or contingent)	Severely stochastic	Deductive inference	Generates an array of alternative events of different "quality."	Alternatives are usually in the form of *scenarios* and not too precise; action-ability depends on number of alternatives presented and their degree of "difference."	Usually quite high (as output is intended to generate "events" of logical rather than objective probability).
Heuristic (or meta-hypothetical)	Indeterminate	Intuitionistic/metaphysical	Generation of broad heuristics or learning-based paradigms to discipline subsequent informational pursuit.	These are prescriptive only in a methodological sense, not a substantive one.	The heuristic does not carry any pretentions to accuracy or realism, per se.

*For a more detailed explanation of these various analytical bases, which really constitute epistemological alternatives, see appropriate sections of my A GENERAL SYSTEMS PHILOSOPHY FOR THE SOCIAL AND BEHAVIORAL SCIENCES (New York: George Braziller, 1973).

Figure 5.14 Table of instrumental properties.

indicates, instrumental categories differ on several critical dimensions. The precision of the output generated by the instrument classes refers to the "narrowness" of numerical or qualitative intervals separating the various "events" generated (or the mathematical precision of the single "event" generated under the optimization category, i.e., the number of significant digits). The *actionability* of the output refers to its ultimate utility insofar as dictating contingent (estimate dependent) "actions" are concerned. Clearly, for both the severely and moderately stochastic cases, the ability of the information to direct subsequent action depends on the number of alternatives outlined and their degree of difference in qualitative terms. The usual condition of scarce resources makes it impossible for us to preadapt to many, significantly different, alternative events assigned significant probabilities of occurrence. This is the inherent limitation of the utility of game-based or contingency-predicated analytical procedures, as with war-games, etc.[5] *Prescriptiveness* is a subdimension of actionability, and refers to the degree of detail in contingency-based actions allowed by the model's informational content.

In summary then, we can suggest that there will be some *vector of analytical congruence* which can be grossly defined between our four analytical ideal-types and the various instrument classes we defined, as in Figure 5.15. The main diagonal represents this *vector of congruence*, where the given analytical ideal-type is associated with that instrumental subset expected to deal most effectively and efficiently with it. To the right of the main diagonal we strike a condition termed *inefficiency*, reflecting a probable misallocation of analytical resources. For here we are using instruments designed to deal with a more complex analytical state than that indicated, and these more powerful instruments will have a higher cost per unit of information associated with them. For example, nonlinear algorithms are more expensive to operate than linear, given any number of state-variables to be manipulated. Thus, we might possibly employ stochastic tools to solve an essentially deterministic situation, but we will reach any terminal error level at a

INSTRUMENT TYPE	SYSTEM TYPE			
	Deterministic	*Moderately Stochastic*	*Severely Stochastic*	*Indeterminate*
Optimization	X		Area of Ineffectiveness: due to high probability of error as a result of the use of too "weak" an instrument.	
Inferential/ extrapolative		X		
Contingent/ game-based	Area of Inefficiency: due to use of too powerful an instrument, "overkill" (which is a misallocation of analytical resources).		X	
Heuristic/ metahypothetical				X

X = congruent association

Figure 5.15 Typology of instrumental congruences.

higher cost than had we used more economical (and more expeditious) optimization instruments, etc.

To the left of the main diagonal in the figure falls a more serious situation . . . *ineffectiveness*. The implication here is that we are employing analytical instruments that are not powerful enough to resolve the properties of the problem at hand, suggesting that whatever eventual error level we do achieve will be unacceptable or considerably higher than necessary. Thus for example, the economist employing "shock models" to treat complex phenomena simply trades off analytical expediency against ultimate rectitude.[6] Any policy decisions made on the basis of that model's output will, then, inhere a significant probability of being dysfunctional, for it will have been predicated on considerable oversimplification of real-world system properties.

5.5 ANALYTICAL AND INFORMATIONAL BASES

The assertions of the previous section may become somewhat clearer when we note that *information*, per se, is always a product of some instrument (e.g., a mathematical statistical, logical, or theoretical model) operating on data (e.g., elements drawn from the empirical or historical record pertinent to some phenomenon or system). Ultimately, then, the information output from a system analysis exercise—in the form of a purportedly predictive or descriptive model or allegory—will owe part of its substance to fact (data, empirical observation, direct experience) and part to the model used to manipulate this data. As was noted early in Chapter 1, there are basically two types of models available to us. First there are what might be called the *inductive* models, those that simply extrapolate or project the properties of some data base, or which develop inferences or generalizations predicated on the empirical data base.

The other broad category of model would be the *deductive* class, where little reliance is placed on data, per se, and much reliance is placed on such nonempirical devices as intuition, judgement, logic, metaphysics, etc. There is no stigma attached to the use of instruments of this latter class where scientific discipline is maintained (in ways that will be made clear in Chapter 7), yet where judgment and speculation begin to displace fact, we must generally place less reliance on the accuracy of any "information" so developed. Yet, as we have tried to point out consistently, systems or phenomena that depart successively more widely from the criterion of determinism become successively less amenable to empirical observation, measurement, or manipulation, and therefore lend themselves less and less well to the generation of any meaningful, reasonably accurate, empirical data base. In this sense, then, we expect that the information pertinent to a system—that is, the final substance of the output from an analysis process—will differ considerably for systems from different analytical categories. This is made clear in Figure 5.16, where we use the two polar ideal-types from Chapter 4 (the mechanism and gestalt) as antonymical cases.

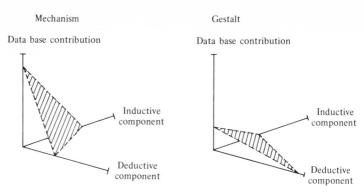

Figure 5.16 Polar informational states.

With respect to Figure 5.16, we can only suggest again what we have already pointed out . . . that the greater the reliance on deductive as opposed to empirical (data base) or inductive components, the greater will be the expected error associated with any informational constructs we develop. This ultimately boils down to a simple tautology, for what it really means is that complex systems are more difficult to predict or describe than simple ones, etc., and the larger *expected* error component is one of the prices we pay for adhering to the dictate of analytical congruence. But *expected* error means that we are forewarned against the surprises the system will hold in store for us . . . and for the system scientist, the old cliche is very meaningful: *forewarned is forearmed.*

The criterion of analytical congruence thus says that stochastic or indeterminate systems should be recognized as such, and treated appropriately, and this means giving explicit credit to their instability, unpredictability, and inherent complexity. In this sense, then, an information base associated with a highly complex system that took the form of that associated with the mechanism of Figure 5.16 would be a sure sign that the system analyst has sinned against congruence . . . that he has traded off accuracy and scientific rectitude against analytical experience. We shall return to this point rather early in the next chapter, simply leaving the thought here that a graphic portrayal of the "origins" of the information used to underlie a system model may be quite revealing as to the *quality* of the system analysis process that produced that information. Thus, where we know that the system under treatment or study is a complex one, we would like to see the information base generate an iconograph like that for the gestalt in the previous figure.

In general then, we must consider that the various instrument categories available to us—each especially congruent with one or another analytical ideal-type— will have significantly different error characteristics, as shown in Figure 5.17.

We may further defend this construct by recognizing that each of the instrumental categories we have set out is derived from an effectively unique analytical

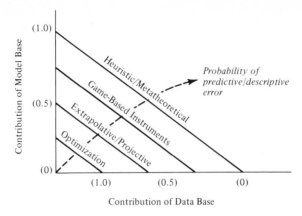

Figure 5.17 **Comparative error characteristics.**

base. That is, each of the four instrumental categories reflects the assumptions of a different *epistemology*, each housing different tenets about the locus of knowledge, and the proper procedures for acquiring it. These four analytical bases to which the various instrument categories respond pretty well exhaust the different analytical strategies associated with modern science, and they may be defined as follows:

1. *Positivistic Modality*—where no logical, mathematical, or statistical model mediates between the data base and the ultimate allegory, such that there is an almost perfect correlation between the components of the original data base and the components of the ultimate allegory. Alternatively, the positivistic modality is indicated by the fact that every element of the allegory is itself deterministic, being assigned no significant probability of departing from the "assigned value".

2. *Inductivist Modality*—where the reliance on the original data base is still extremely strong, but where some "model" has intervened such that the morphological correlation between data base and allegory is dampened. In general, inductivist allegories will be extensions or extrapolations of the elements of the data base, such that the parametric or coefficient values assigned the allegory are products of statistical inference, etc.

3. *Deductivist Modality*—where the reliance on the empirical data base is rather weak, such that there is only limited morphological correlation between the components of the ultimate allegory and the components of the original data base. In other words, deductive instruments introduce significant qualitative changes that mediate between the data base and the allegory or system model.

4. *Heuristic Modality*—where there is no data base from which to work that has any relevance for the problem at hand (or only isolated and uninte-

grated scraps of historical-empirical evidence). Hence, under this modality we deliberately fabricate possible futures and develop initially artificial (i.e., fictional or analytic) frameworks within which a subsequently disciplined learning exercise may take place.

Without going into great detail here (which I have done elsewhere, as is indicated by the footnote to Figure 5.14), it should be clear from these abbreviated definitions that there is now the possibility of developing a typology of analytical congruences similar to the table of instrumental congruences developed earlier. Hence, Figure 5.18.

ANALYTICAL MODALITY	IDEAL-TYPE			
	Deterministic	Moderately Stochastic	Severely Stochastic	Indeterminate
Positivistic	Optimization		*Area of* *Ineffectiveness*	
Inductivist		Extrapolative/ projective		
Deductivist	*Area of* *Inefficiency*		Game-based/ contingent	
Heuristic				Metahypothet-ical/learning based

Figure 5.18 Typology of analytical congruences.

This figure represents the central construct in our work on the concept of congruence. It simply suggests that essentially deterministic systems may be effectively approached using optimization techniques, and that these optimization techniques are agents of what we have called the positivistic analytical modality (e.g., that which demands a hypothesis-free approach to problems, and where the basic analytical task will be trial-and-error manipulation of the system's properties until the optimum is converged on). By the same token, if the system at hand is moderately stochastic, then generally speaking we can develop predictive and/or descriptive models whose substance is largely in the form of inductive or statistical inferences drawn from some empirical/historical data base. As the system at hand begins to approximate the properties of severe stochasticity, our reliance on empirical data, and inductive/statistical inferences drawn from that data, should begin to decline, being replaced by such essentially deductive instruments as game-based formulations or certain types of simulation instruments . . . instruments that yield expectedly less accurate and less precise information than their positivist or inductivist counterparts, but that nevertheless openly reflect the real complexity of such entities.

And, when the system at hand begins to approximate that worst of all worlds— the effectively indeterminate ideal-type—then we have little recourse except to the heuristic modality, with its basis in what are called metatheoretical operations. The concept of a heuristic, and the substance of heuristic processes, are probably relatively unfamiliar to the majority of readers . . . and there are very few adequate references to which one can turn.[7] Therefore, it's worthwhile here to try to convey some rudiments.

5.5.1 Heuristics and Heuristic Processes

A heuristic is usually deliberately nonapodictical (that is, unamenable to empirical validation). Its utility is found in its ability to lend some tentative, *a priori* constraint to an otherwise ill-bounded search space. The heuristic can do this in one or both of two ways: (a) it can narrow the relevant search space by fixing our immediate attention on a limited number of exploratory paths from among the infinitude of trajectories available to us, or (b) it can narrow the search space by imposing certain *a priori* restrictions on the properties of the problem or phenomenon under treatment or study. In either case, the initially specified investigatory paths, or the assumptive constraints on the properties of the entity, are viewed as *hypothetical* rather than axiomatic. In most cases they will be very hypothetical, being largely fabricative constructs with a very low probability of being accurate descriptions of reality. Rather, they are simply to get us started. As such, heuristics become intelligible as metahypotheses . . . as collections of individual hypotheses that are deductive in nature and carry a low probability of accuracy. As the metahypothesis is a loosely ordered aggregate of these individual hypotheses, it (as an integrated construct) carries almost no probability of accuracy and hence is never itself subjected to empirical validation exercises (as are normal hypotheses, per se). In this sense, then, the four ideal-type integrated systems developed in Chapter 4 serve essentially as heuristics to direct further inquiry, and only secondarily as constructs designed to reflect real-world conditions.

Thus, the heuristic serves to lend some *a priori*, tentative order to otherwise indeterminate phenomena, and thus become very broad but also "improbable" starting-state conditions for the analysis of very complex systems. But in addition to its substantive properties which serve to hypothetically close a search space, a heuristic must also carry some methodological significance. Mainly, it must allow us to distinguish between a good search trajectory and one that is not promising, between one that promises to put us on a positive learning curve, and one that is likely to be merely tangential. Were the heuristic merely a traditional hypothesis, to be validated or invalidated by a set of experimental procedures, then this methodological component would be missing, for there are really only two cases to consider: if the experiments tend to the predictions generated by the hypothesis, then we have a move toward validation; if the experiments indicate a result adverse to expectations predicated by the hypothesis, then we have a *prima facie* case for invalidation. But the very substance of a metahypothesis is allowed to change in response to what experiments indicate, so that we are not simply validating or invalidating a fixed construct, but successively improving it. Thus, a "promising" investigatory trajectory is one that yields "clues" of two varieties: (a) clues that tend to support or reject one or more of our hypotheses (e.g., the hypothetico-deductive constructs from which a heuristic is composed), or (b) clues that lend to indications as to how the hypotheses may be restructured in the light of emerging information . . . and that therefore lead to new investigatory trajectories. In a sense, then, a heuristic serves as the constantly changing referent for a search process through some ill-defined space, initially housing our *a priori* expectations and subsequently altering these in the light of *a posteriori* evidence (or experience) that is gained in the course of the empirical trajectories followed. Thus a heuristic initiates a heuristic process, and is not its end product. This deserves some explanation.

A heuristic *process* is essentially non-algorithmic, one where even the desired concluding state (e.g., the properties of a problem solution or a "success") may be initially very loosely or fuzzily formulated. The heuristic that is used to initiate an analysis process, thus simply serves as an admittedly improbable (but logically possible) starting-state condition. It also contains, either explicitly or implicitly, the criteria to indicate whether we are getting "hotter" or "colder" (. . . the criteria for convergence on a solution. But, in the course of the heuristic process, both these criteria and the substance of the heuristic itself are expected to change, depending on the particular trajectories we follow and our sensitivity in selecting promising paths. Hence we have a problem-solving procedure that is *a priori* virtually unconstrained, engined by unbounded *opportunism.* Nothing is denied us except fixity, and nothing can prevent our finally attaining a solution except lack of tenacity, insight, time, or resources (which, in many cases, will be decisive factors, as the coming chapter will make clear). And because there is this lack of *a priori* constraint, and this emphasis on opportunistically exploiting whatever promises the constantly "emergent" situations may offer at successive points-in-time, Walter Reitman was able to make this very critical point in regard to heuristic processes.

> One may solve one's problems not only by getting what one wants, but by wanting what one gets.[8]

Thus, in a true heuristic process, goals (e.g., success criteria, solution criteria, concluding-state conditions) would remain susceptible to alteration, continuously responsive to increasing perceptual data or conceptual insights. This plasticity of these elements seems to make the heuristic process an appropriate referent for what is generally called creativity, and in extreme cases, genius; and thus appears to serve as that modality under which many of the truly great deflection points in intellectual history have been generated.[9]

In its more popular but adulterated form, the heuristic process is *a priori* equipped with a relatively firm "goal" that it is to achieve (which is tantamount to suggesting that there is some uniquely predefinable "solution space" we must eventually locate from among the entire search space). Here, then, we have fixed criteria for success or solution or termination of the search process, and what largely remains "heuristic" about such an exercise is that fact that the search trajectories are still determined largely opportunistically rather than algorithmically. Thus, the truly heuristic process differs in important respects from Stafford Beer's formulation.

> A heuristic specifies a method of behaving which will tend towards a goal which cannot be completely specified because we know what it is but not where it is.[10]

What might better be said is that, in this particular case, the heuristic *cum* starting-state condition specifies the concluding-state condition's properties, and a heuristic search method will now be employed to attempt a convergence toward that *a priori* defined concluding state. But such a formulation is entirely consistent with Beer's advocacy of a totally "cybernetic" approach to system behavior, for cybernetic processes (almost without exception) demand that the goal be invariant in terms of its basic structural properties. In this sense, the cybernetician's version of the heuristic process might be considered a pseudo-heuristic process in our terms. Moreover, the cybernetic formulation does not respond to the "state of the art" knowledge about the behavior of intelligent, "purposive" systems that is coming to light largely through the work of system analysts such as Ackoff and Emery.[11] In their conception, a purposive system would be an *impaired* (pathological) entity were it not able to alter the nature of the goals toward which it is aiming on the basis of successive information acquisitions. In more specific terms, as the reader might already sense, Beer's "heuristic" system would really be amenable to formulation in terms of our severely stochastic ideal-type (i.e., the type-III system of Chapter 4) whereas the true purposive system, unconstrained on all dimensions and fully responsive to accumulative experiences and information, would properly constitute a Type IV system, per se.

A heuristic process may thus be thought of as a disciplined trial-and-error process aiming at gradually striking some adequate "state," or at ultimately arriving at some prespecified "solution space" in the case of the quasi-heuristic exercise. In either case, a heuristic process becomes an exercise in *successive improvement*, where we may learn from both successes and failures (and where the criteria for success and failure may vary with what we have previously learned or what we expect to be able to learn in the future). In this sense, the concept of "social learning" developed by Edgar Dunn may be considered a properly heuristic process, though somewhat looser in formulation than those we shall offer in Chapter 7.[12]

Social learning is a fundamentally iterative and exploratory series of experiments in social action, where predictions about the results of those actions become "developmental hypotheses" to be pursued through a process of "evolutionary experimentation." In short, the collection of predictions pertinent to a social system, in contemplation of a postulated action, become roughly the equivalent of a scenario-based problem definition model, providing, in Dunn's terms, " . . . a finger of light pointing out some aspects of the future terrain, but becomming dimmer and less reliable as it approaches the time horizon." Thus, under the tutelage of the social learning paradigm, problem-solving becomes a process of hypothesis-formulation and testing, an " . . . iterative, sequential series of adaptions of an adaptable, goal-seeking, self-activating system." If we were to add the words "goal-setting" as a complement to these other properties, we would have the *heuristic system*, the most complex of the generic types with which the system analyst need be concerned.

In summary, then, a true heuristic process is characterized by the generation of a tentative metahypothesis (*qua* heuristic) which will carry both substantive and methodological significance for us, and which will thereby serve as the starting-state condition for the analysis of an effectively indeterminate system or phenomenon. The heuristic guides us onto an initially "improbable" investigatory trajectory, in the hopes of finding some information there—or incurring some experience—that will enable us to refine the hypothetico-deductive components of which the heuristic is comprised, and in the hopes of pointing the way toward some more positive or promising trajectory for the next iteration of our search process. Constantly, what we have learned in the course of our experiential or empirical adventures will be fed back to modify any aspect of the original heuristic, including the solution, success, or conclusional specifications. The net result is a constant *metamorphosis* of the heuristic, through feedback, but also a constant flow-forward. Thus, the heuristic process is *concatenative* rather than merely recursive, for seldom (if ever) should we reactivate a search trajectory already explored. And because the goal remains emergent rather than concrete, this search process is fundamentally different from the algorithmically-driven search processes that constitute the heart of system optimization techniques or numerical computer methods . . . and which the cybernetician's concept of the heuristic process at least partially approximates.*

With this basic introduction to heuristics and heuristic processes, we are now in a position to conclude this work on the logic of the system analysis process. For, as we shall now see, the system analysis paradigm we want to present is, in terms of its basic engination, a heuristic one.

---

*In this respect, we are thinking particularly of those search processes directed at finding an optimum (max-min) solution to some system, or attempting to converge on the roots of a polynomial, etc., through successive closure of the feasible solution space. Generally speaking, problems of the former type are those which are undertaken in the name of optimization, whereas formulations of the latter type search processes constitute the field of numerical methods (when coupled with the generation of computational methods in general).

5.6 THE SYSTEM ANALYSIS PARADIGM

In moving toward this chapter's concluding construct, it is well to remind the reader that "scientific" methods need not be abandoned at any level of phenomenal complexity. Thus, in its way—in the face of effectively indeterminate problems—the heuristic modality is as scientific as the positivistic is with respect to effectively deterministic phenomena, etc. Such is the way of congruence. Thus, what is scientific when facing any problem, is the attempt to inject as much discipline and precision as possible at each step in the analysis process, but not to the point where we subvert reality. In the broadest sense, then, science may be thought of as the process of gradually transforming *a priori* less well-understood phenomena into *a posteriori* better and more precisely defined (and more predictable) phenomena. Even for inherently indeterminate phenomena, the imposition of a heuristic formulation of some kind is generally a considerable improvement over abject intuition or speculation . . . or neglect. Thus, the system analysis process may be thought of as a transformation process where successively better models of phenomena are obtained by going through a procedural sequence like that shown in Figure 5.19.

The substance of the system analysis paradigm, as given in the figure, should be readily clear to all at this point, for it really introduces nothing new except a sequencing operation. Basically, it suggests that were we to begin with the challenge to develop either a predictive or descriptive model of some effectively indeterminate phenomenon (as opposed to an inherently indeterminate one), we would initially treat it by the generation of a heuristic of some sort . . . this in the ambition to provide the initial constraints and guidance established for heuristics in the previous subsection. In terms of the levels of analysis with which we have been working, this step would at least provide us with some indication of which state-variables are likely to be determinants of the system or problem at hand, and hence lend us some *a priori* order. Given this array of logically most probable state-variables,* and whatever other substantive constraints on the search space the heuristic tentatively introduces, we are now in a position to treat the phenomenon as a severely stochastic one.

At this point, we leave the metatheoretical domain and attempt to introduce some deduced relational substance into the emerging model, usually through simulation-based, game-based, or adaptive programming techniques (which at least allow us to specify the range of logically probable, relational alternatives to be considered . . . and hence a set of qualitatively unique system states or configurations). At this point, we must then attempt to isolate that particular state alternative that is *a priori* most probable in our estimation. But in some cases

---

*The determination of logically most-probable state-variable arrays or system configurations (relational states) is disciplined by subjective probabilities coupled with a Delphi process, a subject discussed in detail in Chapter 6.

	INDETERMINACY	SEVERE STOCHASTICITY	MODERATE STOCHASTICITY	DETERMINACY
Analytical Task	Generation of heuristics or a metatheoretical envelope to tentatively bound "search space."	Development of array of logically probable system states (qualitative alternatives).	Generation of inductive inferences or sets of statistically-disciplined extrapolations or projections.	Development of optimization algorithms or fully determined predictive/descriptive models of system behavior.
Results of Analysis	Should identify the most logically probable array of *state-variables*.	Should isolate the particular *relational* configuration that is most likely to occur, given state variables.	Should isolate "ranges" within which specific *parametric or coefficient* values are expected to fall.	Should converge on specific parametric and coefficient values.
Appropriate Instrument	Hypothetico-deductive method; Delphi process.	Hypothetico-deductive method (or inductive inference, where permissible), disciplined by use of subjective probabilities or adaptive programming algorithms.	Use of a Bayesian process whereby subjective probabilities are gradually transformed into objective indices, such that a range of alternatives—all belonging to the same qualitative set—is generated.	Use of positivistic instruments . . . particularly controlled empirical manipulation and experimentation (e.g., hypothesis-free, analytic methods).

Figure 5.19 The system analysis paradigm.

the "states" which the system may assume may be periodic or otherwise precedented in nature, in which instance we may develop event-probability distributions that are predicated on inductive inferences (and therefore indexed with
historical probabilities of occurrence). At any rate, the particular relational
state (configuration) that achieves the highest objective or subjective probability
of accuracy now becomes *the* expected qualitative state of the system, and we
thus transform our severely stochastic problem into a moderately stochastic one
(naturally, where subjective as opposed to empirical probabilities are employed
in making this selection from among state-alternatives, the convergence is an
analytical expedient whose validity will subsequently be empirically validated, a
process treated in the next chapter).

With a moderately-stochastic system, we are now in a position to use the extrapolative or projective instruments (e.g., statistical or inductive inference-based
devices) that will allow us to specify probabilistic *ranges* within which parametric and magnitudinal coefficient values are expected to fall. We then inaugurate
empirical experiments that will, hopefully, force a convergence on a single point
value within these ranges, perhaps through a Bayesian process.[13] Once we have
such convergences for all parameters and all coefficients, our system has been
effectively translated from a moderately stochastic into a deterministic system.
At this point, the single most probable parametric and coefficient values are
coupled with the state-variable array and relational states agreed on in earlier
phases, and our model-building task is complete. In effect, then, we have transformed an effectively indeterminate system into an ultimately deterministic one
through the system analysis process just outlined.

In Chapter 6 the technology of this process will be amplified and elaborated,
especially within the context of a general problem-solving paradigm and a paradigm for formative system design. But before going to this more detailed level,
there are three strategic equivocations we should introduce, pertinent to what we
have just done. The first equivocation is fairly obvious: at any point in the system analysis process the *inherent* properties of the system under investigation
may prohibit us from proceeding further. Thus, for an inherently (as opposed to
effectively) indeterminate system, the best we can do is to provide that broad
metatheoretical (heuristic) envelope; for an inherently severely stochastic system, the best we can do is to define the range of logically (or empirically) probable alternative event-states, being unable to cause a convergence on any single
alternative; for an inherently moderately-stochastic system, the best we can do
is to specify the "ranges," being unable to effect the isolation of a single point
value within that range.

In somewhat the same way, certain systems will allow us to develop an *a
priori* information base that may obviate the necessity for going through all the
steps. Thus, for example, an effectively deterministic problem would be approached under the positivistic analytical modality, in which case our only step
is the empirical trial-and-error determination of 'stable' parametric and coeffi-

cient values . . . for the positivist platform denies the appropriateness of any theoretical (hypothetical) predicates, and hence the first three steps in the system analysis paradigm would be gratuitous.

The second equivocation is a bit more subtle, evolving largely from the discussions in the first chapter. This refers to the criteria we established for a "good" model, particularly the fact that the connections among its various components should be nonelliptical . . . logically consistent and formulated according to the formal laws of deductive inference (or, for essentially extrapolative or projective constructs, according to the laws of inductive inference). What this means, in practice, is that empirical validation exercises aimed at lower-level components of the model will automatically reflect on the validity (or invalidity) of the higher-level model components . . . for these higher-level components are, in effect, the formal premises from which the lower-level components were deduced (or induced). Thus we have an integrated construct, one where the relationships among the various levels are clearly and precisely specified, such that higher-order components become *hypotheses* whose probable accuracy is reflected in the extent to which lower-order components derived from them are shown empirically to be valid. This *reciprocity of inference* and the *apodictical* quality of the construct as a whole—this latter term meaning that our construct is susceptible to empirical validation in all aspects—are "necessary" properties of proper system models . . . a point we shall make much of in the coming chapter when we introduce the empirical "learning loop" concept as a requisite step in any model-building process, but an element omitted from the generic system analysis paradigm presented here.

Before ending this section on the logic of system analysis, there is a third equivocation to be made. In most cases, not all aspects of any system will be reducible to deterministic formulation. That is, there will likely be some mix of deterministic and stochastic components, as some system properties are often more analytically tractable than others. When this occurs, there is really no theoretical or procedural problem . . . it simply means that the model will contain some probabilistic components in company with deterministic ones. Under the system analysis paradigm, we are simply asked to bring as much precision and discipline to the entity under treatment as its properties will admit . . . and nothing is said about all system aspects having to wind up in the same analytical category (e.g., determinism, moderate stochasticity, etc.). In fact, as the reader will hopefully recall from Section 4.3, the formulation of the general system iconograph and the general system typology (Figures 4.3 and 4.4) specifically allowed for system dimensions to vary in terms of their analytical tractability.

In summary then, we have tried to show that all the instruments in the system science arsenal—all the analytical modalities available to modern scientists, problem-solvers, and decision-makers—have both positive and necessary roles to play within the confines of the system analysis process. Moreover, we have tried to isolate some of the ways in which allegories or models predictated on one or another of these instruments will differ, and in this respect show them to be *congruent* only in the face of specific phenomenal attributes. Particularly, the informational output from the various instrumental categories will be expected to differ on the following dimensions:

- The proportion of the information output dependent on empirically predicated *data*, per se.
- The proportion of the informational output dependent upon the operation of logical, mathematical, statistical, verbal, or other instrumental vehicles.
- The extent to which the instrumental mediators are themselves empirically *validated*, or the extent to which they are judgmental, intuitionalistic, or otherwise a *prioristic* in origin.
- The marginal productivity of the instruments employed, in terms of their informational output in relation to expenditures of analytical resources.
- The absolute effectiveness of the instrumentation used, reflected in the ultimate error levels of our allegories.

Most critically, however, we have tried to deduce the congruent associations between instrument types and systemic ideal-types, as the latter are the driving determinants of analysis, at least in the following terms:

- The probability of any *a priori* informational stock fully exhausting the postulated properties of the real is greatest for the essential mechanism (i.e., the Type-I system), least for the essential gestalt (Type-IV system).
- Similarly, the probability of any *a posteriori* informational state adequately exhausting the postulated properties of the real state diminishes as the phenomenon at hand departs from the properties associated with the Type-I entity, etc.
- The cost of reducing the probability of predictive and/or causal error associated with the allegorization of some phenomenon by any given increment will vary inversely with the extent to which that phenomenon approaches the properties of the Type-IV system.
- Finally, the greater the approximation of the entity which we are trying to capture analytically to the essentially deterministic ideal-type, the greater the probability that components of the model predicated on extrapolative or projective instruments operating on an historical data base will be accurate.

It is to a further defense and elaboration of the instrumental aspects of the system sciences to which we now turn, especially to the development of some procedural models. Yet as we leave this work on analytical congruence, it should be clear that the system scientist's call for a *syncretic* methodology—for one enabling a complementary mix of quantitative and qualitative, inductive and deductive instruments—is greatly preferred to any methodology that attempts to employ one modality to the effective exclusion of the other. For neither of these modalities, *alone*, can guide the system scientist either properly or efficiently through all the fields he must be prepared to wander.

5.6 NOTES AND REFERENCES

1. See Robert Merton's *Social Theory and Social Structure* (New York: Free Press, 1968), particularly p. 139ff.
2. For more on the trivialization of science via positivism, see Anatol Rapoport's "The Search for Simplicity," in *The Relevance of General System Theory* (New York: George Braziller, 1972), pp. 15-30.
3. There is an emerging branch of mathematical system theory that attempts to define disciplined ways in which qualitative variables, e.g., "fuzzy" sets, may be handled. A good introduction to this area is given in L.A. Zadeh's "Fuzzy Sets and Systems," in *Proceedings of the Symposium of System Theory* (New York: Polytechnic Institute of Brooklyn, 1965), pp. 29-37.
4. An extremely interesting, though somewhat mathematical, version of a learning paradigm—Bayesian based—is given in K.S. Fu's "Learning System Theory," in *System Theory*. ed. Zadeh and Polak (New York: McGraw-Hill, 1969), pp. 425-463. This paper also contains an excellent bibliography, especially valuable for those new to the field.
5. In Chapter 8 we shall talk about the stochastic-state modality, a problem-solving paradigm based on an expansion of game theory and simulation techniques. Here we might simply note that the concept of game-based modeling, and the springboard for modern studies in that area, was provided by John von Neumann and Oscar Morgenstern in their *Theory of Games and Economic Behavior* (Princeton: Princeton University Press, 1947)
6. Jacob Marschak, "Economic Measurements for Policy and Prediction," in *Studies in Econometric Methods*, ed. Hood and Koopmans (New Haven: Yale University Press, 1953). Note especially his defense of the "shock model" concept as a way in which economists can protect themselves against criticism from decision- or policy-makers using their predictions as premises.
7. There are, however, some extremely interesting if somewhat tentative explorations that have been made. Among them would be the following: Newell, Shaw, and Simon's, "Elements in a Theory of Human Problem Solving," *Psychology Review*, **65** (1958); Newell and Simon's *Human Problem Solving* (Englewood Cliffs: Prentice-Hall, 1972); W.R. Reitman, "Heuristic Decision Procedures, Open Constraints and the Structure of Ill-Defined Problems," *Human Judgments and Optimality*, ed. Shelly and Bryan (New York: John Wiley & Sons, 1964); and Frank George's *Models of Thinking* (London: George Allen and Unwin, 1970).
8. Reitman, *op. cit.*, p. 308.
9. In this regard, see the remarkable book by Arthur Koestler, *The Act of Creation* (New York: Macmillan Publishing Company, 1964), especially Appendix II.
10. Stafford Beer, *The Brain of the Firm* (London: Allen Lane, 1972).
11. Russel Ackoff and Fred Emery's *On Purposeful Systems* (Chicago: Aldine Publishing Company, 1972), especially Chapters 4-8.
12. Edgar Dunn, *Social and Economic Development: A Process of Social Learning* (Baltimore: Johns Hopkins Press, 1971).

13. Good discussions of Bayesian processes may be found in many places, among them: Ho and Lee, "A Bayesian Approach to Problems in Stochastic Estimation and Control," *IEEE Transactions in Automatic Control*, **AC-9** (1964); Robert Schlaifer, *Probabilities and Statistics for Business Decisions* (New York: McGraw-Hill, 1959); and William Feller, *An Introduction to Probability Theory and its Applications*, 3rd ed., vol. 1 (New York: John Wiley & Sons, 1968).

6

System Architecture: A Platform for Complex Problem-Solving

6.0 INTRODUCTION

There are basically three major applications for system analysis: (a) problem-solving, (b) policy-setting, and (c) decision-making. In this chapter, we shall be providing a "technology" for the first of these areas, whereas the second and third areas will be treated in Chapter 7.

We approach the general problem-solving area by introducing what we shall refer to as the "prescriptive model-building process." This, basically, entails looking at problems as systems in their own right, and viewing the development of solutions as tantamount to the development of problem-solving systems. In terms of procedures, the prescriptive model-building process first demands that we develop a descriptive/predictive model of the problem to be solved, to serve as a reference for the design of the system that is to solve it. The problem-solving system then becomes "prescriptive" in the strictest sense of the word, serving to offset the undesirable properties of the system we have elected (or which we have been forced) to attack . . . hopefully.

The instruments and techniques appropriate for the analysis and design of complex systems are collected under what we shall call the *system architecture* platform. In introducing its attributes, we shall thus have our first opportunity to say something about the tactical aspects of large-scale system analysis and design projects, and hence take our first step toward "operationalizing" the system analysis paradigm introduced in the previous chapter.

The system architecture platform is applicable to phenomena falling into any of our analytical categories developed from Chapter 4 (deterministic, moderately stochastic, severely stochastic, or indeterminate). What differs, basically, is the expedience of the problem-solving or system-design process, and the rapidity with which we complete our tasks. For essentially mechanical (e.g., deterministic) problems, the system analyst will have little trouble working through the various analytical tasks set out. But the factors inhibiting both problem definition and system design in the organic (e.g., indeterminate) domain will

192

deny the analyst any neatly linear or monolithic path. Rather, the exercises he goes through will be reflexive and recursive, folding back on one another and carrying him through some often tortuous and time-consuming "learning loops" before he finally emerges with an adequate system design. Thus, in a sense, system architecture is the prescriptive model-building process applied to effectively indeterminate problems, much as standard system engineering could be described as the prescriptive model-building process aimed at solving essentially mechanical or deterministic problems. So, as this chapter will hopefully make clear, system architecture can be considered as a first if somewhat halting step toward that "new methodology" Julius Stulman has asked to be developed.

... a new methodology for thinking, one that leads us from the simple viewpoint to a system of thinking, from system to an organization of systems to synthesis, and from synthesis ultimately into metamorphosis—in other words, a methodology of integrated thought and action in which there is a continuing feedback and flow forward that brings constant and continual change to all parts of the system.[1]

In terms of its basic properties, the system architecture paradigm would incorporate virtually all the instruments introduced in Chapter 5, with special emphasis on the deductive-based tools. Important among these would be the *Delphi* process, a procedure for the systematic collection and manipulation of presumably expert or relevant opinion pertinent to some problem or phenomenon. The Delphi process represents a well-developed and widely applied technology, one on which there is a substantial and still growing literature.[2] Here we shall be exploring its use in the context of complex problem-solving and normative system building (e.g., creating therapeutic systems or "utopian" futures). With respect to this latter task, which we undertake in Section 6.4, we also have recourse to the techniques of *defactualization* . . . the technology of constructing artificial futures predicated on disciplined conjecture and speculation. Again, there is some significant literature available to us in this area, including works by scholars such as Simon, de Jouvenal, and Ozbekhan.[3]

Employing these devices—coupled with others such as heuristics, subjective probabilities, event-probability distributions, Bayesian statistics, adaptive programming, etc.—system architecture will emerge as a paradigm especially congruent with the solution of highly complex problems, *qua* systems, where the solutions also take the form of systems.

6.1 THE PRESCRIPTIVE MODEL-BUILDING PROCESS

In Chapter 5 we viewed the scientist as a model-builder. We saw that the models he constructs may serve several ambitions: explanation, description, prediction, or causal reconstruction. Now we want to add a fifth ambition, one especially pertinent for the applied scientist . . . *prescription.* Prescriptive models purport to structure a solution to a problem which is itself defined as a system. In short, prescriptive models house the design criteria for problem-solving systems. Thus, the efforts of the applied system scientist—and the loci of his contributions to the world at large—will be mainly in the nexus between problems and problem-solving systems. Specifically, he will generally try to construct a descriptive/predictive model of some phenomenon demanding treatment, solution, therapy, or some other action (to wit, a problem); this problem-definition model will then become the referent against which a model for a problem-solving system will be generated. The problem-definition model will be used to generate the performance requirements for the problem-solving system model. In this sense, then, the applied system scientist acts as a direct link between the world of academics and the world of administration, between the community of contemplation and the community of action.

As we have tried to show, the relative ease or complexity of constructing the problem-definition model will depend largely on the extent to which the problem at hand approximates the characteristics of the "mechanical" ideal-type of Chapter 1 (see Figures 1.1 or 6.1) or the Type-I (deterministic) system of Chapter 4 . . . the extent to which the system at hand exhibits properties that are empirically accessible, capable of being translated into measurable, quantitative surrogates, and capable of being manipulated within what amounts to a controlled laboratory experiment. But also, for the predictor of system "states," the raw time interval between the point of analysis and point at which predictions are to apply (the horizon) determines, in large part, the inherent complexity of the projective-extrapolative task. Where the interval between prediction and the horizon is extremely large, our ability to rely on extrapolations from an empirical data base may be seriously undermined, more so to the extent that the system and/or environment in question are nonstable or susceptible to change. At that point, we must introduce qualitatively unprecedented properties into our predictive scenario, properties that could not have been derived, as such, from historical phenomenal behavior or structure. In such a case, even when our model-building ambitions are strictly descriptive or static, we face the necessity of entering broad discontinuities (or structural-causal gaps) into our emerging model. For when the system is an "open" one, certain determinants of system states may be transparent or inaccessible to the empiricist (e.g., too far removed in time or space), or he will not be able to assume with any degree of confidence that the unobserved portions of a system's structure will be neat extrapolations or projections of the empirically observed. And when we introduce the predictive ambition, and thus consider dynamic as opposed to static analysis, the analyst treating an inherently complex system may not make the assumption that the system's future states will be any neat, allegorizable function of the system's historical states. But all this we already know from previous work.

Yet to refresh these points, Figure 6.1 redefines the two most universal phe-

PROPERTY DIMENSIONS	MECHANICAL IDEAL-TYPE [Type I System: Essential Mechanism]	ORGANIC IDEAL-TYPE Type IV System: Essential Gestalt
Interface conditions with environment	• Closed system • Autarchic ecological ideal-type	• Open system • Heuristic ecological ideal-type
Structural or domain characteristics	• Additive or linear in nature • Segmented structurally and functionally • Neatly hierarchical	• Synergistic or nonlinear • Fully differentiated • Nonhierarchical (reticulated)
Dynamic attributes	• Stationary on micro level (e.g., finite or steady state) • Homogeneous or homeostatic on macro level (stable input-output relationships)	• Nonstationary on micro level (e.g., stochastic-state or equifinal system) • Unstable in terms of input-output relationships (macro function) through time
Normative analytical properties	• Empirically accessible • Amenable to quantification • Amenable to experimental manipulation	• At least partially empirically inaccessible • Unamenable to precise surrogation • Experimentally intractable
Amenability to inductive inference	Given starting-state conditions, future states may be induced (extrapolated) with a high degree of confidence . . . system's future is a calculable function of system's past.	System's future is unlikely to be any calculable function of historical system states; unobserved portions of system's domain are unlikely to be neat projections of observed portions.

Figure 6.1 Antonymical ideal-types

nomenal ideal-types, the *mechanistic* and the *organic*, using some generic system referents from Chapters 2 and 3. In considering these, the reader might wish to note that the organic ideal-type leads to the condition of indeterminancy and that, moreover, it seems to be a more proper general reference for the social, behavioral, and political sciences than the mechanistic referent.

From even the most casual review of Figure 6.1, it should be clear that a problem approximating the properties of the organic ideal-type will be considerably more difficult to model or allegorize than a problem that is essentially mechanical in nature. And where the problem is an organic one, the expected imprecision and error inherent in the problem-definition model will make the design of a problem-solving system a probabalistic exercise, for the solution system must use the problem-definition model as its reference. In this sense, then, the worst of all possible analytical words is that which finds us trying to design an essentially *organic* system to solve an essentially *organic* problem . . . and so often, the existence of the latter implies the necessity for the former.

In fact, the problem-solver facing an effectively organic phenomenon will face difficulty at virtually all points in the prescriptive model-building exercise . . . which, in essence, becomes a generalized problem-solving process. There are, of course, no lack of paradigms purporting to set out the procedural conditions for problem-solving. But when we consider that the proper problem-definition model will project conditions of the problem at the point where we intend to take action—or at the point where we can legitimately intervene—and that a problem-solving system will have to be responsive to these projections, then a problem-solving paradigm like that proposed by the policy-scientist, Harold Lasswell, becomes attractive. For Lasswell, an " . . . adequate strategy of problem solving encompasses five intellectual tasks," which he defines as:

"Goal clarification: What future states are to be realized as far as possible in the social process?

"Trend description: To what extent have past and recent events approximated the preferred terminal states? What discrepancies are there? How great are they?

"Analysis of conditions: What factors have conditioned the direction and magnitude of the trends described?

"Projection of developments: If current policies are continued, what is the probable future of goal realizations or discrepanices?

"Invention, evaluation, and selection of alternatives: What intermediate objectives and strategies will optimize the realization of preferred goals?"*

But for our purposes here, we are less interested in a strategic problem-solving paradigm than in one that sets out the *tactical* procedures to be followed in the development of the prescriptive models of which we have been speaking. In this sense, then, consider Figure 6.2 which sets out a problem-solving/model-building paradigm more appropriate for our immediate uses.

We note from the figure, that the first step is the isolation or development of those major structural factors (e.g., state-variables) that are expected to be the major determinants of the problem. Normally, we shall then take a second step that reduces these major problem determinants to causal sequences that allegorize the way in which they themselves are determined . . . that is, we go through a system reduction exercise that eventually arrives at the lowest-order determinants of the problem, establishing these in a series of subproblem models which depict the relationships among the subdeterminants in terms of both magnitude and direction of influence.

The third step in the construction of a problem definition model is then a synthesis exercise, the point where we attempt to allegorize the relationships between the major problem determinants themselves . . . which generally involves the transposition of the various linearized (serialized) subproblem models into a causally significant *network* construct with pretentions to both holisticity and predictivity. Thus, at this stage, we have the basic structural description of the problem *qua* system: the array of state-variables, their causal sequences, and the set of relationships prevailing among these state-variables. To translate this structural (descriptive) model into a predictive one, it is necessary to proceed to

*Quoted from *A Pre-view of Policy Sciences* (New York: Elsevier, 1971), p. 39.

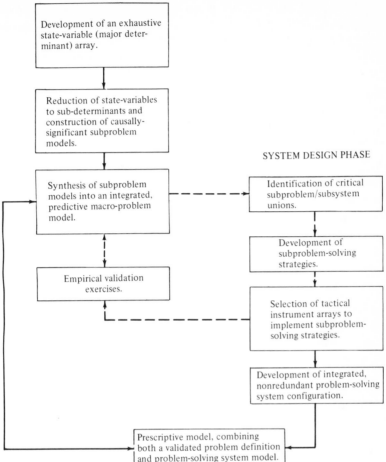

Figure 6.2   The prescriptive model-building process.

the two lower levels of analysis. Specifically, we must, with reference to some future point in time, assign the state-variables specific values, and then do the same for the coefficients of relationship. The result is a model that is capable of projecting problem properties and predicting future system states.

With the problem-definition model in hand, the design of the problem-solving system tends also to become an exercise in successive system synthesis. As the figure shows, the fourth of our prescriptive model-building tasks involves the identification of those subproblems most in demand of treatment, and the association of a subsystem with each of these. Thus, the problem-solving system is an initially *modularized* one (for reasons which will be made apparent later), where each subsystem is dedicated to the solution of a specific subproblem.

The fifth and sixth of the prescriptive model-building tasks then are developing a sub-problem-solving strategy to be associated with each subsystem, and selecting tactical instruments that will hopefully result in the successful implementation of the subproblem-solving strategies. The seventh step is a critical one, for here we inaugurate the empirical validation exercises or learning loops that will either tend to support or negate the previous activities . . . the process of field testing the prior hypotheses *cum* model components. The next step, once the empirical trials or learning loops have been run, is the integration of the heretofore modularized system, with the intention of introducing system efficiency by eliminating redundancies at all levels. Finally, as in Figure 6.2, the problem definition and system models are co-joined into a dual, integrated "field" construct.*

While subsequent sections of this chapter will amplify the logic of this paradigm, it is well here to suggest once again that the properties of the problem at hand will have a definite impact on the expedience, efficiency, and ultimate accuracy of our prescriptive model-building exercises. In fact, we may be rather specific here, for as a problem begins to depart from the mechanistic criteria, the prescriptive model-builder will have to be prepared to operate in the face of difficulties which sorely limit his ability to produce adequate problem-definition models.

First, there will usually be a lack of indentifiable, definable boundaries for organic problem systems due to the constant interchange of forces and material with the environment. This means that some problem determinants will be unidentifiable at any point in time, being spatially or temporally removed from the immediate problem vicinity. Moreover, the dynamic causal sequences leading to the problem's "state" may be expected to be unallegorizable because of:

- components' capability for equifinal behavior (getting to an event by different paths).
- reflexivity, by which every variable in the problem may legitimately be expected to exert determining force on any other.
- some of the forces determining the problem state will be transparent, especially those attitudinal and behavioral determinants which can be only reflectively observed (through their impact on observable parts).

Finally, the future states of a problem will be largely unpredictable because of structural/dynamic indeterminacies, and because organic system components have the capability for initiating strategic behavior to counteract, in possibly unpredictable ways, any move made by the problem-solving system.

When the problem at hand entails such complexity, the design of a congruent problem-solving system will also be considerably complicated. That is, there may be a tendency for problem-solving systems to reflect, at least partially, the

*In this context a field construct treats, simultaneously, the behavior of two or more interacting (interfaced) systems.

inherent complexity of the problem. Thus, for example, we earlier associated Type-IV systems with complicated, unprecedented problems, whereas the simpler Type-I system was suggested as sufficient to meet and manage essentially mechanical problems. So, as the problem at hand begins to depart from the criteria of mechanisticity, we expect the following confoundations to occur in the system design process.

First, because of the inability to accurately determine the future "states" the problem-system might evidence, there is a probability that any problem-solving strategy we elect to implement will prove dysfunctional. That is, we may have predicated our treatment on an event that will not in fact occur. Secondly, because of the wide behavioral-reactive repertoire available to components of nonmechanical systems—evidenced especially in their facility for "strategic" behavior—any therapeutic instrument we elect to impose may prove dysfunctional because:

- of the lack of empirically validated correlations between instruments and effects within the context of organic entities.
- of the possibility that instruments employed in an organically structured entity (i.e., a reflexive-recursive system context) may interfere with each other.

Finally, state-changes may occur more rapidly in the system we are treating than can be adjusted for in the problem-solving system, introducing the possibility that the problem system and the problem-solving system will be chronically out-of-phase.

These confounding factors act to make the problem-solving task in the essentially organic domain something other than the neat, expedient, and relatively monolithic task that it becomes in the mechanical domain. For in following our paradigm for effectively organic cases, the system analyst makes many turns, tries many different trajectories, and gets involved in many tangents. Moreover, his exercise is characterized by much time spent in the learning loop shown in Figure 6.2. But aside from this, the inherent complexity of the problem itself, and the reflective complexity of the system designed to solve it, demands that the system *architect* employ a very different set of tactics, instruments, and tools than his system *engineering* counterpart, a point which leads us directly to the next section.

6.2 THE SYSTEM ARCHITECTURE REPERTOIRE

The system architecture approach permits the system scientist, researcher, decision-maker, or policy-setter to maintain a "scientific" integrity in the face of the worst of all possible operational worlds: that where an essentially *organic* problem must be attacked by a system which will, itself, be effectively *organic*. The scientific aspect of the system architecture approach, in such a situation, is reflected in the table Figure 6.3. It establishes those instruments most appropriate for each of the eight steps in the prescriptive model-building process introduced in Section 6.1, thus harking back to the concept of analytical congruence introduced in Chapter 5.

As we can see, the procedural and instrumental aspects of the system architecture approach presumes the operational difficulties with organic phenomena set out in Section 6.1. In effect, it presumes that the system scientist, administrator, decision-maker, or policy-maker forced to operate in the organic domain will face indeterminancy on all fronts, at least initially, and that only the explicit recognition of what we do not know will eventually lead us to knowledge, per se. Thus, in the early phases of a problem-solving (prescriptive model-building) process, we must usually be content to work at a rather high level of abstraction and generality, and consider virtually all our initial constructs as tentative rather than axiomatic. At first, we may merely establish the broad directional (e.g., static-comparative) relationships between problem components. And initially, our problem definition process and system design process will most likely be focused on the most critical step in the problem-solving paradigm: identifying the relevant determinants of the problem and the broad structural properties that the problem-solving system is most likely to require for its effectiveness. Thus, all our *a priori* problem-solving tasks will be undertaken within the spirit of the hypothetico-deductive method described earlier.

This will affect the precision of our work. Rather than employing empirically-generated, precisely quantified variables or values, etc., we shall at first have to be satisfied with looser, cruder formulations. Similarly, in the initial *a priori* phases of our problem-solving exercises, we shall probably have to do without

ANALYTICAL TASK	CONGRUENT INSTRUMENTAL AND ANALYTICAL ASSOCIATIONS
1. Development of an array of state-variables to exhaust the problem's structural properties.	The most logically probable array of state-variables may be determined by a *Delphi*-type process, disciplined by subjective probabilities.
2. Development of predictive subproblem models (e.g., causal sequences determining state-variable values).	In most cases, such models may be generated with reference to *intradisciplinary* constructs existing within relevant disciplines . . . in many cases, competitive explanatory constructs will be available, so a *Delphi*-based selection process will have to be inaugurated.
3. Development of an integrated, predictive problem-model.	This step will usually involve the development of an initially most logically probable *scenario*, rather broad in its initial formulation. This scenario will serve a *heuristic* cause, simply serving to lend some *a priori* order to expectations about the way in which the integrated problem will be generated from its constituent subproblems, and the overall "states" it might exhibit.

ANALYTICAL TASK	CONGRUENT INSTRUMENTAL AND ANALYTICAL ASSOCIATIONS
4. Development of subproblem/subsystem ordered pairs (modules).	The generation of these problem-system "modules" will demand some sort of *system reduction* scheme to generate mutually exclusive, exhaustive, and fully "reduced" arrays of problems demanding treatment (as will be described in a subsequent subsection).
5. Development of subproblem-solving strategies.	Organic problems involve components capable of initiating "strategic" behavior, and changes introduced in one part of the problem will affect other parts, so the use of *game-based models* is dictated here (both to predict local effects and to try to precapture possible transmitted effects).
6. Development of subsystem instrument arrays.	For each of the alternative strategies developed, a most probably effective instrument array will have to be *inferred*, usually by referring to existing agent-effect models within pertinent disciplines (intradisciplinary cause-effect models).
7. Empirical Validation Exercises.	All the deductions (or inferences) made in the first six steps must now be subjected to empirical validation via a Bayesian-type "learning" process, involving: (a) The controlled implementation of those strategies and instrument arrays elected for inclusion during the *a priori* stage. (b) Successive empirical observation on the subproblem and subsystem properties of interest. (c) Feedback of results so that *a priori* subjective-probability distributions are gradually transformed into *a posteriori* objective ones, as completely as possible. (d) Iterations of observation and feed-back processes until *a posteriori* distributions *converge* on an empirically proven "best" strategy, instrument array and problem construct, etc. (e) Where divergence is indicated, empirical data may be used to modify the *a priori* models and a new testing-modification sequence initiated.
8. Development of an integrated macro-system model.	The finalization of the problem-solving system design will involve a *system synthesis* process. This is generally accomplished through the operations of *convergence* algorithms on two dimensions: (a) that which finds a consensus of judgment or opinion about problem and/or system properties that are unamenable to empirical access or measurement; (b) that which, wherever possible, drives the translation of initially subjective probabilities into objective ones. The net result should be a system model that gradually finds modularity (partitioning) giving way to integration, with a consequent increase in efficiency due to reduction in structural, resource, or treatment redundancies.

Figure 6.3 The System Architecture Repertoire.

objectively-generated, neatly continuous probability distributions and be content with more primitive artifices (e.g., broadly defined dichotomies or trichotomies of ideal-types that can support taxonomic analyses).* But gradually we hope to find these initially crude model components giving way to more elegant and precise ones. For as we move further along in the process, we should be developing more relevant and complete data bases from our concatenative empirical validation exercises. Our central dictate is simply this: *wherever the nature of the problem or system admits, we must make every effort to translate initially subjective probabilities into objective, empirically-generated ones, and to transform static, imprecise, directional coefficients into magnitudinal (quantified) ones.* Yet, never must we be so enamoured of the apparent neatness of mathematical or statistical formulations that we artificially constrain the problem to fit them. Ultimately then, working always within permissible quantitative and empirical boundaries (though always trying to extend them), we can hope to arrive at sets of what Robert Merton has called "theories of the middle range,"

> ... theories that lie between the minor but necessary working hypotheses that evolve in abundance from day-to-day research and the all-inclusive systematic efforts to develop a unified theory that will explain all the observed uniformities of social behavior, social organization and social change.[4]

It is system architecture's potential for deriving such models which concerns us most here, along with its potential for improving the efficacy (and secondarily, the efficiency) of the real-world problem-solving systems we can help build. Our discussion of the approach's operational aspects will thus reflect this duality of interest. Finally, neither systems architecture nor the instruments employed will have any significance beyond the sensitivity and integrity of the individuals employing them, for as Martin Shubik has wisely pointed out,

> ... it would be both foolish and presumptuous to present the new advances in mathematical method in the humanistic sciences as panaceas. They mark an extension of our ability to handle ideas and test concepts that cannot otherwise be examined easily. . . . They do not, per se, take the place of the well-read social scientist with broad factual knowledge, but they complement his capacities in a vital matter.[5]

At any rate, as has been so often suggested, one begins an analytical attack on complex problems or systems by trying to get some first, rough discipline or structure. An instrument that is admirably well-suited to this task for most analytical situations is the Delphi process. Because it is a process unfamiliar to many, even very sophisticated problem-solvers (and also because we will be

---

*Note that for essentially "mechanical" problems, recourse to the system architecture instruments would hardly be warranted, for they would be instances of "overkill" (see, again, Figure 5.15).

modifying some of its properties for our own purposes in these pages), we'll have to spend some time outlining its characteristics and potentials. For it, along with other more widely known instruments in the system architecture repertoire (e.g.,Bayesian analysis, adaptive programming, simulation), constitutes our first line of defense against indeterminacy.

6.2.1 Notes on the Delphi Process

The Delphi process is a rather well-developed technique for dealing with nonmechanistic, nondeterministic phenomena. It, according to Berstein and Cetron,

> ... could be described as an elegant method for developing a consensus [by] the systematic solicitation of expert opinion [and by] the polling of experts representing the controlling factors and from these data developing a consensus which can be used in planning. Its advantage consists in the systematic treatment of data that include the experts' intuitive assessment of imponderables.[6]

There are, of course, plenty of "imponderables" in the organic domain, so the Delphi approach becomes especially promising as an input generator for our complex problem-solving and system architecture activities. Clearly, the opinions solicited may take many forms. They may represent the probability of certain events occurring, or perhaps their desirability. They may represent opinions as to the likelihood of certain complex, compound event-sets accurately reflecting future states of the world, or they may simply represent collections of ordered values or affective positions among diverse populations. Thus, in addition to expert opinion, Delphi processes may also systematically collect and manipulate values or "utopian" variables, and use them as inputs to model-building processes of any ambition (normative, predictive, prescriptive, etc.). For the purposes here, then, Delphi may be considered to be a device by which we collect, codify, and direct essentially deductive or hypothetico-deductive inputs. The utility of the Delphi process is especially well demonstrated in long-range forecasting exercises. The reason for this is one with which we are already familiar: as the time horizon of interest grows successively further away from the present, the relevance of experience or empirical data pertinent to historical or current properties declines rapidly. In short, as the time horizon increases, the probability that the future state of some system will be a simple function of its historical states is radically reduced. Hence, for forecasting or predictive exercises, Delphi represents a much-needed alternative to simple extrapolation.

Naturally, systems that tend to be steady-state, stationary, or are essentially "mechanical" rather than organic in nature would be less susceptible to this generalization, and therefore more amenable to forecasting via extrapolation.

But for most systems of any complexity—and we must here include virtually all non-trivial social, economic, or political phenomena, etc.—the probable accuracy of extrapolative forecasts will rather quickly go from dubious to ludicrous. For this reason, the Delphi process provides a judgmental or "deductive" base for long-range forecasts, one which may include experiential or empirical expectations but is in no way restricted to them. In fact, as the complexity of the phenomenon at hand increases, or as the time horizon expands, the deductive relative to the inductive-empirical component in Delphi processes must be expected to increase.* In effect, then, the Delphi process allows us to transform deductively-predicated phenomenon (i.e., concepts) into legitimately "scientific" inputs, much as empirical techniques allow us to capture sense-data (i.e., percepts) that will drive model-building exercises directed at simpler phenomena.

In addition to solicitation and ordering of opinions, expectations, or judgments, the Delphi process also is, as was just mentioned, an excellent vehicle for the systematic solicitation of, and ordering of, axiological (value-driven) or affective positions. These axiological or affective positions are also nonempirical in origin, or if originally empirically-predicated, have since become *a priorisms* (as is the case with biases, prejudices, and many "learned" attitudes, values, or beliefs that are carried beyond the context of their generation). While affective and axiological phenomena are empirically elusive, they nevertheless are *real* determinants of some systems' behavior, and as a consequence must be considered in decision-making or policy-setting activities. It is, indeed, a naive system analyst or designer who feels he can ignore these "transparent" phenomena with impunity, despite the fact that they are often difficult to collect with accuracy, and usually amenable only to relatively imprecise formulation.

In summary, then, the Delphi process' utility is found in its ability to capture deductively-predicated or conceptual "data," thus allowing us to compensate for the paucity of relevant empirical or objective information pertinent to very complex systems or relatively far futures. It was in this sense, then, that we suggested that a Delphi process might be inaugurated to generate the array of state-variables that are expected to be the set of determinants for some effectively organic problems. Recall that one of the properties of an organic phenomenon was its "openness" on the ecological dimension. Earlier we suggested that open systems present an analytical problem because determinants may be far removed from the physical location of the system, or removed in time from the point of analysis. Thus, in the open, organic domain, "causes" are potentially obscure, and effects may resonate far out into space or the future. As such, not all of the state-variables comprising a system will be empirically accessible at the point of analysis; others will have to be *deduced*, with a Delphi panel (perhaps representing diverse opinions and backgrounds, etc.) polled as to their opinion about those state-variables that should be incorporated into the emerging problem

*See again our discussion of informational bases in Section 5.5.

definition model. In effect, then, the Delphi process aims at producing a most likely array of state-variables to serve as the foundation for a problem-definition model, and will systematically collect and order a diversity of opinion about the probability of certain factors being actual determinants of the problem at hand.

As for the use of the Delphi process in the second and third steps of the prescriptive model-building paradigm, it is simply necessary to note that the Delphi process may be directed at the solicitation of opinion about the probable accuracy or relevance of conceptual constructs, theories, formulas, or hypotheses, etc., as well as individual factors (state-variables) as was the case above. Thus, when we are attempting to elect the best subproblem model to be entered into the emerging problem definition model—and where two or more competitive constructs pretend to be *the* explanation for the particular problem component being considered—expert opinion may be systematically solicited and ordered to select the expectedly "best" of these competitive alternatives.

In a later section we shall see why such selections often have to be made, and will be more specific as to how they are to be made; here we simply suggest that the Delphi process is not restricted to any particular class or level of information, but may operate at all four of the "levels of analysis" we earlier spelled out. Thus, at the relational level, that primarily associated with the third model-building task (where we attempt to synthesize an integrated, predictive model of the problem from its subproblem constituents), the Delphi process allows us to poll a diverse audience for their opinions about the likely accuracy and relevance of the various alternative relational states that might prevail, or about the overall configuration that the problem *qua* system is likely to exhibit at the point of concern (e.g., at the predictive horizon).

This latter process, in a sense, is roughly equivalent to the solicitation of opinion about the relevance and accuracy of alternative *scenarios*, constructs attempting to capture and order properties of complex "wholes." These scenarios differ from descriptive models, per se, in that they represent what might be, rather than what is just "likely" to be. Moreover, scenarios are usually of the "if : then" type of formulation, and are thus exercises in the elaboration of possibilities as well as just probabilities. They thus serve to set out the array of qualitative "state" alternatives that might be expected to occur, given some initial state conditions, and thus become fundamental for the treatment of severely stochastic systems (as per the earlier definition of these systems as capable of giving rise to a limited number of state alternatives which differ not merely in degree, as with moderately stochastic systems, but in fundamental quality).* Shortly we shall also use the scenario as the vehicle for ordering not just our expectations, but our desires as well; they thus will take on a "utopian" aspect in Section 7.3. At any rate, in step three of the prescriptive model-building process—considering that no empirical experiments or trials have yet been run—a Delphi exercise may be directed at defining the various configurations or states

*The logic of "administering" such systems will be dealt with in Chapter 8.

which the problem might exhibit, and toward the selection of one of these as the most likely of the alternatives.

6.2.2 Subjective Probabilities and the Concept of Convergence

The discipline inherent in the Delphi process—and the device that allows us to make "best" selections from among competing alternatives at all points in the problem-definition process—is the *subjective probability*. Subjective probabilities engineer any *convergence* we may achieve in opinions or judgments about elements of a truly complex (organic) problem. In short, in the *a priori* phases of system analysis or system design efforts, subjective probabilities play the same role as objective probabilities do in *a posteriori* problem-solving or system design exercises.

To begin with, it is clear that both long-range forcasting and complex system analysis exercises will be characterized—at least in initial phases—by the construction of models whose components are primarily deductive rather than inductive in origin. This implies a critical difference in procedure between such efforts and those undertaken in the mechanistic (e.g., deterministic) domain, a difference that becomes most explicit when we note the essentially different probability indices used to maintain the scientific integrity of the exercises.

Thus, whenever we are able to employ inductive inference in any of its guises (e.g., statistical extrapolation, qualitative projection, data base amplification, ampliative logic, etc.), our activities may be disciplined through the employment of *objective probabilities* . . . those derived from empirical analysis or controlled experimentation. Thus, a prescriptive model undertaken in the mechanistic domain will have each of its components indexed with an empirically generated index-of-accuracy (or confidence). This suggests, in turn, that the aggregated model will also carry with it an empirically predicated index-of-accuracy (or, in the inverse, an aggregated probability of error). We distinguish inductive models from deductive models largely by the fact that the predictions made by the inductive model, or its descriptive components, are traceable to some empirical data base, such that no essentially unprecedented qualitative components are introduced. Deductive models, as we already know, do introduce qualitatively new components between the original data base and the ultimate predictive—descriptive implications, such that at least some of the components of the model owe their origin less to facts than to instances of judgment, speculation, *a prioristic* reasoning, or subjective analysis (e.g., idiographic or intuitive operations).*

Clearly, these deductive models are the only alternative left to us (at least initially) in the organic domain, where the phenomena we encounter tend to exhibit spatial and temporal discontinuities in both structure and behavior. Under such conditions, the relevant, exhaustive, and accurate data base required

*See, again, Section 5.5.

for inductive operations is either lacking or irrelevant. Thus the danger of *a priori* error inherent in deductive processes may be more than offset by the error potential associated with the inductive presumption that the seeds of the future are accessible in the analysis of the past (or that the properties of an unobserved cross-sectional segment are inferentially present in the observed aspects of the phenomenon). In short, then, there is simply no inherent law dictating that inductively predicated models will always carry a lower probability of error than deductively predicated ones.

This point becomes especially significant when we realize that the inherent quality, actionability, or utility of any model becomes intelligible in terms of an abstract construct that does not distinguish between inductive and deductive predications, a construct with which we are already familiar. This construct is reproduced in Figure 6.4, where the gradual transformation of the event-probability distribution (from a less favorable expected "variance" state to a more favorable one) gives rise to the favorable learning curve.

Recalling the logic of Chapter 5, we can immediately see that the *a posteriori* event-probability distribution represents an improvement over the *a priori*, for in the former there are fewer events that are assigned any significant probability of occurrence, and these events are implicitly less diverse in their nature than those associated with the *a priori* distribution. Hence, as the *a priori* event-probability distribution is gradually transformed to the *a posteriori*—presumably as we expend greater analytical resources and/or take more observations on properties of interest—we generate a positive learning curve . . . one which reflects the lower expected probability of error associated with the *a posteriori* state (see Section 5.2).

The critical point is this: every model we build, as scientists, will be comprised of components that are susceptible to the analytical device just outlined. For the entry of any component into a model represents some sort of selection from among alternatives that might have been entered. Thus, any aspect of a model may be indexed by an expected probability of error which, in turn, is derived from the imposition of an event-probability distribution on the array of alternatives considered. The expected accuracy of our selection is indicated directly by

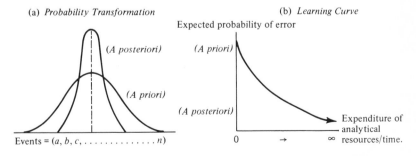

Figure 6.4 Relations between probability distributions and learning curves.

the variance associated with the event-probability distribution, with the ambition of analysis and research to cause the kind of transformation indicated in Figure 6.4. The aggregate expected probability of error associated with the model as a whole will then be some function of the event-probability distributions associated with each component of the model. Thus, a high-quality model will be that which generates an aggregate event-probability distribution approximating the *a posteriori* curve in the illustration. For, whether the model is intended as predictive, prescriptive, or reconstructive, the *a posteriori* state represents a situation of greater assurity and confidence than the *a priori*.

Clearly, the rate at which we cause such a transformation, and the ultimate level of expected error we can hope to achieve, depends in part on the level of analytical resources or time we are willing to invest, but depends primarily on the inherent analytical tractability of the phenomenon being modeled (the extent to which it meets the mechanistic criteria). But the transformation concept is equally valid in both the mechanistic and organic domains, or in either the inductive or deductive approaches. For the mechanics of the transformation operation do not distinguish between event-probability distributions that are the product of objectively or subjectively generated indices of expected accuracy. In short, it makes no difference to the statistical operations whether the probabilities being manipulated are empirical or judgmental in origin. Thus, a "good" model will simply be one that, at each point, enjoys the lowest possible variance in event-probability distributions imposed on its various elements . . . which simply means, in effect, that our confidence in the particular alternative model-component selected at all points is as high as it can legitimately be.

In general, then the condition for a good model is that it exhibit a minimal "internal" variance. When the model is an essentially deductive *(a priori)* one, then this internal variance is obtained by minimizing the variance in subjectively driven event-probability distributions surrounding each model component; when the model is an essentially empirical one, then the event-probability distributions should reflect minimal variance in objective probability indices. In neither case does this say anything about the *operational* effectiveness of the models we build . . . for we cannot know about this until after the event we are trying to predict has already occurred; resulting in some "external" variance between predicted and actual events. Thus, in all model-building cases, it is internal variance which we try to minimize, even in the recognition that internal and external variance may not always be strongly correlated.*

When we move from mechanistic to organic problems, then, or from short-range to long-range forecasts, what changes are not the criteria for a good model, but the nature of the probability indices used to drive the event-probability distributions disciplining our "selection" decisions. And as we know, in any model-

---

*External variance is not available to us at the time we are constructing the model. Thus, our expectations need not reflect reality, and hence the possibility for a weak correlation between internal (expectation-driven) and external (reality-driven) variance.

building exercise, it is important to translate, as fully as possible, subjective probabilities into objective ones. This is precisely the task that Step 7 of the prescriptive model-building paradigm performs; for the "empirical learning loops" we undertake there are the exercises that gradually transform our problem-definition and problem-solving system models from *a priori* to *a posteriori* ones. As should already be clear, the extent to which this transformation can be performed will depend on the analytical catagory to which the problem and/or system *inherently* belongs, with inherently deterministic entities allowing us a complete transformation, and the other three categories successively reducing the extent to which objective probabilities may be substituted from subjective.

The subjective probabilities in the *a priori* phases of our model-building exercises in the organic domain thus provide much the same contribution as the objective probabilities would in the mechanistic domain. Both enable us to audit our learning progress in terms of the learning curves generated during our analysis operations; both help yield the criteria necessary for distinguishing a poor model from a good one; both assist us in generating the constant trade-offs which must be made between ultimate rectitude and expediency, between economics and academics . . . and both serve to yield a map of our information, or lack of it, pertinent to some phenomenon or class of phenomena. In summary then, subjective probabilities serve to codify and discipline judgment and speculation in much the same way that objective probabilities serve to codify and discipline experience and observation. And we tend to associate the subjective probabilities with the organic domain largely because, at the onset of analytical exercises, experience tends to become irrelevant and observation either impossible or gratuitous.

There are two final points to make here. The first point is that subjective probabilities may be obtained in several different ways, and that much current literature has sprung up suggesting how reasonably unbiased indices may be generated.[7] The second point concerns the fact that we couple the Delphi process with subjective probabilities because, in the system architecture scheme we are interested in obtaining a convergence (or consensus) of opinion, judgment, or expectations, etc.* The fundamental reason for this is that we employ the Delphi process to generate inputs for formal models, whereas others may employ it simply to sample opinion and, in fact, are not concerned with any divergences that appear. The end point of the system architecture model is *action*; that is, the results of the system analysis exercise are to be used as decision or policy premises. As such, it is the function of the system architecture approach to eliminate divergence if possible, and to reduce it in all instances. Hence our emphasis on the use of subjective probabilities to gain a convergence that, in the normal Delphi process, is not a necessary condition for success.

*In fact, consensus or convergence is the vehicle by which we minimize "internal" variance.

6.3 ARCHITECTING PROBLEM-SOLVING SYSTEMS

We may now proceed to explore some of the key operational aspects of system architecture in the first of its applications: *complex problem-solving.* Here, basically, we shall be offering some direct suggestions as to how the system architecture instruments may be employed within the broad framework of the prescriptive model-building process introduced earlier.

As suggested, the rate and efficiency of the learning process in the course of a problem-solving exercise will be reflected in the rapidity of convergences on low-variance event-probability distributions surrounding the structural and dynamic components of the emerging model. Analytical efficiency will be determined by several factors: the rate at which we converge on an expectedly exhaustive yet manageable array of state-variables purportedly acting as determinants of the problem, on the rapidity of our convergence on a set of ostensibly accurate causal sub-models, and on the ultimate efficiency of the synthesis process that finds us producing an integrated, predictive model from the isolated subproblem models. The overall quality of the problem definition model will depend on our ability to maximize the incidence of empirical as opposed to subjective constructs, which implies the gradual replacement of deductively predicated model components by inductively predicated ones . . . a natural consequence of a secularly favorable learning curve.

In the real world, however, the transition from subjective to objective probabilities and from speculative to empirically validated model components will not be easily made . . . not, that is, in the organic domain. In the first place, our major sources for model components—the social and behavioral sciences—are afflicted by the two debilitating problems discussed in Chapter 1, polarization and parochialization. Polarization tends to lead to constructs that are either empirically predicated but often trivial, or of sweeping ramification but highly speculative (or non-apodictical). When model-building ambitions are prescriptive in nature, carrying with them either policy or action implications for the real-world, neither type of construct can be employed without considerable modification. For, in most cases, empirical manageability and statistical discipline will have been gained at the expense of reality, usually by artificially isolating a phenomenon from confounding factors in the environment or from its natural relationship with other phenomena. By the same token, the speculatively-based models, while specific enough in their action implications, will usually be predicated on first-premises or assumptions that are empirically unvalidated, which will make the model's prescriptions or predictions erroneous to the extent that the initial premises are in error. Thus, the prescriptive model-builder will spend considerable time affecting a compromise between polarized constructs, trading-off the empirical precision of the one against the realism in terms of scope of the other. In the course of producing these quantitative-qualitative hybrids, the model-builder will be forced, at least initially, to index them with subjective as opposed to objective probabilities, something which the mechanistic problem-solver need not worry about because of the wealth of empirically validated constructs at his disposal in the physical, biological, or engineering sciences.

A second problem emerges with the recognition that our social and behavioral sciences are largely *parochial* in nature, affecting academic demarcations that are simply not present in real-world phenomena. Thus, socioeconomic development becomes intelligible to the sociologist largely in terms of social variables, to the economist largely in terms of economic variables, and to the behavioral scientist largely in terms of such empirically transparent factors as "values" or other axiological phenomena. In reality, development depends upon some mix of all three classes of factors, yet the parochialization of our disciplines has left us with rather precise but effectively irrelevant *intra*disciplinary models that, before they can become useful to the prescriptive model-builder, must be interconnected by the generation of appropriate *inter*disciplinary interface models. Obviously, these interdisciplinary interface models may have to be deduced, being unprecedented in origin, carrying substantive implications which themselves have little empirical prediction. As such, their construction must be guided by a Delphi-based process aimed at generating explanatory alternatives. These are then placed within the confines of an event-probability distribution engineered by subjective probabilities, ultimating, hopefully, in a consensus of presumably expert opinion about their respective adequacy. In short, the interconnection of parochialized constructs is a major service that the hypothetico-deductive modality may perform within the prescriptive model-building process, and one of the prime targets for the use of subjective probabilities as disciplining factors.

A third area in which our system architecture instruments provide something of a saving grace to the organic problem-solver is in the necessity for selecting among essentially competitive social and behavioral science constructs. This becomes especially important when we recognize that there is really not just *one* psychology or *one* sociology or *one* economics, but several, each of which purports generally to be *the* accurate interpretation of the field. Thus, when the model-builder must decide how to treat some axiological or behavioral factor in an emerging problem definition model, he may get radically different answers depending on which of the alternative psychological "schools" he queries. If he turns to the behaviorist school, he may get an allegory that is considerably different from that offered by the structuralist or gestaltist schools for effectively the same phenomenon. The same case would follow for most economic, social, or political issues. Wherever such competitive explanations exist, a decision must be made as to which, if any, to accept. Such a decision may be engineered by subjective probabilities driving a Delphi poll. More often than not however, the model-builder may have to develop some sort of a *syncretic* or eclectic alternative, encompassing aspects drawn from the two or more competitors. Here, again, this must be an essentially hypothetico-deductive exercise, one aimed at producing a qualitatively new entity, and hence becoming susceptible to indexing by subjective probabilities.

Whenever we strike instances of parochialization, polarization or competing explanatory models, we would, in the absence of the Delphi process and the concept of convergence, be forced to introduce a discontinuity or logical gap into the emerging problem definition model. Yet the employment of these instruments allows us to develop reasonably linearized models by isolating, from among all alternatives, the particular construct that enjoys the *highest logical probability* of being an accurate explanation for the phenomenon (problem aspect) at hand. The value of this logical probability index would be determined by the *degree of convergence* or consensus we are able to develop among the pollees engaged in a Delphi process, for the degree of convergence obtained would be directly reflected in the morphology of the resultant event-probability distribution pertinent to that aspect of the problem . . . in the variance of that distribution. Thus, our *confidence* in the accuracy of the model components we introduce into our emerging problem definition model is always available to us in surrogate form through the subjective probabilities employed, just as confidence in an empirical hypothesis or formulation is given by objective probability indices predicated on calculated variances.

Thus, the Delphi → subjective probability → convergence sequence may be employed at any level of analysis, and with respect to any aspect of the problem definition model-building process, a point which we may now make somewhat more explicit.

6.3.1 The Problem Definition Process

The ultimate problem definition model must be integrated to the extent that the real-world problem is integrated; its scope must reflect that of the real-world problem in terms of the structural determinants incorporated and considered; its dynamic aspects must adequately allegorize the range of processual interrelationships the problem-system exhibits in the real-world. Given such a model, we are then in a position to develop the design criteria for the problem-solving system, criteria reflecting not only the problem's structural and dynamic properties at any single point in time, but one that is sensitive to possible responses of the problem's components to actions initiated by the system.

In working toward the realization of this integrated, predictive model, we will have access to several resources:

(a) The range of existing social science model and data bases that purport to allegorize various social, economic, political, or behavioral phenomena we might encounter.

(b) The array of system design and analysis tools entered in the system architecture repertoire, along with those mathematical and statistical instruments we can safely borrow from the physical and engineering sciences for certain operations.

(c) Where existing instruments and models fail us or promise to be ineffective, we have recourse to the most basic of all analytical instruments . . . disciplined deductive inference and empirically-reinforced "learning" processes.

At any rate, as we have just seen, as the problem at hand departs from essentially mechanistic criteria (e.g., amenability to empirical observation, precise quantification, and experimental manipulation), existing sociobehavioral, political, or economic constructs become less applicable, forcing us to rely more and more on resources from the second and third of the above categories. This is due to factors which we have already mentioned . . . the tendency for most social and behavioral science constructs to be affected variously by polarization or parochialization.

Most analysts will quickly find, as the problem definition process begins, that many of the constructs on which they might draw—existing social and behavioral science models, hypotheses, paradigms, formulations, "laws", etc.—will be formulated largely in verbal terms, and will consider only broad directional cause-effect correlations (as with, for example, the comparative-statics models in economics or the ideal-types *cum* hypotheses of modern macrosociology). The net result is that an examination of the existing model bases available to us reflects the tendency to partition real-world phenomena into factor categories that parallel academic departments, and the consequent tendency to treat subjects falling within these various factor-classes as if they were *really* isolated from interactions and codependencies with variables falling within the purview of other academic disciplines.

But these models, albeit parochial, can be of direct use to us. First, they can serve as the basic vehicles for the identification of those structural factors that are expected to be "determinants" of the problem at hand. Secondly, they can be used to provide us with existing allegories of the process by which problem determinants obtain specific values (qualitative or quantitative) in the real-world . . . but only those determinants that admit to intradisciplinary explanation. Where problem determinants are themselves determined by variables (or subdeterminants) that are the property of several different disciplines, as is usually the case in the organic domain, we are going to have to provide *interdisciplinary interface models* so that the causal sequences may reflect the real-world interdeterminacy and reflexivity which our departmentalization of academic faculties ignores.

Suppose, for example, that our job was to design a system to solve a regional underdevelopment problem. In defining the problem, we would strike several major determinants we would have to deal with, among them the capital-labor ratio. Now, there is no lack of models in the literature of economics purporting to allegorize the way in which a specific capital-labor ratio is obtained. However, these models incorporate, for the most part, only economic factors as sub-determinants (e.g., the regional capital investment function, the investment incentive schedule, size of labor force, distribution of skills, prevailing salary schedules relative to skills, etc.). But, if we were to try to use these models as the basis for a development strategy, we would find that the values of some of the capital-labor ratio's subdeterminants (and hence the value of the capital-labor ratio itself) depends on noneconomic variables. For example, one determinant of the size of the labor force relative to the employable population will be the structure of the social values among the employable population. In some societies, work is valued in an ideoreligious sense; in others, it is considered fundamentally sacrilegious. If, now, we were to review the literature of sociology, we would strike verbal paradigms purporting to isolate the social and ideological predicates of a particular work ethic. Thus, we would have two logically (if not mathematically) deterministic models, one purporting to allegorize the process by which a particular capital-labor ratio is obtained, the other allegorizing the process by which a particular work attitude might have evolved.

To use these two models in the context of an integrated, predictive problem definition, we must supply an interface between them, suggesting the way in which the prevailing work ethic acts, among other factors, to determine labor force size, and the reverse. This interface between sociological economic factors becomes, then, a submodel in the emerging interdisciplinary macroproblem model. Here, we may use deductive inference in the development of interdisciplinary interface models which relate two previously isolated subdeterminants of the problem-system (where the subdeterminants are usually associated with different academic disciplines).

But the emerging problem definition model also demands the development of *macro interfaces.* These allegorize the direction and magnitude of the interrelationship among major problem determinants, the final step in the construction of a fully integrated, predictive model of the problem as a whole. Here, for example, we would have to consider the nature of the interaction between the basic high-order political, economic, social, and behavioral variables comprising a regional economic system (e.g., the relationship between the distribution of political power within the region and the capital-labor ratio). For the most part, these macro interfaces will be the most difficult of the constructs, as many of the interrelationships may become obvious only through intensive deductive analysis and "logical" simulation exercises. Yet, to neglect the almost staggering reflexivity present in most social, political, or economic problem contexts is the surest way to arrive at problem models that have neglected real-world complexities in favor of the analytical paths of least resistance. In summary then, we must develop *realistic* problem models in the organic domain by providing deduced interface models at two levels: first, the level at which subdeterminants (i.e., determinants of major determinants) are entered into the model; secondly, at the level where the major determinants of the problem are to be interrelated.

Thus, eventually, we arrive at a reticulated causal network, with subdeterminants being linked via micro-interface models to form subproblem models, these subproblem models gradually being linked into a fully integrated problem model via successively higher level and more encompassing macro-interface models. The problem definition process can then become intelligible in terms of successive reduction and synthesis processes, where the ultimate relevance and accuracy of the macro-problem model we arrive at depends on the rectitude of the *selection decisions* that have had to be made at each of the various model-building stages:

1. The selection of a *determinant array* which as fully as possible exhausts those structural factors that will actually comprise the problem at hand.
2. The selection, from among all alternatives, of those *intradisciplinary models* that most accurately allegorize the causal sequence leading to values for each of the determinants identified above.
3. The selection of those *micro-interface models* that most accurately allegorize the nature of the interrelationships among heretofore isolated sub-determinants involved in the causal sequences just developed.
4. The selection of *macro-interface* models that most accurately allegorize the nature of the interrelationships among the several sub-problem models developed immediately above.

Naturally, as we move toward the fully synthesized macro-problem model, we want to be able to estimate its validity at all points. So, each of the various structural and dynamic factors involved in the emerging problem definition will be indexed with either an empirically or deductively derived probability of rectitude. Quite clearly, a great majority of our analytical efforts will eventually be spent in translating these rather more speculative "logical" probability indices into objective ones, by subjecting their associated model components to empirical validation, we must constantly reevaluate our deductive and inferential premises so that we can arrive at logical probabilities that reflect successively higher conditions of reliability, accuracy, and relevance.

In summary, then, our objective in this problem definition process is to arrive at an integrated problem allegory which is indexed at all points with the highest feasible (logical or objective) probabilities of rectitude. We shall now attempt to clarify some of the methods by which this can be achieved, beginning with a discussion of the role played by the first of our system architecture instruments, consensus statistics.

6.3.1.1 The Potential of Consensus Statistics As we have already suggested, the basic input for the development of interdisciplinary or syncretistic model components will come from the Delphi process described earlier. It, as we saw, was an excellent device for trying to lend some tentative order or discipline to the imponderables that often constitute the basis for "organic" problems. These, lacking the structure of mechanistic problems and therefore allowing us scant opportunity for the injection of empirically-predicated models, hypotheses, or "laws", etc., force us to turn to essentially deductive devices, such that the *a priori* problem definition model will generally be a collection of loosely connected hypothetico-deductive constructs.

Although our use of consensus statistics will be slightly different depending on whether we are trying to develop the structural determinant array, select a "best" intradisciplinary model to allegorize some member of that array, or define a "best" macro-interface model, the basic strategy will remain the same. For the first of these tasks, we want the determinant array to be as exhaustive and broadly inclusive as possible, yet it must also be of manageable proportion. We must, then, inaugurate a method that will allow us to identify some *n* most probable state-variables from among the universe of potential determinants. There are basically three steps we can go through here:

1. The selection of an *initial array* by incorporating variables encountered in the literature of the various disciplines we think might somehow be involved.
2. Then, through the submission of this list to various expert individuals or groups who are asked to *add* whatever factors they think were left out of the master array, we arrive at an *additive array.*
3. At this point, we can impose a frequency distribution on the additive array by noting the cross correlations (unions) derived from one or all of the following survey procedures:
   (a) Where the entire group of respondents (experts) are given the entire additive array and asked to rank the *n* factors they think will have the highest probability of exerting the greatest impact on the problem as a whole.
   (b) Where the additive array is stratified into disciplinary classes (e.g., economic variables, sociological variables, etc.) as are the respondents— e.g., economists, sociologists, etc.—. The experts are then asked to rank only those variables in their respective areas.
   (c) Where the stratification procedure is used (as above) but where experts are asked to rank only those variables that are *not* derived from their respective subject areas (e.g., economists selecting the *n* most expectedly critical social variables, political variables, behavioral variables, etc.).

Thus, we emerge with an *a priori* most logically exhaustive determinant array, each component of which has been assigned a probability index reflecting the consensus as to its importance or probable impact on the problem as a whole.

As for the problem of selecting intradisciplinary (parochial) models, where there exists only one model purporting to explain a problem phenomenon, this should be submitted to the multidisciplinary panel (established above) for validation, such that a logical probability of accuracy can be assigned it on the basis of the number of "acceptances" it receives. Where two or more competitive models are found, a decision has to be made as to which should be incorporated into the emerging macro model. A polling process similar to that given above can be inaugurated which (either by stratifying respondents or just using an unstratified panel) assigns logical probabilities to each of the alternative, competitive models on the basis of some combination of the following:

- The number of mentions each receives in the literature of the field.
- The aggregated rank it earns in a survey of experts.
- The extent to which the model has been validated in the field (if at all).

We would emerge, then, with the alternatives arrayed in a frequency distribution similar to that developed to select a determinant array. This frequency distribution (histogram) may then be translated into a probability distribution, assigning each alternative a value reflecting the "consensus" as to its probable validity.

Figure 6.5 is an example of such a distribution curve. The normative decision action would be to initially adopt that intradisciplinary model which receives the highest number of mentions (subject to two confoundations we will introduce shortly).

For the construction of interface models, we are concerned with the integration of variables from hitherto unrelated disciplines into a subproblem model (e.g., the causal sequence of a major problem determinant or state-variable). In selecting a model to allegorize the nature of the interrelationship between two subdeterminants, we may proceed by first making a rough cut at the interface model or at the causal or codeterminate relationship we (as analysts) expect will prevail. This can be sent out as a straw-man for the experts to shoot at and modify according to their own judgment. We can then incorporate those modifications most frequently mentioned and recycle the modified interface model back through the panel, this time asking that they assign it a logical probability index reflecting its perceived appropriateness. If the model receives a sufficiently high index, it is entered in the macro-problem model; if not additional iterations must be performed.

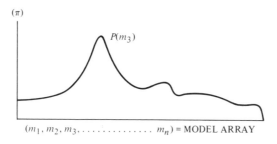

Figure 6.5 Subjective probability distribution.

Essentially the same process can be gone through for the development of those macro-interface models that would establish the most probable interrelationships among the major structural variables of the problem-system. For the development of the macro model is largely just a synthesis process conducted at a somewhat higher level than the one we just went through. If we are extremely fortunate—if we can manage to avoid two very prevalent confoundations we shall introduce shortly—consensus statistics operating on existing model bases and data bases should enable us to arrive at a neat, most logically probable causal network, in that the model so developed will be that which has the highest *a priori* probability of being an accurately predictive allegory of the problem we are to attack. But this expectation of logical determinacy, and this neat network structure will be very rare indeed in the organic context, for most problems will pose both stochastic and indeterminate confoundations very early in the definition process.

6.3.1.2 Treating the Confoundations The first indication of degeneracy in the relatively neat process we have just described will involve logical stochasticity, the case where the consensus process returns two or more competitive models as significantly probable allegories for explaining the problem phenomenon at hand. So, rather than the logically deterministic case involving a consensus-generated probability distribution with only one peak, we emerge with a multi-peak distribution. When this occurs—where there is no clear-cut favorite and no way of merging the models to form an acceptable hybrid—we must introduce a *stochastic branch* into the developing problem definition model. This will indicate that we expect either one or two (or more) alternative events to occur at that point in the model. Each of the alternatives are assigned an associated logical probability index and our neat, logically deterministic network is interrupted by these multiple contingencies at the point of the branch.

These stochastic branches must eventually be subjected to empirical validation exercises (perhaps in a Bayesian framework) so that the *a priori* stochastic probability distributions can gradually be translated into *a posteriori* deterministic ones and the monolithic quality of the model reinstated. In other words, we presume that successive empirical observations taken on the phenomenon of interest will eventually cause the concatenating probability distributions to converge on the alternatives.

But there is an even more serious confoundation with which we must be prepared to deal. This is logical indeterminacy, which can emerge at some point in the developing problem definition because the number of alternative models identified as "significant" in the consensus process is simply too large to permit the development of stochastic contingencies, or because the consensus process has returned *no* model that is expected to be an adequate predictive allegory for the phenomenon at hand. In either case, the range of alternatives that might occur is so great that it cannot be made manageable within the confines of the developing macro model. At that point, we must enter a *discontinuity*, interrupting the concatenating causal-structural sequence and, when we do this, we can introduce the second and third instruments in the system architecture repertoire: deductive inference and disciplined, successive approximation or "learning" processes.[8]

The former involves the development of two allegories that represent polar opposite outcomes (the "best" and "worst" of all possible worlds). These will provide us with two effectively antonymical causal submodels, the parameters of which may be established by a consensus statistics process such as that described for the interface models. These models need not be "realistic," but they must be constructed so that there is a significantly high probability that the real outcome will fall somewhere within the range proscribed by the polars.

When one of these indeterminate discontinuities emerges, the succeeding causal and structural components become subject to severe uncertainty. So it is critical that the problem definers temporarily abandon their deductive exercises and subject the *a priori* indeterminate phenomenon to an empirical investigation at the earliest possible moment (either by constructing a laboratory-type experiment or by inaugurating a monitoring process to watch developing real-world conditions). In this way, *a priori* indeterminate phenomenon may gradually be made manageable in terms of a more constrained, actionable, and directive stochastic branch, assuming that the inherent properties of the phenomenon permit this.

In this way, a learning-based successive approximation process is brought into play, underlying the effort to assign empirically-derived *a posteriori* probability distributions to phenomena that were initially described by stochastic or indeterminate distributions. The basic epistemological rationale for the disciplined "learning" approach, represented most popularly by Bayesian-type processes, is that the value of information about an *a priori* ill-structured situation can be increased through time by successive empirical observations taken on properties of interest, with current estimates being made responsive to the concatenating series of prior estimates. We shall have a great deal more to say about this shortly.

Where, sadly, such an empirical convergence process is infeasible, we have recourse to two other, less desirable techniques. First, we can consider the construction of logical simulation models which allegorize the way all succeeding problem components will behave should the real-world "event" tend toward one or another of the deduced polar opposites. In other words, we artificially turn the indeterminate discontinuity into a stochastic branch with two contingent causal trajectories. Necessarily, the model will be gross and have an extremely high probability of being inaccurate, affecting adversely the probable rectitude of all successive constructs. Moreover, in the end, the effort might be shown to have been gratuitous if neither of the polar opposites is approached significantly closely. The other alternative is a sort of statistical hedge and involves the development of a hybrid model that as nearly as possible reflects the median conditions formed by the two polar opposites. The advantage of such a logical compromise is that it will yield, *a priori*, a minimal expected-value for the variance between predicted and actual outcomes. The disadvantage is that this minimized expected-value is simply a statistical straw-man and may not at all reflect the tendency of the real-world process to seek the median between the artificial antonyms.

We can now see why efforts to translate all these components into an effectively integrated and predictive problem model will become something more than an exercise in deterministic synthesis, where all components will be interrelated in a well-behaved finite-state system.[9] Rather, the almost inescapable indeterminacies we must deal with will tend to make the synthesis process dependent on our ability to develop complex and often analytically unwieldy stochastic or dynamic programming models. In short, only by recognizing and acting on the legitimate expectation that several different events might occur at various points in the problem process can our macro models adequately reflect the nature of most real-world social, economic, and behavioral problems.

The stochastic or dynamic programming option here provides us with several allegorical and analytical advantages in these problem contexts. First, it isolates those points in the integrated problem definition that are most *a priori* precarious, thus prescribing a priority scheme for the empirical validation exercises that must follow. Secondly, it introduces some operational and predictive flexibility into the model at points where the problem's structural conditions (i.e., state-variable or relational properties) are most likely to change, and where a limited repertoire of most probable changes can be preidentified. Thirdly, it treats analytical error explicitly, reflecting accurately the irrevocable out-of-phase condition in the interfaces between real-world problems and analytical models. Finally, in conjunction with this last point, it makes the further modification of the model a virtual operational necessity, overriding the analysts' reluctance to tamper with deterministic models despite changes in the emerging real-world situation.

6.3.2 The System Design Process

It can be suggested that a normative theoretical foundation for organizational design was laid down in an "ends-given" scheme implicit in the work of Max Weber. As David Mechanic says of Weber's work,

> Weber's argument has at least four ideas of considerable importance to organizational decision-making. The ideas, often forgotten by policy-makers, are these:
> 1. Given clearly defined ends, evaluation can be made of the extent to which various alternative means achieve these ends.
> 2. It is possible to assess the extent to which the accomplishment of some ends interferes with the accomplishment of other ends.

3. In evaluating the application of means to ends, it is not only possible to assess the extent to which the means are successful in achieving the end under scrutiny, but also what other consequences would result if particular means are applied.

4. Inaction must always be treated as an alternative means, since inaction clearly has consequences, and in this sense, inaction is a form of action.[10]

If we accept this assessment of Weber's contribution, we find that the essential components of a "normative" decision-making paradigm have been with us far longer than we thought, replete with concepts of instrumental competition, evaluation of alternatives, transmission of dysfunctional effects, and the "action" implications of delay. Here also may be the historical precedent for the social scientists' excessive preoccupation with internal efficiency at the expense of the far more analytically demanding problem definition process, for the ends-given assumption legitimates the insulation we encounter in so many modern system analysis paradigms.*

Nevertheless, Weber's ideas are critical to the internal aspects of the system design process. For we must consider that any means (e.g., strategy, tactic, or specific instrument) we elect to treat a problem aspect might interfere with some other instrument being used in some other problem area, or may have short-run benefits but introduce long-run dysfunctions (as, for example, where a beneficial drug induces an addiction which remains after the symptoms it was treating have disappeared). Weber also warns us that we may be forced to trade off the probable consequences of acting quickly in error (in the absence of information which could have been obtained at a later time) against the probability that the problem we are concerned with will degenerate to a more serious state while we are delaying intervention.

So far as internal efficiency matters are concerned, Weber's concepts are more than adequate. Yet, if we are to promise an ultimate system design that is both effective and efficient with respect to a constantly changing problem entity, our system design process has to look outward at all points. This suggests that effectiveness in the problem-system interfaces must be given precedence over internal efficiency criteria. It also suggests that the most appropriate operational objective in socioeconomic and sociopolitical system design contexts is minimization of the probability of translating inescapable errors into action† ... our heuristic objective.

With these dictates in mind, our system design process will be based, as was the problem definition process just described, on a disciplined reduction and

*In many such paradigms, the objectives to be achieved, and hence the performance criteria the system must meet, seem to have appeared by some *a priori* miracle rather than by the kind of problem definition process just described.

†As we shall see, risk minimization and performance optimization often become competitive ends in social, political, and economic operational contexts, just as system effectiveness and efficiency can be competitive (where one can be achieved only at the expense of the other.

successive synthesis approach, where: (a) initially isolated subsystems are gradually brought together into an integrated, adaptive system macro model;[11] (b) where each of the components of this macro model will have to be indexed with a probability of rectitude, initially most likely to be a "logical" index; (c) where empirical efforts will be directed at translating these *a priori* logical probabilities into *a posteriori* objective ones, modifying our original deductions or inferences as to expected system behavior where actual and predicted results diverge significantly; (d) where, at all points, we will be examining the predictive accuracy of the *a priori* problem definition model, for this is the reference for our system design criteria. Toward this end, the system design process might best involve procedural and tactical steps such as the following:

1. The establishment of a subsystem (an effectively isolated component of the emerging system) to deal with each of the major subproblems isolated during the problem definition process. A priority scheme would suggest that the first subsystem assignments would be made to the most causally critical of the subproblems (those which are perceived, according to the problem macro model, to have the greatest determinacy on the properties of the problem as a whole). Each subsystem would then be the focus for selecting and implementing a subproblem-solving strategy.

2. The assignment of an array of subproblem-solving instruments to each of the subsystems, designed to implement a previously selected subproblem-solving strategy. The instruments assigned initially should be those receiving the highest logical probabilities of effectiveness, where these probability indices may be developed via a consensus statistics process such as that described for the problem definition process. Here, then, we are trying to predict the nature of the interface conditions which will emerge when a component of our system attacks an aspect of the problem.

3. The inauguration of empirical field tests where the performance of each subsystem is observed in a "laboratory" context, with the key interface variables subjected to formal measurement.* This should improve the validity of our problem definition model by identifying and then modifying those points where predicted and actual outcomes show significant departures. The empirical trials will also help objectify our predictions about instrumental effectiveness and efficiency, enabling us to produce a validated system model to accompany the gradually refined problem model.

4. As these empirical validation exercises proceed at the various subproblem subsystem interfaces, we will be attempting to move to the point where we can do two final things. First, we should be able to estimate, with empirical predication, the potential aggregate effect of the system as a whole on the problem as a whole, and we should be able to introduce strategic or instru-

---

*Even if such tests must be conducted on empirically-accessible *surrogates* for transparent factors or variables.

mental modifications at the emergent weak points. Secondly, we should be able to move toward the integration of the system into an operational configuration that is, in aggregate, at least adequately effective (with neither significant over- or under-capacity) and as efficient as possible. In short, the integrated macro-system model should assist us in eliminating any structural, resource, or treatment redundancies.

Because we have already introduced several of the system architecture instruments that will have to be used in complex system design processes (specifically, consensus statistics, deductive inference, successive approximation, and the concept of stochastic programming), we can concentrate here only on the operational implications of those architecture concepts and tools unique to the system design process, namely: the importance of modularity; the use of game-based analytical instruments in the development of subproblem-solving strategies; the contributions expected of the empirical validation exercises; and the broader aspects of the final macro-system "optimization" process.

6.3.2.1 In Defense of Modularity During the problem definition phase we reduced the overall problem into a series of effectively isolated subproblem models, each being an integrated (interdisciplinary, where necessary) causal sequence underlying one or another of the major structural components of the problem. Here, we want to partition the problem-solving system into specific subsystems, each dedicated to the solution of a specific subproblem. There are several reasons for this. First, during the system design stage, modularity permits us to work with more detailed, accessible units of analysis. This type of reduction is permissible to the extent that we can accurately model the interrelationships among these subsystems and thus arrive later at a structurally-functionally adequate approximation of the system as a whole. During the operational stage, this partitioning of the system into semi-autonomous subsystems localizes dysfunctional reverberations which might occur as the result of inescapable problem analysis and system-building errors, acting as a buffer against their transmission to the system as a whole. It is at this point where the design trade-offs become most explicit, as a partitioned system must be expected to be initially less efficient than a fully integrated one. Yet these losses in potential efficiency must be expected to be more than offset by the reduction in the expected value of errors were they allowed to concatenate freely throughout the problem-solving system.

Modularization, the construction of effectively isolated subsystem-subproblem interfaces, also permits us to develop priority schedules which should maximize both the information and development leverage associated with complex design programs. Information leverage is maximized by making those most critical (or representative) interfaces the first investigated empirically, on the implication that the data thus emerging will be used to minimize potential dysfunctions associated with subsequent modules.* By concentrating our "learning" toward the initial stages of implementation, we thus expect to effectively minimize the costs associated with *a priori* errors which would otherwise have been translated into action, with all the irrevocable dysfunction that would entail. On the other hand, development leverage is effectively maximized by implementing those most critical subsystems first, so that subsequent subsystems may work in partially cleared areas.[12] This is desirable in most complex problem-solving processes because certain adjustments or modifications are prerequisite to the effectiveness of other efforts. By delaying the inauguration of such dependent subsystem programs, we minimize the overall costs of the problem solution effort.

Finally, modularity can considerably increase the efficiency and economy of computational exercises we go through; for, particularly in optimization, the amount of computer time used is almost logarithmically related to the number of independent variables we are working with. Practically then, modularity can be a way of economizing on scarce analytical resources.[13]

In summary, then, we partition the system into various subproblem-subsystem modules and schedule them for implementation according to their expected analytical or operational value, resolving any valuational conflicts via the already familiar consensus process.

6.3.2.2 The Game-Based Process The efficacy of the system as a whole will depend primarily on the effectiveness of the individual subsystems with respect to their subproblems. This, in turn, depends on three factors: (1) the rectitude of the subproblem-solving strategies employed; (2) the effectiveness of the tactical instruments employed in the effort to implement those strategies; and (3) the ability to avoid conditions of suboptimization or adverse interference among the modules.

So far as the identification of a logically most effective strategy is concerned, most socioeconomic or sociopolitical problem-system confrontations will benefit from the adoption of a game-based approach. There are three reasons for this. First, if the problem component involves human beings or other volitional elements, there is the possibility that they may act *strategically* to try to offset any changes we try to impose. Some of the reactions will be "foreseeable" and therefore amenable to treatment within a game context (though usually not amenable to strict mathematical analysis).† Secondly, if we propose to try to change a certain problem property, we must consider the possibility that compensating or secondary reactions may be released somewhere else (e.g., raising welfare payments to make New York City residents more comfortable brings in migrants

---

*We consider information leverage to be the ratio of the reduction in the expected value of error associated with a given information increment and the costs associated with the realization of that information, both components on a dollar dimension.
†For a more detailed analysis of the value of game-based approaches, see Section 8.2.2.3.

from other areas; improving traffic control in an urban area can result in making driving more attractive to people who previously used public transportation, thus actually worsening the situation). Finally, there is a strong possibility that those systems relying heavily on the contribution of human beings will be unpredictable at the problem-system interface, for the problem components can affect system components just as system components affect problem components. For example, it is not unusual to find social workers displacing organizational values and sympathies for those of their clients, thus departing from the normative performance criteria laid down by the system designers.

In these situations, we are forced to try to deductively infer what reactions the implementation of a given strategy might evoke, considering both functional and dysfunctional possibilities. We strike, then, situations similar to those giving rise to the stochastic branches and indeterminate discontinuities raised during the problem definition process, but somewhat more complicated in that they involve two-party rather than single-party predictions. But the development of game-based models permits us to formally preaccount for the most significant of these cause-effect alternatives, the formality owing to the assignment of consensus-derived *a priori* probabilities of rectitude assigned each predefinable outcome. through the now familiar consensus statistics process).

So, the normative follow-up procedure would be to first implement that strategy which was assigned the highest of these *a priori* probabilities of rectitude. But to actually validate the effectiveness of any given strategy, we must first operationalize it by assigning a set of tactical instruments to see it carried out. Thus, for example, we might have a social development strategy that suggests the displacement of archaic or dysfunctional values with a potentially more productive set. The development of an instrument array, then, might involve the identification of the various means that might realize the strategy (e.g., propaganda, moral suasion, dramatization-emotionalization, reward-penalty schemes, enforced reeducation processes).

Quite clearly, we can begin by developing an *a priori* probability distribution reflecting expectations about the differential effectiveness and efficiency parameters expected of each of the alternative instruments we might employ (or each alternative set of instruments where more than one is required to carry out the selected strategy). The standard consensus statistics exercise introduced in the problem definition process may be used to derive this initial distribution. Once this is done, we must inaugurate an empirical validation exercise directed at gaining objective support for our deductions about instrumental performance.

6.3.2.3 The Empirical Validation Process Where the number of instrumental alternatives is very large, we will probably have to settle for a "satisfactory" rather than an optimal solution.[14] This involves our empirically examining the cost-effectiveness ratios associated with the various alternatives until one is found that seems to be at least adequate. We would, of course, begin our empirical validation with that instrument or set of instruments receiving the highest logical probability of effectiveness/efficiency. Where there are only a few alternatives, we might introduce each into an empirical observation and measurement context, selecting that which achieves the highest overall performance level for entry into the final system configuration. At any rate, we can employ a Bayesian-type learning process here because our logical probabilities are the theoretical equivalent of the *a priori* probabilities upon which the Bayesian technique is predicated; and our deductively generated, empirically unvalidated models represent various preidentifiable and alternative states of the world that might legitimately be expected to occur. Thus, our system designer should meet the criteria Martin Beckman has outlined for the Bayesian decision-maker.

In order to act even initially he is supposed to have some prior information as reflected in an *a priori* subjective probability distribution. From observations made as the decision process moves along the decision maker will calculate *a posteriori* probabilities by means of Bayes' principle, thus revising his subjective probabilities in the light of experience.[15]

This tool, then, becomes the basic platform by which we translate the *a priori* logical probabilities associated with each aspect of the problem and/or system into empirically-derived *a posteriori* ones, enabling us to audit and control our successive approximation and learning processes at all points, a facility critical to the contribution expected of the systems architecture approach.

These empirical validation operations must first be directed toward the elimination of discontinuities in the *a priori* problem definition model. The suggested sequence of the validation operations is that which provides the greatest information leverage with respect to the problem definition model as a whole. Secondly, the noninherent stochastic branches in the problem model should be treated. Then we must subject the various subproblem-solving strategies to empirical validation, formally observing interface conditions which emerge.

This examination of the reactions set in motion by the trial implementation of the selected instrument array will largely answer for the rectitude of the problem constructs and strategies, for they are the premises on which the instrument selection was predicated. So the way in which individual problem components behave when faced with the change-agents introduced becomes the most critical foci for the empirical validation process. For when desired problem modifications are converged on, within a reasonable amount of time and with a reasonable expenditure of resources, all prior analytical constructs are thereby legitimated (at least probabilistically). Exactly what constitutes a "reasonable" amount of time or expenditure is a somewhat hazy concept, yet we can suggest that there should be a constant and significant reduction in the spread of the probability distributions reflecting probable instrumental effectiveness . . . that successive estimates on parameters of interest should converge steadily toward a resolution value rather than waver or oscillate.

Where such a convergence is not forthcoming, or where successive estimates do not behave well, we must assume that our premises are in error somewhere. There are, of course, at least three possibilities. First, that the instruments selected to implement the strategy in force were ill-assigned, suggesting that our *a priori* instrument-effect expectations were in error. Secondly, the selected strategy may have been an inappropriate one, suggesting that our game models need modification or refinement, leading to a new set of criteria for instrument selection. Thirdly, and most seriously, the problem definition constructs might have been erroneous, requiring redevelopment of both the particular subproblem being worked on and all dependent or subsequent problem definition components. This would give rise to a new set of subsystem performance requirements to be met by new strategies, etc. We cannot, however, be too prescriptive here, but can suggest that the greater the divergence between predicted and actual outcomes, the greater the probability that this latter error has occurred.

In general, time and resource expenditures may be minimized in the face of nonconvergence or nonvalidation by introducing most localized changes first (e.g., by starting with instrumental changes until reasonable possibilities are exhausted, then introducing a new strategy, and so forth). At any rate, the inventory of empirical data we have been building may guide us in all redefinition areas, gradually minimizing the reliance which must be placed on unvalidated deductive or inferential constructs.

6.3.2.4 System Integration and Optimization Implicitly, at all points in the system design process, we have been building toward a fully-integrated system model at the macro level, much as we did in the problem definition phase.

But, we have also been concerned up to this point primarily with the introduction of effectiveness into the emerging system, not having mentioned *efficiency* explicitly. Yet, obviously, efficiency is a critical design objective and can only be achieved through the construction of a model which permits us to:

1. Dispose of any possibly inimical or competitive relationships between the various subsystem/problem component modules (e.g., where one subsystem is doing its work at the expense of another).
2. Identify any resource redundancies among the various subsystems that could be eliminated without weakening the system's partitioning.
3. Eliminate any treatment redundancies, such that no two subsystems are undertaking identical functions or duplicating effects unnecessarily.

These are, broadly speaking, classic symptoms of the suboptimality that might accompany non-integrated, reductionistic (or *ad hoc*) system configurations.

Following the course we have outlined should permit us to gradually objectify more and more of the heretofore speculative problem or system elements. In the process, the use of effectively-deterministic analytical instruments becomes more and more justified, and our quantitative manipulations become both more meaningful and manageable, even for very large constructs. In this sense, then, the system integration activity becomes one of successively synthesizing larger and larger segments of the previously partitioned system within an instrumental framework that is gradually relying less on stochastic or deductive techniques and more on deterministic, optimization methods. Thus, as the demands on our mathematical sophistication increase with the number of system increments which must be simultaneously considered, they are at the same time reduced by the introduction of more and more model elements that can be handled deterministically. So, overall, we must look to the day when we have access to algorithms that are built on a combination of simulation and optimization techniques, the former being used only when the latter are infeasible.[16]

Only then can we arrive at a point where the construction of an integrated, predictive macro-system model becomes manageable within the current state of the mathematical programming and model building art, thereby allowing us to pursue system efficiency through analysis rather than experiential trial and error.

6.4 AN AMPLIFICATION OF THE SELECTION LOGIC

As we have been stressing, the problem-solving process involves a long sequence of "decisions" about which model components, from among the universe of alternatives available, will be elected for entry into the emerging problem definitions and system-design models. We have also suggested that, wherever possible, selections be made on the basis of objective (i.e., empirical; experiential) factors rather than judgemental, subjective, or logical factors. Yet, where the problem at hand is an essentially "organic," indeterminate one, our *a priori* problem and system constructs will primarily be products of "deductive" rather than inductive inference . . . only subsequently being transformed, to the extent possible, into validated *a posteriori* constructs.

Thus, our first step in the solution of a complex problem is the isolation of an array of state-variables that, as a set, promises to have the highest *logical probability* of exhausting the actual determinants (e.g., structural components) of the problem at hand . . . some of which, for "organic" entities, may be rather far removed in time or space. Thus, we inaugurate a Delphi process that systematically collects and orders "opinion" about problem determinants, emerging with an array of state-variables each member of which carries some probability of likelihood (e.g., an estimate of the expected accuracy of our judgements that it will, indeed, prove to be an actual determinant). These indices may be assigned either by the number of "mentions" each receives, or by some weighted index which ranks the state-variable candidates according to the expected *intensity* of their impact on the "state" of the problem *qua* system. The first distribution will normally exhibit a high degree of variance in opinion, which subse-

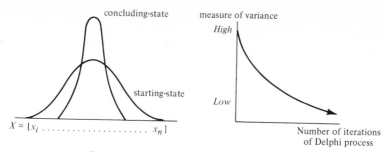

Figure 6.6 The Delphi transformation process.

quent iterations of the Delphi process should reduce. The degree to which variance declines, as a function of the number of iterations of the Delphi process, would be a measure of the efficacy (and efficiency) of that device as a *syncretic* model-building technique . . . as a reduction in variance would indicate that our major objective—subjective or "deductive" consensus—is gradually being obtained. Hence we have a transformational illustration with which we are already well familiar, given as Figure 6.6. In the figure, the dimensions of the event-probability distribution are the array of state-variables which have been assigned significant logical probabilities of being actual determinants, $X = [x_i \ldots x_n]$. The *a posteriori* or concluding-state distribution shows that successive iterations of the Delphi process have caused a convergence of opinion, eliminating some from consideration and heightening the intensity of consensus about the probability (or intensity of impact) of those that remain. The result is, as we know from earlier work, that a reduction in variance is tantamount to a reduction in the *expected probability of error*, such that the curve on the right may be thought of as a "favorable" learning curve.

At any rate, the set of x_i's which remains in the concluding-state distribution would be that set of n factors (n being some manageable number) which, in aggregate, have the highest "likelihood" of being actual determinants. Now, given this "universe" of factors, we may proceed with the development of some alternative problem definition models, *qua* heuristics through: (a) the selection of a subset of consistent x_i's from among the universe available (where consistency means that the factors entered are mutually compatible); and (b) the imposition of some "order" on these subsets which means, in effect, the establishment of a postulated set of relationship conditions among those state-variables constituting a particular heuristic alternative. Thus, we have proper system models defined at the state-variable and relational levels.

In many cases, we shall probably emerge with two or more heuristics, to the extent that there is a divergence of background, information, experience, or interests among the model-building team. These may differ either in terms of the specific subsets of state variables selected, or in terms of the functional relationships imposed on them. Thus, we might emerge with something like this:

ALTERNATIVE *A PRIORI* HEURISTIC PROBLEM DEFINITION MODELS

$$A = f_a \, [X_a]$$
$$B = f_b \, [X_b]$$

.
.
.

$$M = f_m \, [X_m] \, ;$$

where X_a, X_b, and $X_m \subset X$ (the universe) and where $f_a \neq f_b \neq f_m$.

Alternative heuristics are thus those where either the subset of determinants differ from those in other formulations, or where the relationship imposed (the f_i's) is different, assuming that the set of determinants is the same. In most cases, heuristic problem definition models will differ on both these dimensions. In any case, all will be assigned some "index" of likelihood as being *the* best allegory for the problem at hand, an index which will be assigned either on the basis of the gross number of acceptances each receives among those polled, or according to some scheme that includes weighting factors (to measure intensity of acceptance).

These aggregate likelihood indices (assigned to heuristics as wholes) are really products of lower-order indices. These result from the fact that there is usually a *clustering* effect of some kind operating in model-building groups, such that subsets among the group form on the basis of differentially shared backgrounds, interests, or axiological predicates, etc. (the most obvious of the clusters would be formed along disciplinary lines). This clustering effect may be partially offset by stratifying panels into subsets that represent different backgrounds and interests, or values, etc. Nevertheless, the alternative scenarios will usually result from the fact that there will not be unanimity among panel members as a whole, and that there will usually be divergences of opinion about the rectitude of model components *within* strata or clusters. But the clustering and stratification schemes differ in important respects, as follows:

	WITHIN MODEL VARIANCE	BETWEEN MODEL VARIANCE
Cluster	Low	High
Stratification	High	Low

That is, under a clustering scheme, we tend to put similar panel members together into a model-building team (e.g., all economists or all sociologists or all environmentalists); under the stratification scheme, we tend to form teams of opposites. The net result is that the models built by clustered teams will vary greatly in aggregate, but will have high degree of consensus (e.g., low variance) internally . . . for the premises under which clustered teams operate vary greatly *between* the teams, but little if at all *within* the teams. Just the opposite is true of the stratification effect. There we will have a high degree of divergence within terms, and a low degree of divergence among teams, with the net result that the models built will vary little between each other, but have high degrees of internal variance.

As a general rule, clusters will tend to form naturally, whereas strata have to be deliberately invoked . . . something that may prove to be dysfunctional if recrimination and acrimony occurs within groups.

For the sake of efficiency in the heuristic-building phase of the problem-solving process, then, it is usually better to allow the formation of these spontaneous clusters, and then concentrate on the elimination of differences between these constructs as wholes at a subsequent point. For the models are built from clustered teams will each seem both feasible and highly likely to occur from the standpoint of those who built them, but will probably be highly unpalatable and unlikely from the standpoint of other clusters. Thus we have reasonably disciplined, "finished" products toward which objective argument may be directed, whereas groups containing acrimonious components will have severe difficulty in actually *completing* anything substantial.

To make this point somewhat clearer, consider Figure 6.7. What we tend to find is that the aggregate probability distribution functions for alternative *a priori* problem definition models (*qua* heuristics) tend to be products of the *means* of the event-probability distributions, reflecting the expected likelihood of the various alternative heuristics (which in turn reflects the degree of consensus within the model-building cluster or stratum as to the likelihood of that con-

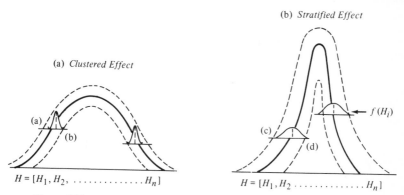

(b) *Stratified Effect*

(a) *Clustered Effect*

$f(H_i)$

$H = [H_1, H_2, \ldots\ldots\ldots\ldots H_n]$

$H = [H_1, H_2 \ldots\ldots\ldots\ldots H_n]$

Where: $[H]$ = the set of alternative heuristics (*a priori* problem definition models), and: $f(H_i)$ = the marginal probability density function for the event, H_i.

Figure 6.7   Results of clustered as opposed to stratified. Model-building structures.

struct). In the clustered case, then, we have a situation where a larger number of alternative scenarios are proposed (such that the aggregate variance in likelihood is greater for the "flatter" clustered distribution) but where the consensus as to the individual rectitude of these alternatives is strong (which means that each of the alternatives in the clustered case will carry a rather low expected value of error). Just the opposite situation prevails with respect to the stratified distribution; there we have fewer "events" assigned significant probabilities—with less variance in the aggregate distribution due to their tendency to be redundant with one another due to the stratification process—but each of the alternatives carries with it a much higher expected value of error (and hence internal variance) than do the alternatives in the clustered case.

That neither of these situations is really satisfactory may be seen by calculating the overall variance associated with the constructs (e.g., computing variance as the product of the *within* and *between* variance).[17] The net result is that both cases would carry about the same total variance, with the lower within variance associated with the clustered case (indicated by the fact that $[b - a] < [d - c]$) being offset by the lower aggregate probability of occurrence being assigned each alternative . . . as is indicated by the "flatter" aggregate distribution.

What we eventually want to emerge with is, of course, an aggregate event-probability distribution like that in Figure 6.8. We could achieve this distribution in either of two ways, relative to the distributions of Figure 6.7. First, we could inaugurate Delphi processes that will reduce the *within-heuristic* variance associated with each of the few alternatives remaining in the stratified distribution (by forcing a consensus within the model-building groups). This, in effect, means heightening the marginal probability density functions for all remaining H_i's. This reduces the expected value of error associated with each alternative, and hence results in more "peaked" superimpositional probability functions. Second, we could take the low "within variance" alternatives of the clustered distribution and inaugurate Delphi processes that cause the aggregate probability density function to "peak" . . . thereby eliminating some of the less likely alternatives, and correspondingly increasing the likelihood of those remaining.

The net result, in either case, is the same . . . we have reduced a high-variance, high-expected-error situation to a lower-variance, lower-expected-error situation, with the end result that some single, most logically probable heuristic (e.g., the *a priori* problem definition model) is gradually converged on, which itself carries a sufficient probability of adequacy. Thus, in Figure 6.8, both the aggregate and marginal probability density functions reflect an improvement.

In many cases, and we shall not labor the point here, the ultimate construct (e.g., the H_i that is finally agreed to be the most "likely" estimator for actual problem properties) might emerge as some sort of compromisive "hybrid," where agreement is obtained at the expense of either precision or actionability. The result of *democratic* model-building processes is often a construct that, while it has very little probability of proving absolutely wrong as a representation of

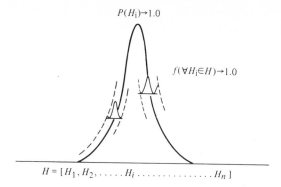

Figure 6.8 The idealized event-probability distribution.

some phenomenon, also has almost no probability of being right. And where such constructs are to become premises for decision or policy action, the fact of a subjective convergence or consensus will have little bearing on the actual rectitude of the model, and hence may be a disservice to the community the system analysts and policy-makers represent.

A very important distinction, then, would be between models that obtain a convergence through compromise, and those that are truly *syncretic* or rationally (and sapiently) discerning. These strictly compromisive hybrids, like so many essentially political formulations, will generally trade off ultimate rectitude against short-run procedural expedience. And there is really no defense against this except for the fundamental integrity of the team leaders, so we can offer no "technology" for escaping these degenerative Delphi processes . . . just a caution to be alert for their presence.

In summary of this section, then, the within-heuristic variances emerge from the fact that there will be divergences of opinion—especially between and to an expectedly lesser extent within clusters—about the likelihood (probable accuracy) of any individual state-variables that might be entered into an alternative prob-lem definition model, and also about the probable accuracy of the functional relationships imposed on the subset of state-variables employed for each of the alternative heuristics. Thus, each of the models is itself a product of a sequence of decisions with respect to the following:

1. Likelihood $(x_i \| x_i^c)$, for $\forall x_i \in W_j \| X_j$, for $\forall X_j \in X_j$

2. Likelihood $(f_i \| f_i^c)$, for $\forall f_i \in F_j$, for $\forall X_j \in X$

Where: X is the set of alternative *a priori* problem definition models assigned significant probabilities of occurrence.

In the first formulation, each of the x_i's represents a specific state-variable associated with some W_j which is a proper subset of the universe of state-variables, $[W]$. The subsets thus become the array of state-variables constituting the major structural properties (i.e., determinants) of some X_j, which is one of the alternative *a priori* problem definition models constituting the set of all such models, X. For each set of state-variables (each W_j), there will be some function imposing an "ordered" relationship among all x_i's, this being F_j. This F_j may now be thought of as a set containing all the individual functional relationships "ordering" each set of interacting state-variables, the f_i's.

Thus, in the problem definition process, we are asked to make decisions about the likelihood (probability of accuracy) of each of the state-variables actually being a determinant of the problem at hand (*given* the presence of the other state-variables constituting the subset of which the particular x_i is an element). In much the same way, we are asked to make decisions about the likelihood of some particular function, f_i, being the relationship between some interacting set of state-variables, given the functions relating other elements of the set F_j to which the particular f_i belongs. Hence, the likelihood indices we assign are really *conditional* probabilities, conditional in that we recognize that no state-variables may be entirely isolated from any other and that no individual functional relationship has real significance unless it is associated with the others of which the "system" is comprised.

When we then allow ourselves to work with successively more encompassing sets of state-variables and functions, so that larger and larger components of the aggregate system are analyzed simultaneously, we are going through the process of system synthesis . . . a very demanding and difficult procedure when conducted according to formal rules . . . for modern mathematics (and modern man, as well) has considerable difficulty in dealing with units of analysis containing more than just a few variables connected by a very limited number of functions. So, though the conditional formulation is always to be preferred, it is unlikely to be followed except where the system or problem at hand meets the empirical/positivist criteria we set out in Chapter 1.* For the complex case, the subjective probabilities associated with each component (both structural and functional) of the emerging *a priori* problem definition model—and later the *a priori* system design model—will probably be set quite casually, which is entirely consonant with its role as a starting-state condition. It is only in the *a posteriori* phase, to which we shall shortly turn, that the empirical estimation of conditional probabilities becomes important, and that the successive integration of interactive system components becomes an imperative rather than an ideal.

Finally, the likelihood indices we will associate with each of the alternative heuristic problem definition models will then be some product of the likelihood indices assigned the several structural and functional components . . . and the variance of these aggregate estimates will reflect the degree of divergence in the subjective probabilities (likelihood indices) assigned the components. Thus we

---

*And it is precisely in such a case where the more sophisticated analytical tools are not needed anyway.

are now at the point where we have one, or perhaps several, alternative *a priori* problem definition models, and must now set about transforming them into empirically-validated, *a posteriori* ones. It is here that the action-research aspect of the system architecture platform can help us. And though we have already broadly viewed the *a priori* → *a posteriori* transformation process, it is worthwhile revisiting its operations and looking in greater detail at the analytical "utility" of action-research.

6.5 THE UTILITY OF ACTION-RESEARCH

In the strictest sense, the system architecture approach to problem-solving emerges as an example of *action-research* . . . a "learning while doing" scheme especially appropriate in the face of complex phenomena. Under action-research, a system that is initially too complex to allow us to make any accurate *a priori* assertions concerning the actual effects of prescriptive actions which we might take, becomes a target for restricted (modular) empirical experimentation. Under this scheme, "actions" are introduced not merely in the hope that they will produce some desired effect, but in a way which ensures that whatever happens, our information about the problem (and hence about the requirements for solution) increases. In short, our actions become elements of a hypothesis, and agents for inquiry as well as effect.

The action-research aspect of the system architecture approach is found in its eventual concentration on the emerging interface between two initially hypothetical constructs: the problem definition model and the problem-solving system design model. Given the expected properties of the problem, as reflected in the first construct, we are able to deduce what actions should produce desired changes; that is, we deduce the prescriptive aspects of the system by making reference to the properties of the *a priori* problem definition model, and secondarily develop cause-effect (action-outcome) sequences for each of the subproblems. Now, because all the components of the problem/problem-solving system models are formally connected (through the laws of deductive inference), we may treat our "actions" as hypotheses that will be validated if our expectations about problem properties are true, and if our prescriptive predictions are true (subject, obviously, to our ability to control for confoundations).

If the actions we inaugurate have the expected result, this is tantamount to a validation of the empirical validity of the prior constructs on which the prescriptions were based . . . for the subproblem-solving "tactics" are the lowest level components of a long and complex hypothetico-deductive chain. If, however, the actions we inaugurate in the hopes that some therapeutic effect will be achieved do not produce the expected or desired result, then we must look for points where our hypotheses are in error. Thus, when an unexpected result accompanies the inauguration of an action, it should help us locate the errors in the premises on which that action was predicated, and thus serves as an empirically-significant invalidation of some hypothesis (either in the problem definition model or somewhere in the system design model). In this sense, then, actions undertaken in the system architecture framework become agents of research, and the ultimate tests of the empirical rectitude of our problem definition and system design constructs . . . and they clearly become the basic vehicles by which initially unvalidated constructs become gradually translated into objectively validated ones. In abbreviated, graphic form, what we have said here is summarized in Figure 6.9.

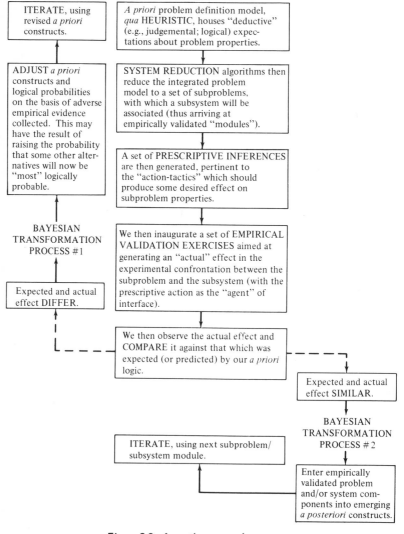

Figure 6.9 An action-research process.

As the figure shows, action-research involves a constant interchange between judgment and experience, with the results of the latter (derived from the experiments pertinent to actions) being fed back to either modify or validate the hypothetical model components. Thus, experiments with actions that produce predicted/desired results give us greater confidence in the hypothetical premises on which the predicted results were based, and hence allow us to gradually replace the subjective or logical probabilities assigned those model components with objective ones. By the same token, when the action fails to achieve the results that the hypothetical sequence would predict, then either the definition of the subproblem's properties was in error to some extent, or our prescriptive inference was incorrect (e.g., the action-effect sequence we predicted, given the problem properties, was inaccurately generated). In such a case, the failure of the predicted outcome to occur would be passed through a Bayesian process (which acts to combine subjective and objective probabilities into a hybrid probability index), that would then reduce the probability index assigned to either the problem or prescriptive hypothesis and, in the process, raise the probability of some alternative explanation being true.

In short, then, our action-trials (experimental implementations) should produce information that will lead to one of two analytical adjustments: (1) the failure of our *a priori* expectations to be empirically validated would lead to a change in the structure (morphology) of the basic event-probability distributions themselves . . . retarding the ill-conceived hypothesis and advancing some alternative; or (2) the empirical validation of our *a priori* expectations would cause us to gradually transform the subjective probability indices into objective ones, with the resultant objective indices reflecting the statistical significance of the experimental results. Clearly, then, the heuristic process described in Section 5.5.1 (evolving into the system analysis paradigm of Section 5.6) and the prescriptive model-building process just described are exercises in action-research whenever the problem or system at hand is a nondeterministic one. And, without question, the correlation between action-research exercises and the ultimate success of our problem-solving efforts must be expected to increase as the entity under investigation or treatment increasingly departs from the mechanistic-deterministic criteria earlier set out.

Thus, in its role as an action-research platform, system architecture emerges as a broadly defined procedural "algorithm" within which individual users may try to set their own problems and resolve their own procedural and methodological issues. It relies on no instrument that is yet uninvented, and it does not ask magic of our intellects. Neither is systems architecture any kind of a scientific evolution. It is simply a relatively common-sense way of structuring instruments and concepts that others have laid down and brought to operationality in somewhat less general contexts. It is then, a context-independent paradigm for approaching those very complex problems that will not admit to traditional, less humble, or more constrained methodologies.

Moreover, the adoption of the essential logic of this scheme should assist social, behavioral, or administrative scientists in obtaining really meaningful research grants; for to the grant administrator, the discipline and control and accountability aspects of systems architecture make it very attractive indeed. In addition, it provides sponsors a running indication of the progress of our learning, and may in fact be able to objectify some aspects through the use of the learning-curve concept developed in Chapter 5. In short, under this scheme, we scientists promise not simply to change society, but to first understand it. And considering the failure of most of our notably evangelistic crusades (e.g., those broadly financed and much publicized community action programs for the War on Poverty), this reemphasis may be most comforting.

It is the opportunity for science to simultaneously reeducate itself *and* make an impact on the real-world that marks systems architecture as a potentially positive platform. There is so much that we may learn under its aegis. First we will learn something about the quality of our existing social science models, quality being measured roughly by the variance between predicted and actual events. But, along with this, we will be gradually building up an inventory of validated models to displace those existing constructs that failed the validation exercises. In this way, we will be directly making an impression on some of the major theoretical foundations of the various social sciences, for we will be subjecting some of the (often implicit) deductive premises of the respective disciplines to field experiments in a real-world context, something that individual hypothesis-tests in contrived analytical situations do not do.

Secondly, we may hope to learn something about the process of constructing interdisciplinary interface models; something about the ways in which we can unite the parochial, often introspective models of the individual disciplines into operationally relevant allegories. And, again, a by-product is the development of an inventory of such models, all of which will have been empirically validated and many of which will probably be appropriate in subsequent problem-solving exercises. Thirdly, we may eventually impose quantitative coefficients on many models that will have been originally only static (or directional) in nature. In this sense, then, we will be gradually transforming many of our heretofore rhetorical constructs into models that can be manipulated in a mathematical framework. This, in turn, will permit us to become rather more precise and efficient in the generation of actionable prescriptions for the real-world.

These three points lead to an important operational corollary: the ability to move away from analytical operations predicated on stochasticity or interdeterminacy, toward determinacy. This, after all, is the aim of all science. We stressed a "disciplined" learning process so that results from one development experience or problem-solving process can be transmitted to others, much in the way that the physical and engineering sciences have "learned" their way toward a concatenated, nomothetic model base. Indeed, it may be that the constant complaining we have done about the inherent intractability of social science subjects compared to those of the "hard" sciences has more reflected the historically undisciplined nature of our methodological approach than the inherently greater complexity of the subjects with which we deal.

Finally, the last of our learning opportunities is concerned with methodological aspects, with isolating from among the entire array of strategic, tactical, and instrumental alternatives available to us, those that are "objectively" expected to perform best in the various problem situations we can identify. We learn about this by subjecting different instruments to replicable experiments designed to measure their relative cost-effectiveness, recording and broadcasting the results, and describing the mathematical properties of the resultant learning curves in universalistic terms.

So, in the most fundamental sense, all our work in this chapter has been directed toward the provision of an extremely broad, perhaps immature array of heuristics. And these, if they do not act directly to amplify the system sciences' contributions to the world at large, will hopefully at least set out some of the conditions and directions by which we may expect to learn how to better serve those who depend on us . . . even if this means we might occasionally serve ourselves less well.

We may now move on to Chapter 7 and discuss the other two applications of system analysis logic: policy-setting and decision-making. In the process, we shall be amplifying some of the points made here, for both of these tasks may be viewed as special cases of problem-solving in general.

6.6 NOTES AND REFERENCES

1. Julius Stulman, *Evolving Mankind's Future* (Philadelphia: J. B. Lippincott Co., 1969).
2. Joseph P. Martino, *Technological Forecasting for Decisionmaking* (New York: American Elsevier Publishing Co., 1972), or Olaf Helmer, *Social Technology* (Basic Books, 1966).
3. Herbert Simon, *The Sciences of the Artificial* (Cambridge, Mass.: MIT Press, 1969); Bertrand de Jouvenal, *The Art of Conjecture* (New York: Basic Books, 1967; and Hasan Ozberhan, "The Emerging Methodology of Planning," *Fields Within Fields . . . Within Fields*, **10** (June 1974).
4. Robert Merton, *Social Theory and Social Structure* (New York: Free Press, 1968), p. 39.
5. Martin Schubik, *Readings in Game Theory and Political Behavior* (New York; Doubleday & Co., 1954), p. 3.
6. Bernstein and Cetron, "SEER: A Delphic Approach to Information Processing," *Technological Forecasting*, **1** no. 1 (June 1969), pp. 33–54.
7. See Robert Schlaifer, *Probability and Statistics for Business Decisions* (New York: McGraw-Hill, 1959).
8. In a sense, we are seeking a concensus in much the same way that we might try to seek a specific optimum were our problem one that involved the manipulation of quantitative, as opposed to axiological or qualitative, variables. For a generic appreciation of successive "learning" processes, see

Charles C. Ying's "Learning By Doing—An Adaptive Approach to Multi-period Decisions," *Operations Research*, **15** no. 5 (September–October 1969); or D. J. Wilde's *Optimum Seeking Methods* (Englewood Cliffs: Prentice-Hall, 1964). The mathematical sophisticate might also want to see Dupac's "A Dynamic Stochastic Approximation Process," *Annals of Mathematical Statistics*, **28** no. 4 (1957), pp. 1003–1010.

9. Recall that the finite-state system is essentially one where, for any given set of starting-state conditions, there will be one and only one outcome. In effect then, finite-state system networks or models will be linear, serial, and monolithic, free of the stochastic branches and indeterminate discontinuities of stochastic-state models. For more on the finite-state phenomenon, see A. Gill, *Introduction to the Theory of Finite State Machines* (New York: McGraw-Hill, 1962).

10. David Mechanic, "Some Considerations in the Methodology of Organizational Studies," *The Social Science of Organizations* (Englewood Cliffs: Prentice-Hall, 1963), pp. 137–182.

11. An "adaptive model," as used here, refers to one whose structural and dynamic properties are plastic and responsive to manipulations in the face of changing endogenous or exogenous conditions. Such models reflect the "normative" cognitive processes of man himself rather than the synthetic, rigid models we encounter in the deterministic sciences. For examples, see Jocob Marschak's "On Adaptive Programming: Statistical Control of Time Standards," *Management Science*, **9** no. 4 (1963), p. 137f, and Richard E. Bellman's "Some Applications of the Theory of Dynamic Programming," *Operations Research*, **2** no. 3 (1954), pp. 275–288.

12. Development leverage is measured as the ratio of net system effectiveness (the change in problem-system parameters) relative to a given level of cost associated with that achievement. Thus we economize on overall costs by delaying some modules' implementation until certain prerequisital modules have been implemented. Generally, those *most critical* modules should be implemented first, these generally being those which will treat those problem properties (or subproblems) that appear to be the most central "nodes" in the emerging macro-problem model (viewed here as a network). The basic concept of development leverage does not come from a systems theorist, but from the brilliant and prolific development economist, Albert O. Hirschman. See particularly the first several chapters in his *The Strategy of Economic Development* (New Haven: Yale University Press, 1958).

13. For a detailed analysis of some of these points, especially the error reduction associated with modularity, see Arthur E. Ferdinand's "A Theory of System Complexity," *International Journal of General Systems*, **1** no. 1 (1974), followed by my commentary for the nonmathematician.

14. See Chapter 5 of Herbert Simon's *Administrative Behavior* (New York: Macmillan Publishing Company, 1957) for the concept of "satisficing."

15. Martin Beckmann, *Dynamic Programming of Economic Decisions* (New York: Springer-Verlag New York, 1968), p. 76.

16. Some work in the area of joint simulation/optimization models has been done under the aegis of the Rand Corporation. See, Karr, et al., *Simoptimization Research—Phase I*, No. 65-P2.0-1, C.A.C.I. (Santa Monica, California, 1965).

17. In this respect, see Dean Jamison's "Bayesian Information Usage," *Information and Inference*, ed. Hintikka and Suppes, (Dordrecht, Holland: D. Reidel Publishing Co., 1970), pp. 28–57.

7

Policy-Setting and Decision-Making: Extending the Bounds of Rationality

7.0 INTRODUCTION

In this chapter we want to explore two critical applications of systems analysis, beyond general problem-solving. The first of these applications is *policy-setting*, the second is *decision-making*. In both instances, we shall try to present those points which are effectively unique to the system sciences' treatment of these tasks, giving references where the reader may find information about what might be called the "traditional" approaches.

Policies are generally agreed to be extremely broad, usually long-range, formulation-based dictates for action. In a negative sense, they represent a restraint on the action-space available to individuals or systems, or in some way serve to limit the repertoire of desired behavior. In operation, policies serve as a broad strategic envelope within which decisions are made, and, in effect, provide certain *a priori* premises for the normal decision-maker. Thus, for example, a state or nation may have an environmental policy that demands conservation; the existence of this policy then constrains the decision-space available to individual businessmen, government agents, etc., or anyone else dealing with any aspect of the environment. It thus serves to limit the prerogatives available to systems that might have an impact on the environment. Without going into great detail, all policies have a very special property as a class of phenomena: all reflect assertions about desirable system properties, and hopefully serve the cause of transition from less favorable to more favorable system states . . . either through prescription or proscription.

In short, policies are *normative* in nature, and always involve a preference given to one state-alternative at the expense of all others that might have been elected as most desirable. Thus, *normative systems* may be thought of as ends (system states) that policies are designed to attain, and thus reflect "ordered" sets of idealized attributes pertinent to some future point-in-time. To this extent, policy-setting becomes the rational activity associated with the isolation of those means by which a transition from a less favorable to a more favorable state may be *most efficiently* effected within some bounded time interval.

In the first part of this chapter, then, we shall be offering what is essentially a variation on the system architecture scheme presented in the previous chapter, this time turning our attention toward the design of normative systems rather than problem-solving systems. This, in essence, involves the "creation of favorable futures," with policies emerging as the basic *action-vehicles* by which favorable futures are generated from less favorable existing systems, etc. Thus, normative system design involves the specification of desirable system properties, and the isolation of action proposals (*qua* policies) which have the highest probability of forcing the desired transition.

In terms of basic procedures, the normative system-building process will be similar to the problem-solving system design process. Here, however, the generation of a *most likely* problem definition model, as a referent for the system design, will be replaced by a *most desirable* set of system properties, with the normative system designed to achieve the desirable system state (much as the problem-solving system was designed to effect a solution relative to the predictive problem model). Thus, while the basic action-research logic of the normative system design process will be familiar, the sequence of steps and a few of the system architecture instruments will be new; as Figure 7.1 indicates.

The "technology" of this process will, then, primarily occupy us in the first section of this chapter, and will constitute the system approach to rationalized policy-setting.

The transition from policy-setting to decision-making is a relatively neat one. As suggested, policies become premises for decisions, and hence serve to reduce the feasible solution-space within which the rational decision-maker must search for an optimal (or, more feasibly, a satisfactory action-alternative). In normal terms, decision-making is conceived of as the selection of an expectedly best course of action from among all alternatives, given criteria for decision success. The decision-making process, then, is somewhat more constrained than the problem-solving process we went through (where the criteria for solution had to be evolved and were not *a priori* "given"), and is considerably less complicated than the policy-setting process where effectively axiological or subjective factors must be manipulated and isolated as to "desired" ends. The decision-maker has a much narrower, better-defined and more neatly-bounded search-space than either his policy-setting or problem-solving counterparts. His is not so much the task of system design, as it is the task of system maintenance, and not so much the task of isolating optimal or adequate strategies, as it is the task of converging on preset system parameters in the most efficient way possible. Thus, decision-making involves a precise criteria for success, and involves a search-space bounded by policy constraints from some higher level authority.

In normal instances, as we shall later define them, the decision-maker most often deals with problems existing at lower system levels, whereas policy-setters usually deal with problems associated with the highest levels of the system. In actual fact, this might mean that the problems demanding treatment by decision-makers, per se, are likely to be effectively moderately stochastic or deterministic;

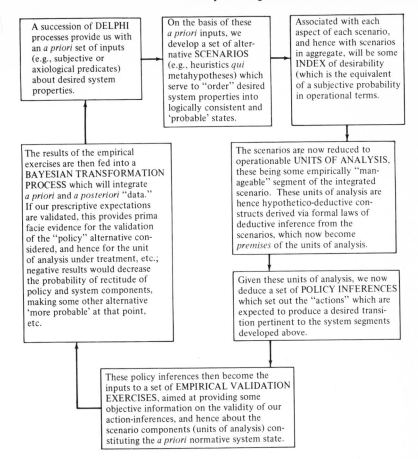

A succession of DELPHI processes provide us with an *a priori* set of inputs (e.g., subjective or axiological predicates) about desired system properties.

On the basis of these *a priori* inputs, we develop a set of alternative SCENARIOS (e.g., heuristics *qui* metahypotheses) which serve to "order" desired system properties into logically consistent and 'probable' states.

Associated with each aspect of each scenario, and hence with scenarios in aggregate, will be some INDEX of desirability (which is the equivalent of a subjective probability in operational terms.

The results of the empirical exercises are then fed into a BAYESIAN TRANSFORMATION PROCESS which will integrate *a priori* and *a posteriori* "data." If our prescriptive expectations are validated, this provides prima facie evidence for the validation of the "policy" alternative considered, and hence for the unit of analysis under treatment, etc.; negative results would decrease the probability of rectitude of policy and system components, making some other alternative 'more probable' at that point, etc.

The scenarios are now reduced to operationable UNITS OF ANALYSIS, these being some empirically "manageable" segment of the integrated scenario. These units of analysis are hence hypothetico-deductive constructs derived via formal laws of deductive inference from the scenarios, which now become *premises* of the units of analysis.

Given these units of analysis, we now deduce a set of POLICY INFERENCES which set out the "actions" which are expected to produce a desired transition pertinent to the system segments developed above.

These policy inferences then become the inputs to a set of EMPIRICAL VALIDATION EXERCISES, aimed at providing some objective information on the validity of our action-inferences, and hence about the scenario components (units of analysis) constituting the *a priori* normative system state.

Figure 7.1   The normative system architecture process.

whereas those that must be faced by policy-setters are more likely to be of a higher order of complexity (severely stochastic or indeterminate). Thus, decision-making becomes the application of the principles of microeconomics, usually intelligible in terms of neat structures such as cost-benefit analysis. But, as we shall see soon enough, an adequate appreciation of the decision-making task really depends on an understanding of what might be involved in rationalized policy-setting, the subject to which we now turn our attention.

7.1 NORMATIVE SYSTEM ARCHITECTURE

In the simplest possible terms, the normative system design process involves the following:

(a) The specification of a set of "utopian" properties which a favorable future would entail . . . "ordered" in terms of a hypothetico-deductive system model (often in scenario form).

(b) The development of a descriptive model of the existing system, or at least those aspects that are pertinent to the normative model.

(c) The specification of the "differences" between existent system properties (or expected system properties, in the absence of action on our part) and the normative system properties.

(d) The isolation of a set of action-proposals—policies—that promise to have the highest probability of causing an efficient transition from the less favorable existing/extrapolative system state to the normative one, pertinent to some time horizon.

In this sense, then, the architecture of normative systems becomes roughly equivalent to the "creation of the future," and directly relevant to the task of rationalized policy-setting.

It is in this area of policy-setting and normative system design, then, that the imagination, sensitivity, and "deductive" authority of the system scientist become especially critical, and converge directly on the interests of the social theorist, the political scientist, or others who are concerned with the basic integrity and improvement of the broad bases of civilization. It is here, then, that the system scientist becomes the sociopolitical or socioeconomic or sociotechnical architect, and not simply a system engineer or a computer expert. It is here that he ceases to deal with numbers or mechanical functions and processes, and turns his hand to the manipulation of concepts, philosophical constructs, axiological variables, and the systematic treatment of "imponderables." It is here that he moves furthest away from that which exists or that which is statistically probable, and becomes concerned, instead, with that which is possible or that which is desirable.

7.1.1 The Normative System-Building Paradigm

A methodology applicable to constructing futures must give vent to imagination on the one hand, and on the other, still accommodate whatever empirical or experiential factors emerge either in the course of the system building exercise or in the interval between our analysis and the culmination of the future at the horizon of interest. But the methodology must also seek to minimize the probability of analytical error being translated into irrevocably dysfunctional actions.

The basic strategy for normative system-building, then, involves the explication of that which is deemed desirable in the future, but also the recognition of that which emerges as inevitable or highly probable, irrespective of its desirability. Such an approach would be consonant with the recognition that the algorithm that finds us setting goals, devising strategies to achieve those goals, and then moving ever closer toward convergence is a highly unrealistic one in the real-world, and probably dysfunctional as well, for several reasons.

First, in a complex, protean world (such as post-industrialism is purported to be and such as the present proves itself daily), goals set far in advance of some horizon of interest may tend to neglect opportunities that will only emerge subsequently. This is especially true of goals or objectives set on the basis of predictions about future states of the world, for predictions become gratuitious to the extent that the system at hand is a complex one, and to the extent that the distance between the development of predictions and the horizon of interest increases.* Thus, wherever possible, goals should be established in *formula terms* rather than as point estimates, and should refer to properties that will gradually become inherent in the system rather than to superficial parameters (e.g., instead of establishing a goal as the realization of some x% rate of return by some period, a formula goal might be read as an effort to maximize the resilience or responsiveness of the system by invoking structural changes, perhaps as with Toffler's concept of the "adhocracy)."[1]

Secondly, there must be a recognition that linear strategies—those that anticipate a direct drive toward some objective—are seldom realized in the real-world. Rather, behavior tends to be heuristic in nature, and a future-building methodology must take explicit cognizance of this procedural modality and deny the impulse to develop rigid prediction-based planning and control schemes. Rather, the emphasis should be on real-time monitoring and feedback exercises, with the criteria for success constantly being reevaluated and altered in light of changing contextual conditions. Indeed, in the world of the future, which is being approached heuristically rather than algorithmically, there is a distinct advantage which Walter Reitman has pointed out, ". . . one may solve one's problems not only by getting what one wants, but by wanting what one gets."[2] In a world where we know only how to seek goals, and have not the capability to constantly adjust them, the actual future will hold only frustration and suboptimality. Thus, while the forecaster or traditional predictor of futures may bemoan the fact that there is no determinism out there, the "rational" system will recognize that where there is no determinism, there is also no lack of opportunity. And for such a system, prediction will become a great deal less important than alertness, resilience, and versatility.†

What we want, then, is a methodological procedure that frees us from the extrapolative constraints that bind the mechanistic, inductive forecaster, per se, but that also militates against the abjectly intuitive and idiosyncratic constructs of the science fiction writers or teratological Cassandras which enjoy such prestige in the popular media. Thus, our methodology must not only be able to create the future, but must be able to *manage* the future.

7.1.2 The Procedural Aspects of the Paradigm

Given all the methodological considerations just discussed, it is possible to construct a procedural paradigm which would serve as a fairly promising reference

---

*That is, either the inherent complexity of the system or the length between point of prediction and horizon can act to dilute the validity of extrapolative forecasts.
†These properties, among others, constitute the heuristic administrative modality we shall be discussing in Chapter 8.

for those involved in the "creation" of futures. In diagram form, the paradigm would involve the eight steps given in Figure 7.2. As the reader might readily recognize, some of the tasks here are reminiscent of the system architecture paradigm given in Figure 6.9. But there are at least three elements in the normative system-building paradigm that will require some elaboration: (a) scenario-building, (b) construction of problem "network" models, and (c) generation of action proposals and the utility of learning loops.

7.1.2.1 Scenario-Building As was indicated by Figure 7.2, our normative system-building exercise begins with the construction of a syncretistic scenario

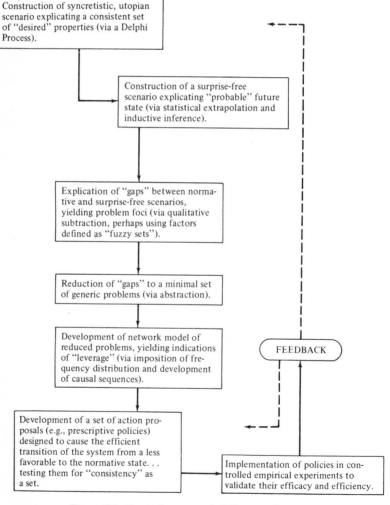

Figure 7.2 Normative system-building paradigm.

which will accommodate a diversity of needs and desires. This scenario should serve to emphasize similarities in axiological or affective predicates, not merely explicate differences. This means that it should be constructed at a level of abstraction that, as nearly as possible, works backward from superficial positions to fundamental societal attributes. The device by which we may do this would be a simple variation on the basic Delphi process. But here, rather than searching for opinions or for probabilistic expectations about events, we would try to structure a set of properties that could be integrated into a normative future ... properties based on the criterion of desirability rather than likelihood, for example.

Given this set of utopian or normative future properties, we might set about collecting a set of expectations about the future independent of any action that we might take. This might be the development of a "business as usual" scenario, or of the type which Harold Linstone has referred to as *surprise-free*.[3] The normative and the surprise-free scenario would differ in an important respect. The normative scenario will usually be predicated largely on hypothetico-deductive instruments generating nonempirical "information"; the surprise-free scenario may legitimately be based largely on extrapolative or projective information derived from present or historical (empirical) data. The normative scenario, then, will often be a product of intellect and discernment, whereas the surprise-free one will generally be a more or less mechanical exercise in statistical analysis coupled with limited uses of inductive inference which, again, simply extends the properties inherent in some empirical or experiential data base, introducing changes which are matters of *degree* rather than of quality.

We have already had a discussion of the procedures and promises associated with the use of the Delphi process as a system architecture instrument (see, again, Section 6.2.1). Here, then, we simply note that while the normal Delphi process will value "divergences" which might emerge in constructing our scenarios, we must search for the same kind of "convergences" that we did in the problem-solving system exercises of Chapter 6 . . . hence our syncretic ambition throughout.

In any exercise of significance, we must expect to meet with the *clustering* effect noted in Section 6.5, divergences based on essentially different background assumptions and, here especially, different axiological or "affective" predicates. Thus, when participants are asked about a normative future through the Delphi process, we should find alternative constructs emerging, just as we found alternative *a priori* problem definition models in the problem-solving exercise. These different scenarios, based on the "natural" clusters which emerge, should enable us to locate the axes of recrimination (if any) among participants, and make opaque the often transparent "metahypotheses" on which divergences of opinion or evaluation rest. This is the first step in gaining a consensus where divergences are a matter of value or idiosyncratic perception rather than a matter of "objective" argumentation. Thus we might direct the

Delphi process at the development of cluster-based normative scenarios. Given these, we could then set about trying to develop some sort of "syncretic' hybrid"—perhaps at a level of abstraction where the axiological arguments no longer hold sway. At the very least, we would be able to pose these cluster-based scenarios as products of "background assumptions" that can be measured, however indirectly, by the kind of techniques offered by Mitroff and Turoff.[4]

Where, however, divergences are more likely to be "objective" or "rational" in origin rather than affective or axiological, then we would probably want to develop stratified scenarios . . . which can benefit from argumentation from different backgrounds and experiential sets. Thus, while the normative scenarios are probably better conducted as clustered exercises, the extrapolative or surprise-free scenarios would better be conducted as stratification-based model-building exercises (particularly where the strata would represent thoroughly *interdisciplinary* teams). For those not clear on the logic here, a rereading of Section 6.5 would be helpful, as the points we made there will be largely applicable to that which follows (e.g., the reader might substitute "scenarios" for the heuristic *a priori* problem definition models we used there, and substitute indices of desirability for likelihood operators). At any rate, because we seek a consensus—and because we want to be able to "measure" our progress toward it in terms of learning curves that measure decreases in variance of indices of desirability (or likelihood, for the extrapolative scenario)—we would want to pose Delphi-based questions in some form that will permit a fairly precise response, perhaps using an answer continuum something like the following:

$$\begin{array}{cccc} | & | & | & | \\ 100 & 75 & 25 & \emptyset \end{array} \quad \text{(Probability/Desirability Index)}$$

Each respondent is asked to place a check mark at the point on the continuum that best describes his expectations about the probability or desirability of the event (or item) in question. The aggregate of all such responses, for each iteration of the Delphi process, will thus represent a frequency distribution with proper statistical properties, proper in the sense that it will yield a formal measure of variance. The questions should be phrased in such a way that affective or objective origins of disputation may be isolated (e.g., asking "leading" questions or questions with a strong but subtle valuational bias). On subsequent iterations of the Delphi process, when essentially the same issues are raised, perhaps however in different form, a measure of the decrease (hopefully) in variance can be obtained, which should enable us to roughly evaluate the effectiveness of the strategy or tactics by which we are trying to establish a consensus. Thus, through the course of a scenario-building exercise, it is the variance of responses with which we shall be concerned, for this is the best guide we have as to the means by which a consensus might be obtained. We shall not specify any of these means here, except to note that behavioral scientists concerned with consensus and conflict-elimination have methods that are at our disposal, and the comparative effectiveness of these methods can be audited by the above procedure. Thus, the consensus-seeking process might be viewed as an action-research experiment in its own right, shifting instruments in response to empirically derived variance estimates.

It should be mentioned here that response-by-continuum (e.g., asking for responses in the form illustrated above) lends us another capability which is extremely important, and which has been treated in greater detail elsewhere.* Specifically, the frequency distributions that emerge from the successive iterations of the Delphi process, aimed at securing indices of desirability pertinent to future properties, may be thought of as subjective (*a priori*) probabilities, and may be treated as such. In short, in operational terms, expectations about the likelihood of an event occurring, and estimations of the desirability of events, become intelligible in exactly the same terms. In fact, we may usually expect to generate fairly accurate surrogates for desirability of events by asking about their probability of occurrence, this in the sense that respondents are often likely to assign the highest likelihood estimates to events that they themselves value. There is some advantage in this surrogation approach, especially where social conventions might act to impede true responses. For example, a respondent might really prefer that in the future his contact with members of minority groups be minimized, but he would be reluctant to be tied to such a statement; asked, however, about the likelihood of homogeneous communities, we may get a reasonable basis for inference about desirability. Naturally, some local testing would have to be done to determine the extent to which expectations about probability of occurrence and estimations of desirability are truly correlated, with the reliability of inferences being adjusted accordingly. As a general rule, however, there should be some opportunity during the course of the Delphi process to gain indices of both likelihood and desirability.

The net result of this process will be a scenario, that, at each point may be thought of as involving a selection from among all alternatives that might have been included. In this sense, a scenario emerges as a proper model, with each of its components being assigned some index of either desirability (in the case of the normative scenario) or probability of occurrence (in the case of the extrapolative or surprise-free scenario). In graphic terms, we may think of each component of the scenarios as being represented by an event-probability distribution, similar to that shown in Figure 7.3(a). The events on which the probability distribution is imposed may represent anything we wish, pertinent to some scenario under construction (that is, the e_i's may be variables, relationships, functions, complex events, parameter values, etc., or any other component). Of the two curves in (a), the *a priori* (presumed to be that which exists after the first Delphi iteration and prior to the first attempt at consensus) is less favorable in terms of variance than is the *a posteriori* (which is presumed to exist after some n iterations of the Delphi and consensus-seeking process).

The transformation from the *a priori* to the *a posteriori* curve as a result of our

*See, again, Section 5.2.

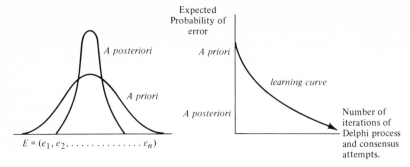

Figure 7.3 Event-probability distribution and associated learning curve.

polling and consensus-seeking operations results in the favorable learning curve in (b). We may now interpret these constructs in the following two ways:

1. *For the Normative Scenario.* Suppose that the event set [*E*] is an array of mutually exclusive attributes pertinent to some aspect of the future, such that the two curves should be read as products of respondents' estimations of the desirability of these alternatives. In the *a priori* state there is a considerably greater divergence than in the *a posteriori*, with the numerically calculated variance acting as an imputed measure of the degree of consensus obtained. The "learning curve" in (b) thus reflects the rate at which this consensus has been gained, such that the curve in that diagram may now be thought to represent the variance in estimations of desirability among those contributing to the scenario-building exercise.

2. *For the Extrapolative Scenario.* Here the *a priori* and *a posteriori* curves represent expectations about the likelihood of occurrence of the events constituting set [*E*], such that the *a posteriori* curve assigns respectively higher probabilities of occurrence to a sharply decreased set of alternatives. Thus the "learning curve" in (b) may be read as written: measuring the probability of expected error associated with the aggregation of predictions. In short, we have converged gradually on a consensus of opinion about what will occur, whereas in the normative exercise we converged on a set of opinions about what is desirable.

In both of the above cases, we have used a statistical surrogation process to discipline the inputs from Delphi participants, and to gain an empirical appreciation of the *efficiency* of our model-building and consensus-seeking process. The normative scenario will, then, constitute a complex model that at all points has been assigned specific indices of consensus as to the desirability of the components entered. For the extrapolative or surprise-free scenario, we have a model that, at all points, contains those components that have been assigned the highest probabilities of occurrence by the participants. The net result should be a normative scenario with the highest logical probability of accurately encompassing the desires of participants, and an extrapolative scenario that, relative to all others we might have built, has the highest probability of accurately reflecting the future *in the absence of any therapeutic or directional actions we might take.* In other words, this latter scenario represents what we think will happen if we do not interfere, or if we abrogate our opportunity to create the future.

There are two other aspects of the scenario-building process which we should note here, although these are mentioned in virtually all treatises on the subject. The first is that the normative and extrapolative scenarios should represent logically consistent models. Thus, as Joseph Martino suggests,

> a scenario is more than just a set of forecasts about some future time. It is a picture of an internally consistent situation, which, in turn, is the plausible outcome of a sequence of events. Naturally there is no rigorous test for plausibility. . . . The scenario thus occupies a position somewhere between a collection of forecasts whose interrelationships have not been examined, and a mathematical model whose internal consistency is rigorously demonstrable.[5]

While there are no hard and fast rules for establishing consistency, it is nevertheless useful to have at hand some sort of instrument for examining the nature of the interaction between system components, an exercise that is naturally aided by having an interdisciplinary flavor to the scenario-building team and concentrating some attention on the interfaces that appear among components of the emerging models.

Secondly, the utility of the normative scenario-building process stems from the simple realization that if we were able to start from scratch, very few systems would be designed the way they have naturally evolved. Therefore, it sometimes pays simply to ignore what exists and turn instead to a disciplined exploration of what should exist. Little has been gained from the large number of incredibly costly studies aimed at "finding out what's wrong with system x." The response that the system scientist might make to such an assignment is: "Compared to what?"

Without the normative predecessor, studies of existing systems lack a referent and therefore can accomplish little (yet empirical science's domination of research technology has lent such studies a patina of legitimacy, despite their long record of sterility).

7.1.2.2 Toward the Problem Network The completion of the normative and extrapolative scenarios now allows us to concentrate on the differences between what we want to occur and what we expect will occur in the absence of action on our part. These differences thus represent "gaps" that must gradually be closed if the properties of the normative scenario are to be realized. It is important, therefore, that the normative and extrapolative scenarios be built on exactly the same dimensions, such that they represent essentially different states for the same essential system. In short, expectations and estimations of desirability should, where possible, be generated in pairs with respect to a set of system components that remain constant through both exercises.

Thus, for each aspect of the future, there will be a set of ordered pairs of properties, with the first element in the pair representing the desired property, and the second representing the property expected to exist, given inaction. We won't go into detail here, but it should be obvious to system scientists that defining properties in terms of ordered pairs lends us some valuable mathematical capabilities and allows us to treat the two scenarios as formal state-alternatives for a formally defined system.[6] Where the elements of each pair are essentially similar, the "gap" will be negligible and this particular system aspect may thus be removed from immediate attention.

However, before we finalize our action proposals, we must again review any elements that were set aside. For new conditions might be introduced that will prevent the extrapolative value from converging on the desired. The logic here is simple but critical . . . in interfering with those aspects of the system deemed to be dysfunctional, we might very well introduce changes that prevent desired events from taking place through the extrapolative mechanism. In short, when we change any aspect of the system, we must reassess the impact these changes might have on aspects of the system with which we did not wish to interfere.

At any rate, the generation of the "gaps" which do exist might be viewed as a problem in *qualitative subtraction*, where we are basically interested in isolating that set of properties which is *not shared* by the two scenarios (relative to each of the dimensions of the scenarios or to each system component being considered).* As far as formal procedures for this exercise, there is an increasing literature on what is known as "fuzzy" set theory, which is the attempt to deal mathematically with qualitative variables.[7] The result of this subtractive exercise should, then, be a set of ordered differences that now may be thought to represent problems, per se.

But for a scenario of any significant size, much less for those directed at large-scale systems such as regional socioeconomic systems or urban areas, etc., the number of problems *cum* gaps will be enormous. True, we have eliminated for the moment those aspects of the system where desired and extrapolated ends were the same (e.g., where the trend is adequately favorable or where a favorable system aspect is expected to remain secularly stable), but we must now perform a further reduction.

We want, in effect, to arrive at an array of problems that exhausts the "gaps" isolated above, and that contains the fewest possible elements or entries. We do this by looking for ways to phrase problems such that all those which we arrive at will be mutually exclusive and pertain to the largest possible number of specific instances (e.g., gaps). In a sense, then, the problem definitions that are sought here will be arrived at by a process of *successive abstraction*. With this

---

*Of course, for factors that are quantifiable, mathematical as opposed to qualitative manipulations are used.

process we are constructing generic problem referents that perform much the same function as theories or laws: they introduce efficiency into our explanatory process by allowing us to account for the largest number of specific (unreduced) phenomena with the fewest possible unique formulations.

In operational terms, this successive abstraction process would be conducted by searching the several gaps for elements of *isomorphy* or attributal similarities. The search for, and exploitation of, instances of isomorphy is one of the best described procedures of system science, so there are ample references to which the reader may turn for specific guidance.[8]

The general strategy, however, relies mainly on the intellectual tenacity and sensitivity of the participants, and on the ability to absolve the problems *cum* gaps of their contextual or superficial properties so that instances of isomorphism may be uncovered. In short, the method here would be to take the gaps previously isolated and gradually strip away as many *modifiers* as possible. The result should be the fewest number of mutually exclusive generic problem definitions that in substance, exhaust as fully as possible the gaps from which they were generated.

The next step is the analysis of these generic problem referents, and the imposition of some sort of *causal order* on them. We would first calculate the number of specific gaps (e.g., unreduced problems) to which each of the generic problems refers, thus giving a rough measure of the degree of abstraction associated with each element of the reduced problem array. When this is done for all generic problems, we may develop a simple frequency distribution which will often have a valuable property for us, for when the various generic problems are arrayed as the event-set in the frequency distribution, the amplitude of the resultant curves imposed on each element in that set (each generic problem) gives us a measure of the relative *system leverage* it exerts. That is, the frequency distribution will point out those problems that, when operated on or treated, are likely to have the greatest overall therapeutic effect on the system as a whole. In short, the measure of abstraction associated with each of the generic problem referents is also a measure of its influence on the *state* of the system, with those generic problems encompassing the largest number of specific gaps being those which carry the greatest expected leverage. Hence, in the histogram shown in Figure 7.4, Problem $[p_2]$ carries imputedly greater leverage than any of the others, being the generic referent for the largest number of unreduced problems (or having appeared as a factor in the largest number of specific gaps).

We would next search for some sort of *causal order* among the various generic problems we have defined. All must be directly or indirectly related, or else the system with which we are working is not a *proper* system. The task is then to allegorize the nature of these relationships, and these will generally fall into one of two broad categories: hierarchical or reticulated networks. If the ordering of influences among problems is of the former type, then we will be able to develop a causal *tree* (e.g., a partially ordered set) where problems may be arrayed on

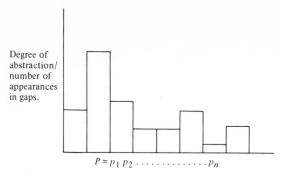

Degree of abstraction/ number of appearances in gaps.

$P = p_1 \, p_2 \, \ldots \ldots \ldots \ldots p_n$

Figure 7.4 Sample histogram.

levels such that problems on a lower level are deemed to be "causes" of problems on the next higher level, and so forth.

The net result of such a structure is a rather neatly linear relationship among the various problems, with micro problems gradually giving way to intermediate level problems which finally merge into a macro problem. In order to be a true hierarchy, we might impose a constraint that prohibits higher-order problems from affecting lower-order ones, or perhaps a constraint that acts against reflexivity among the various problems (as reflexivity would abrogate the linearity and unidirectional causality we like to see in proper hierarchies). At any rate, there are many sources of information about the properties of hierarchies, properties that must be met by the generic problems if the hierarchical modality is to be employed to lend them an ordering. (See Section 2.4.1.)

The reticulated network represents a more complex set of relationships, one where the various problems are equipotential (i.e., all may affect each other). A reticulated network thus does not possess the neatly algorithmic properties of proper hierarchical structures, and so becomes very much more difficult to model. (See Section 2.4.2.) Under this structure, one must conceive of the problems being related in a network fashion where each of the various problems represents a *node*, from which many different paths of interaction may radiate. As the reader might rightly expect, then, problems taking on a reticular form are generally associated with systems whose components have a wider behavioral repertoire than do the components of hierarchical systems. That this is so may easily be verified by comparing some of the formulations of modern network theory against their hierarchical counterparts.

With the completion of these causal orderings, the results from the frequency distribution should be reexamined. The problems that received the greatest number of appearances in the histogram of the first step should be those with the greatest number of connections in the reticular model (or, where the hierarchical structure is imposed, should be at the highest levels of causality . . . influencing the greatest number of other problems). In this way we have a check on our derivation of problems from gaps and an additional verification of the consistency of our reduction logic. And we may now proceed to the last of our procedural steps.

7.1.2.3 Generation of Action-Proposals and Learning Loops

The models just generated will serve as the input to the last of our steps . . . the generation of a set of action proposals that will cause the transition from an unfavorable system state to a favorable system state at some point in the future. From the work just completed, we know something about the order in which action-proposals should be generated, and also about the sequence in which they should be executed. Obviously, those problems shown to exert the greatest leverage (e.g., those with the highest number of appearances in the histogram, those representing most "highly connected" nodes in the reticular formulation, or those at the highest causal levels in the hierarchical structure) should be the first attacked. Thus, with respect to the frequency distribution just set out, Problem $[p_2]$ of Figure 7.4 would be the first for which an action-proposal (solution strategy) would be developed. The causal ordering model—in either the reticular or hierarchical form, whichever was deemed most appropriate—would then be used as the basis for a *simulation* of the effects of the solution strategy on the system as a whole. The results of the first iteration of the simulation model would then be to isolate any redefinitions in the other problems associated with the simulated implementation of the solution to the first problem. In short, we want to know what effects our action with respect to Problem $[p_2]$ would have on the other problems . . . so that, for each of them, a solution strategy could be devised in light of the solution to the prior problem. We would then have to iterate the simulation until we were able to incorporate the entire array of problems to be solved, together with the parameters of their solution strategies.* This is done simply to be certain that in solving one problem, we do not create others, or exacerbate the system situation in some way.

In beginning with that problem deemed to exert the greatest leverage on the system, we may emerge with an aggregate solution strategy (pertinent to the simultaneous solution of all problems) that promises to be most effective and efficient in making the desired system transition. In some cases, however, particularly where a hierarchical problem structure was uncovered, we may think about introducing solutions *sequentially* . . . implementing them in a sequence that, at each step, isolates the problem which at that point-in-time promises to exert the greatest therapeutic leverage when solved.

In either case, iterations of the simulation model should give us a *logical* pointer to the necessary conditions for each solution step, and the indication of which particular problem will emerge as the best target for attack at that itera-

---

*Again, as was suggested in the previous chapter, the expedience of multi-variable simulations depends greatly on the ratio of deterministic to stochastic components.

tion. Thus, the causal orderings of the problems give us the basis to make a most efficient transition, such that expenditures of developmental resources will produce an expectedly "optimal" effect, both in aggregate and at each point in the solution process.

There is now a final aspect of the normative system-building paradigm to be considered . . . the inauguration of *empirical learning loops*. As was earlier mentioned, the normative scenario was considered to be a "metahypothesis," a product of many different hypothetico-deductive elements linked together in a consistent system of concepts (where the consistency here may be considered to mean that the laws of deductive inference were followed more or less closely in relating the various components). In a similar way, the extrapolative (surprise-free) scenario is also a metahypothesis, though it is not strictly a hypothetico-deductive one because at least some of its substance is owing to the projection of empirical data and experimental bases (thus making it primarily an inductive construct whose components, or at least many of them, may be indexed with objective probabilities of accuracy based on statistical or inductive laws).

The problem network models were evolved directly from these two scenarios through the processes of qualitative subtraction and successive abstraction described earlier. Thus, in the strictest sense, the problem network model may be thought of as a *surrogate* for the normative scenario, for it simply has caused a reordering and redefinition of elements that were not found in the union between the normative and extrapolative constructs (e.g., those properties associated with the normative scenario that were not present in the extrapolative).* Thus, our manipulation of the problem network model in the face of simulated solutions is roughly the equivalent of operating on the normative scenario itself, though the number of factors associated with the former will normally be vastly greater than those comprising the reduced network model. In this way, very large-scale systems may usually be reduced to more manageable entities without too much loss in rectitude . . . providing that the normative scenario can ultimately be *resynthesized* from the problem network models to which it was reduced (which can be done to the extent that the reduction procedure is a fairly algorithmic one). Hence, the reduction process we support not only allows us to isolate those aspects of a potentially very large system that demand treatment if some normative system state is to be realized, but enable us to develop a considerably simplified surrogate on which we can perform analytical operations such as simulation, thus allowing us to economize greatly on the *costs* of analysis.

The added attraction of this reduction process is that we have a unit of analysis (e.g., the hierarchical or network model) that is highly amenable as a referent for empirical experiments aimed at validating (in surrogate form) the hypothetico-

---

*For this reason, it is important to try to construct normative scenarios in positive terms, such that they can be translated eventually into structural-functional properties. In short, negative scenario elements (e.g., elimination of prejudice; less unemployment) are to be avoided in the context of the present paradigm.

deductive components of the scenario, and our expectations about therapeutic actions we might take. In this sense, the strategies we evolve in the form of action-proposals now become hypotheses, per se, and the process of their implementation now becomes intelligible in terms of a reasonably well controlled *experiment*. The results of these empirical trials will then be fed back to the network model, and if our expectations were in error, appropriate modifications must be made in that model. And because the reduced network model can be resynthesized into the normative scenario, we are able to allow our experiments on solution strategies to have a direct bearing on our normative construct way up the line, allowing modifications necessary in the network model to resonate back toward their origin in the much larger, less-empirically tractable construct. The result of the hypothesis-experimentation-feedback process is what we have sought all along ... the gradual transformation of initially hypothetical constructs into empirically validated ones, which in effect means the gradual transformation of the subjective probabilities associated with the normative scenario into objective probabilities.

It is this latter property that lends the paradigm outlined here its status as an *action-research* platform, one that enables us to learn, in a disciplined way, while having a positive effect in the world at large. Its other properties make it appropriate for handling complex, as opposed to simple systems, and for the treatment of extremely large-scale systems for which few substantive methodological directions yet exist (even in the literature, much less in operation). But the construct and technology of normative system-building is far from mature, so that what we have done here can really be considered as only the first step toward a procedural system which is perhaps not yet completely operational, but which will surely emerge from the tentative foundations being laid by the system scientist in the company of the long-range forecasters and social theorists.

In summary, this normative system-building process—and this system-based approach to policy-setting—is a very demanding and somewhat "idealistic" construct in its own right ... much like the scenarios it is intended to help generate. Thus, it may represent more what could or should be done than what is immediately feasible or immediately likely. But at least it represents a start toward a methodology useful for those who believe that we control the future and are responsible for it, a position which, thankfully, seems to be taken more and more often (especially as regards environmental issues). It also represents, hopefully, an alternative to the long succession of *management by crisis* under which most social, political, and economic systems seem to labor, and does give us an opportunity to handle those axiological, judgmental, and subjective factors that existing system design algorithms cannot accommodate.

At any rate, the normative system-building paradigm represents a theoretically rationalized approach to policy-setting, and while it may not be the best we can do (it surely will be superceded by more sophisticated constructs at some point), it nevertheless represents a "disciplined" approach to the subject. And it explicitly gives to *policies* the action-potential they so richly deserve.

7.2 DEFINING THE DOMAIN OF DECISION-MAKING

Decisions take place within an envelope of constraints laid down by policies. That is, policies serve to broadly constrain the feasible search and solutions spaces within which decision-makers, per se, are expected to operate. In more specific terms, policies lead to broad, qualitatively unique system states, defined at the state-variable and relational levels, and thus serve as transitory vehicles. As such, they establish the broad structural-functional attributes of the system that then become *a priori* constraints for the lower-order decision-maker.

Policies thus represent what might be called *strategic* decisions, whereas proper decision-making takes place on a *tactical* level. We shall, in later sections, make the differences between these two types of system analysis exercises more specific, contenting ourselves here with the rather gross differentiation given in Figure 7.5.

In terms of the logic we have developed thus far in Chapters 5 and 6, and the first sections of this chapter, policies are *expectedly* vehicles for achieving a system state where the attributes of this particular system state are derived from the axiological and subjective inputs to the normative system-building process just outlined. In effect, the normative system-building process takes an initially "indeterminate" situation and structures it to be a severely stochastic one (involving several "logically" probable or desirable system states); next, it isolates one from among these several system states for intended implementation, this being the particular alternative awarded the highest *a priori* probability of desirability/feasibility, etc.; finally, policies become initially "hypothetical" instruments of transition from a less-favorable to this expectedly most-favorable state ...hypotheses whose actual effectiveness and efficiency will be a matter for continual monitoring and empirical observation.

In terms of our system analysis logic, then, we now have a set of state-variables

ATTRIBUTES	POLICY-SETTING	DECISION-MAKING
Level of analysis	State-variable and relational	Parametric and coefficient
Instrumental emphasis	Deductive and heuristic	Statistical and inductive
Character of inputs	Subjective, judgmental, logical and axiological	Objective, universalistic, and empirical
Analytical category	Severely stochastic	Moderately stochastic
Nature of output	Hypothetico-deductive prescriptions	Deterministic or range functions; point or interval values

Figure 7.5 Policy and decision attributes.

which have had a tentative "order" imposed on them, with a set of action-proposals *qua* prescriptive policies aiming to have this particular system state realized at some future point in time. With the state-variable and relational attributes of the system *defined*, what now remains for the completion of a proper system model is the assignment of "values" to the state-variables (e.g., parametric assignments) and the assignment of specific magnitudinal coefficients to the elements of the relational set defining the nature of the influence among the state-variables. These, as we will recall, are established largely as the isolation of specific quantitative values all occurring within a single qualitative set . . . and are generally set as matters of "fact" rather than opinion or judgment. The net result, then, is that by the time we are ready to establish the parametric and coefficient aspects of a system, we have moved into the moderately stochastic analytical domain, and are ready to displace deductive instruments with inductive inference and empirically-predicated statistical analysis. And at this point we pass from the policy-setting task to the decision domain.

An example is in order here. Suppose, for argument's sake, that one of the aspects of some normative scenario we developed was the utilization of a higher percentage of the regional available labor-force. Let us further suppose that there were several policies which emerged as potential candidates for achieving this normative (desired) end:

1. Increase economic growth in the region by providing investment incentives.
2. Inaugurate a subsidy system for underemployed groups, perhaps by agreeing to assume a certain portion of their salaries.
3. Invoke incentives to underemployed groups or classes of unemployables to migrate out of the region to some other region (perhaps by making travel funds available, etc., or by reducing welfare or unemployment provisions).
4. Increasing the tax rates or regional tariffs associated with the importation or purchase of capital equipment . . . thereby attempting to lower the overall capital-labor ratio.

Let us further suppose, that for various reasons, there was a consensus of opinion or judgment that the last of the policy alternatives was the most "desirable" and feasible with respect to the problem of reducing regional unemployment levels. Note that the selection of this policy alternative (or, for that matter, any of the others) introduces new qualitative components into the system, and thus necessitates a system redefinition at the state-variable and/or relational level.

We may now enter the *decision domain*, per se. The reason for this is simple. The basic structural aspects of this subsegment of the normative system are established *a priori* in terms of the decision to elect a particular qualitative alternative: increasing the tax rate on purchase or importation of capital equipment in the hopes of making labor more "attractive" as a means of production (at least in those areas where labor and equipment are effective substitutes within some range). The issue facing the decision-maker is thus not a qualitative one, but an essentially quantitative one: the development of a macro function (e.g., input-output equation) which will indicate the relationship between an x% increase in the equipment tax and a y% decrease in the capital labor ratio ... where the basic qualitative structural aspects of the system (e.g., the micro level) remain effectively transparent.

In short, the tactical decision now becomes not a matter of deciding on a basic strategy or course of action, but a matter of deciding "how much" action to take. His is then the responsibility for deciding on a particular tax rate, from among all *quantitative* alternatives, on the basis of a generic function relating inputs (e.g., tax increases) to outputs (e.g., reductions in the capital-labor ratio). In gross effect, then, this difference expressed here between policy and decision analysis corresponds in detail to the difference we earlier set out between moderately and severely stochastic systems, per se (See, again, Section 3.2).

In general, then, the decision-maker deals with problems which can be resolved largely through the use of statistical instruments. For in the course of moving from policy to decision problems, the data to be operated on is gradually transformed from subjective to objective. Judgmental or "affective" inputs decline in favor of hard facts or empirical elements. Accordingly, the congruent instruments cease to be deductively predicated and become those that generate inductive inferences. In summary, then, if system architecture offered a method of handling indeterminacy, and the normative system-building paradigm was able to accommodate severely stochastic problems, the decision mechanism offers a disciplined set of procedures for dealing with moderate stochasticity and for determining most likely magnitudes (e.g., point-in-time parametric or coefficient values) and best tactical moves predicted on those magnitudes.

7.3 TOWARD A DECISION PARADIGM

The requirement for a decision may initiate either with the decision-maker himself or with some superordinate. In any case, he initiates the decision process, per se, by articulating his expectations about the relationships expected to prevail between the various informational states (stocks) first introduced in Section 5.1.

There, it will be recalled, we worked with three stocks or "sets" of information. The first, the *real* set, contains the system analyst's expectations about the "limits" of information available, and hence may be thought to set the criteria for analytical success and the point at which the analysis process will be completed. As was mentioned earlier, this real informational set is the reference against which the adequacy of our *a priori* and *a posteriori* information sets are compared, and is a complex product of judgment, speculation, experience, and ultimately of epistemological predicates (or biases). The second, the *a priori* informational set, on the other hand, contains what we think we already know about the problem or system at hand, and therefore establishes the "starting state" conditions for the analysis process. The contents of this *a priori* set, as with the real, is a complex product of judgmental or subjective factors, and empirical-experiential or objective components. Those set elements that have no historical precedent (e.g., that do not reflect actual experiences with similar systems or problems or are not taken from some empirically-predicated historical data base) are hence deductive in nature. Those which do reflect experience or historical fact are essentially inductive . . . this because, in the act of entering them into the *a priori* set of some problem or system of current interest, we make necessary assumptions about the degree of "correlation" between the contexts in which the data or experiences were originally generated and the current context. If the contextual conditions are seen to be highly similar, then the authority or confidence we lend these inductively-predicated elements of the *a priori* set will be rather high; similarly, as the correlation between historical and current contexts is perceived to decline, we assign successively less confidence to the inductively-predicated elements of the *a priori* set.

The third, the *a posteriori* informational set(s), are those that are developed as a result of explicit, formal analysis . . . either empirical or logical (e.g., Gedanken experiments, deductive analysis) in nature. At any rate, *a posteriori* information is always associated with the current expenditure of analytical resources (whereas the *a priori* informational elements carry only historical or "sunk" costs, if any). At any rate, we now have at hand the components for a *general* decision model, diagrammed in Figure 7.6.

The story that this figure tells us is an admittedly simplistic one (ignoring factors that will be introduced into a more sophisticated version in a later section). Nevertheless, its elementary logic is useful for us, and might be summarized as follows:

(a) Initially, the decision-maker may (usually illegimately) perceive an effective identity between his *a priori* state at time t_0 and the postulated real state.* When this is the case, he takes immediate decision action, drawing his premises from the *a priori* information stock.

(b) If this identity is not perceived, he inaugurates an analysis exercise. An *a posteriori* information stock is then produced that, at each iteration of the process, is compared against the real for identity. If identity is not perceived, the decision-maker will look at the difference between the information stock at time t, relative to that which was obtained at time $t - 1$ (associated with the previous iteration).

*As we have suggested, the probability of the *a priori* informational state adequately exhausting the properties of the *real* decreases radically when the system or problem at hand begins to depart from the criteria for the essential mechanism (e.g., the deterministic ideal-type).

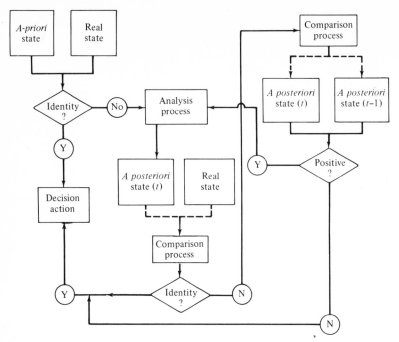

Figure 7.6   The general system decision model.

(c) So long as the relationship continues expectedly positive, the analysis process will be continued. Should the learning curve turn negative or become
uneconomic (such that the relationship between successive information
stocks is perceived unfavorable relative to costs), a decision is made using
whatever premises can be drawn from the existing information stock at
that point.

This is the basic logic of the analysis process. Given these, it is now a fairly
simple task to determine under what set of conditions the policy-setter or
decision-maker (or system analyst) will make the decision to acquire *additional*
information. These conditions are:

(a) There is a perceived significant variance between the existing stock of information (either *a priori* or *a posteriori*) and the postulated "real" stock
of information.
(b) There is expected to be a positive marginal product associated with the
acquistion of the next increment of information.
(c) There is no requirement that the decision be made immediately. In other
words, the permissible decision-horizon is still some distance away.
(d) If we are in the *a posteriori* state, a final condition is that there be some
substantive and positive difference between the information stock at time
t and time $t - 1$. That is, we must have a "history" of successive improve-

ment in our informational acquistion via the system analysis process. If successive observations on parameters or properties of interest have yielded no new information, we can assume that we have hit some kind of analytical *ceiling*, or that the properties of the subject system are changing more rapidly than we can encompass using the specific analysis instruments and strategies involved. In this case, we can either take decision action on the basis of what we have, or explore the possibility of inaugurating a new research strategy or a new analytical modality. (Discussed in Section 7.3.3).

The above model is "general" in that it does not explicitly distinguish between strategic (policy-oriented) decisions and tactical (moderately stochastic) decisions. But it must be clear that the difference between these two decision modalities rests largely in a simple fact: the output from any prior policy-setting exercises (e.g., strategic decision analyses) will be inputs to the *real* and *a priori* informational sets for the tactical decision-maker, per se. Thus, while the decision logic remains essentially similar for both policy-setting and tactical decision-making activities, the "richness" of detail and substance in the *real* and *a priori* sets for the latter serve to considerably restrain the gross solution and search space which must be considered. The bounds of the policy-setting process are both much wider and less well-defined (as is consistent with the fact that such exercises refer to higher-order system levels than do tactical decision exercises).

7.3.1 The Substantive Decision Model

The simplicity of the previous model (diagrammed in Figure 7.6) has cost us something in terms of reality . . . it fails to consider some points that will now be included in a somewhat more complex construct. This we shall call the *substantive decision model*, and its components are displayed graphically in Figure 7.7.

The logic of this model is really just an extension of the general system decision model introduced as Figure 7.6. The decision-maker enters at the point where he puts forward his expectations about the relationship between the *a priori* and real informational states (stocks). If they are perceived to be identical—that is, if he feels that the information he already has adequately exhausts the properties of the real state, then he may proceed directly to enact a decision, using the *a priori* information stock as the basis for the selection of an action alternative. The only situations under which this route may be taken by the "rational" decision-maker are cases where the problem at hand is one that is fully precedented, such that an *a priori* decision may simply be replicated. Such a situation, however, really argues against the logic of the decision-making process . . . for it is only in cases where a problem is an effectively deterministic one that *a priori* experience can exhaust the analytical demands that the system sciences would make. Wherever the problem at hand is a proper target for decision-making (e.g., a moderately stochastic one), taking the *a priori* route

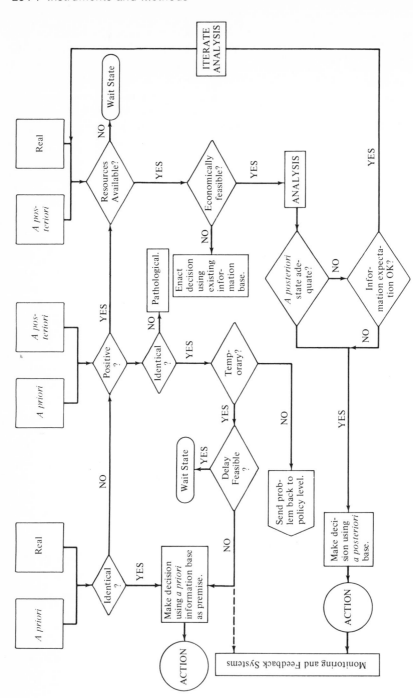

Figure 7.7 The substantive decision model.

simply represents either a situation of irrational arrogance or a conscious decision to trade-off analytical expedience against ultimate rectitude. In short, the *a priori* path in the substantive decision model is generally an unconscionable or "prescientific" one.

In the "normative" situation, then, the decision-maker will not assume an identity between his *a priori* and the real state, and will hence move to the next block, this one testing his expectations about the relationship between the *a priori* and *a posteriori* states. If he perceives that the *a posteriori* state will have an advantage over the *a priori*, then he would move into the analysis phase. But let us stop for a moment and consider another incongruent path, that resulting from a perceived identity between the existing *a priori* information stock and the potential *a posteriori* stock(s).

If there is a situation where the conduct of a formal analysis exercise is not expected to improve on the quality and substance of existing information bases, there are two possible "rational" explanations. First, it could be that the problem which has been assigned the decision-maker is an inappropriate one . . . e.g., it might be an inherently indeterminate or severely stochastic situation, which his statistical and extrapolative instruments are not prepared to handle (and which, as the reader will recall, are proper targets, at least initially, for *a prioristic*-deductive instruments). In this case, the decision-maker might quite properly note that there is nothing that empirical analysis can help him with at this point, and simply elect to return the problem to the policy-making level (which handles severely stochastic entities).

On the other hand, he may simply feel that the *a posteriori's* failure to provide an expected advantage over the *a priori* is a temporal phenomenon, perhaps due to the existence of some *exogenous* factors that time might repair. For example, he might simply require some instrument that has not yet been developed or fully matured; or, a more common circumstance, there might have to be some time involved in "legitimation" before any analysis can proceed (as many social systems and humans have to be approached rather slowly and carefully if information is going to be made available to investigators). When one of these latter situations prevails, then the decision-maker might elect to see if a delay is possible—that is, if circumstances will permit his postponing the analysis phase in the hopes that a favorable set of conditions might eventually emerge to make the *a posteriori* state potentially more attractive as an alternative to the *a priori*.

If, however, there is a demand that a decision action be taken immediately— such that delay becomes infeasible—then the decision-maker will simply have to accept the risk, and inaugurate a decision alternative on the basis of the *a priori* information state. Under such a situation, the decision-maker would probably inaugurate a rather elaborate monitoring and feedback scheme of some sort to test the validity of the decision . . . for he will know that the probability of accuracy (or optimality) associated with an *a priori* selection under these circumstances is insufficiently high to allow him the luxury of simply taking action and forgetting it (note, however, we have not made the inclusion of the monitoring-feedback provision part of the repertoire of the decision-maker who assumed an identity between the real and *a priori* states, for he would probably lack the humility to monitor his decisions anyway).

There is a generally infeasible situation which we must also consider, that associated with taking the NO path from the box that asked about the identity between the *a priori* and *a posteriori* states. Following this path indicates that the decision-maker expects that formal analysis will actually result in an erosion of information relative to the real state . . . i.e., that the production of an *a posteriori* information stock would be a regressive move. Note that we have termed this a pathological *situation*, possibly associated with those who have a distinct prejudice against empirical or positivistic techniques (e.g., Kant, who intensely distrusted any "sense data" to the point where he believed that anything that could be perceived would be delusionary).[9] This particular path, then, holds little interest except for those who study irrational decision behavior.

We now move on to the question-box that asks about the relationship between the *a posteriori* and the *real* informational states (after having ascertained from an earlier step that the relationship between the *a priori* and *a posteriori* favors the latter in the decision-maker's expectations). In short, we are now operating on the assumption that the decision-maker expects that a formal analysis will yield a closer approximation to the real problem or system properties than will the *a priori* information stock, and hence will inaugurate an analysis process, per se. But he must first go through some usually simple exercises to determine whether or not analysis is *feasible*.

There are two conditions under which we might effect the *NO* path from this box. First, if the resources to conduct the analysis are not currently available, given that these resources are endogenous (e.g., within the control of the decision-maker). If he expects that they will be available at some future point-in-time, he would enter a "wait state," going on to perform parallel tasks until the analysis for the problem at hand can be inaugurated. The second condition under which analysis might not be feasible is an economic equivocation . . . the cost of obtaining the additional information might simply not be worth the expenditure of analytical resources required to obtain it. Under this condition, the decision-maker would simply make the decision selection using the existing information stock as the premise. The calculations of economic feasibility are extremely important . . . and we shall devote the next section of this chapter to an amplification of the logic we have already presented in Section 5.2.

If, now, analysis is deemed to be feasible—both in terms of the favorable marginal product expected from the production of an *a posteriori* information state (stock) and in terms of immediately available analytical resources—we then proceed directly to the development of an *a posteriori* information state. In terms of the present context, this means that the decision-maker will set about collecting (or have his system analysts collect) empirical data pertinent to the precise valuation of the parametric and coefficient aspects needed to complete the *model** of the system or phenomenon at hand. In short, the decision-maker is going to be conducting the "empirical learning loops" of which we have so often spoken, this time they are directed at converging on numerical or precise qualitative system properties at the parametric and coefficient levels (as decision-making, per se, is restricted to these lower-level system analysis tasks in the framework we have been using). After some positive expenditure of analytical resources, an *a posteriori* information state is generated that sets forth the currently "best" parametric and coefficient estimates, each estimator equipped with some empirically-generated probability of accuracy.

Now the decision-maker will have formulated some desired level of confidence for his model components, which may be thought of as a *desired probability of accuracy* (1.0–the expected probability of error). In terms of the event-probability distributions we have worked with so often, this means that there is a certain level of *variance* that he will tolerate (both in aggregate and for any or all components of the emerging model). Now, if the actual *a posteriori* information state at this point-in-time meets or exceeds this criterion, then it will be used to provide the premises for a decision action. However, if the actual *a posteriori* information state contains too high a variance (e.g., has components that carry probabilities of accuracy below the desired level), then the analysis process must be reiterated.

But before he actually makes the decision to reiterate the analysis process, the "rational" decision-maker will want to examine the *learning curves* that his previous iterations have generated. It is through a process of learning curve analysis–a process we shall reinvestigate in the next section of this chapter– that the decision-maker calculates the probability that another iteration *using the same instruments* will produce an increase in the information stock, or whether a shift to some other analytical modality might be indicated . . . or indeed, whether he has exhausted the information potential of this system or problem and must simply take action on the basis of the existing *a posteriori* information base. This case might occur where the system or problem under treatment was an *inherently* moderately stochastic one, such that no amount of analytical expenditure will cause a convergence on a set of nonprobabilistic (e.g., deterministic) coefficient and parametric values.

At any rate, the iteration path is elected when the learning curve analysis produces an expectation that another iteration of the analysis process–using some specific instrumental set (either the same or different than that used in the previous iteration)–will indeed produce an increase in information and a higher

---

*In this context, the "model" would probably try to capture the expected impact of some alternative decision action on some particular system, much as we did at the interface between problem/problem-solving system components in the system architecture paradigm of Chapter 6.

rate of exhaustion of the properties of the real state. In such a situation, we would find him winding his way back through the tests for resource availability and economic feasibility before actually proceeding to inaugurate the next iteration of the analysis process, etc. Eventually, he would hopefully emerge with an *a posteriori* information base which meets his confidence requirements, and proceed from there to a decision enaction . . . and hence on to the monitoring and feedback exercises once an action has been inaugurated.

7.3.2 Amplification of the Decision Logic

On the normative path of the substantive decision model, the decision-maker was forced to make many "internal" decisions, among them:

1. What could legitimately be expected from the production of an *a posteriori* information stock (S), relative to the properties of the real state (R).
2. Whether he has sufficient resources to produce an adequate *a posteriori* information stock, given his desired level of confidence (which sets out the upper limit probabilities of error associated with components of the information stock $[D = d_1 \ldots d_n]$).
3. Whether the production of some *a posteriori* information stock (S_t) is a good "economic" investment.
4. Whether, given that some existing *a posteriori* information stock (S_t) is inadequate—with respect to the confidence criteria—an iteration of the analysis process should be inaugurated.
5. Whether, given the "learning" performance in previous iterations(s), a change in instruments or tactics is indicated (and, of course, a decision about what changes might be most appropriate or promising).

There can be no question that these are decisions of enormous complexity, and that most decision-makers will be content to make them casually. But, in previous chapters, we have at hand some devices that might help us here. Obviously, the first decision can be approached, at least tentatively, by reviewing the work we did in Chapter 5 pertinent to analytical congruence. Particularly, we already know roughly what kind of performance to expect from each category of instruments pertinent to the various analytical categories into which real world phenomena might fall (e.g., what extrapolative instruments can expect to accomplish in the face of effectively moderately stochastic problems or systems).

As for the second decision—that dealing with the resource requirements of analysis—the decision-maker is going to have to construct some sort of learning curve, as these are the devices which attempt to relate "rates" and ultimate "levels" of information acquisition with respect to expenditure of analytical resources. We are familiar with their basic properties from Chapter 5, but will have to go into more detail here. The third decision, regarding economic feasibility, is also a learning curve question, where we add a denominator in the form of the expected "costs" of acquiring information relative to its imputed value (again an exercise with which we are conceptually familiar from Section 5.2).

Decision four, asking about "adequacy" of the information stock relative to some desired level of confidence, becomes intelligible largely in terms of event-probability distributions. For the morphology of these, as we have many times seen, translates directly into estimates of *variance* which in turn become estimates of the expected accuracy of model (or informational) components. But we shall look at this process again in the pages which follow. Finally, the fifth decision will demand use of the differential characteristics of the various instrument categories with which we are already familiar (from Figure 5.14). It, again, is a task that depends on the generation and analysis of learning curves (both expected and empirically-predicated), as basically do all of the other "internal" decisions. So part of the work which we will be doing here will be familiar to us, part new. At any rate, the place to begin is with a brief recapitulation of some points from earlier sections.

Particularly, recall from our discussions in Chapter 5, that the *rate* of learning about a phenomenon (e.g., the rate at which knowledge is obtained, pertinent to the development of some formal model) depends jointly on: (a) the analytical category to which the model belongs and (b) the congruence of the analytical instruments employed . . . which means treating the phenomenon with that particular instrumental category which promises to be most efficient and effective in producing relevant information. The results of these earlier discussions are summarized in Fig. 7.8.

With the elements of Figure 7.8 in mind, we may now say something about the "internal" decisions associated with the substantive decision model. These inter-

SYSTEM TYPE	CONGRUENT INSTRUMENT CATEGORY	NATURE OF INFORMATIONAL OUTPUT	LEVEL OF ANALYSIS
Deterministic	Optimization techniques	Generates a single, unique solution for any set of predicates (i.e., linear programming models).	Evaluates parameters and coefficients.
Moderately stochastic	Extrapolative/ projective techniques	Generates a "range" within which true value is expected to fall (e.g., statistical estimation/Markov processes).	Estimates probabilistic parameter and coefficient values . . . predicts precedented (iterative) system states.
Severely stochastic	Game-based deductive techniques	Postulates a set of logically probable alternative system states (e.g., scenario-building; adaptive programming).	Operates at the relational level, working with qualitative system configurations.
Indeterminate	Metatheoretical/ heuristic techniques	Sets initial limits (tentative and speculative) on *search* space, and specifies criteria for learning.	Works primarily at basic state-variable level.

Figure 7.8 Summary of system analysis logic

nal decisions, in abbreviation, are the following: (a) make a decision (take action); (b) iterate the analysis process using an existing set of instruments in an effort to produce a better relationship between desired and actual error levels; and (c) abandon the existing set of analytical instruments for another (i.e., exercise a modality shift).

In the simple set terms we have been using, the decision-maker's desired level of confidence may be reflected in the tolerable difference between the *real* and *a posteriori* informational states:

$$P(\text{error})_z = f(R - S_z)$$

where: S_z is the stock of information that will yield a probability of error equal to or lower than some $[d]$, such that the level of confidence of the decision-maker is greater than or equal to $(1.0 - d)$.

The actually achieved probability of error, after some n iterations of the analysis process, would be formulated as:

$$P(\text{error})_y = f(R - S_{y_n}).$$

These definitions permit us to say something about the conditions under which the decision (action) and iteration alternatives might be exercised. What we want to suggest is summarized in Figure 7.9. From the origin of the diagram to the point (a), the decision-maker might be expected to tolerate the difference between desired and actual information stocks . . . with the probability of tolerance (and hence the probability of taking immediate action through the making of a decision) declining toward (a). Beyond (a), the probability of iterating analysis predominates . . . for the difference between the desired and actual stocks is too high to warrant taking action, but not so high as to cast doubt on the capability of the existing information set to produce useful information.*

The conditions under which the third decision would be taken—the decision to shift analytical modalities by bringing in a new set of instruments—cannot be disposed of so easily. For this decision must be predicated on a dynamic factor . . . the rate at which the actual information stock (and hence the actual error level) is approaching the desired information stock (and hence the desired level of confidence). In short, the decision to shift modalities becomes a function like that shown in Figure 7.10.

Simply, the higher the rate at which the existing instrumental modality is exhausting the properties of the real state, the lower will be the probability that

---

*This set of assertions would remain the same whether or not we allowed the real information set (and hence the desired stock of information) to vary . . . that is, we need not assume that the properties of the real state are fixed and unresponsive to increasingly rich *a posteriori* information stocks. Indeed, under the heuristic analytical approach we have been espousing, a variable real state would be an imperative (though for most lower level decision situations, per se, the real state may be assumed fixed).

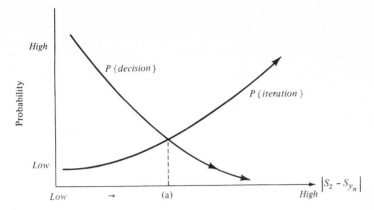

Figure 7.9 Probability of internal decisions.

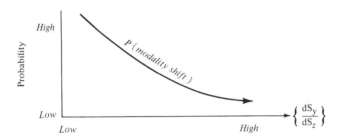

Figure 7.10 Probability of modality shift.

a modality shift will be inaugurated. Thus, it is primarily when we are making unsatisfactory progress that a modality shift becomes significantly probable ... when the successive iterations of the analysis process just simply fail to cause an adequately rapid convergence between the desired and actual information stocks and error levels. But to make this somewhat clearer, we're going to have to know more about the growth properties of information.

7.3.3 The Logic of Shifting Instrumental Modalities

The growth of information under any single instrumental modality should behave roughly according to the following function:

$$G(n) = f(n - 1, \sigma, L_{R_\sigma}) + C(\sigma, t, n - 1, n)$$

provided that:

$$\frac{dL_{R_\sigma}}{dn} \leqslant \frac{dG(n)}{dn}$$

where G(n) is a function of the following parameters:

(a) σ is the analytical ideal-type that the system or problem at hand approximates (i.e., deterministic, moderately stochastic, severely stochastic, or indeterminate).

(b) n is the n'th iteration, and $n - 1$ refers to the just previous iteration.

(c) t is the time interval between successive iterations.

(d) L_{R_σ} is the theoretical limit of the real state.

The component $f(n - 1, \sigma, L_{R_\sigma})$ is the growth of information attributed directly to the expenditure of analytical resources—the results of formal analysis—whereas the component $C(\sigma, t, n - 1, n)$ is a cumulative function.

Suppose, now, that we are faced with a system that is effectively indeterminate, but inherently deterministic. According to the criteria of congruence introduced earlier—and with reference again to the sequential system analysis model illustrated in Figure 5.19—we know that we shall initiate analysis using heuristic or methatheoretical instruments, then shift to game-based or adaptive instruments, move through the extrapolative and projective instruments pertinent to a system that has been reduced to moderate stochasticity, and finally use the optimization instruments pertinent to a deterministic entity. The result should be a roughly "optimal" information growth function . . . *if* we have been alert to the points where modality shifts should have been made in the face of cumulative information growth that transfers the phenomenon from one to another analytical category. In short, the efficiency of the aggregate learning process depends on being able to read the empirically emerging learning curves, and thus recognizing the "optimal" points for modality shifts. In this respect, consider the following function:*

$$G = \sum_{\sigma=1}^{4} G_\sigma(n) = \sum_{\sigma=1}^{4} \sum_{n=1}^{N} f(n - 1, \sigma, L_{R_\sigma}) + C(\sigma, t_1, n - 1, n)$$

subject to:

$$\frac{dL_{R_\sigma}}{dK(\sigma)} \leqslant \frac{dG_\sigma}{dK(\sigma)}$$

*Note that this formulation is easily transformed into the more familiar natural growth curve.

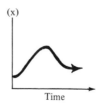

(x)

Time

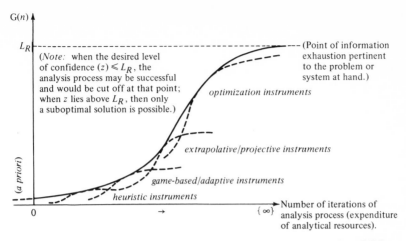

Figure 7.11 Cumulative information function: multiple instrumental modalities.

where $K(\sigma)$ is the iteration used in the modality. This formulation should lead to a diagrammatic information growth curve much like that in Figure 7.11, where departures from the "optimal" learning curve are relatively slight on the assumption that the analysts conducting the exercise were alert to the properties of the analytical ideal-types that real-world entities approximate and were sensitive to the system logic outlined in previous sections.

Figure 7.11 thus shows a sequential—effectively optimal—contribution by each of the four instrumental modalities available to the system scientist, brought into play at the appropriate time in the analytical sequence. Let us now consider a technique that might help us make these optimal modality shifts indicated at the deflection point of figure 7.11. The method available to us is a simple one . . . we simply conceive of the emerging *a posteriori* information stocks as loosely defined but still "proper" sets of attributes (e.g., collections of either quantitative or qualitative elements). In the course of a favorable learning process, we should be able to note *differences* between successive *a posteriori* information stocks, with the magnitude of the differences being a rough measure of the extent to which we are acquiring new information. The efficiency of the learning process is then measured by the rate of change in the first differences between successive information stocks, relative to expenditures of analytical resources (through, for simplicity sake, we may use the surrogate n, this being the number of iterations of the analysis process).

The "internal" decision rule pertinent to modality shifts within a decision-making process is illustrated in Figure 7.12. and shows that by making a timely shift from extrapolative/projective instruments to optimization techniques, an effectively "optimal" learning curve is obtained. It is simply a cumulative growth curve for a decision problem. Remember that we have suggested that

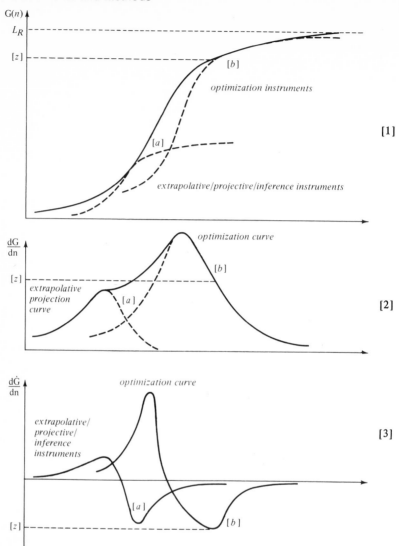

Figure 7.12 Cumulative and derivative learning curves.

decision-making, per se, always, takes place in the face of moderately stochastic problems or entities. Therefore, we must consider only one modality shift ... that where we abandon extrapolative or projective (i.e., inductive inference) instruments and move into the optimization domain ... given that the system is an inherently deterministic one. The dashed line indicates the actual learning trajectory we follow, with the solid line simply being a continuous approximation. Thus, at the point (*a*), we have noted a decline in the first differences between successive information stocks *given* the use, up to that point, of extrapolative/projective/inference techniques (e.g., statistical inference; Markov processes; regression-correlation analysis).

At that point, then, we suggest that we are beginning to exhaust the potential of that instrumental category, the implication being that we have gradually caused a convergence on some specific parametric or coefficient values (to the point where the event-probability distribution imposed on the "range" of alternatives is peaking rapidly, and hence moving gradually toward an aggregate variance which approaches zero. In short, at point (a), we have translated the problem from a moderately stochastic one into an effectively deterministic one (providing that our convergence on specific values is accomplished with a sufficiently high confidence . . . i.e., statistical probability of accuracy).

Beyond (a), we have moved into the use of optimization instruments that, as the trajectory of Curve 7.12-1 shows, rapidly exhausts the informational potential of the problem or phenomenon at hand, which is equivalent to reducing the expected probability of error of our allegory to zero. In short, at the point (b), the *a posteriori* informational stock may be said to have adequately exhausted the properties of the *real* . . . and the desired level of confidence of our analysis (z) has been reached. At this point, then, according to the components of the substantive decision model, the decision-maker will now select a course of action and inaugurate it . . . subsequently employing some sort of monitoring/feedback scheme to keep a constant empirical eye on the results of the "action" in the real-world (and as the reader might expect, we would caution the decision-maker that the sophistication of his monitoring and feedback system—and the frequency of sampling, etc.—should be somehow related to the calculated degree of confidence associated with the decision inaugurated or, more generally, to the residual value of expected cost).

Turning now to Curve 7.12-2, we note that this curve is really the derivative of the cumulative curve (roughly charting the first differences). Note, however, that this curve is really a product of two subcurves, the first (the left-most) being that charting the expected information function for extrapolative/projective instruments, the second being the curve for optimization instruments. Note that, by making the modality shift at [a] in Curve 7.12-1, we have avoided moving onto those areas of the two curves where decreasing marginal information returns set in. In short, by keeping alert to the morphology of the empirical learning curves (summarizing successive differences in the information stocks), we have followed an actual learning trajectory that is effectively "optimal" and a signal improvement on trying to have a single instrument set do all the analytical work for us.

The final illustration, Curve 7.12-3, is then the second derivative of the cumulative growth curve. It reflects the "acceleration" of the information growth function and gives us an analytical solution to the modality shift problem. Note that where the second difference of the extrapolative/projective/inference curve reaches a minimum at [a], then the modality shift should take place. Similarly, when the curve for the optimization instruments falls to a minimum at [b], then we halt the analysis process and move toward the enaction of a decision (using the actual *a posteriori* information stock available at that point to derive premises for the decision). The implication is that we have finally reached the point where the total information available about the problem has been adequately exhausted, such that additional iterations of the analysis process would simply provide increments of information which cost more to produce than they are worth (given the desired level of confidence that the decision-maker is working with . . . assumed to rest at the point [z] on the vertical axes of the figures).*

As a final note, it should be evident that we may also bring into consideration the expected economic worth of information as a criterion for "internal" decisions within the decision-making process. As we saw from Chapter 5, it is possible to get an *imputed value* for information (in dollar terms or some acceptable surrogate), by evaluating the expected impact of an increment of information on the expected value of an error associated with some model we are building. Thus, when the analyst is able to project with fair accuracy what the difference in information stocks will be, pertinent to another iteration of the analysis process or with respect to some modality shift, he already has at hand the capability to translate this expected informational difference into an expected marginal product (in dollar terms). He should also be able to get some sort of rough estimate of the cost—in terms of analytical expenditures—that will be required to produce that increment (usually with reference to historical or *a priori* analysis processes). In this sense, then, we might look at a formulation like the following:

$$\frac{\$EV\,[S]_{n \to n+1}}{\$EV\,[C]_{n \to n+1}} = \quad \text{(the expected marginal product, in dollar terms, of the } n+1\text{'th iteration of the analysis process).}$$

where: [C] is the cost estimate.

Thus, for each *a posteriori* information stock, there will be some dollar-value that reflects the worth of the emerging model to the decision-maker, at some n. There will also be some cost associated with each *a posteriori* information stock. It is useful to include this cost factor, not simply for its contribution to the determination of the marginal product of information increments, but also because there will often be some aggregate budget limit on analytical expenditures. Thus, in the real-world, many decision-makers might cut off the analysis process well before some adequate level of analysis has been obtained, simply because the budget has run out. However, being able to provide the funding

---

*It should be noted that essentially the same logic would be used to calculate the points at which the heuristic/metatheoritical instrumental set should be displaced by the game-based, and the point at which the former should give way to extrapolative/projective instruments.

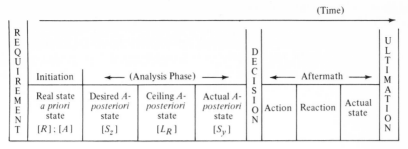

R E Q U I R E M E N T	Initiation	◄— (Analysis Phase) —►			D E C I S I O N	◄— Aftermath —►			U L T I M A T I O N
	Real state *a priori* state	Desired *A-posteriori* state	Ceiling *A-posteriori* state	Actual *A-posteriori* state		Action	Reaction	Actual state	
	$[R] : [A]$	$[S_z]$	$[L_R]$	$[S_y]$					

Figure 7.13   Decision process.

sources with an adequately defensible set of expectations about incremental productivity of any additional funds they might make available, might help analytical budgets become variable rather fixed constraints. And, as an obvious point to the above, were direct dollar conversions impossible or difficult to make with respect to "internal" decisions, the analyst always has the option of switching to *utility* variables; they would be manipulated in exactly the same way as dollar values.

In summary, then, we have now been through the logic and procedures of a system based decision-making paradigm, as shown in great abbreviation in Figure 7.13. With the decision-making logic now in hand—coupled with the policy-setting and problem-solving logics earlier introduced—we are now in a position to move to the concluding chapter of our work . . . the point where we explore the system approach to system administration and control.

7.4 NOTES AND REFERENCES

1. See the section on "The Coming Adhocracy" in Alvin Toffler's *Future Shock* (New York: Random House, 1970).
2. W. R. Reitman, "Heuristic Decision Procedures, Open Constraints and the Structure of Ill-Defined Problems," *Human Judgments and Optimality*, ed. Shelly and Bryan (New York, John Wiley & Sons, 1964).
3. Harold Linstone, "Four American Futures: Reflections on the Role of Planning," *Technological Forecasting and Social Change*, 4 no. 1 (1972).
4. Mitroff and Turoff's "On Measuring Conceptual Errors in Large-Scale Social Experiments: The Future as Decision," *Technological Forecasting and Social Change*, 6 no. 4 (1974).
5. John P. Martino, *Technological Forecasting for Decisionmaking* (New York: American Elsevier Publishing Co., 1972), p. 267.
6. In essence, formal systems are treated as giving rise to ordered inputs and outputs. In this respect, see L. A. Zadeh's "The Concepts of System, Aggregate, and State in System Theory," *System Theory*, ed. Zadeh and Polak (New York: McGraw-Hill, 1969).
7. L. A. Zadeh, "Outline of a New Approach to the Analysis of Complex Sys-

tems and Decision Processes," *IEEE Transactions on Systems, Man and Cybernetics*, **SMC-3** no. 1 (January 1973).

8. A good conceptual introduction to this area of systems is given in Anatol Rapoport's "The Search for Simplicity," *The Relevance of General System Theory*, ed. Ervin Laszlo (New York: George Braziller, 1972). Or, look again at Chapters 2 and 3 of this book.

9. Fernand van Steenberghen, *Epistemology* (New York: Joseph F. Wagner, 1949), p. 279ff.

8

Towards a General Theory of System Control and Administration

8.0 INTRODUCTION

We have now come to the final point of concern with the system sciences, the point at which we explore their conceptual contribution to the control and administration of socio-economic systems . . . business organizations, governmental agencies, service, creative or educational enterprises, etc. In the course of outlining this contribution, we shall be bringing together the ideal-types defined in previous chapters—plus the decision-making, policy-setting, and problem-solving technologies of Chapters 6 and 7—and using these to generate an array of control and administrative modalities. Figure 8.1 shows the major relationships with which we shall be concerned.

These correlations between system type and control and administrative modalities take on special significance for us when we recognize that most complex socioeconomic systems usually become at least moderately intelligible in terms of a pyramidal construct like that in Figure 8.2. As a result, different levels of socioeconomic systems tend to approximate different ideal-type referents, and thus become susceptible to treatment modalities.

Figure 8.2 is a particularly important construct for us, for it suggests that the ideal-type referents we earlier developed (Section 4.5) operate *within* complex systems as well as among systems viewed as wholes. The alert system manager, then, will demand that each of the several subsystems or levels of his organization be treated by that modality that is congruent. For there is no *single* best management method, nor any *single* best system control modality, any more than there was any *single* system approach. Rather, rationality in the administrative and control arenas consists in making the proper associations between properties of the entity to be managed, and the various modalities available. In short, just as we used Chapter 5 to introduce the concept of analytical congruence, we shall use this eighth and final chapter to introduce congruence with respect to administrative and control modalities.

One more preliminary note before proceeding with the elaboration of the

IDEAL-TYPE REFERENT	CONGRUENT CONTROL MODALITY	CONGRUENT ADMINISTRATIVE MODALITY	COGNITIVE BASIS
Deterministic (type-I system)	Ritual/dogma institutionalization	Finite-state system analysis	Optimization (often through trial-and-error).
Moderately stochastic (type-II system)	Implied or direct coercion/rules; programmation	Servocybernetic programming	Decision theory
Severely stochastic (type-III system)	Rational advantage/ objective audits	Stochastic-state techniques	Policy science
Indeterminate (type-IV system)	Self-regulation/ ethical codes	Heuristic approach	System architecture

Figure 8.1 Table of correlations between ideal-types and control, administrative, and cognitive modalities.

various modalities. System control and administration are areas that are usually handled in rather parochial fashion by the several traditional disciplines. For example, system control—to the traditional engineer—means simply the employment of Laplace transforms and first-order differential equations in a feedback scheme. In much the same way, the management "scientist" within schools of business is often the fellow for whom system administration means simply applying the tools of optimization or extrapolation, such that management becomes roughly the equivalent of applied mathematics (though applied mathematics of a much less sophisticated order than usually employed by physicists or others in the truly hard sciences). To yet another, and perhaps even larger group of manage-

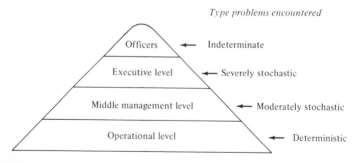

Figure 8.2 The hierarchical interpretation of the normative socioeconomic enterprise.

ment theorists, system administration is simply an exercise in applied behavioral science . . . in short, human relations.

Now, while all three of these approaches have much to recommend them, none alone is a truly *general* approach to system administration and control. For a general approach would have to knit together the relevant portions of the model bases of all three: (a) the empirical precision and discipline of the engineer where the system at hand (or some subsystem) is essentially deterministic in nature; (b) the concepts of rationality and quantification available from the operations researcher *qua* management scientist, and especially their extension into "econometrics," extrapolative forecasting, inventory optimization, linear programming, and other devices for effectively handling moderately stochastic problems, or managing and controlling essentially stochastic system components and systems; and (c) the sensitivity to the "human" component from the behavioral and social scientist, to be much valued and drawn upon except where systems are entirely mechanical or automated in nature.

Thus, the systems approach to system control and administration, like the systems approach to science in general, is eclectic, borrowing, ordering, and extending contributions from many different sources in the determination to achieve a constant congruence between problem and instruments, and between system and treatment. In this sense, we may then begin this chapter by looking first at the concepts of system control that are derived—however indirectly—from the social and behavioral sciences, leaving the remaining sections of this chapter to treat administrative modalities and, in the process, inject some engineering and operations research concepts. The net result, hopefully, will take two forms: First, it will provide the first tentative steps toward a truly generalized theory of system administration and control; secondly, it will provide the reader with an opportunity to see how the various system concepts we have developed can be brought together in a reasonably well ordered, at least partially integrated, whole.

8.1 THE SOCIOBEHAVIORAL ASPECTS OF SYSTEM ADMINISTRATION AND CONTROL

For the strict social or behavioral scientist, understandably enough, system administration and control consists largely in finding ways to "manage" the human components of enterprise. From the system science perspective, we can suggest that the sociobehavioral aspects of system control might best be approached as outlined in Figure 8.3. This figure takes the four ideal-type integrated systems we first developed in Chapter 4 and sets out the effectively unique control correlations associated with each.

The origins of the correlations in the figure, as the reader might suspect, are deep and difficult to trace, but they clearly would have a great deal to do with the various ecological (or "survival") postures associated with the ideal-type systems. As the reader will recall from Chapter 4, each system type faced an effec-

SYSTEM TYPE	PREDOMINANT CONTROL INSTRUMENT	PREDOMINANT CONTROL MODE	NORMATIVE BASIS FOR AUTHORITY	BEHAVIORAL OBJECTIVE SOUGHT
I	Dogma	Ritualistic	Tradition/ mystery	Obedience and mechanisticity
II	Coercion/ esprit	Algorithmic	Position	Programmability/ predictivity
III	Rational advantage	Objective (*a posteriori*) audit; plans	Expertise or interest	Innovation; assiduity
IV	Ethical or professional codes, etc.	Autoregulation; peer evaluation	Individual (via credentials; professional membership, etc.)	Creativity

Figure 8.3 Table of differential control modalities.

tively unique set of environmental conditions in an effectively unique way and—as Figure 8.4 attempts to show—each system thereby gains a unique ecological advantage (accompanied, of course, by some liabilities as well).

The logic pertinent to environmental and system interface conditions is familiar to us, largely because of the work we did with *fields* in the last section of Chapter 4. Here we wish to extend this logic, because the ecological *mission* forced on (or elected by) a socioeconomic system will largely determine which particular control instruments will be most effective and efficient in dealing with that system's constituents. Each of the control modalities available to us will vary considerably in their precision, exactitude, cost-effectiveness, and reliability. Most essentially however, the modalities will tend to produce organizational behaviors that are distinctly different. Thus, for example, the first modality, ritual and dogma, tends to produce an organization whose components may be expected to behave deterministically. On the other hand, the ethical and autoregulative modality will tend, normatively, to allow components a behavioral latitude that marks them as effectively indeterminate. In short, then, we are here going to be interested in the most fundamental of organizational problems: how to get people to do what we want them to do with the least associated expenditure of resources, time, or energy.

8.1.1 The General Control Typology

The model that will guide our work takes the form of a metahypothesis which purports to set out the *congruent* associations between our various organizational

SYSTEM TYPE	ECOLOGICAL TYPE	ECOLOGICAL OBJECTIVE	ECOLOGICAL ADVANTAGE	PROBABLE SOURCE OF ECOLOGICAL ERROR
I	Autarchic	To institute essentially automatic (ritualized or mechanized) responses to a highly limited, precedented stimuli-set.	Automaticity in the face of an invariant set of environmental conditions.	Atavism, in that the system remains rigid even in the face of major environmental alterations.
II	Symbiont	To establish a set of algorithmic responses to a highly constrained stimuli-set and to maintain operational consistency throughout the entire system domain (among all functional parts).	Maximum internal efficiency and operative control in the face of routine, but often critical, performance demands.	Obsolescence, in that the system may tend to maintain internal consistency at the expense of environmental congruence.
III	Dominant	To make most efficient use of resources in a succession of variant short-runs ... to most thoroughly and expeditiously take advantage of emerging opportunities for exploitation.	Effective optimality over the long-run by exercising a continual trade-off between versatility and mechanisticity, between external congruence and internal efficiency.	Misallocation of resources due to the time-lag between recognition of a new opportunity and internal readjustment (plus some danger that an adverse innovation or strategic change will be implemented).
IV	Heuristic	To ensure an effective response to unprecedented situations; to instill creativity rather than mechanisticity.	Adaptivity in the face of nonroutine and unpredictable exogenous forces or influences through maximum structural and functional plasticity.	Dissolution, in that the largely autonomous parts are only weakly cohered ... moreover, the constant quest for innovational responses entails a high probability of an error of commission.

Figure 8.4   Table of ecological implications.

CONTROL INSTRUMENT/ CONTROL MODALITY:	SYSTEM IDEAL-TYPES			
	Type-IV	Type-I	Type-II	Type-III
Ethics/auto-regulation	X			*Ineffectiveness*
Dogma/ritualism		X		
Coercion/algorithms			X	
Rational advantage/objective audits	*Inefficiency*			X

Figure 8.5   Table of control correlations.

ideal-types and the array of control modalities available to the system administrator. These associations are summarized in Figure 8.5. The typology of Figure 8.5 may be interpreted as follows:

• There is a *vector of congruence* which purports to set out the most efficient and effective instrument for exercising control given the four ideal-type systems.

• To the left of the vector we strike conditions of *inefficiency*, such that the instrument we elect to employ costs more (in terms of resources or energy expended) than is theoretically required to realize control for the system type indicated.

• To the right of the vector are the more serious instances of *ineffectiveness*, where the instrument elected is simply not powerful enough to realize control over the associated system type.

In iteration then, our general control model contends that the following associations are those which will emerge most frequently in the real world:

Type-IV System ⟶ Ethics/Autoregulation

Type-I System ⟶ Dogma/Ritualism

Type-II System ⟶ Coercion/Algorithms

Type-III System ⟶ Rational Advantage/Audits

But before we begin to discuss these correlations in detail, we want to note an ancillary aspect of the model: the several control modalities are arrayed in terms of expected cost per-unit-of-effect. For when we consider the purportedly least expensive modality—ethical codes associated with autoregulation—we find control bases that are generally rhetorical or intangible in nature. The Hippocratic oath, for example, considering the measure of control it has exercised over two millenia, is perhaps the most remarkably economically efficient instrument we can isolate;

similarly, the informal code of ethics that constrains professorial prerogatives carries no direct cost to colleges or universities . . . and the instrument by which professional codes are executed, by which professional integrity is maintained, is usually peer-evaluation which operates only on an exception basis and usually without any direct budgetary support.[1]

The employment of dogmatic and ritualistic instruments in the Type-I system is somewhat more expensive, for some institutional groundwork must be laid. Moral or religious authority—often reified in the form of dogmatic or superstition-driven dictates—demands such material accouterments as vestments, altars, temples, statues, miracles, or other trappings that lend essentially transparent ideological forces some moment and mass. This is as true of the feathers and medicine pouch of the shaman as it is of the massive infrastructure of the several great churches. However, the direct expenses associated with the reification of moral power into dogmatic and ritualistic control are usually historical. That is, they may be prorated over many previous years or even centuries. So in a marginal sense, cost of control eventually begins to be quite small in relation to the aggregate concatenation of power available to mature, ideologically-predicated institutions. Today's Catholic priest benefits by the labor of countless generations before him, and from the accumulations of centuries of tithes. Likewise, the power reified in the shaman of fifty years ago was seeded perhaps twelve centuries earlier in west-central Mexico or eastern Siberia.

It is when we consider Type-II and -III systems; the coercive and rational-advantage modalities, that issues of direct cost emerge and become definitive in the control calculus. If coercion is to be effective, we must maintain some reification of power in the form of standing instruments: i.e., armies, police forces, prison guards, proctors. The expenses associated with the exercise of coercive control are usually proportionate to the degree of inimicality exhibited by the population to be controlled and positively related (though not always directly) to its size. At any rate, the utility of coercion depends on the ability to maintain the pretense of force, and this demands that it occasionally be exercised or that the instruments be concrete and visible. Coercion can be a remarkably cheap control instrument when it induces slave labor, or adolescent obedience to a bully, for example. But there are two ancillary factors which may make coercion a mixed blessing:

(a) The tendency for coercion to concatenate in legitimation from one sector to another, or more simply, the tendency for coercion to beget coercion. The Egyptian masters of the Mamelukes learned this to their regret, as have many aristocracies of wealth, ascription,* or ideology.

---

*In ascriptive systems, rewards from society are predicated largely on the social class into which one is born, rather than on one's individual characteristics. Hence, such systems have low social and economic mobility.

(b) There is the problem that performance levels by individuals housed in a coercive system depend on the constant presence of the instruments of coercion; for when the motivation to perform is solely externalized, performance levels will decline in their absence.

Thus, the potential of recrimination and the necessity for a constant presence make coercion a potentially costly modality to employ.

The costs associated with the provision of rational advantage to *a priori* nonideologically, nonethically motivated individuals are usually both direct and proportional to performance expectations. The concept of control via rational advantage is simply the extension of the *bargaining* concept into the exchange of material rewards for material performances . . . an exchange denominated by some universalistic base such as dollars, etc. Thus in most organizations, budgetary provision for salaries and trappings of status tend to increase with the level of the hierarchy at which the person to be controlled is resident. Usually, the amount of reward given an individual is predicated on some objectively determined (i.e., audited) measure of his contribution to the organization he has elected to serve. The promise of higher rewards for incrementally greater output is a prime motivating factor, and may be translated into a control concept when this positive relationship is made explicit (either positively or negatively).

Quite obviously the correlations we have made between the organizational types and control modalities are largely just normative at this point. Moreover, they do not have the strategic flexibility we require; for the alert and imaginative controller will be one who tries to supplant, to the extent possible, those control instruments whose effectiveness is most costly with those whose effect can be realized with lower associated expenditures of resources. Particularly, costs of control within an organization will decrease, in aggregate, when ideological or ethical instruments can be made to displace coercion or rational advantage. But such displacements may draw support from a phenomenon which lies well outside the scope of any single organization: the empirically observable trade-off between social and economic benefits. More simply, the tendency for some individuals, and for some socioeconomic systems, to deliberately sacrifice cost-carrying economic rewards for essentially cost-free social rewards. Obviously, the wise administrator is one who knows how to invent and implement these costless motivators, thereby considerably increasing the overall efficiency of his control system in cost-benefit terms, etc.[2] At any rate, we may now proceed to a brief discussion of each of the modalities (recalling, as well, that the various control instruments and the points made here are appropriate to subsystems within complex systems, as well as to systems as wholes).

8.1.2 The Mechanism and Ritualism

Initially, the effectiveness of dogmatic instruments of control is enhanced by the existence of certain attributes we associated with our Type-I systems: (a) on the domain dimension, we note their predominantly *segmented* structure as opposed to the fully differentiated structure of more modern organizations; and (b) on the ecological, there is the *autarchic* posture which develops in the face of a placid, consistent environment. These provide a fertile ground for ritualistic-dogmatic constructs, which in turn tend to lend the Type-I system its essentially *mechanical* (i.e., deterministic) quality on the dynamic dimension.

The primary prerequisite for dogmatic control is thus the essentially placid milieu. Environmental sameness or consistency, through long periods of time, evolves a system that tends to be self-sufficient in virtually all sectors. Such systems have been sheltered (deliberately or inadvertently) from the secularizing influences of science and the industrial revolution, both of which act to reduce the "mysterious" aspects of existence for the developed cultures.

In the absence of purportedly rational explanations for natural events, the tendency is to create appealing inventions.[3] As one cynic has said: "We had to invent God so he could invent us." The pantheism of primitive, isolated societies thus serves essentially the same functions as do the empirically-predicated, purportedly rational explanations of science for more modern societies. Where we see the operation of gravity or Newtonian-Keplerian physics, they see some deific influence or an instance of anthropomorphism. At any rate, dogma assumes significance as a control instrument only when the population to be controlled is amicably disposed toward mystical or exegetical* predicates. People who do not believe in the infallibility of the Pope will not be amenable to control by the threat of excommunication. Similarly, individuals who deplore nationalism will not respond to patriotic pleas.

Under the guise of the dogmatic modality, at least when it is carried to its logical conclusion, an individual's behavior is almost guaranteed to be congruent with the "welfare" of the system of which he is a part. One rather obvious reason for this is that systems employing the dogmatic modality as the predominant control mode are resident in contexts that often provide only two alternatives for the individuals . . . adherence or exile (with exile meaning sure death or incredible deprivation). For, within the area populated by a system having an effectively "autarchic" ecological dimension (as we earlier defined it), there will probably be no other sociocultural or socioeconomic alternative accessible to the outcast.†

---

*Exegetical predicates are derived from supposedly sacred or revelatory bases (e.g., the Ten Commandments).

†Although very little is known about it, it appears that there may be some method in the apparent madness with which primitive societies set their boundaries. We have always been tempted to test the hypothesis that these boundaries were located in such a way that before the individual exiled from one tribe or village could effectively reach another, the probability of his survival would be very low. Such a scheme would not only result in the subject system being *the* only viable alternative in a given field, but would also explain in part the inordinately high association between exile and death in the minds of many primitives. The theory may gain some empirical credibility from the apparently widespread tolerance with which exiles are welcomed into those tribes they do finally manage to reach.

Moreover, the systems we encounter that are predominantly controlled under the dogmatic modality are usually agrarian in nature. Agrarian systems usually foster an aristocracy of some sort, be it one of power like that of the 19th century Zulus,[4] one of ascription like that of England, or one of morality like that of the Dukhobors or early Mormons. In each of these cases, the identity of the individual is generally not an issue, as one's schedule of roles, rewards, and benefits is essentially fixed at birth. Lacking effective vehicles for differentiation, premises for individual conflict with the society at large are minimized, as is the motivation to generate innovations (as innovations in such a system, even if strictly economic or military in application, would also tend to threaten the social fabric, which is intolerable). In short, the relationship between social and economic benefits is deemed fixed and invariant and sacred, with the social rather than economic factors representing the primary determinants so far as any single individual is concerned.

To continue, the autarchic system, responding to an isolated, effectively consistent set of ecological demands, is most efficient when the responses required for coping with that array of demands are effectively automatic . . . made so by the ritualistic, automatistic character lent all survival activities, from war to marriage to harvest to death and to distribution of spoils and wealth. In this sense, we can see that the autarchic, dogmatically-controlled system is the social sciences' counterpart to the finite-state automata of the engineers or the strictly deterministic phenomena of the classical physicists. Indeed, the behavioral predicates for such socioeconomic systems are available from the ideological "map" we draw of such systems, in the same way that the behavioral predicates of a machine are available from the designers' blueprints . . . and the "maturity" of a dogmatic socioeconomic system is generally indicated by the depth of mechanization.*

However, were the dogmatic modality solely restricted to those living under agrarian dominion in isolated areas of the world, it would not concern us here as much as it does. But situations in which dogma is the predominant control instrument are distributed across many contexts, largely because of its widely recognized "economy," and also because of the inherent susceptibility of many people to mysterious authorities (that absolve so many of us from the discomfort of being sapient, and the responsibilities of being free). Under the aegis of dogma then, we will find the most tireless and tractable objects of control. They will often toil without pay, kill without mercy, believe without equivocation, and sacrifice without remorse; the Type-I system is the home of *homo-sentient*. Here, automaticity of response, programmability, and predictability are the organizational reifications of social sentience.

But sentience is not solely restricted to primitive agrarian systems; it lurks always just beneath even the most urbane and blasé socioeconomic patina. As a

*That is, by the extent to which behaviors of system members are automated or constrained by programmed criteria.

consequence, there waits always the opportunity to exploit the sentient potential by supplementing wages with a "mission," or displacing coercion with mysticism. Thus, on the behavioral dimension, dogma breeds determinism, as surely as does institutionalization on the sociological dimension. The net result is man *cum* hierodule and the socioeconomic system *cum* mechanism . . . which in turn both nurtures and is supported by structural segmentation.

Segmentation, as we already suggested, implies a lack of differentiation and hence individualization among system components, with the fully-segmented system lacking functional specialization also. Thus, in the primitive system, a man may be a herder one day, a warrior the next, a fisherman the next, a spirit-body the next, etc. All these roles may be fully programmed, such that when the proper ecological switch is thrown old roles are automatically discarded in favor of the new. The emphasis is primarily on instantaneous obedience and response to a *few* preprogrammable exogenous events that might occur (e.g., an invasion, the appearance of the rains, the awning of the wheat, the migration of the buffalo). To the extent that the range of events requiring adaptation or response is limited, and to the extent that the events are precedented (i.e., periodic), institutionalization proceeds via ritualization. The individual tends to see himself only indirectly, as a momentary reflection of the part assigned him in a temporal drama, and the need for both coercive or material control instruments declines accordingly.

Thus, the primary instruments of control in the other systems are largely gratuitous within the context of the Type-I system. This system has the advantage of allowing ritual and dogma to virtually automate behavior, such that the probability of departures from ritually-predicated expectations is virtually nil. The depth at which roles are implanted, the social ostracism which accompanies departures from those roles, the insularity and abject parochialism of the socialization process, and the lack of effective social alternatives . . . all these lend the Type-I system the highest possible analytical and administrative tractability.

In overview then, dogma-driven systems are generally restricted to milieux that permit or recommend ecological autarchy, and to systems whose structures are fully-segmented (such that a single set of control instruments can control virtually the entire system, thus reducing both the complexity and cost of coordinating the system and maintaining its integrity). When these conditions exist, the opportunity to induce automatic responses among system components is both feasible and compelling. And to the extent that all men are at least partially susceptible to affective instruments, the administrator of nonprimitive systems cannot neglect the potential of the dogmatic/ritualisitc modality. In this regard, we have as examples both the grass-roots political party and its social counterpart, the charitable organization, engined almost exclusively by axiological or ideological factors (political or moral persuasions). Were rational advantage (i.e., wages) the only means of motivation or control at our disposal, neither the political party nor the broadbased charitable organization could exist.

8.1.3 The Bureaucracy and the Coercive Compromise

Recall that the Type-II system, of which the bureaucracy is an agent, is characterized by:

Ecological Type	Symbiont
Domain Type	Structurally Segmented/ Functionally Differentiated
Dynamic Type	Non-equifinal
Analytical State	Moderately Stochastic

Given these properties, we suggested that the congruent control instrument would be *coercion*, and that the control mode we would most often find would be by way of programmatic processual *algorithms*. Because of the critical nature of such systems—their relative importance in the conduct of the affairs of socioeconomic and sociopolitical man—we want to be quite certain that the basis for these correlations is appealing.

The bureaucratic ideal-type originally postulated by Weber has been perhaps the most procrusteanly applied construct of the organizational sciences.[5] Most business firms, when viewed as something more than attenuated assembly lines, *do not* fall within the confines of the bureaucracy as Weber defined it. Rather, as we will try to show in the next section, the bureaucratic ideal-type is inimical in many ways to the operational demands made on the modern business organization (though it may have very well served as a model for some nineteenth century industries). At any rate, the correlations we wish to draw between the bureaucratic ideal-type and the coercive instrumental modality come clear by inference: what circumstances enable us to account for a system that can take two individuals, give them equal rank and pay, and then send one to fight in the jungles of Asis while the other plays in the band at Fort Ord? What accounts for the viability of a system that can take two priests, give them equal rank and pay, and then send one to the backlands of Brazil or the jungles of Peru, and let the other remain in the comfort of a parish in Beverly Hills or Newport? And the answer is . . . the structurally-segmented/functionally-differentiated organization, with some potential for coercion at its disposal.

As a general rule, the systems we associate with the bureaucratic ideal-type have some sort of *ranking* or caste provision that serves as a method of cohering otherwise superficially different entities. Within the Church, we have the orders, and ranks within orders; within the military, we have the universal rank criteria; within government sectors we have the American civil service system with its standardized G.S. levels, etc. To some extent, the parts (i.e., members) of such a system are interchangeable, so that migration from one functional area to another is frequent. There are limits, however: a surgeon-major will not assume command of a line unit over the head of a line-captain; a G.S.-16 will not presume to dictate technical procedures to a G.S.-15 working in the area of atomic energy structures; a colonial bishop will not, as a rule, presume to dictate to a member of a strong missionary order. Occasionally mediating between absolute rank and formal authority, then, are such factors as technical expertise or membership in particularly elite units (e.g., the S.S.; the White House staff).

Another feature of many systems approximating our ideal Type-II attributes is the existence of *uniforms* of some kind, often with subuniforms. The uniform, first, serves to distinguish members of the system from nonmembers, and secondly may serve to distinguish members of the several subsystems from one another. In this respect the uniform may act as a lever for the injection of ideological or affective aspects of control. The screaming eagle of the famous American paratrooper regiment, the unique shield decorations of the various Zulu regiments, the black uniforms of the S.S., the blue and gold of U.C.L.A.'s basketballers, the rough, dun robes of the Franciscans, the heraldic emblems of the Crusaders and European knights, the club jackets among high school students, the green berets of elite army units in Vietnam, the tartan of the Black Watch, the fraternity pin, the dark suit and white shirt of the old-line IBM'er . . . all contributing to the process of identity by virtue of system or subsystem membership and, in many cases, requisite for the viability of the system.

In some instances, intrasystem competition among various subsystems or commensal units is extremely keen. Within the old British Colonial army, it was a poor proposition to let certain regiments camp within proximity of one another; similarly, elements of U.S. paratroop units and marines continuously fought with one another—almost on sight—in the various leave towns of Japan and Vietnam. In Brazil and Portugal particularly, the Franciscans and Jesuits conducted a running ideological and political battle. Indeed, one of the prices we must pay for *esprit de corps* seems to be this type of intrasystem conflict. It certainly has its healthy aspects, as has been occasionally demonstrated in the demarcation and encouragement of competition among various agricultural communes in both Russia and China. As a general rule then, we expect to find individuals more intensely associating with immediate units of membership (e.g., a demarcated subsystem) than with the bureaucratic macro system itself.

From the standpoint of macro system effectiveness, such intrasystem competition is a God-send. In the face of equal pay for unequal tasks, in the face of deliberate subordination of individual identity to some organizational abstraction, in the face of efforts to isolate the members of the system from the outside world, in the face of the distinct economic and material deprivation which is often associated with such systems, the injection of a strong ideological/affective component is a necessity. This can be cultivated by allowing visible indices of subsystem uniqueness, awarding of unit citations, etc., and by the rewarding of individuals for activities conducted on behalf of the unit of membership. Thus, Roger Young could get the Medal of Honor, whereas Billy Mitchell got a courtmartial.

Again speaking generally, the control of such systems is via algorithmic rules through the establishment of programmed procedures for the conduct of virtually every task that must be performed somewhere within the system. Maintenance or adherence to these algorithms is supported by the threat of coercive reaction to departures. Courtmartial, excommunication, demotion, the potential for transferring an individual to a less favorable geographic or functional sector . . . all of these, along with the possible recrimination of the member's of the heretical individual's own unit (i.e., via the Kangaroo Court), are instruments of coercion we find associated with almost every bureaucratic system. But these must be used as exceptions. For the efficacy of the bureaucratic subsystems generally depends more fully on the continued leverage that can be exerted by the internalization of the "mission," or through the affective power of unit pride, *esprit de corps*, and collective competition. Thus, it is usually more efficient to have soldiers fighting for an ideal or for the dignity of their unit than to keep them forward by putting a sergeant at their back; it is more efficient to have a church's missionaries inbued with a "vocation," than to keep them in the jungles by threat of excommunication.

As we have suggested, the rigors of membership in such a coercive-algorithmic, deindividualizing system are at least partially off-set by the social benefits that come hand-in-hand with membership (especially in a demarcated subsystem). By virtue of the effective ideological or physical isolation of such units, and because of the emphasis on unit-tasks rather than individual tasks, the members tend to become very close, and sometimes even homogeneous. Paradoxically, the strength of the internal (commensal) relationships may tend to increase as the exogenous pressures on the unit increase. In effect then, potential economic and material benefits are either inadvertently or (in some cases) deliberately traded off against the social benefits associated with membership in a demarcated system or subsystem. Individual objectives and values tend to become subordinate to the reputation, welfare, and *esprit* of the group; this occurs most quickly, perhaps, in those groups that have a tradition, old flags, cannon-shot mess kits, martyrs, or historical relics.

Most of the attributes we have assigned to the Type-II system are obvious when we consider the symbiont ecological posture it entails. Initially, to be in a symbiont system role, the system must be performing some function that is deemed useful to the broader system of which it is a part. National defense, education of the young, maintenance of domestic order, administration of national functions, provision of spiritual succor, and containment of asocial elements are all functions we associate with the bureaucratic type, per se. And these are all *critical* functions . . . necessary, to a lesser or greater extent, for the integrity of the wider system itself.[*] They are also functions that can be reduced to a set of programmatic, algorithmic processes which are distributed among the

---

[*]These services, hence, appear to have highly inelastic demands, both intra- and interculturally.

various system components, to be effectuated when the proper external stimuli occur as an "event" demanding response.

So the premium, among such systems, is on responsiveness and predictability of performances from system components. The criticality of the missions performed by such systems do not allow the luxury either for equivocation of orders or for questioning of commands by subordinate subsystems or their personnel. To prepare for critical contingencies, the containing force must be trained to perform much like a machine . . . with maximum expedience and obedience, and with minimum unpredictability. Hence the reliance on rehearsals, specialization of function, and supremacy of authority inhering in occupants of any higher-order position. And hence the reliance on implied or manifest coercion as a constant complement to whatever ideological or rational control instruments the system might have available.

The algorithmic attribute we associate with Type-II systems does two things: first, it tends to inject strong automaticity into the dynamic dimension; secondly, it tends to discourage potentially dysfunctional innovations or individual actions. It also permits, wherever possible, a single set of rules to discipline functionally or geographically differentiated entities, such that there tend to be manuals of rules and policies which cohere the system as a whole, with subcodes and formulations and processes defining more specific activities for the demarcated units themselves. Hence, the "book" is the first and last resort of the bureaucratic administrator, be he or she clergyperson, military officer, or agency head, and most decision-making takes place largely via simple *exegesis*.*

Along with the processual algorithms defining procedures relative to specific functions, there are usually rigid command and communication channels, with individual units discouraged from setting up informal arrangements with other intrasystem units (which is *encouraged* within the Type-III system we shall discuss in the next section). And finally, because the effectiveness of the system as a whole depends on the performance of the individual units adhering to programmed procedures, the efficiency of the system is usually related to the *exhaustiveness* of the algorithmic base of the system . . . the extent to which all "events" that might occur have been assigned preprogrammed, effectively automatic responses.

But recall that the symbiont system is one that we defined as having essentially one role to perform, and the system can grow and be valued only to the extent that role is deemed functional. With the mission of handling or responding to a single event or highly correlated set of events, there is no advantage in stressing individual responsibility and potential disaster in encouraging individual initiative or innovation. Hence, strict centralization of authority and the careful demarca-

---

*I.e., by searching through the appropriate *book* for supportive or directive bases for decisions.

tion of delegated authority (often in the form of detailed job descriptions) is not only justified, but probably the best way to ensure optimality of performance for the system as a whole.* And to the extent that performance demands will tend to be essentially iterative or precedented in nature (marking responses as precedented), the promotion of individuals may rightly proceed on the basis of *seniority*, for there will indeed be great merit in experience as opposed to imagination or innate intellect. Time both provides a familiarity with the small number of iterative demands that fall on the member of the Type-II system, and helps ensure that the individual with greater time-in-unit will probably be more thoroughly institutionalized. This emphasis on seniority obviates promotion by merit, for where tasks are carefully compartmentalized and fully algorithmic, individual merit is effectively irrelevant. Hence there is a very special and powerful social benefit that attaches itself to such systems: *security*. This is one of the Type-II system's most powerful appeals.

The intensity with which the attributes we have set out will inhere in any particular system will depend quite strongly on the relative rigor and sensitivity of the mission. Thus we expect H.E.W. or the Bureau of Fisheries to be less strictly approximate to the bureaucratic ideal-type than the First Division of the Army, the C.I.A., or the New York City Riot Squads.

In summary then, the ecological demands associated with the symbiont system permit the identification of detailed plans that then are used as the basis for processual control of the system as a whole, with various preprogrammed tasks being distributed among the various subsystems. In general, the same type of organizational structure prevails throughout the system, despite the fact that the individual subsystems may have very different functional submissions to perform. Usually, specialization is on a group rather than an individual basis, so that the group itself is the primary focus of the individual's ambitions and objectives. To the extent that the mission imposed on a subsystem is hostile or dangerous, programmaticity and potential for coercion become valued system attributes. Rank and uniform are virtual prerequisites, and rank often follows seniority.

8.1.4 The Competitive System and the Technocratic Imperative

The problem, of course, is that the public sector seems to try to meet virtually every contingency with a bureaucratic system. This is a problem because, as we now know, the very structural and functional properties which make the Type-II

---

*We can note that when there is a conflict between superior and subordinates in a Type-II system, the subordinates are *a priori* presumed to be at fault. Moreover, there are usually strict regulations covering the *decorum* which subordinates must maintain when dealing with a superior (e.g., saluting officers). In Type-III systems, on the other hand, the superior who has problems with a significant proportion of his subordinates is himself likely to be in difficulty, for most Type-III systems set constraints on the superior's behavior toward subordinates, exactly the reverse of the Type-II situation.

system entirely congruent for some missions make it ill-suited to others. Thus, while the bureaucratic modality is properly at home with the demands made on the infantry or in the traditional secondary manufacturing arena, it does discredit to less programmable, less highly-structured situations (such as those faced by the neighborhood policeman,* the social service worker, or the high school teacher).

But if the public sector may lag a bit in achieving congruence between mission and organizational properties, certain segments of the commercial sector have been evolving toward distinctly nonbureaucratic systems, especially in technologically-based or tertiary industries.[6] For the forces converging on many modern commercial enterprises are neither iterative nor precedented . . . and hence not entirely predictable. And when external conditions are significantly unpredictable, preordained processual algorithms lose their significance and the mechanisticity inherent in the bureaucratic ideal-type becomes dysfunctional. At some point then, the tractability of the ecological domain decreases to the point where the bureaucratic ideal-type is no longer appropriate . . . and this may very well be at the point where the environment itself moves from moderate to severe stochasticity. For clearly, as the environmental forces of the system's milieu become less well-behaved, a greater premium is placed on a system's ability to respond with agility and quickness, to generate creative responses to newly emerged events or opportunities. And, to the extent that the system is subject to exogenous forces at all levels, rather than having lower-order components effectively insulated as in the Type-II system, creativity and originality and responsiveness must be distributed throughout the organization, not just concentrated at the very highest decision-making levels; hence, the premium on decentralization, innovation, and relative merit we will find associated with Type-III systems.

We must also note the Type-III system's emphasis on full-differentiation, such that different functions are normally performed by differently organized entities. Uniquely structured subsystems come in and out of being, as new processing demands dictate, or as new opportunities for exploitation emerge, with the premium placed on their quick identification and rapid attack. This is a very different strategy than the conservative "subsistence" one we associate with Type-I systems or the mechanization of a single, predefinable array of essentially invariant responses associated with the Type-II system. Moreover, this *differentiated* structure of the Type-III system suggests that affective/ ideological or coercive instruments will probably not be too effective, for the fully-differentiated system is almost totally secularized, and therefore largely reliant on rationalistic control instruments applied selectively to individuals.

---

*As most police officers will testify, the actual mission which they perform on the streets— where success depends so much on judgment, imagination, and "creation" of solutions—is hardly one assisted much by the bureaucratic trappings of the station house or the department itself.

One does not, for example, search for ideological engines motivating employees of shoe factories or airline personnel or computer technicians. One does not expect to find any commensal aspects in modern industrial corporations as one sometimes finds in the communities of coal miners, soldiers, the old immigrant proletariats, or even among certain institutional populations. Instead we find certain (often weak) social correlations among members of the same demarcated work-units (e.g., departments; crews), but these often do not extend beyond a beer on Friday afternoon. On a joint socioeconomic dimension, the members of the Type-III system tend to exist in a nuclearized, individuated world, with very little expectation of, or opportunity to realize, social benefits within their work confines.

Where there are few, if any, social benefits to be accumulated on the job, the stress on rationalistic or materialistic rewards is highest. Wages often become a surrogate for lack of amenities and social rewards, so that there is almost a constant and often acrimonious bargaining going on between workers and management. After all, if there is nothing to be gained from the job except money, and if the correlation between social benefits and economic remuneration is deemed both positive and direct, we should hardly expect anything except such bargaining behavior . . . where any level of compensation which happens to exist is always perceived as inferior to that which *could* exist. Nor should we then be surprised at the casting of this bargaining into a *zero-sum game* context, where not only management but also one's colleagues and other workers are viewed as direct competitors.[7]

At the higher levels of the organization, however, there may be some complementation between social and economic inducements . . . even if the social benefits are only delusory or surrogational. Before there were so many white collar workers, the white collar was an effective "carrot," often resulting in long hours of work and great assiduity for pay actually less than that enjoyed by the blue collar workers. On another dimension, the key to the executive washroom and the array of other pseudosocial benefits available to the "organization man" are largely inexpensive but relatively effective instruments for provoking assiduity on the job. But such differentiations can be afforded only by those at the higher levels of the organization, for even the most naive and exploitative administrator knows the futility of efforts to differentiate the plant-floor or blue collar proletariat. Thus with pseudosocial instruments impotent, and with coercion outlawed, the payroll check is about the only instrument left.

Strictly rationalistic instruments (e.g., money and rugs on the office floor) tend to induce employee *mobility* rather than loyalty. Simply, labor follows differential benefit levels, and these (unlike affective benefits) are usually not restricted to any particular system in a field. Thus there is the substantial turnover among the employees of Type-III systems. There is also less emphasis on long-run security as a benefit; and in many cases there is no provision for security at all except among members of strong unions (largely because Type-III systems discount seniority against merit).[8] As the Type-III organization is itself an exploitative vehicle, individuals in such systems tend to view themselves in an exploitative relationship to the employing organization. Thus, the intensity of association between individual and system declines as we move from the Type-I toward the Type-III system, and so, therefore, does the coefficient of control we can expect to exercise.

There is another interesting property common to most Type-III systems . . . the attempt to foster internal competition among employees (for jobs, rewards, status, recognition, etc.). This goes beyond the largely morale-oriented, unit-based internal competition of the Type-II system, and usually reflects the hope that this will make the organization itself more ecologically competitive. Athletic teams, for example, award starting positions on the basis of demonstrated ability; promotion within the strict Type-III organization generally is predicated on past performance, objectively audited; jobs are awarded or positions assigned not on the basis of simple seniority (as with the Type-II system) or on the ascriptive basis (as with the Type-I system), but ostensibly on the basis of merit . . . which means either good grades in school for the recruit, or a "good record" for the veteran. The grade-oriented educational system, the early predication of promotion in school on the basis of performance, parents' admonitions about success now being the best indication of happiness later . . . all these serve to prepare us for entrance into a universalistic, merit-oriented system. Of course, some success, and perhaps an increasing amount, is predicated not on "doing," per se, but on appearing to do (or appearing to have done). To this extent, the neat ideal-type world of Max Weber becomes gradually transmogrified into the dramaturgical world of Goffman, a critical shift indeed.[9]

As a rule however, the Type-III system attempts to place the right man in the right job just as, in carrying out its fully differentiated structural role, it tries to design organizational substructures most congruent with designated functional roles. So what we want to portray for the Type-III system is a situation of constant experimentation, change, innovation, and differentiation.

Such a portrait is entirely consistent with the disturbed, nonplacid, and protean milieu in which the Type-III system resides; for it employs comparative excellence as the arbiter of survival. The complex and constant alterations in the character and distribution of resources in such a field, with several different systems competing for the same resource stock or market, tends to reward rapid adjustments in the structure of the organization. Thus the success of the Type-III system will depend largely on its ability to read immediate (and sometimes long-run) futures. In addition, the competitive nature of the milieu demands that the organization constantly innovate and adjust; hence, the ceaseless hiring and firing or displacement of personnel, and the constant structuring, restructuring, creation or disbanding of entire units or processual technologies. These are all activities of the systems whose survival depends always on their having relatively less waste, error, or inefficiency than their competitors.*

---

*In professional sports, where a team is restricted to a certain number of active players on its roster, this situation becomes particularly severe for the individual of only marginal capabilities (who would most likely be protected in an essentially Type-II system).

The system aiming for dominance in a complex and changing milieu sees its overall effectiveness and efficiency dependent on getting the most out of every constituent . . . individual employees, subsystems, divisions, etc. The only mechanism for achieving this (lacking affective or ideological levers and given the absence of any code of ethics for the corporate manager or line-worker) is the reliance on Adam Smith's "invisible hand"—enlightened self-interest—coupled with a reward schedule that promises that the better the individual's objectively-determined performance, the greater the return on his time.

In this rationalistic context, it is critical that performance be measured in terms of some effectively measurable end agreed to beforehand by both controller and controllee. All organizational resources and personnel are thus viewed as instruments to be approached on the basis of their marginal productivity, with the required or base level of performance generally a compromise between what the supervisor thinks is possible and what the employee thinks is reasonable (or what the union will tolerate in organized shops). There is, in effect, no need for bringing in abstracts like optimality, but a strict tendency to stress "satisficing," much in the sense that Herbert Simon has suggested.[10] Thus for the member of such an organization, the "end" is usually given in terms of a particular rate-of-return for a profit/loss center, or a production quota for a line supervisor or worker, etc. With the end explicated and "set in concrete," auditing becomes the primary control vehicle, with actual attainments compared against desired goals in as close to real-time as is necessary or economic.

As such, the major cognitive attributes of such a system become both apparent and legitimate: (a) the emphasis on planning accompanied by the emphasis on prediction of probable future environmental (e.g., market) states; (b) the translation of these broad plans into successively more detailed ones, with the operational criteria derived directly from desired performance levels; (c) the concentration on the calculus of satisfactory performance determined via an audit process; and (d) the residence of the entire system in a "rationalized" setting, where every possible event is numericalized and/or objectified, and where affective or subjective factors are not supposed (normatively) to intrude.

Overall then, such systems trade on the pecuniary equity that has been fostered in most modern nations through the industrialization phenomenon, accompanied by nuclearization of the family, the belief that social benefits follow only from economic achievements, the primacy of a sacerdotalized work ethic, and the reliance on universalistic and objective criteria for self-worth (the most expedient and accessible of which are materialistic measures). And, in such a world, the ceaseless search is always for "more," both at the organization level and at the level of the individual himself.

8.1.5 The Gestalt and Autoregulation

The Type-IV system is as yet a relatively rare phenomenon, with the following properties:

Ecological Type	Dependent
Domain Type	Structurally-Differentiated/ Functionally-Segmented
Dynamic Type	Heuristic
Control Instrument	Ethical and Professional Codes
Control Modality	Autoregulation
Analytical State	Indeterminate

The ecological milieu in which the Type-IV system operates is one which contains a significant number of effectively unpredictable events that may impinge on the system (and demand adaption or response). As such, the dynamic dimension of the Type-IV system will tend to take on a heuristic or opportunistic (occasionally hysteric) overtone. The inability to predict and define events—the inability to construct an adequately exhaustive yet still manageable array of probable futures—obviates the emphasis on planning associated with Type-III systems. This, in turn, makes management by preprogrammed algorithms or fixed objectives rather more gratuitous than effective. Under these circumstances, the system must rely most heavily on the personal integrity or commitment of the individuals comprising it, for the option to exercise direct or even objectively retrospective control is largely absent.

Thus, the Type-IV system will generally be the least viable of the entities we may encounter, for it is the least likely to exist independently of the specific individuals it contains. That is, it is most dependent on the idiosyncratic, moment-in-time qualities of its members ... their skills, their aptitudes, their personal proclivities, and talents. To this extent, an unfavorable or ill-equipped member is a serious affair, and the only effective control the system can exercise is through careful and stringent recruiting and selection processes. Thus, to some extent, the infeasibility of continuous objective control is offset by rather more thorough screening processes and more demanding sets of qualifications. To this extent, one must show credentials to enter such an organization, and these credentials are generally in the form of some professional preparation.

The Type-IV system is, as we suggested, a relatively new phenomenon. It seems to have had its origin in several distinct causes: (a) the failure of bureaucratized agencies to deal effectively with gestalt-like social, economic, behavioral, and political problems; (b) the gradual but striking shift from secondary to tertiary industry in the highly developed countries; (c) the demand for expert consulting and staff organizations to lend specialized assistance in the face of an increasingly complex technologized milieu in all sectors: political, social, and economic; and (d) the increasing emphasis lent educational or intellectual as opposed to experiential attributes in an environment increasingly characterized by unprecedented events (demanding creative rather than iterative or precedented responses).

In the world of the professional, both ends and means are assessed idiographically. The "think tank," the research organization, the research-oriented university faculty, aesthetic enterprise (i.e., modern theater companies, interior decorators) usually recognize the critical nature of individual inputs . . . substitutions generally demand organizational or processual modifications, unlike member substitutions conducted in any of the preceeding system types. To obtain creativity, one must offer the least constraint, which means that procedural or policy discipline in the Type-IV system is normatively the lowest, as is the emphasis on objective or universalistic performance criteria. This means that the organizational loyalty of the members is probably lowest, as when the scientist or C.P.A. accords more worth to professional considerations than to corporate or organizational ends. Attempts to exercise control usually lead to defections, except where alternatives are extremely scarce (which is less apt to be the case with the member of a Type-IV system than with the member of one of the other system types). Professionals, in addition to being unresponsive to coercive efforts, generally have a low regard for transparent attempts to employ ideological instruments, except for certain grand societal abstracts that do not lend themselves well to specific actions. Finally, the tendency to set professional recognition and personal considerations atop material rewards (a phenomenon supported by increasingly 'adequate' base salaries in the educational and social service sectors, etc.) makes incremental control via rational instruments somewhat dubious.

Hence, at least so far as immediate administrative prescriptions are concerned, we treat the members of such organizations with kid gloves, often making administrative positions deliberately subordinate in status to professional or creative positions (e.g., the dean of a faculty, the business administrator of an artistic company, the manager of a research project are often less prestigious and less well-paid than the operational professionals). This, coupled with the ineffectuality of the other instruments, leaves only autoregulation as an appropriate control modality, where control on the individuals is both indirect and usually nonspecific. This modality relies on one of two vehicles for its effectiveness: (a) peer evaluation; or (b) the existence of codes of ethics that set tacit constraints on professionals' behavior.

These are relied on due to the nature of the tasks to be performed within the confines of the Type-IV system. Owing to the indeterminate nature of task demands and the emphasis on personal capabilities and talents in their realization, tasks cannot be *a priori* algorithmic and performance criteria cannot be made rigid. Nor can any type of objective audit be performed except by a group of peers carrying purportedly the same basic set of professional qualifications; and even these may be loath to attack a colleague except in the most extreme cases. In short then, the price one must pay for the internalized motivation, professionalism, and strong creativity necessary for the survival of the Type-IV system is loss of control.

The lack of structural constraints on the domain dimension we associate with such systems contributes to this uncontrollability, but at the same time promotes effectiveness in dealing with very complex, unprecedented situations. Work tends to be done either in seclusion or through informal patterns of interaction which often shift too rapidly to be allegorized. And because members of such an organization tend to be viewed as assets by the organization itself, attempts to dictate chains of command can be self-defeating, just as the attempt to enforce strict processual paradigms can lead to frustration, defection, or downright disobedience. In short, the effective administrator of a Type-IV system has a role considerably different in nature than the others we have proposed: his job may not be so much to direct the enterprise and its personnel, as to provide the kind of milieu which allows the personnel to direct themselves, to act more or less as a buffer between organizational exigencies and the latitude of the employees, to protect them from bureaucratic aggravations and, occasionally, from the personality and temperamental excesses which so often haunt creative enterprises.

Yet as we implied earlier, the Type-IV system is a case of organizational "overkill" except where system success (i.e., the mission) depends on creative and idiosyncratic as opposed to algorithmic or universalistic criteria . . . or where there is simply no advantage to be gained from ritualization, mechanization, or objectification. For the more sophisticated or intellectually demanding tasks facing post-industrial society, or for the more fluid and aesthetically-dependent tasks performed in the tertiary industry sector, the Type-IV system seems especially appropriate, and perhaps uniquely so. In medicine, law, higher education, research, resocialization, therapy, and art we will likely find the Type-IV system. And the demand of the developed nations for something more than faster cars or brighter television sets or bigger planes seems to suggest that the Type-IV system will become more and more prevalent as an organizational modality.

By way of summary, these discussions carry us to the point where we may explore aspects of system administration, having now some concepts pertinent to the control of the human components of socioeconomic systems. What is perhaps most important, we now have at hand the basis for a set of admittedly speculative assertions about the predictability or tractability of the human components in systems, assertions summarized in Figure 8.6.

8.2 TOWARD AN ARRAY OF ADMINISTRATIVE MODALITIES

We are now in a position to consider opportunities for complementation between the human relations and technological schools of administrative theory . . . for we must understand that the *congruence* of any administrative approach which we take to any organization must somehow consider the relative capital-labor ratio. For the extent to which machines may be (or have been) substituted for people is usually a critical factor in determining the administrative

SYSTEM TYPE	FACTORS PROMOTING ADHERENCE BY MEMBERSHIPS	EXPECTED COEFFICIENT OF CONTROL
I	No socioeconomic alternatives in the accessible milieu; acculturation and institutionalization.	Highest
II	Security of position; identity via group membership; primacy of collective reputation and pride; economic, social or corporal coercion.	Moderately high
III	Economic and immediate material benefits.	Relatively low (except when alternatives are scarce, etc.)
IV	Peer recognition; self-actualization; idiographic rewards.	Lowest

Figure 8.6 Table of assertions about tractability.

tractability of an enterprise. We potentially inject more determinacy into our enterprise as we displace men with machines, which greatly simplifies not only the production processes themselves but the scheduling, marketing, logistical, and financial operations as well. And there is, of course, a subtle ancillary benefit whose importance has not been lost on alert administrators: increasing the capital-labor ratio associated with an entire industry may make unions more tractable and the remaining workers more "loyal" and assiduous.

In short then, the firm whose production process (or, more properly, production function) owes greatly more to the capital-equipment input than the labor input, is likely to be able to approach administrative problems as if they were effectively deterministic, and therefore make decisions in a very different framework than the firm whose output relies primarily on the input of less highly disciplined, less constrainable, and less predictable human components. Thus, for example, the fully-automated petroleum cracking plant is greatly simpler to both allegorize (i.e., model) and manage than the enterprise that relies for its viability on a balanced man-machine process. Extending this, the enterprise driven by man-machine systems is likely to be more administratively tractable than the firm that has no mechanical aspects to its processes, such that the "indeterminate" human component drives the entire production process (as with creative, professional, or most tertiary or service organizations). This latter type enterprise will be least susceptible to any principles of management that deny stochastic agents primary determinacy and least amenable to quantitative treatment, but *most* responsive to injections of behavioral science and human relations considerations. By the same token, for the essentially mechanical, capital-driven enterprise, management will rely most heavily on engineering skills, and be least concerned with behavioral interpretations of managerial functions. And, as the saving grace for the "principles of management" men, it appears that what we earlier described as the normative bureaucratic system will be reasonably amenable to universalistic constraints in the form of conceptual devices such as span-of-control or to structural prescriptions such as "no subordinate should report to more than one supervisor," etc. So just as we had, in the last chapter, several different analytical modalities responding to the several different analytical ideal-types, we must here suggest that there will be several unique administrative modalities, each especially well-suited to one or another of the organizational ideal-types that were isolated in the first chapter.

8.2.1 Some Peremptory Propositions

Essentially the same factors that determined a system's analytical tractability will at least partially determine its *administrative tractability*. The critical foci are the properties that: (a) allow us to use effectively positivistic methods in treating an enterprise; (b) allow us to assume, legitimately, that the system's future behavior will be an essential replicate of its historical behavior; (c) allow us to assume that the system's unobserved properties will be morphological extensions of the empirically accessed properties. In this context, we offer the following propositions:

1. The more placid the environment in which a system is resident *and* the more constrained and selective that system's interchanges with that environment, the greater the probability that the system's future ecological "states" will be some calculable function of its present and/or historical states. In other words, the transforms that take place on the ecological dimension are quite likely to be manageable within a relatively simple analytical framework. In fact, if environmental and interchange properties alter only quantitatively, a simple extrapolative transform function might well serve our purposes.

2. The more tractable the domain of a system (presuming properties of homogeneity, symmetry, accessibility, etc.), the greater the probability that unobserved portions will be some calculable function of the empirically observed portion. Thus, simple statistical inference processes or projective techniques might be appropriate.

3. The more tractable the dynamic dimension of a system, the greater the probability that future processual "states" will be quantitative rather than qualitative variants of the present (and/or historical). That is, the coefficients of our functional or causal constructs might change, but the morphology of the basic relationships and processual states is likely to be relatively invariant through time.

The obvious analytical corollary to these propositions is this:

The greater the tractability of any dimension of a subject system, the greater the probability that its future properties will be adequately captured by empirically-based analytical methods (e.g., inductive projections and statistical inferences). Conversely, the greater the intractability of any dimension of any subject system, the lower the probability that that dimension's future state will be any calculable function of its empirically observable properties; hence, the lower the analytical relevance of historical data bases and the repertoire of empirically-predicated analytical techniques.

Now the relationship between analytical and administrative tractability of a subject system is this: to the extent that empirically-predicated inductive and inferential techniques become less relevant, the decision premises which are available to the decision-maker become less precise and accurate. Therefore, there is a higher level of expected error associated with any decision we might make. For deterministic tools become irrelevant to the extent that the system at hand departs from mechanistic criteria (i.e., as the system becomes inherently less predictable due to its reduced amenability to observation, measurement, and controlled manipulation). As this occurs, we substitute stochastic or deductive instruments for the deterministic. These produce less directive and less well-validated decision premises, such that there is an inherently high risk of dysfunction associated with decisions predicated mainly on deductive analysis (dysfunction being a product of undesired consequences stemming from a decision action we have taken).

In this way we arrive at a fourth proposition, this one directly related to administrative modalities:

4. The greater the correlation between the properties of a subject system and those of the Type-I referents, the greater will be the proportion of decisions that can be legitimately based on precedent. Conversely, the more the system at hand approximates a Type-IV referents, the greater must be the proportional reliance on unprecedented or innovative decisions.

Simply, in well-behaved, stable organizations, the majority of the decisions are well-precedented. In legal decisions, for example, administrators tend to examine historical data bases and replicate premises, thus entering an element of automaticity into the administrative and control aspects of the organization. We identify such systems because of the high qualitative correlation between historical and current decisions. But this, of course, implies that there is a high correlation between past and present contexts, between past and present exogenous conditions. So long as this condition is met, precedent permits the inculcation of great efficiency into the administrative and control mechanisms of a system, with decisions tending to perpetuate themselves through time until they become institutionalized, ritualistic. To this extent, the "strategic" or intellectual demands on the decision-maker decline to a comfortable minimum and the managerial decision-making function tends to become analogous to the "conservative," precedent-seeking algorithms of, say, the judicial system.[11]

IF: System's properties are predominantly:	Tractable	Intractable
. . . the most congruent analytical mode is:	Empirically-predicated inductive analysis	Deductive analysis
The most probably effective administrative mode is:	Precedent	Heuristicism
Because the environmental context of the system is most likely to be essentially:	Placid	Turbulent
The decision-making criterion should be:	Maximization over a succession of short-runs	Minimization of secular risk
The system should be structured to achieve:	Maximum efficiency (programmaticity)	Maximum responsiveness and resilience (plasticity)
With the predominant internal control instrument being:	Algorithmic rules	Autoregulation
Because "parts" will be:	Highly dependent	Highly autonomous

Figure 8.7 Table of polar administrative prescriptions.

But, the man trying to manage a Type-IV system finds himself having to make unprecedented, often irrevocable decisions in the face of considerable uncertainty. As the appropriateness of his historical data bases and prior decisions declines, his reliance on deductive alternatives must increase proportionately, for *disciplined* decisions must be made even under conditions of great uncertainty and anxiety. It was to support decisions under such conditions that we earlier set out analytical paradigms such as the system architecture approach or the normative system-building (and policy-setting) scheme of Chapters 6 and 7, respectively.

Thus, as we earlier suggested, systems inhering very different properties will demand very different administrative modalities, a point lent substance in Figure 8.7.

We can be a great deal more explicit, however, for there will be unique administrative properties associated with *each* of our four systemic ideal-types, not merely the two polar opposites. Recalling our points about the dynamic dimensions of each of the four systemic ideal-types,* we arrive at the associations of Figure 8.8.

*See, again, Section 4.4.

SYSTEMIC IDEAL-TYPE	ANALYTICAL STATE	DYNAMIC IDEAL-TYPE	ASSOCIATED CONTROL ASPECTS
I. Primitive system	Deterministic	Mechanical	Dogma/ritual
II. Bureaucratic system	Moderately stochastic	Nonequifinal	Implied coercion/ algorithms/*esprit*
III. Competitive system	Severely stochastic	Equifinal	Rational advantage/ objective audits
IV. Emergent or professional system	Indeterminate	Heuristic	Autoregulation/ethical codes

Figure 8.8 Typology of dynamic correlations.

Recall, also, that each of the systemic ideal-types has a definite ecological posture it maintains that, in turn, determines the domain aspects of the system, as illustrated in Figure 8.9. Continuing with our typological summaries, we easily note that the recollection of the logic underlying these associations leads us directly to an association of unique administrative properties with each of the four systemic ideal-types, as in Figure 8.10.

Now, for our purposes here, we need not repeat any of the contentions about sociobehavioral control aspects made in the first sections of this chapter, but may begin to concentrate, instead, on some of the quasi-technical aspects of system administration, per se. Primarily, we shall be interested in introducing the broad *cognitive* bases underlying the treatment of entities approximating one or another of our ideal-types . . . we are interested in developing the "intellectual" components of the modalities.

In this sense then, we want to concentrate on the decision-making aspects of organizations that have both the ambition and potential for scientific adminis-

SYSTEMIC IDEAL-TYPE	ECOLOGICAL POSTURE	DOMAIN IDEAL-TYPE
I	Autarchic	Fully segmented
II	Symbiont	Structurally segmented/ functionally differentiated
III	Dominant	Fully differentiated
IV	Dependent	Structurally differentiated/ functionally segmented

Figure 8.9 Table of domain correlations.

SYSTEMIC IDEAL-TYPE	MORPHOLOGY OF THE ADMINISTRATIVE SYSTEM	DECISION LATITUDE (AUTONOMY) ALLOWED "PARTS"	DECISION-MAKING PREMISES
I	Coextensive with the social structure	*None:* all behavior programmed via dogma-driven ritual	Mystery, dogma, or exegesis
II	Hierarchical and centralized	*Little:* most decisions are highly constrained, the constraints dependent on "level of organization"	Precedent, tradition, and legislated premises (i.e., rules and tables of procedures)
III	Decentralized (except for major policy direction)	*Moderate:* within assigned sphere of influence or expertise	Rational or scientific in origin . . . i.e., objective
IV	Amorphous and adhocratic[12]	*High:* there are often formal sanctions against constraints	Intuitive or idiographic

Figure 8.10   Table of administrative properties.

tration, whether it be in pursuit of some elusive and idealistic "optima" or, more realistically, in pursuit of Simon's *satisfactory* solutions.[13] A somewhat new perspective is required, however; the perspective which sees administration of an organization as a problem involving the development of objectively rationalized reactions to problems that emerge both within and without the organization. More specifically, the administrative subsystem of an organization is concerned with the prediction of the behavior of external and internal factors, and with the generation of effective/efficient responses to those factors within the confines of whatever objective functions the organization has elected to fulfill (or which have been imposed on it by some superior system).

At any rate, we now want to partition the range of problems an organization may expect to encounter into four by now very familiar categories, as done in Figure 8.11.

Now, within the confines of our concern with administrative decision-making,

SYSTEM TYPE	PROBLEM CLASS
I. *Deterministic:* For any given array of premises (including starting-state conditions and the array of change-agents to be introduced), there is one and only one system-state that can be assigned any significant probability of occurrence (simply, such a system has only one behavior alternative associated with any alternative action we might define).	*Certainty* . . . as in the effort to maximize the output from a finite-state automatic production system where output levels are directly and calculably related to input levels.
II. *Moderately Stochastic:* For any given array of premises we can define, there is one and only one array of state-variables that will occur but more than one array of parameter or coefficient values which must be assigned significant probabilities of occurrence.	*Probabilisticity* . . . when, for example, a demand level for a precedented product may assume any value within some precisely defined range of values or where the only "events" of any significance all belong to the same qualitative set; where system relationships vary over some range of magnitudes rather than varying in basic nature.
III. *Severely Stochastic:* Given any premises-set we might define, there are two or more predefinable alternative system-states that can be assigned significant probabilities of occurrence, the degree of "severity" depending on the number of alternatives that have been assigned significant *a priori* occurrence probabilities.	*Risk* . . . where two or more qualitatively different events have significant probabilities of occurrence (e.g., winning or losing a contract; solving or not solving a problem; acquiescence or rebellion among employees faced with procedural changes, etc.)
IV. *Indeterminate:* Given any premises-set we might define, there is no adequately predefinable system-state that can be assigned any significant probability of occurrence, indicating that we expect some as yet to be defined system-state to occur.	*Meta-Risk* . . . where we have no sufficiently precise idea what state-of-the world will occur, but can only be sure that something we haven't yet thought of will be "the" event.

Figure 8.11 Table of problemic ideal-types.

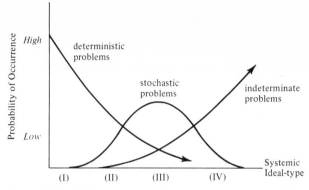

Figure 8.12 Distribution of problem types among system types.

we can set the normative relationship between the problemic ideal-types defined in Figure 8.11 and the various organizational ideal-types shown in Figure 8.12.

As so much of our earlier work has been intended to make clear, we expect that essentially deterministic problems will predominate in the inherently simpler system types (the primitive and bureaucratic) and emerge only as a rare luxury in the Type-III and Type-IV systems. Similarly, we expect effectively indeterminate problems to be most frequently encountered within the confines of the Type-IV system, less frequently within the competitive-dominant Type-III system. Finally, stochastic problems will be most frequently encountered in the Type-II and Type-III system, hence the normal curve for these. And, had we broken out the severely and moderately stochastic subcases, we would expect the former to be heavily skewed toward the Type-III system, the latter predominant in association with the Type-II entity.

But, there is another deductively predicated proposition we wish to offer, this one concerning the probable distribution of the various problem categories *within* any complex organization, as illustrated in Figure 8.13. We must expect

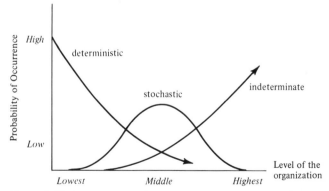

Figure 8.13 Distribution of problems within the normative organization.

that within any organization, the complexity of problems to be faced and solved by decision-makers will normatively increase with the level of the organizational hierarchy.

What this suggests is, that while every administrator will have some planning, some predicting, some evaluation, and some controlling to do, etc., the conditions under which these tasks will be performed will alter considerably with the level of the organization at which the administrator is resident. Specifically, as we move upward in the normative organization, we can expect the following to occur:

(a) The number of variables that must be considered for any given problem will increase.

(b) The number of nondetermined exogenous variables will increase.

(c) Planning will involve the development of greater numbers of unique alternative "states."

(d) Analysis of alternatives will involve the simultaneous manipulation of greater numbers of essentially ill-behaved variables and arrays.

(e) Fewer of the logically probable alternatives (i.e., interaction-patterns among the state-variables relational functions) will be *a priori* determined or "given."

(f) Any predictions or decision premises finally accepted will owe more to judgmental than empirical/factual bases.

In other words, the decision-maker at the lower levels of the organization will deal with more fully-premised decision problems, where there is only a very limited judgmental latitude allowed him. It is as if we successively curtailed the number of nonspecific, *a priori* unresolved premises available to decision-makers as we move down the hierarchy of the organization, permitting them only more highly precedented (e.g., routine), factually-predicated decisions (where an optimal solution is not only feasible but almost inescapable within the exogenously-set confines we pass on). We provide, as it were, an *envelope of certainty*, which becomes more and more strict as it extends downward. Conversely, as it extends upward; it becomes more amorphous. More decision factors must be treated exogenously and often assigned values predicated more on opinion than on fact. As this occurs, the "range" of alternative events to be considered accelerates and the probability distribution imposed on them attenuates.

Thus, in the *normative* organizational context (that characterized by hierarchical or pyramidal structure), the nature of the decision-making activities must alter with the level at which they take place. Most generally, as we have already suggested, the amount of relevant, factual, or objective data available to develop unambiguous (i.e., deterministic) decision alternatives will be highest at the lowest levels of the organization, tailing off as we move upward. Secondly, the relative complexity of the decisions that must be made also increases as we

move upward, reflecting the well-documented transition from *operational* to *managerial* to *executive* decisions as we rise through a pyramidal organization.

Ancillary to these general comments are some hypotheses which should be fairly obvious by now. First, if we have a computer-driven management information system, we would expect that it would, of itself, be able to assume many lower-level decision-making functions, managing those processes that are essentially deterministic in nature and that are capable of being effectively reduced to meaningful quantitative terms. But the information system *cum* decision-maker would decline in appropriateness as we move upward and begin to encounter severely stochastic or even indeterminate decision situations. Secondly, we can suggest that the codification of information—its reduction from detailed data streams to statistical indices and from there to broad indicators or trend variables—increases as we move upward in the pyramid or hierarchy. Finally, the response-time allowed decision-makers generally increases as we move higher in the organization, a fact that reflects not only the greater complexity of problems faced at the higher level but the longer-range implications of decisions associated with these levels. All told, then, we expect to find empirical data bases relevant for decision-making heavily skewed toward the lower levels of the normative organization (which implies that the judgmental component or non-empirical decision-bases will be skewed toward the higher levels). Figure 8.14 expresses this point graphically.

This, of course, simply reflects our assertion (by way of a heuristic, if you will) that deterministic processes or problems will be heavily concentrated at lower levels of organizations, etc. And when we recall from Chapter 3 that information is a quantum product of *both* raw data and manipulative models (e.g., statistical or mathematical algorithms; verbal paradigms), we are on the track of a proposition central to administrative theory: the level of error expected to be associated with the decisions made by administrators will depend not only on the intensity of resources applied to their study (i.e., the cost in terms of time, energy, dollars, etc., of the predictive/descriptive allegory of the

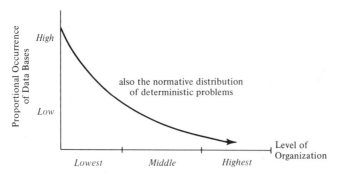

Figure 8.14 Distribution of organizational data bases.

	SYSTEM CLASSES			
	Deterministic	Moderately Stochastic	Severely Stochastic	Indeterminate
PROBLEM CLASS	Certainty	Probabilistic	Risk	Meta-risk
ASSOCIATED INSTRUMENT CLASS	Optimization	Extrapolative	Game-based; simulative	Heuristic
ANALYTICAL BASE	Positivistic	Inductivistic	Deductivistic	Intuitive/ metaphysical
RELATIVE CONTRIBUTION OF: (a) Factual or data component	Highest	High	Low	Lowest
(b) Judgmental or model component	Lowest	Low	High	Highest
POST-DECISION TASKS	None, once "steady-state" has been identified	Periodic monitoring to identify "true" parameter	Controlled experiment to identify "true" state	Exhaustive empirical "learning" exercises

Figure 8.15   Table of decision properties.

problem system), but also on the analytical ideal-type category to which the problem to be solved belongs.

There does not seem to be any way to escape the increasing irrelevance of data bases as problems depart from the criteria for *inherent* determinacy or moderate stochasticity. There is no way, therefore, to escape the increasing probability of predictive/prescriptive error associated with the allegories we build to try to analytically discipline *inherently* stochastic or indeterminate entities. The major source of this predictive/prescriptive error is the inescapably greater reliance on *a prioristic* or judgmental informational predicates for these stochastic entities. In this light consider Figure 8.15, where the various systemic or organizational ideal-types are arrayed in columns, and the various correlatives of interest in rows.

In summary of our work thus far then, we emerge with the suggestion that, as the system at hand departs from the criteria associated with the Type-I organizational ideal-type (the autarchic, segmented, and essentially "mechanical" primitive organization), we must expect that the decision-making demands placed on the administrative subsystem will become more complex. Moreover, *within* any organization, the complexity of decision-making tasks will increase as we move from lower to higher levels.

8.2.2   The Array of Administrative Modalities

Though it is impossible to be extremely precise at this point, we do want to introduce some kind of tentative structure to guide our discussions of adminis-

trative modalities available to the decision-maker, a structure responsive to the groundwork we have laid thus far. Figure 8.16 seems to provide us with what we need. As the figure indicates, each of the administrative modalities we shall be defining will be primarily appropriate to one or another of our analytical (i.e., problemic) ideal-types, and therefore primarily associated with one or another of the organizational ideal-types.

8.2.2.1 The Finite-State System Engineering Modality
Of the four modalities to be treated, the finite-state system engineering modality will require the least elaboration. This is because the finite-state modality is the administrative *null-hypothesis*. It suggests, in effect, that the principles of microeconomics provide the theoretical envelope within which administrative operations should take place, and that the actual process of decision-making is best undertaken using the tools and techniques of deterministic engineering (i.e., those which purport to effect optimality). In short then, the finite-state modality draws an explicit correlation between the engineer's concept of an "optimal" mechanism and the microeconomist's concept of the optimal enterprise. Moreover, for enterprises that owe the majority of their processing to machines or physical mechanisms of some sort (as with, for example, an automated production line or a computer-driven chemical cracking plant), all decisions may be made largely within a deterministic engineering domain . . . at least theoretically. The concepts underlying such an approach are admirably well treated in the existing literature, as are the instruments necessary to implement the approach. And, where the entity we are dealing with may be assumed to be sufficiently simple (i.e., significantly approximate to the deterministic analytical ideal-type or the effective mechanism), this approach is entirely warranted.

In general, however, the finite-state system engineering modality (coupled with the principles of microeconomics) will become operationally difficult to apply as we move to higher levels within a modern enterprise, or as the enterprise itself begins to depart from the criteria we earlier established for the Type-I organizational ideal-type (e.g., a simple, highly selective ecological dimension; no equifinal potential available to the parts). In short, the situations that permit us to make assumptions of determinacy and "engineer" aspects of an organization will be very limited.

Nevertheless, at the lowest levels of most enterprises, there will be ample opportunity to employ this modality. For example, we tend to use a disciplined trial-and-error empirical analysis to set the effectively optimal parameters associated with the input-output ratios of automated production processes and "efficiency studies" for other processes. In the same way, the system engineers working with an enterprise's computer will operate as if it is possible to develop optimal input schedules and configurations, such that the investment in the information system will produce an effectively optimal (i.e., maximal) output in terms of data quantity. Additionally, most of the exercises in plant lay-out, in-plant logistics, and other largely mechanical-technical aspects of production

ADMINISTRATIVE MODALITY	ASSOCIATED PROBLEM TYPE	ASSOCIATED INSTRUMENTAL BASE	AREAS OF APPLICABILITY
Finite-state system engineering	Deterministic	Optimization techniques	Type-I systems and "mechanical" subsystems within other organizations
Servocybernetic approach	Moderately stochastic	Econometric and statistical models	Type-II systems; highest levels of Type-I systems and lowest levels of Type-III
Stochastic-state	Severely stochastic	Game-theoretical and dynamic programming techniques; simulation models	Type-III systems; lower levels of Type-IV systems
Heuristic	Indeterminate	Learning models	Type-IV system

Figure 8.16 Distribution of administrative modalities.

belong to the engineers and technically sophisticated staff men. These people are generally equipped with a range of instruments that purport to deal deterministically with finite-state processes (e.g., the optimization instruments of chemical, production, and industrial engineering; linear programming models that will effectively optimize transportation and delivery algorithms, etc).

That such instruments may be yielding answers or schedules that have little probability of being exactly realized in practice is of little concern, for at this level of the enterprise, the exogenous variables passed down from higher levels act to effectively eliminate stochastic considerations from the engineer's calculus. In other words, the constraining assumptions that he receives in terms of necessary production schedules, budget restrictions, and demand and supply forecasts, etc., essentially insulate his activities from perturbations that will arise in the real-world and properly be the concern of others within the enterprise. The system engineering modality may be employed to insure that whatever criteria are passed down in the form of expected performance levels are realized with the least associated cost in terms of resources and inputs expended. In effect then, it may be the envelope of assumptions passed down that enables so many lower-level operations in an enterprise to be effectively treated via the finite-state system engineering modality, and thus susceptible to the abstractions of microeconomics.

By way of a note, we sought implicitly to associate this modality primarily with Type-I systems—those with autarchic ecological postures, essentially segmented domains and dynamic dimensions that tend to exhibit mechanical properties. Moreover, we earlier gave as examples of Type-I socioeconomic systems the primitive subsistence cultures and such phenomenon as charitable and political organizations based on a cell-like structure. To a certain extent, and perhaps only poorly in some instances, the assumptive nets which constrain lower-order units of modern enterprise (and the frequently encountered interchangeability of units of production in these subsystems) tend to make the analogy between the primitive system and the plant process not entirely inadmissible. At any rate, we would be hard-pressed to isolate better examples of "engineered," effectively optimal systems than the ritualized, highly programmed "automata" that intense institutionalization has bred in many primitive cultures. The environmental "givens" of the sociocultural system are roughly equivalent to the exogenous "givens" that constrain the technological subsystem.

The essential point of comparison between these phenomena is, however, the tendency for exogenous factors to allow deterministic assumptions, and hence allow us the luxury of assuming that applications of finite-state system engineering tools and optimization techniques will, indeed, give us exactly what we want, when we want it. In short then, the analogy between the primitive sociocultural system and the lower-level processing subsystem in a modern organization is complete at the point where we realize that the components of both systems are effectively constrained from inaugurating unexpected behaviors; those of the sociocultural system because of the thoroughness of institutionalization and acculturation, those of its technological counterpart because of the limited behavioral repertoires available to the components of essentially mechanical systems.

8.2.2.2 The Servo Modality By way of introduction, recall that in Section 8.1 we approached the problem of organizational control from the standpoint of the social scientist. Here we may approach the same problem from the standpoint of the engineer.[15] The servo model (a variation on the cybernetic theme) has often been considered the *only* paradigm needed as a reference for system coordination, integration, and operation. While this may be essentially true for systems approximating those that engineers like to build, or for socioeconomic systems predicated more on algorithms than innovation, it is hardly appropriate to all organizational contexts. Yet as a primary paradigm for Type-II system administration, and as an operative concept when approaching essentially moderately stochastic problems within any organization, the servo modality has great merit. Graphically, the model's properties are shown in Figure 8.17.

Here, broadly as possible, are the generic operational attributes associated with the servo modality:

1. There is some process we are interested in controlling, represented by the large triangle in the diagram (this "process" may be almost anything: a production operation, an organizational subsystem, a chemical reaction, an income-redistribution plan, etc.).
2. Preselected, critical parameters of the process are to be monitored constantly by a set of appropriate sensors (e.g., visual, thermal, statistical,

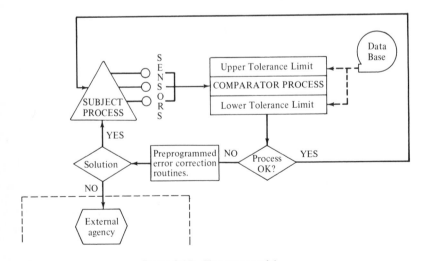

Figure 8.17 The servo model.

electronic, etc.). These sensors capture the point-in-time "values" of the critical parameters.

3. These "values" are then passed off to some kind of comparator process, that ascertains whether or not they are within some preestablished, tolerable limits (the values of which are stored in a memory or data file to which the comparator process has access). For example, we may be trying to control a chemical reaction where there are certain acidity limits permissible for the output; if a small computer were used as the comparator, it would accept readings taken by an appropriate sensor and then compare the "real" or actual acidity against the preestablished tolerance limits stored in its memory.

4. There is next a decision that must be made: is the parametric value associated with the process within or outside the permissible limits? If it is within limits, then nothing further is done . . . we set our control system ready to receive the next reading from the sensors. If the actual parameter is not within permissible limits, then we must take some action.

5. The action we want to take initially is this: compare the actual departure from the tolerance limits (magnitude and direction of parametric deviation) against a set of deviances for which we have preprogrammed error correction routines available (e.g., for the chemical process described above, we may have anticipated an occasional increase of the acidity index to some x level, and have a preprogrammed error correction routine that adds enough alkaline base to bring the process back within tolerable limits on the next pass).

6. However, the actual parameter may not be one for which we have preprogrammed a solution; when this is the case, the closed-system automaticity of the servo-control process must be broken, and a call for help initiated to a superordinate (e.g., a decision-maker equipped to handle nonroutine departures from the tolerance limits). He then examines the actual parameter relative to the prespecified and takes some sort of "judgmental" action:

   (a) He may take the problem to *his* superordinate if it is not within his domain.
   (b) He may make a nonprogrammed correction in the process, altering its basic structural or functional properties for future runs.
   (c) He may alter the calibration of the sensors.
   (d) He may alter the permissible tolerance limits stored in the data base so that a larger deviation will be required to cause an error condition to be recognized.

In short then, under the servo concept, organizational control becomes equivalent to process control.

Now the operational economies associated with any servo-control process are found on two dimensions. First, there is *system response time.* This is measured as the interval (in time) between the occurrence of a parametric departure from the tolerable limits and the correction of the process malfunction which led to that error. In more explicit terms, we are concerned with factors such as:

- The frequency of the sensing of critical parameters.
- The speed with which the logical compare operations or arithmetic compare operations can be performed.
- The sensitivity (resolution power) of the sensors.
- The range of parametric departures for which we have preprogrammed solutions.
- The efficiency of these solution routines.
- The inherent "error" probabilities associated with the process itself.

The second dimension of concern is the *ratio of routine to nonroutine parametric deviations.* Above we suggested that the essential "economy" of the servo-control process depends on the "efficiency" of the error recognition and correction routines. Clearly, this efficiency will be greatest for those preprogrammed solutions that take place (automatically) within the confines of the control system itself. But this automatic feature will depend primarily on the ratio of routine to nonroutine errors generated by the process. The greater the number of parametric departures subject to automatic, preprogrammed solution, the greater the operational relevance of the servo approach.

Underlying these two dimensions is the relationship between time-to-correction (response time) and the probable "cost" or loss associated with any process error. The lower the response time (that is, the longer we allow a process error to continue unchecked), the greater the expected loss (cost of dysfunction). Additionally, the longer a process has been permitted to run out of control, the more costly it is to correct. The most expedient (if not the most rigorous) way to illustrate these contentions is to treat parametric departures (or process errors) in *trajectory* terms, as in Figure 8.18. The concatenating character of the cost or loss associated with any given parametric error is illustrated by the fact that the curve *ab* is shorter than the curve *cd*, and thus carries a lower cost. Note also that the inauguration of a given error correction routine at time t_1 returns the deviant process to a normal level at time t_2, and that the same correction routine applied at time t_3 takes longer to work; the interval between time t_1 and time t_2 being less than that between time t_3 and time t_4 (the angles at *a* and *c* are equal, indicating "identical" strategies of correction).

Thus far, we have spoken about the servo approach with respect to processes that can be adequately managed within a *moderately stochastic* framework, where some parameter(s) of interest may vary within some predefinable tolerance range and where, implicitly, correction strategies can be developed along some continuum. Thus, we have been concerned with a single "state" involving a continuous distribution of some parameter of interest. This represents a situa-

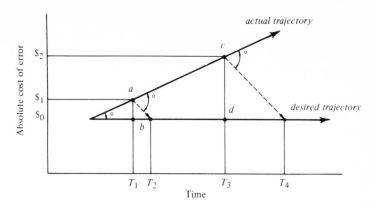

Figure 8.18 The trajectory model.

tion where, for every significant magnitude and direction of deviation of the process parameter from some preestablished tolerance interval, there will be some uniquely determinable correction strategy to bring the process back into control (i.e., a finite-state relationship between process errors and rectification processes).

The broader decision-making significance of the servo modality may be illustrated by an example. Let's presume that we, as system analysts, have been given the job of optimizing the production process with respect to some commodity a company is producing. And; let's further suppose that we are equipped with an information system that has an "intelligent" computer at its core, with some satellite computers and communications gear scattered throughout the organization (an assumption which is valid for most large organizations, business or otherwise). Now, the optimization of a production process involves two things. First, it involves raising the output/input ratio (marginal productivity) of the process itself to an effective maximum; secondly, it involves scheduling production output levels so that, for the period in question, there is a minimal "waste" factor (caused by producing too much of the product or, on the other hand, by producing too little such that potential sales revenue is foregone). Thus, aside from essentially endogenous factors (e.g., available man-power, raw material inventories), the optimization of this production process will depend on our ability to correctly estimate the real-world *demand* for the product, and our ability to adjust our aggregate output accordingly. The distribution of demand across the time-interval in question then becomes the primary control variable for a servo approach to this problem. Assuming that our product has a history, servo logic will dictate a scheme like the following.

Initially, we have to start production according to the statistical "best bet" about next period's demand. This means, effectively, that we have to look at the historical demand record and develop a statistically disciplined projection. Thus, the first demand projection we want to issue the production department, a projection on which it will develop its initial production schedule, is that demand level which receives the highest *a priori* probability of occurrence. Now, the "limits" to be used by the servo process can be set in the following way: the "mean" value for demand from the distribution "null" hypothesis. The upper and lower tolerance limits will then be those that are sufficiently far removed from "mean" to indicate a significant departure from expectations. Thus, an "out-of-control" situation will occur when there is a statistically significant departure of "real" values from the expected. These departures will dictate changes in the production schedule.

The actual operation of the optimization/control process will look like this:

1. We initiate the production, distribution, and sales effort on the basis of the mean value.

2. At selected intervals (at some given frequency), we collect actual sales data from the various field marketing locations and feed them into the storage unit for the central computer.

3. At periodic intervals, an *a posteriori* probability distribution is constructed on these "actual" values.

4. Using a Bayesian-type algorithm which has been programmed into the computer, the *a posteriori* distribution is superimposed on the *a priori* and a new, hybrid distribution is developed.

5. The "mean" of this new distribution is compared to that of the *a priori* and, if a statistically significant departure is apparent, a process-correction program is called to restructure production.

6. The computer can be equipped to translate directional and magnitudinal departures (within a certain limit) into up-dated production schedules that reflect the departure of the real-world demand values from expected. To do this, the computer needs to be equipped with an algorithm relating demand projections to production levels, much as we would have to be equipped were we to do the calculations ourselves.

7. This "continuous" error correction process will be permissible only within some range, as "automatic" corrections cannot be preprogrammed over extremely wide ranges. So, when a deviation exceeding some "routine" magnitude is realized, the interface between the automated control process (the computer-driven system) and the decision-maker is exercised, for he might have to counter with "state" changes which involve radically different production algorithms, resource requirements, or product investment schedules.

8. Within the realm of "routine" corrections, the servo-control system can calculate an updated production schedule and send it to the small satellite computer in the production department (which will inaugurate a lower level servo-control process to see that the new schedule is met most efficiently). By the same token, any other organizational segments affected by the production schedule change can be updated (e.g., a system should be

able to initiate limited changes in raw-materials inventories or order schedules associated with the process at hand). In this way, then, the entire organization begins to become intelligible in terms of a *hierarchy of processes*
that are capable of being administered almost entirely within the "automated" confines of the information system, per se; providing the processes are essentially moderately stochastic in nature.

Thus, for any problem meeting the criteria of moderate stochasticity, the administration control problem reflects the logic developed in the previous chapter
on information economics. For what we have done here is to suggest how to effectively optimize some function dependent on a moderately stochastic variable
by exercising the servo modality's capabilities for gradual production of successively more "realistic" estimates of the true parameter. This process then becomes intelligible in terms of Figure 8.19.

What has happened in Figure 8.19 is this: as the number of observations taken
on the demand parameter increased, it became more and more apparent that the
a priori mean of 750 units was a serious over-estimate. Hence, through time, the
a posteriori distributions began to become more intense around a lower mean of
600 units. At the same time, the expected cost-of-error associated with the production operation (e.g., dysfunction via over- or under-runs) began to decrease,
as the *a posteriori* generated probability continued to concentrate more toward a
lower estimate of the true parameter. The efficiency of our learning process is
given roughly by the slope of the transformation $(\partial p/\partial n)$.

In summary then, the servo modality has much to recommend it in its role as
an administrative device in the face of moderate stochasticity. However, as we
try to apply it to cases of successively greater complexity, operational confoundations enter at many points:

(a) The number of variables whose parameters will have to be monitored
(sensed) will increase.
(b) The precision and reliability of "sensed" estimates will decrease.

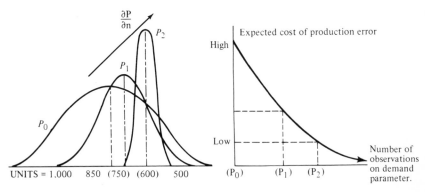

Figure 8.19 Estimation convergence function.

(c) The complexity of the "limits" to be introduced will increase (from individual parameters with very precise values to broad qualitative alternatives).

(d) The limits of *tolerable process behavior* will become broader; the permissible range of nonactionable departures will normatively increase (the broader the process' structural, functional, or resource implications the more careful we want to be about making process alterations).

(e) The probability of any "departure" falling within routine, automatic correction-procedure limits will decrease; hence, the activation of the interface between the information system and the judgmental decision-maker will increase.

(f) The probability of dysfunctions associated with any non-routine correction strategy we implement will increase.

So as the process or system at hand departs from moderate stochasticity, we become increasingly unable to establish sensors that will have the required degree of precision, increasingly unable to identify a truly exhaustive set of parameters that can be reduced to quantitative terms, increasingly unable to set reasonable "narrow" tolerance limits . . . and unable to establish a set of preprogrammed, automatic error correction routines that will be sufficiently broad to exhaust the array of real-world events which can emerge whenever the system or process to be administered is a severely stochastic one.

8.2.2.3 The Stochastic-State Modality Within limits that we shall shortly make explicit, the servo paradigm can serve as a tentative and initial model for treating severely stochastic organizations or processes. Here, however, we not only have to consider parametric or coefficient properties of systems—those manageable within mathematical or statistical frameworks—but broad qualitative properties associated with the state-variable and relational levels of systems. But at least with the severly stochastic situation (as opposed to the indeterminate) we have a strong *a priori* idea about the "range" of alternative states which might obtain. In most decision situations, barring the luxury of delaying a decision pending more investigation of the process we are trying to predict or entity we are trying to control, we will elect to act on that "state" which receives the highest *a priori* probability of occurrence. We would then monitor the emerging real-world properties of the situation until an empirically-predicated convergence on a "true" state were obtained. To this extent then, the servo modality remains applicable as a theoretical mask.

Generally speaking, we consider *state* changes to take place in one of two ways:

(a) By the introduction of new state-variables, such that the basic structure of the entity or process at hand is altered.

(b) By the possibility of significantly different relationship conditions occurring among the various state-variables.

A problem that might meet our *severely stochastic* criteria is the prediction of meteorological phenomena. Alternative states may be considered to be events such as snow, freezing temperatures, excessive humidity, tornados, etc. In any case, they occur not only because of different parameter values which might be assumed by the various weather determinants but also because of different coefficients of interrelationships that might develop among the state-variables (e.g., snow is a combination of freezing temperatures *and* a certain moisture content of the air). If, for example, we were administering a transportation company, we might have several different action-alternatives associated with the several different weather "states" which might emerge.

Now, the process of arriving at most probably optimal transportation algorithms with respect to different weather "states" that could occur will be an exercise similar to that we went through for the moderately stochastic case, except that here the servo process is characterized by:

- The need to monitor several (or many different state-variables and to collect estimates on them with great frequency.
- The need to monitor coefficient or relational values among the state-variables in addition to parameter values.
- The tolerable process "limits" will represent complex *functions* rather than single parameter values, such that the comparator process will be comparing "states" rather than numerical values.
- Hence, any "routine" error corrections we preprogram will represent complex state-shifts rather than simple process-parameter changes (a significant tendency toward snow, for example, might result in a shift to air rather, than land transportation, a shift with extremely wide ramifications).
- There is a higher probability that *nonroutine* situations will occur, situations requiring judgmental rather than mechanical rectification, because we are dealing with an *inherently* more complex process here than with the moderately stochastic examples of the previous section.
- Because of the considerable resource and cost ramifications of a state-shift, we want to be relatively more certain here that a truly significant departure from normalcy has occurred. Therefore, we will set the tolerable event range more broadly, requiring relatively larger departures to signal an out-of-control process.

At any rate, the abstract provisions of the servo model still may hold here, for we will tend to take initial action on the basis of that particular event which may be assigned the highest *a priori* probability of occurrence. (But for the severely stochastic situation, by definition, these *a priori* probabilities cannot be assigned simply on the basis of projections derived from some record of historical system or process events.) Some sort of monitoring-feedback program is then inaugurated, such that our *a priori* expectations may be modified by the emerging realities of the process or system we are trying to adapt to or exploit in some way. Yet even if the logic still holds, the operational difficulties take a quantum leap when we move from the moderately to the severely stochastic analytical domain and our fundamental administrative strategy must shift to a new modality entirely.

This modality is the stochastic-state approach. It makes use of deductive instruments which are capable of bringing some logical order to a future which is expected to hold events which differ markedly in terms of their qualitative properties, (and not merely in terms of magnitudes). Thus, where the future is unlikely to be merely an extension or repetition of some historical state(s), the statistical instruments associated with moderately stochastic phenomena lose their relevance. In short, the transition from moderate to severe stochasticity demands a shift in analytical modalities as well as a shift in administrative strategy. Particularly, those trying either to analyze or administer a Type-III system should turn to game-theoretical or "contingency" tools capable of generating arrays of *if* → *then* scenarios, each of which carries some logical probability of being *the* future state.[16]

The multiple "state" alternatives generated by the *stochastic process* are critical to a theory of complex system administration. Their essential value lies in the ability to provide, beforehand, means for the control of unsought or undesired consequences that may attend any action we elect to implement. When events come as a complete surprise, they will normally result in a greater loss than there would have been if preprogrammed provisions for their correction had been available to the administrator. In this way, the conception of complex systems as inherently stochastic processes provides an alternative to *management by crisis*.

We are already familiar with the logic underlying this contention. Recall, for example, that the essential mechanism is a constrained system, with a low probability of departures from desired, predicted, or programmed behavior. Not so with more complex organizations, where the actual event which occurs may be entirely independent of desires or expectations. Thus, in Chapter 1, we distinguished between tractable and intractable events on the basis of event-probability distributions like those of Fig. 8.20.

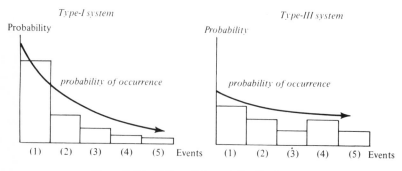

Figure 8.20 Differential event distributions.

In the figure, we have arbitrarily set the identifiable alternative events at five and distributed them along the horizontal axes of the diagrams. The vertical axis of each is merely a probability scale. The diagram for the essential mechanism (the Type-I system) shows the distribution of probabilities across events to be highly skewed to the left, indicating a high probability for event #1 and a radically declining probability for all others. For the Type-III system, however, *all* the events have some rather significant probability of occurrence and the resultant distribution is much flatter.

Moreover, as we suggested, the events of interest in the severely stochastic domain are likely to differ greatly in terms of their properties and implications (whereas in the moderately stochastic domain, events of interest differed only as a matter of degree). When events differ greatly, and when several events have been assigned probabilities of occurrence, then the expected value of an error is extremely high . . . for both the probability of an error and the absolute value of an error are significant.* Thus, for the administrator of a Type-III system, operating under conditions of severe stochasticity, the stochastic-state approach simply gives substance to the old addage that *forewarned is forearmed.*

The point here is simple. Events which entail distinctly different properties will demand distinctly different responses from the organization. In the competitive field in which Type-III systems reside, both opportunities and perils are likely to appear rapidly, and gain momentum quickly. The organization that is unprepared to respond with rapidity will suffer a competitive disadvantage. For this reason, Type-III organizations place a great premium on being able to "read" a potentially complex future . . . for the ability to preidentify events which will occur offers the ability to preadapt.† And preadaption is the *sine qua non* of success in the competitive domain, where the residents play that zero-sum game we have so often spoken of. And the most sophisticated of these competitors (whether commercial or political or ideological) will invest great sums in trying to anticipate a future that other residents of the field are also trying to anticipate and, in some cases, trying to actively influence or structure. These sums will be spent in gathering whatever intelligence is available and in operating those instruments that Section 5.4 specified as congruent with severely stochastic situations (e.g., the game-based and "contingency" models). The result of their efforts should be a reduction in the expected value of an error, through the specifica-

---

*Note that for the moderately stochastic situation, where all the events in question belong to the same qualitative set, the cost of an error associated in selecting a wrong one will generally be lower than were the events greatly different in terms of their quality. This assertion derives from our earlier proposition that it is relatively more serious to make an error at the state-variable or relational levels of analysis than at the coefficient or parametric levels.

†Thus, for example, industrial organizations in many industries will try to get a jump on the competitor by investing in the production of a product for which a market is not yet established, knowing that a correct decision leads to that best of all possible commercial situations . . . *monopoly profits.* And firms do this despite a long list of enterprises driven to bankruptcy by a wrong prediction.

tion of a single qualitative state-of-the-world which can be assigned a satisfactory (if not significant) logical probability of occurrence.

With the entrance of the stochastic-state modality we get our first taste of the *strategic game* played within competitive milieux. To be effective, the modality depends on the range of probable, predefined alternatives, being as comprehensive as necessary, but also as few as possible. The alternatives should be identified with sufficient precision to enable their recognition should they actually occur, and to enable the programming of a relatively specific contingent response. The normative game strategy, then, is to position one's retaliatory resources in relation to the probabilities of occurrence assigned the several alternative events. Care should be taken, though, that such a dissolution of resources does not severely reduce the probability of an ultimately effective response (in which case the resources should be massed at the point of topological intersection among the events, with the relative distance from each being determined with reference to the probabilities of occurrence).

Obviously then, the stochastic-state administrative modality entails considerable risk—risk that the events we can preidentify may not actually occur; risk that in the competitive domain, other systems may be trying to lead us down an ultimately ineffectual tangent by supplying false clues from which our expectations may derive; risk that our own strategic plans may somehow become known; risk that we will not be first with an innovation that proves incrementally more efficient in exploiting some market or resource, or in effecting a dominant advantage. Yet to attempt to deal in such a milieu with only statistical or extrapolative instruments at our disposal—to ignore the mandate for technological innovation and for the construction of sets of strategic moves and countermoves—is to court disaster. In short, the risk is inherent in this type of ecological field, and can only be manipulated within narrow boundaries, never eliminated. And one thing must emerge from this discussion as an absolute: in the competitive domain, it is to the advantage of the parties playing a zero-sum game to make sure that their moves are unprecedented. This makes it imperative that we displace statistical mechanisms with cognition, and extrapolative analysis with invention and imagination. For these deductive skills are the engines of the stochastic-state modality appropriate to those organizations playing politics, war, or that economic game called "share of the market."

Unfortunately, however, one is seldon able to reduce the probability of incurring errors without paying some price. Here we reduce the probability of decision dysfunctions by diffusing probabilities over a range of event alternatives, and thereby lose some direction and actionability. For example, an econometrician might develop a range of GNP estimates that carries with it an extremely high confidence level largely by making the range as large as possible. This can be done quite inexpensively and quickly. On the other hand, it may cost a great deal more to produce a reasonably narrow GNP interval within which we can be adequately sure that the real GNP value will fall. But this smaller interval would provide a far better premise for subsequent decisions (e.g., product demand estimates), with the higher expenses of analysis perhaps being justified by the relatively lower expected error value of decisions associated with the narrower, more actionable range.

So when we begin to consider state alternatives in the severely stochastic context, it is clear that the greater the number of alternatives prespecified, the more difficult it is to adequately prepare for them. Consider the predicament of the army general who asks his staff officers for an estimate of the enemy's most likely future moves. The staff can protect themselves by returning a great list of contingencies, running all the way from immediate retreat back to Bulgaria to an attack with heavy armor in Arkansas. The general, who must decide where to best deploy his forces, is unlikely to be very much impressed by the staff's assertion that they have, in constructing so many logically possible scenarios, effectively eliminated any probability of error associated with their analysis.

Hopefully, we can see that the greater the number of alternatives specified at some significant probability of occurrence, the lower will be the probability that any *one* of them will be adequately provided for should it occur. For the greater the number of contingencies a stochastic-state analysis offers, the greater the resultant dispersion of retaliatory or reactive resources. Further, inasmuch as only one event may ultimately occur, the opportunity cost associated with those resources covering nonoccurring contingencies will be extremely high, just as a general who needs defensive troops must surely feel the loss of having used troops to cover contingent fronts where the enemy never appeared. By carrying the stochastic-state approach to its logical conclusion then—by providing a great diversity of alternative outcomes each with an unsubstantial, but "significant" probability of occurrence—we undermine its functional potential.

Yet the situation for the competitive system is not as difficult as this section might suggest. For, clearly, the normative system-building paradigm of Chapter 7 may itself be used as a stochastic-state instrument,* one able to force a convergence among state alternatives (and hence lend stochastic analyses the 'actionability' component which traditional contingency analyses lack).

Particularly, the stochastic system administrator can use the normative system-building paradigm to attempt to arrive at an adequately exhaustive but still manageable array of qualitatively unique futures, largely because he can control the number of events which are defined and the depth of their definition. In short, there are aspects of the normative system-building/policy-setting scheme that are directly applicable to the administration of Type-III systems, and it is these aspects that can lend an operational substance to the abstract stochastic-state logic.

8.2.2.4 The Heuristic Modality We move from the severely stochastic to the indeterminate case when we find that the number of alternative events to which significant probabilities of occurrence must be assigned is simply too great to be

*As a procedural framework within which dynamic or adaptive programming, or game theory, may be used.

manageable within the stochastic-state modality. Here, clearly, we are faced with a situation of manifest uncertainty. Under conditions of *meta-risk*, then, the decision-maker must abandon any hope of isolating a single most probable event and therefore any single "best" action or response. Nor is the range option much help (see again the event-probability distribution for the Indeterminate Case, section 4.2). The decision-maker's administrative strategy must be almost the direct opposite of his counterpart operating with simpler systems or processes resident in a simpler environmental field. Whereas the latter can at least hope to approach optimality, the man forced to deal with the Type-IV system or with essentially indeterminate problems must adopt an entirely different operational objective—he must act to *minimize the probability of inescapable analytical errors becoming translated into dysfunctional decision or policy actions.*[17]

For him there are no panaceas from technology or science, there is only common sense. And common sense would dictate a set of administrative guidelines something like those that follow (and which constitute the bases for our heuristic administrative modality).

The first dictate is that *all irrevocable commitments of resources and/or action be delayed until the last possible moment* . . . . on the understanding that the value of available information increases through time and, hence, the probability of incurring a decision error declines accordingly. This implies the establishment of priority schemes which see our most "liquid" resources committed and our most recoverable actions implemented during the initial stages of the learning process, saving specific resource investments or irrevocable actions until the decision horizon is approached or until the expected value of a decision error has been reduced to an acceptable (or "floor") level. Operationally, this means that short-run economies of specialization and early implementation might have to be foregone in favor of long-run risk minimization. It also suggests that systems should be designed in a modular mode, with the modules effectively buffered against the transmission of localized errors to other parts of the system. Risk-minimizing modularity here displaces the association of maximum productivity with fully integrated, mechanically interfaced subsystems (which we may legitimately strive toward within less complex and more stable organizational and environmental contexts).

A second common sense dictate is that *plans and planning-based control instruments be abandoned in favor of real-time, feedback-based successive improvement techniques* . . . . on the understanding that in complex and rapidly changing organizational and environmental contexts, yesterday's "optimum" is today's anachronism. With environmental (exogenous) forces altering rapidly and unpredictably, the economies associated with rigid organizational structures and algorithmic processing schemes are going to have to be sacrificed for adaptivity and high-speed responsiveness. Premiums will be placed on what Toffler has called "adhocracies," with their versatile, alterable, multipurpose components. Where control is possible at all, this may suggest that reliance on historical accounting and auditing procedures will eventually be replaced by computer-driven, real-time monitoring schemes, and that the information specialist will gradually find himself spending more and more time on techniques of reducing the delay between the occurrence of an event and its' reporting. Quite simply, then, we are suggesting that the emphasis on operational plans, budgets, and purportedly optimal project management techniques (e.g., PERT) are inapplicable in many nonmechanistic situations, and that the gains in ostensible efficiency they imply can possibly be at the direct expense of ultimate system effectiveness.

A third dictate is that *there be no artificial separation between system analysis, system design, and system administration responsibilities* .... on the understanding that their separation may tend to make managerial effectiveness equivalent to adherence to preestablished operating criteria (usually efficiency-oriented) and discourage attempts at strategic innovation or continuous system modification. One possible way to ensure integration is to devise system design and analysis teams that contain the actual or potential system administrators. They can then be legitimately asked to make the necessarily competitive trade-offs between localized managerial effectiveness and overall system effectiveness. Just as an automotive engineer is better able to modify his automobile's properties to meet changing environmental conditions than is the nontechnical driver, so is the designer-manager better able to devise and implement functional alterations in the face of rapidly changing operational parameters.

This implies some disparagement of the now popular idea of the professional manager, the man who is equally at home managing a chemical plant or a post office or a research and development group. Instead, a premium should be placed on the man who understands the substantive aspects of his system's effectiveness, not just the purportedly universal (context-independent) tools by which output is maximized and expenditures minimized. Thus, we would have no objection to the professional manager being used to administer a benefits distribution function in an automobile plant. But we would have considerable doubt about his efficacy in distributing resources aimed at securing regional economic development or a reduction in ethnic crime rates in the inner city. Effectiveness in these latter areas cannot be neatly quantified in universalistic terms, nor does administrative effectiveness here vary directly with improvements in operational efficiency. We should be dubious, then, of movements to put ex-generals or retired business executives in charge of health, welfare, and education programs, or of any efforts that act to insulate the administrator's performance criteria from the ultimate effectiveness of his system.

As a final dictate, we suggest that *the entire decision-making and administrative process in the indeterminate domain be set in a controlled "learning" context* .... such that *a priori* (unvalidated) expectations or models (i.e., allegories) may gradually be transformed into empirically-predicated, more accurate, *and* actionable *a posteriori* ones. This simply reflects the song we have been singing since the first page of this work: we cannot stop learning about complex socioeconomic entities. Our learning should be continuous, disciplined, and carefully documented; otherwise opportunities to eventually make initially indeterminate situations ultimately more tractable will be lost. Both organizations and the sciences must then document decision errors as well as successes, so that future systems analysts and administrators need not reinvent the wheel with each new project or perturbation. Hence, the "learning" dictate serves the operational demands of indeterminate administrative contexts, but in the wider view promises to lend an empirical authority and precision to the model-building efforts of real-world administrators and academics alike.

The heuristic modality then, in summary, dictates that the administrator working in Type-IV systems or facing indeterminate problems operate in a way which minimizes the expected cost of errors by remaining constantly incredulous and humble, avoiding the temptation to translate *a priori* constructs directly into implementation by skipping the intervening "learning" processes. It asks, further, that the scientist and administrator avoid the neat, comfortable compartmentalization of tasks into those that are properly the sphere of the academician and those that are the province of the manager; it asks that the security of rigid performance criteria be abandoned in favor of flexible, plastic parameters; it cautions us to ignore the technocratic siren-song spilling over from the essentially mechanistic domain, singing the praises of giant-killing, fully-integrated systems that inhere a risk that an ill-conceived part can sterilize the whole . . . a song that has become as addictive to some administrative scientists as it has to most minor government functionaries and junior computer programmers; and it cautions us to ignore, as well, the suasive croonings of those social and behavioral scientists who may be more interested in changing societal behavior than in understanding it.

However, again, nothing in the administrative domain is gained for free. So, in adopting this heuristic administrative modality and accepting the reduction in expected costs of error which it implies, the administrator must be prepared to pay the following prices:

(a) He sacrifices the short-run efficiency and economies associated with fully-integrated, essentially "mechanized" systems (e.g., highly bureaucratic organizations, electromechanical constructs, or other such effectively programmable entities). Instead, he attempts to secure long-run system viability via the development of an organization that is responsive and resilient.

(b) He abandons the opportunity to tightly control his subsystems or organizational components, for as his subsystems become more autonomous in the pursuit of a creative, responsive organization, centralized control mechanisms must gradually give way to autoregulation.

(c) He understands that as programmability and centralization decrease, the probability that the system will spring "leaks" or inaugurate dissipative

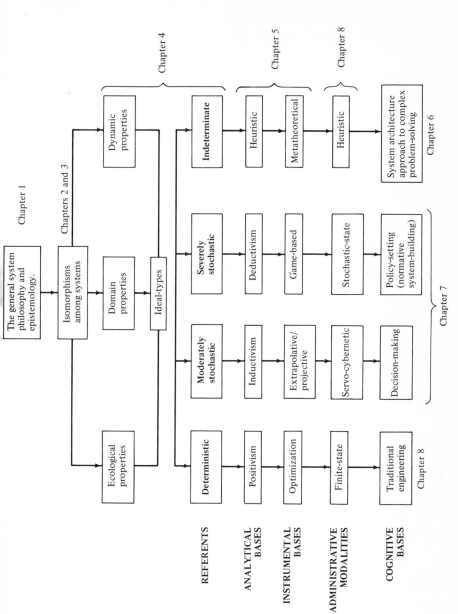

Figure 8.21 The general system "Map."

tendencies increases (as when professional social workers adopt political stances that are inimical to their development agency's survival within the community or when professors, acting under the guise of academic freedom, spend more time in paid consultation than in course preparation).

Thus, administratively, departures from highly controllable, more manipulable organizational modalities is justified only when mechanical or bureaucratic structures will be expected to be ineffective in carrying out the system's ultimate mission.

8.3 A CLOSING NOTE

We have come to the point where we can offer the last of our constructs, Figure 8.21, the *general system map*. The reader will no doubt be glad to know that this map does not show where we're going, but attempts to give an overview of where we've been.

Many of you will walk this same ground again, hopefully with greater thoroughness and alertness than we have done here. So much in this world remains to be done, and we cannot even begin to estimate that which remains to be learned. All that can be hoped is that what has been written here will stimulate others—of greater insight, talent, or energy—to search deeper and wider. The greatest hope for what you have just read is not, then, that it should be conclusive, but that it should be germinal in some small way of better-conceived and better-executed efforts. And, perhaps paradoxically, our fondest hope is that the reader *knows* less now than when he began so many pages ago . . . that he is less certain about the answers and more sensitive to the questions.

8.4 NOTES AND REFERENCES

1. A good treatment of the problems of the professional within a formal organization, and a discussion of some of the difficulties of their control, is given in Blau and Scott's *Formal Organizations*, (San Francisco: Chandler, 1962).
2. There is a short section on the operation aspects of the socioeconomic trade-off in my "Towards an Array of Organizational Control Modalities," *Human Relations*, 27 no. 2 (February 1974).
3. The tendency is always to associate irrationality with primitive systems. But there is an element of irrationality in even the most advanced systems, and among the purportedly most "rational" elements of these societies . . . scientists themselves. For an elaboration of this point, see my "Axiological Predicates of Scientific Enterprise," *General Systems Yearbook*, **XIX** (1974).
4. A brilliant analysis of the sociocultural foundations of a power-based Zulu system has been given in the first part of Donald Morris's *The Washing of the Spears: The Rise and Fall of the Zulu Nation* (New York: Simon and Schuster, 1965). Note, particularly the political power-agents employed by Shaka, on the greatest Zulu chieftains.

5. For an interesting analysis of some of Weber's more practical contributions to organizational theory, see David Mechanic's "Some Considerations in the Methodology of Organizational Studies," *The Social Science of Organization*, ed. Harold J. Leavitt (Englewood Cliffs: Prentice-Hall, 1963), pp. 139-182.

6. There is clearly some attempt to sophisticate the management of public enterprise by abandoning certain clearly dysfunctional aspects of bureaucratic organization, at least among those public agencies that have some nonroutine tasks to perform. For more on this see Eric Trist's "Management and Organization Development in Public Enterprises and Government Agencies," a mimeographed report available through the Management and Behavioral Science Center, Wharton School, University of Pennsylvania (Philadelphia). This paper was prepared for the United Nations Seminar on the Use of Modern Management Techniques in Public Administration of Developing Countries.

7. For information on the theoretical bases and implications of the zero-sum game, see Bierman, Bonini, and Hausman's *Quantitative Analysis for Business Decisions* (Homewood, Ill.; Irwin, 1969), p. 238ff.

8. Naturally, unions have a defense against merit structures when they can "close" a shop. The classical move is to set arbitrated work quotas that the individual will exceed only at the risk of incurring the displeasure of those with whom he works. The competitive organization's preference for objective, individualized performance standards and merit devices, etc., is seldom realized in practice except where unions are weak or absent. Hence, in most modern corporations we look for such mechanisms operating primarily among management, professional, or white collar personnel. More thorough information about such problems may be had from *Industrialism and Industrial Man: The Problems of Labor and Management*, ed. Kerr et al., (Cambridge, Mass.: Harvard University Press, 1960). And for a somewhat jaded but brilliant critique of the impact of the behavioral sciences on industrial organization, see George Strauss's "Some Notes on Power-Equalization," Leavitt, *op. cit.*, pp. 39-84.

9. For more on the dramatalurgical world protrayed and analyzed by Erving Goffman, see his *Asylums* (Garden City, N.Y.: Doubleday, 1961), or his *The Presentation of Self in Everyday Life*, Monograph no. 2 (Edinburgh: University of Edinburgh Press, 1956). For its importance as an alternative paradigm for sociology, see Alvin Gouldner's *The Coming Crisis in Western Sociology* (New York: Basic Books, 1970), pp. 378-90.

10. See, for example, Herbert Simon's *Administrative Behavior* (New York: Macmillan Publishing Company, 1957), especially Chapter 5.

11. For an imaginative discussion of the Supreme Court as a decision-making phenomenon, see Robert A. Solo's *Economic Organizations and Social Systems* (New York: Bobbs-Merrill Co., 1967), pp. 22-28.

12. The adhocratic organization is one which is plastic, resilient, and ephemeral; called into operation or "created" as needs arise. For a discussion of this emergent phenomenon in post-industrial society, see Alvin Toffler's *Future Shock* (New York: Random House, 1970), Chapter 7.

13. Simon, *op. cit.*, Chapter 5. In short, the "satisficer" attempts to reach some apparently adequate solution to problems; this as opposed to the purportedly optimal ambitions of the decision-maker in classical microeconomics.

14. For example, see A. Gill's *Introduction to the Theory of Finite State Machines* (New York: McGraw-Hill, 1962). Of course, finite-state phenomena

occupy only a portion of the engineer's time. Considerably more complex phenomena are sometimes dealt with under the heading of systems engineering.

15. More specifically, engineers tend to be concerned about process control, a subfield of system control in general. For an excellent study of the role of the servoconcept and its adjuncts in process control, see F.G. Shinskey's *Process Control Systems* (New York: McGraw-Hill, 1967).

16. Readers interested in the game theoretical approach might first see Blackwell and Girshick's *Theory of Games and Statistical Decisions* (New York: John Wiley & Sons, 1961).

17. For a more thorough treatment of the rationale behind this strategy, see my "Attacking Organizational Complexity," *Fields Within Fields... Within Fields*, **11** (Spring 1974).

INDEX

Index